The Cuisine of Sacrifice among the Greeks

The Cuisine of Sacrifice among the Greeks

MARCEL DETIENNE

and

JEAN-PIERRE VERNANT

With Essays by

JEAN-LOUIS DURAND, STELLA GEORGOUDI,

FRANÇOIS HARTOG, AND JESPER SVENBRO

Translated by

PAULA WISSING

THE UNIVERSITY OF CHICAGO PRESS
Chicago and London

Marcel Detienne is directeur d'études at the Ecole pratique des Hautes Etudes, Paris. Among his earlier books, *The Creation of Mythology* was published in English translation by the University of Chicago Press in 1986.
Jean-Pierre Vernant is professor at the Collège de France. His previous books include *Myth and Thought among the Greeks* and *The Origins of Greek Thought*, both in English translation.

The University of Chicago Press, Chicago 60637
The University of Chicago Press, Ltd., London
© *1989 by The University of Chicago*
All rights reserved. Published 1989
Printed in the United States of America
98 97 96 95 94 93 92 91 90 89 5 4 3 2 1

First published in Paris as *La cuisine du sacrifice en pays grec,* © Editions Gallimard, 1979.

Library of Congress Cataloging-in-Publication Data

Detienne, Marcel.
    [Cuisine du sacrifice en pays grec. English]
    The cuisine of sacrifice among the Greeks / Marcel Detienne and
Jean-Pierre Vernant; with essays by Jean-Louis Durand . . . [et al.];
translated by Paula Wissing.
    p. cm.
    Translation of: La cuisine du sacrifice en pays grec.
    Bibliography: p.
    Includes index.
    ISBN 0-226-14351-1 (alk. paper).—ISBN 0-226-14353-8 (pbk.:
alk. paper)
    1. Sacred meals—Greece. 2. Sacrifice—Greece. 3. Cults—Greece.
I. Vernant, Jean-Pierre. II. Title.
BL795.S23D4713 1989
292'.38—dc19   88-39143
                                        CIP

Contents

v

Translator's Note

A few words are necessary concerning the citations in the text. Translations of the Greek texts are my own, based on the French, since often the French wording better accorded with the spirit of the discussion than available English versions. I have also translated French secondary sources. For biblical passages, I have utilized the English edition of the Jerusalem Bible throughout.

I would like to express my gratitude to Arthur Adkins and Virginia Seidman for their attention to matters Greek that lay beyond my competence and to Priscilla Murphy for her eye for detail. Any errors or misreadings of the French are, of course, my responsibility.

Culinary Practices and the Spirit of Sacrifice
Marcel Detienne

T HERE are two reasons for our choice of examining the Greeks on the problems of blood sacrifice. First of all, we see in the Greeks a society in which the basic ritual acts in daily practice are of a sacrificial type. For nearly ten centuries, guided by immutable cultic statutes, the Greeks never failed to maintain relations with the divine powers through the highly ritualized killing of animal victims, whose flesh was consumed collectively according to precise strictures. This factual consideration is joined by another, which illuminates the Greek presence within us from the time of the Church Fathers to the sociologists who, with Durkheim and Mauss, study the relationships between religion and society through inquiry focused on the phenomenon of sacrifice.

These two influences converge in the Orphic account of the death of Dionysus and secure for it the honored position of a reference point among sacrificial myths.[1] The plot is simple. A god in the form of a child is jointly slaughtered by all the Titans, the kings of ancient times. Covered with gypsum and wearing masks of white earth, the murderers surround their victim. With careful gestures they show the child fascinating toys: a top, a rhombus, dolls with jointed limbs, knucklebones, and a mirror. And while the child Dionysus contemplates his own image captured in the circle of polished metal, the Titans strike, dismember him, and throw the pieces in a kettle. Then they roast them over a fire. Once the victim's flesh has been prepared, they undertake to devour it all. They just have time to gobble it down, all except the heart, which had been divided into equal parts, before Zeus' lightning comes to punish their crime and reduce the Titan party to smoke and ashes, out of which will be born the human species.

Interpretation is an integral part of this mythological account, which apparently dates from the time of the earliest Orphic writings at the end of the sixth century B.C. On the one hand, this is a story conceived of and invented by theologians devoted to the Orphic way of life, who meant to

1

denounce blood sacrifices and turn men away from the cannibalistic practices they unwittingly carry out (by extension) each time they offer an
animal victim to the gods. Elsewhere, beginning with the Aristotelian
school of the fourth century,[2] a different exegesis focuses on the figure of
the slain Dionysus, leading him toward the horizon on which a general
theory of sacrifice will be built.

At this point we begin to see evidence of a ritualistic reading of the
myth, which will be developed from the beginning of the Christian era on
up to contemporary analyses with their anthropological perspective. For
example, in the fourth century A.D. pamphlet entitled *On the Error of Profane Religions*[3] Firmicus Maternus condemns the custom practiced by the
Cretans of tearing a live bull apart with their teeth. In doing so, he for-
mulates a key interpretation connecting a ritual omophagic model, in
which Dionysus invites the faithful to eat raw animal flesh, with the recognition of the god who appears sometimes in taurine, sometimes in human form, and who is incorporated into the faithful who devour him, or
who offers himself in response to their communional desires. Only recently, working from a perspective that is deliberately open to anthropology but misled by the conviction that it is possible to exhaust the myth by
a faithful accounting of a Dionysiac ritual, E. R. Dodds, author of *The
Greeks and the Irrational*,[4] brings together the story of Pentheus, the
Orphic tale, and other traditions and finds in them a sacramental model
in which the god, present in the form of his animal or human "vehicle," is
torn apart and eaten by the assembled worshipers.

The slaughter of the child Dionysus is an exemplary tale, whose persist-
ence throughout multiple retellings may lead one to wonder whether, as
Wittgenstein says,[5] in the final analysis it does not appeal to some inclination within ourselves; it permits us to connect a series of problems concerning Greek acts and practices of blood sacrifice and in a more general
fashion to inquire about the presuppositions governing the elaboration of
a theory of sacrifice as the central figure of religion and society combined.

*

Only supreme inattention to the details of the account of Dionysus' slaying at the hands of the Titans would lead one to find in it traces of a ritual
connected with eating raw food. The narrative emphasizes the combination of roasting and boiling, which is so odd in this instance (the tale
specifies that what has already been boiled is then roasted) that it provides
the subject and terms of one of the "problemata" in the Aristotelian collection. It is precisely these specifications for cooking which refer in the
myth to the familiar and ritual gestures of the blood sacrifice.[6]

Along with the knife, the spit and kettle together and separately constitute the instruments of a way of eating that Herodotus in his accounts of Egypt places at the heart of the difference, the otherness, that the Greeks perceive in themselves with respect to the Egyptians.[7] By showing their repugnance at using a knife, spit, or kettle belonging to a Greek because he makes sacrifices and eats according to different rules, the Egyptians described by Herodotus reveal to the listeners of the *Histories* an image of themselves in which their sacrificial practice, seen in its instrumental aspect, is circumscribed by its alimentary function. For here we find the first characteristic that justifies the central place of the blood sacrifice in Greek social and religious thought: the absolute coincidence of meat-eating and sacrificial practice.[8] All consumable meat comes from ritually slaughtered animals, and the butcher who sheds the animal's blood bears the same functional name as the sacrificer posted next to the bloody altar.

But sacrifice derives its importance from another function, which reinforces the first: the necessary relationship between the exercise of social relatedness on all *political* levels within the system the Greeks call the city. Political power cannot be exercised without sacrificial practice. Any military or political undertaking—a campaign, engagement with the enemy, the conclusion of a treaty, works commissioned on a temporary basis, the opening of the assembly, or the assumption of office by the magistrates— each must begin with a sacrifice followed by a meal. All citizens holding civil posts regularly offer sacrifices. And until a late date, a city such as Athens maintained a king-archon,[9] one of whose major functions was the administration of all sacrifices instituted by the ancestors and of the body of ritual acts that guarantee the harmonious functioning of society.

Two examples enable us to observe the solidarity between the domain of the political and that of the sacrificial. The first can be seen in the incarceral space temporarily occupied by citizens awaiting the decision of the court or the execution of a sentence. All prisoners share the fire and meals. Sacrifice and meal conjoin to confirm the ephemeral community of the group jailed together. The only one excluded from these food sacrifices is the typically asocial individual rejected by his fellow prisoners, who refuse to light a fire with him and make a place for him in their reduced community.[10]

The second example, by contrast, is found in the act of extending political territory. To found a colony it is sufficient to bring a spit from the home city and a pot with fire in it.[11] The sacrifice thus made possible is not only the act of founding a new political community born of the first. It will become the basis for the filial relations maintained by a colony with

its mother city. Thucydides tells us that the Corinthians hate the people of
Corcyra, a colony of Corinth, because, during the religious ceremonies
when the victim's flesh was being distributed, the citizens of Corcyra neglected to give the first portion to a Corinthian, who should have received
the honored share.[12] Elsewhere, when two cities are bound by an agreement, the distribution of power is made according to their respective participation in the sacrifices. Thus, for two cities of unequal importance,
such as Myania and Hypnia in western Locris, contributions of judges,
foreign ambassadors, soldiers, and local magistrates are levied according
to the number of victims that each must provide in shared cultic activities.[13] Inversely, whoever does not have the right to sacrifice, either as an
individual or in the name of a city, lacks the corresponding political rights,
whether to take part in prestigious contests, such as the Olympics, or to
participate in the assemblies that gather several cities around a temple.
One of the marks of a foreigner is that he is kept away from the altars and
is unable to make sacrifices without the official mediation of a citizen, who
will answer for him before the gods and the local community.[14]

*

To analyze the sacrificial system of a society that places sacrifice at the
center of its dietary practices and politico-religious thought, the Center
for Comparative Research on Ancient Societies has chosen to utilize four
major tactics:

1. The first aims to view the system from "outside," by noting both
the sets of prohibitions and the transgressions that the system authorizes,
so as to define its boundaries. In particular, it is the forms of protest explicit in the different orientations of Greek mysticism that permit us to
discover the implicit rules and major dynamics of the sacrificial system.

2. This external perspective is complemented by the internal analysis
of the sacrificial system: its architecture as seen from within, beginning
with the major mechanisms and their basic values on through the configuration of each of the terms of the sacrificial process. The victim is also
considered: its status and place in the bestiary, the behavior required of it,
and its qualities and defects, as well as an examination—but this time from
within—of exclusionary procedures (animals that are not to be sacrificed,
flesh that is not to be eaten). The methods for dismembering the animal
and the division between the different internal parts and those in some
way constituting the animal's exterior are also examined. Types of cooking
are studied: the respective values of being raw, roasted, and boiled, as well
as the meanings of what rises with the smoke—bone, fat, and aromatics.
Last, the modalities of the distribution and division of the victim's flesh

are analyzed, including the honored portion, the pieces reserved for the priests, the ranking of the animal's skin, head, and feet, the egalitarian model of distribution, casting lots, and the position of women, half-castes, and foreigners with respect to the celebrants. All of these issues tie in with others and raise questions concerning a series of relationships central to Greek thought and symbolism—between men and gods, animals and men, grains and the animal world, or again, between women, the female body, and meat or food.

3. The third approach concerns the political and alimentary vocation inherent in sacrificial practices, which are viewed in relation to other activities such as hunting, warfare, marriage, and agriculture. The nature of the victim, which must be a domestic animal, poses first of all the problem of the relation of sacrifice to hunting on the one hand and agriculture on the other. The blood flowing from the slaughtered animal raises the problem of warfare and the symbolisms engendered by violence. The reference to the earth and cereals is suggested by several aspects of the sacrifice, such as the status of the chosen victim or the function of grains in ritual, for example.

4. The last orientation considers sacrifice a mythic operator in a group of narratives in which performing a sacrifice stands in opposition to or complements hunting, waging war, or cultivating the soil. In this way, for example, we can observe the adventures of Hercules—a monster-killer but also a meat-eater of such voracious appetite that he goes so far as to steal an ox still under the yoke, while elsewhere we find him, this time a recalcitrant victim, in the midst of the cannibalistic sacrifices organized by Busiris, the bloodthirsty king of the Egyptians and most pious of men.

*

Expressed in actions and carried out since time immemorial in eating habits, the sacrificial system eludes clear and explicit analysis. It depends on shared knowledge, the various terms of which the Greeks felt the need to formulate only in marginal milieus where voices of protest were raised and heard. The denials and distortions found there enable us to trace, as if in a broken mirror, the outlines of a secret, implicit system.

At one time it was commonly accepted that there was a marked leaning toward a type of vegetarianism in Orphic and Pythagorean circles—those two major orientations of Greek mysticism. It was thought that abstaining from fleshly food in these sectarian milieus originated solely out of respect for all forms of life. This was a twofold error. On the one hand, it meant misunderstanding the reference to sacrifice in the behavior of nonvegetarians and consequently underestimating the rupture implied by a deliberate avoidance of meat. On the other, it meant following a banal and semantically impoverished line of reasoning and forgetting that Pythagorean cuisine was more subtle than what is conveyed by the term "vegetarian." In reality, the dietary code of sectarian circles reveals the coordinates of each type of protest and situates each one with respect to the dominant politico-religious system and the concurrent orientations of the mystical movement.

Thus the strictest of the Pythagoreans, called the Pure, reject all fleshly food and respect only altars that cannot be stained by blood. They shun all contact with cooks or butchers as well as hunters. The only sacrifices they make to the gods are cakes made from grain, honeycombs, and incense, which are burned on their altars. But in addition to the disciples of Pythagoras who refuse any form of blood sacrifice are those who adopt a more subtle regimen; if they refuse to eat lamb and the flesh of the working ox, they readily dine on a morsel of pork or a slice of kid. In truth, the division between the two groups of Pythagoreans can be understood only in the politico-religious order referred to by culinary options. To refuse to eat meat is not only to behave in a manner different from one's fellows, it is to decide not to carry out the most important act in civil religion. This so-called vegetarianism is a singularly efficacious way of renouncing the world.[15] The ritual practice of sacrifice in the city and dietary behavior in the mystical circle are opposing terms. Consequently, the difference between the two types of Pythagoreans is linked to their respective political positions. The first have taken the path of renunciation: asceticism, mortification of the soul, and the intransigent rejection of any relationship to meat and blood. The others, engaged in the reform and salvation of the city, come to terms with worldly dietary practices and develop a system founded on the separation between meat and nonmeat in which the status of fleshly food is assumed first by the working ox and then the sheep, while the comestible parts of minor victims are considered to be non-fleshly food. Casuists of the sect specify that in the case of victims other than the ox and sheep, meat begins with the heart and womb. Other theologians and ritual experts explain that the goat and pig, the most common sacrificial victims, are deprived of their fleshly attributes because both are guilty of devouring food that the gods reserved for man; the goat grazed upon Dionysus' vine and the pig ravaged Demeter's harvest.[16]

Orphism lacks the tension between this renunciation of the world and the salvation of the city found in the Pythagorean position. The person choosing the Orphic way is a marginal individual destined for a life of wandering and exile from the city, ever since the voice of Orpheus revealed to men in writing that each time a living being is killed, each time an animate being is destroyed, a murder (*phonos*) takes place. Now, the community of men is founded upon murder; it lives by bloodshed. Crime is an institution. The living devour each other; legal cannibalism reigns. The inhabitants of the city imagine that they worship the gods and honor their altars, while the father eats his son and the son gnaws on the mutilated heads of his kin. The diet of the city, the very same one that the Titans, humanity's ancestors, established by eating the child Dionysus, makes cannibalism universal.

The radicalism of the Orphic attitude is accompanied by a systematic critique of official theology and the city's "orthodox" discourse concerning its relations with the gods and the animal world, between nature and the supernatural. All the speculative thought of the Orphic disciples, with its cosmogonies, theogonies, and anthropogonic preoccupations, develops in opposition to the dominant thought of the politico-religious world, in opposition to the officialized parlance of Hesiod and Homer, and in total rupture with the value system found in the Hesiodic account of Prometheus and the first food and blood sacrifice. For, with Prometheus in an ambiguous mediating role between Zeus and man, a world stressing relationship by distance is inaugurated with a sacrifice offered to seal the agreement between the parties. The division is clearly marked on the dietary level: the gods receive the smoke of the charred bones and the perfume of the herbs thrown into the flames, while men receive the fleshy parts of the ox that Prometheus has sacrificed.

Through this founding myth, which is the implicit reference point for all the sacrificial practices of the city as seen in the criticisms by the disciples of Orpheus, the consumption of the meat effects a distance between gods and men in the very movement that accomplishes communication between this earthly world and that of the divine powers. Henceforth the acts of each sacrificer will serve as a reminder that, by eating flesh destined for corruption, men are condemned to hunger and death, while the gods enjoy the privilege of perfumed smoke—the incorruptible substances that the flames of the sacrificial fire have transformed into superior food reserved for the divine powers. This value system underlies the "political" cuisine that Orphism both denies and reveals in its intention of bridging the distance between men and gods and returning to a time of primordial unity. Orpheus chooses escape by the high road, on the side of the gods, by eating only perfectly pure foods such as honey or grains, foods homologous to those that the Orphic liturgy prescribes for each power invoked when it lists the aromatic vapors destined for the gods.[17]

Dionysianism is defined within the same framework as well, at least in one of its major orientations. What, in fact, is omophagia, the dismemberment of a living being hunted down like a wild beast and eaten completely raw, but a way of refusing the human condition as it is defined by the Promethean sacrifice and imposed by the rules of conduct prescribed in the use of the skewer and the caldron? By eating raw meat, the faithful of Dionysus wish to act in the manner of beasts and, in the literal sense of the term, *go wild,* in order to escape the politico-religious condition. This time the desire is attained via the low road, on the side of bestiality.

*

If transgressions reveal the limits of the system with regard to its major prohibitions, only internal rules permit us to discover its underpinnings and describe their workings. Since meat is of primary concern in political sacrifice, the relationship to the animal world plays a fundamental role. A detail from the legend of Pythagoras offers a view of this relationship in the aversion the philosopher of Croton felt for hunters and cooks because for him they both belong to the same criminal species.[18] The confusion between the two is deliberate and puts the totality of the relations into question. In the city the cook, whom the Greeks call *mageiros,* is indissociably both butcher and sacrificer. On the other hand, cooking is never confused with hunting. As a general rule, wild animals are never offered to the gods. In large measure the subversion of Dionysus can be seen in this context. The city wages war on wild animals but sacrifices and consumes only domestic species. The Greeks divide the animal world in two: animals that are hunted for the harm that they can cause, and those that are protected because of the services that men have come to expect from them. The official ethic, codified by Aristotle, teaches that men must use animals for their own ends and that if they renounce this they in turn are in grave danger of leading a bestial life.

Moreover, the services rendered by some animals are only recognized to emphasize their "distant" position from men. From the time of Hesiod, the animal world is the kingdom of unreason, knowing neither justice nor injustice. Therefore, men cannot establish any formal relationship with beings that, from the practice of eating raw food to the allelophagia that makes them devour one another, are dominated by violence. Only some species, such as oxen, sheep, goats, and pigs—the most domesticated because men control their reproduction—although lacking in reason, "exist with a view to the good of man," as Aristotle says, and are on earth to aid man in his work.[19] It is these species that provide the sacrificial victims.

All the ritual acts established by the city aim to maintain the distance between domestic animals and others, as well as the distinction between the butcher-cook and the hunter. Moreover, there is a desire to play down the violence in the sacrificial ceremony, as if from the very outset it were necessary to disclaim any guilt of murder. The animal selected as victim is led without apparent constraint in a procession to the altar at the same pace as the future diners, and the ritual takes care to obtain the animal's consent by a sign of the head. The usual procedure puts the animal in contact with pure water and the fruits of the earth, but suddenly and by surprise. When the cold water splashes on the animal, it shudders; and when the shower of grain touches its head it shakes it to the right and left, which among the Greeks is a sign of agreement. The exegetes of Delphi went so far as to read in the victim's shudders proof that it was pure, healthy, and whole "in soul as well as body."[20] Some legalistic traditions attached to the same temple insist on the ambiguity of the relationship between animal and cereal foods. The oracle at Delphi—this great, ever-active slaughterhouse—probably encouraged the killing of the first victims in order to aid the plants and fruits of the earth that were threatened by the increase of the animal population; but the fear of shedding the blood of a living being led to seeking a sign of its assent at the moment of the libation in order to believe that no injustice had indeed been committed.[21] Inversely, when some animals refuse to move toward the altar or, more rarely, they spontaneously rush forward, often to kill one another, the sacrificial ritual is perverted and corrupted by traits that carry it into the domain of hunting or warfare.[22]

As a general rule the sacrifice is carried out in an atmosphere of uneasy caution, as can be seen in words and gestures laden with ambiguity. Thus in a sacred law from Cos, the victim destined for Hestia is sacrificed only if it has indicated its assent, i.e., if it has lowered its head (*hupokuptein*).[23] Now the same verb, which here means to consent, also has two other senses. It is a term from the vocabulary of supplication; the animal takes the posture of the supplicant placing himself under the protection of Zeus. Similarly, it is a verb of submission: to bend beneath the yoke. Here we must amplify the image of the bond. It is the custom in Greece to allow animals consecrated to the gods to wander freely within the temple enclosures. Thus the animal is designated *aphetos*,[24] "at large." It is free of all bonds and obviously does not labor for man. It does not however cease to belong to the domestic species, but it is no longer tamed and its neck no longer knows the yoke that denotes the working animal. The sacrificial ritual feigns obtaining the victim's tacit renunciation of this discretely supervised freedom by leading it to lower its head as if it were coming of its own accord to submit to the yoke (*hupokuptein*). Once this agreement has been elicited, the animal is struck down—with a blow to the base of the neck in the case of bovines—but always by surprise and in such a manner as to avoid letting the violence done to the victim show. For the same reason, the knife that makes the blood flow is in principle hidden in a basket of grains of barley mixed with salt.[25] Based on these four elements—meat, water, grain, and salt—different symbolic figures emerge that can be remarked in the unfolding of rituals and mythic accounts in which, for example, grains are at times replaced by pebbles, at times by oak leaves. In this way, but on another level, we may consider the proceedings of an Argive funerary ritual. The fire, which has been tainted by death, must be extinguished, and the mourning relatives can only resume eating meat through the medium of grain. To obtain a portion of the sacrificial meat the family must bring the equal amount of grain in exchange. Only afterwards can a pure fire be taken from the neighbors' hearth to consecrate the resumption of the sacrificial cooking that had been suspended during mourning.[26] Cereals precede and prefigure meat and fire because they are naturally cooked by the brightness of the sun. They can serve as a substitute for animal flesh as well as announce the cooking action of the hearth.

After it has been skinned, the animal's body is divided according to a model in which the interior, which is considered analogous to the living, has a dual aspect in contrast to the exterior. First the internal organs are seen in opposition to the rest of the meat. The viscera (liver, lungs, spleen, kidneys, and heart) are the parts engorged with blood, of which they are the product; but another division is also made within the internal parts between the viscera and the entrails contained in the cavity of the lower abdomen, the stomach and intestines, in other words.[27] The ritual insists on the distinction between the viscera and the flesh to be consumed— chronological order and type of cooking—in two ways. The viscera are roasted on skewers in the first phase of the sacrifice and eaten on the spot near the altar by the inner circle of those taking full part in the sacrifice, while the quarters of meat, put to boil in the cauldron, are intended either for a larger feast or for distribution, sometimes over a distance. As for the entrails, prepared as sausages they are consigned to the periphery of the sacrificial meal.

The rule dictating that the boiled follows the roasted is so compelling that by reversing it, the Orphic account of Dionysus (who was boiled and then roasted) undertakes to contest a cultural history, explicit elsewhere, that states that humanity, on the road from "the worse to the better," must have eaten grilled meat before learning the art of stewed dishes.[28]

In a ritual where the acts of cooking only extend those of killing and carving, the sacrificer is both butcher and cook. By law, every sacrifier* is qualified to execute this series of operations. Neither killing nor carving require sacerdotal virtues, any more than they demand specialized technical knowledge. However, in the sociocultural reality from the fifth century B.C. onward, the different operations of the sacrifice are undertaken by one person, the *mageiros,* the butcher-cook-sacrificer, whose functional name denotes the conjunction between the slaughtering of the victims, the sale of meat, and the preparation of fleshly food. The emergence of this functionary, often a public one who is attached to a temple or hired on an annual basis for a given salary, doubtless depends on the importance accorded the slaughtering of the victims in a largely urbanized and demographically developed society. In sacrifices directed toward commensality, the *mageiros* is usually slaughterer as well as cook; and the congruence of these two roles indicates to what extent the offering of a sacrificial victim is regarded and enacted as a way of eating together. The authority of this system can be seen in the fact that the butcher's actions must conform to those of the sacrificer. In other words, all comestible meat must result from a sacrificial killing. Rules specify in fact that the meat sold in shops may come neither from animals that have not been sacrificed nor from those that cannot be sacrificed. Just as imperfect victims are kept away from the altar, animals that have died from sickness or age or have been killed by wild beasts are placed beyond the circle of meats that can be ritually eaten.[29]

Of the three roles assumed by the *mageiros,* that of cook is assuredly the most familiar. Lighting the fire, setting the table, kneading the dough, remembering the salt, vinegar, or oregano—all these are the ordinary gestures accomplished by the cook with as little mystery as those of the butcher, who cuts meat either before the sacrificial table in front of all or behind his counter in the middle of the market, in the public space. The most unfamiliar of the three is certainly the task of the *mageiros*-sacrificer. His professional profile seems to shrink as the space taken by the sacrifice

---

*Following the distinction made by Henri Hubert and Marcel Mauss in *Essai sur la nature et la fonction du sacrifice* (1899), the sacrifier (*sacrifiant*) offers the sacrifice but may employ a ritual specialist, the sacrificer (*sacrificateur*), to carry out the sacrifice for him.—TRANS.

contracts. In the narrow confines of the slaughter of the victim, the *ma-geiros* grows imperceptible to the point where he is no more than an "instrument" by which the sacrificers can ritually kill their victim.

As Guy Berthiaume has noted, on a linguistic level it is impossible to separate the one who is both sacrifier and sacrificer from the one who delegates the killing to a subordinate. In other words, when the *mageiros* is present at a sacrifice, one can never state that he is the one who has dealt the fatal blow. The blurring of distinctions here is fundamental. For what is hidden in this way is the naked act of violence, as if the features, the distinct face of the one who strikes and kills with the ax or knife were best left shrouded in darkness. Is this another game of "hunt the slipper," albeit a less dramatic one than in the spectacle of the Bouphonia—the drama of "Who Killed the Ox?"—in the conclusion of which the "Knife" lets the guilty one disappear and all feelings of culpability fade away, leaving on stage the circle of commensals peacefully engaged in their fleshly meal? [30] Just as in the drama of the working ox, the sacrificial system imposed by the *mageiros* is directed towards its alimentary goal, as if at the very heart of the city's sacrificial mechanism lay the refusal to hear the accusations made by the Greeks of the hinterlands, those disciples of Pythagoras who confuse the *mageiroi* with hunters and reproach them for being murderers and for identifying with the instruments, the weapons that shed the blood.

In this world where only the protesters cry out to denounce the slayer, the *sphageus*[31] hidden in every sacrificer, it is strange to discover at the center of the temple at Delphi a god, the very purifier, praising the knife and surrounding himself with servants armed for killing. The Homeric *Hymn to Apollo* insists upon it. When the Cretans disembark from the ship that the god had turned towards Crissa, their first care before refreshing themselves is to raise an altar, light a fire upon it, and consecrate some white meal, the *alphita leuka*. In this place Apollo has the right only to a libation. But once they have reached the middle of the rocks where the temple will be raised, the sailors, uneasy at seeing neither vines nor pasture, hear Apollo foretell a plentiful table and meat for them: "Let each one of you take his knife in his right hand; it will not stop killing victims."[32] There is more than one worrisome figure in the temple of the Discharger of Arrows, beginning with the Knife, *Makhaireus,* who is the son of Banquet, *Daitas*—a pairing that says a great deal about the sacrificial ambiance at Delphi from Neoptolemus' misadventure to Aesop's miserable end.[33] Without a doubt, nowhere in any temple is the sacrificial weapon more obviously praised. It is the *makhaira,* the cutthroat, that faithful servants presented as sacrificers wear on their belts in the lifesized statues placed near the temple of Apollo *Mageirios* and *Lakeutes* (sacrificer and augur) at Pyla (Cyprus),[34] as well as in Phocis, at the center of the earth.

The commensal meal begins with division. Two systems seem to compete, both in the carving of the meat and its distribution. The first is centered on privilege, the *geras,* the meat privilege. The choice pieces—thigh, hindquarter, shoulder, and tongue—are given to the priest, king, or high magistrates of the city. In this case, the butcher's art is to divide the victim along its natural joints, detaching the limbs one after another.[35] In contrast, in the other system corresponding to the Homeric model of a "meal in equal parts,"[36] the animal, it appears, is divided entirely into pieces of equal weight, which are distributed by lottery.[37] But later in the aristocratic society of the epic the two systems, rather than being mutually exclusive, are combined. Once the choice piece or pieces have been taken, the most meat being awarded to those having a special honor or dignity, the rest of the victim can be distributed in an egalitarian fashion in accordance with a certain isonomic ideology of the city.[38] The ritual marks equality before the meat in two ways: first by lottery, which can apply either to the skewers or the portions of meat, which each are as interchangeable as the rights of the citizens within the circular space of the city. But equality can also be manifested through the sacrificial processes, as for example in the choice of a victim for the sacrifice offered to Zeus by the citizens of the entire community of Cos. Chosen from among the animals that each subgroup presents to the collectivity and submits to the judgment of Zeus' priest Polieus, the victim is brought before the hearth of the city, the Hestia.[39] It is brought to the central point, the *meson,* where common things are placed, in the heart of the circular space and equidistant from all the guests, with respect to which each citizen occupies an interchangeable position. "Placed in the middle," the meat from the animal can be the object of only an equal distribution, wherein the portion eaten by each of the guests consecrates, in alimentary and sacrificial order, his share of political rights that arise from his belonging to the circle of citizens and having in principle the same rights of speech and the exercise of power as the others. Here again, dietary practices reflect the political texture of the sacrifice as well as the type of social relationships involved therein.

*

One of the most obvious consequences of analyzing sacrificial procedures from an anthropological perspective with attention to their place within a network of socio-religious actions, practices, and symbolisms is to question the pertinence of the proposed models to explain the function of sacrifice as an autonomous institution in a specifically religious order. Thus, at the beginning of the century when Henri Hubert and Marcel Mauss propose in their *Essai sur le sacrifice*[40] a theory that aims to account for the complexity and diversity of sacrificial practices in the principal cultures of the world, they offer as its central mechanism a double process of communication between the sacred and the profane by means of a victim called to play a mediating role between the sacrificer and the divinity. The two poles are united by two complementary processes: the first, sacralization, leads from the profane to the sacred, while the other proceeds in the opposite direction, by desacralization. This is so to such a degree that the sacrifice is seen as essentially directed at establishing a relationship between the two separate domains that the chosen victim is able to unite at the same time that it keeps them apart. In 1958 Jean Rudhardt[41] demonstrated how the Maussian model, with its oscillation between sacred and profane, was inadequate in the case of the Greeks, where neither the sacrificer nor the victim is supposed to leave the world at any time; instead participation in a social group or political community authorizes the practice of sacrifice and receives in turn that which confirms the cohesion of the group and the coherence of the community's image with respect to the divine powers.

But Mauss' theory is only one episode in the great undertaking that from Robertson Smith up to Ernst Cassirer produces a unitary figure of sacrifice and places it at the heart of what was then the accepted definition of religion. The illusion regarding totemism during the same period from 1885 to 1920 would not have been so complete if the issue of the totem had not raised, in addition to the problem of the separation between man and the vegetable world, uneasy questions concerning the virtues imputed to some sacrificial rites for maintaining a form of community between man and animal.[42] Because he alternated between animal and human form, and because he existed at the juncture of the old agrarian foundations of the Near East and the new desires of salvation religions, a god such as Dionysus played a major role in the thinking of scholars at the turn of the century. They were careful to distinguish between the wild and repugnant rituals assigned to the "peoples of nature" and the modes of communional relationship whose moral value and spiritual aim brooked no doubt concerning their ties to the sphere of religion. From Robertson Smith and his anthropological analysis of the religion of the Semites, a path is cleared that begins with the biblical world and leads to the hinterlands of Christianity and the spirituality of western reason in the neo-Kantian philosophy of Cassirer. Undoubtedly, in the Christian sphere sacrifice has long been the cultic act that serves as the touchstone of religion and whose efficacy is repeatedly verified in voyage narratives. "It is," says Lafitau in 1724, "as ancient as Religion itself, and as widespread as the Nations subject to Religion, since there is not a one of them in which Sacrifice is not the custom, and among which it is not at the same time a proof of Religion."[43] But it is the arrival of a science of religions in the middle of the nineteenth century that accords sacrifice a theoretical status. One perspective dominates: evolutionism. And in the field of inquiry that emerges to produce a history of the elementary forms of religion, totemism, which is credited with a universal character, appears as the prototype of all sacrificial action. Robertson Smith recognizes the two essential components of the first form of sacrifice in the consumption of the totem animal killed by the clan: the common meal and blood alliance.[44] It was not necessary to wait for Salomon Reinach's loud denunciation of a survival of totemism in the Eucharist[45] to find that in his study Robertson Smith "thought of Christian communion first of all and found in the totem the prefiguration of the sacrificed god." Marcel Mauss had noted this in 1906[46] in distancing himself from the totemic hypothesis, which failed to grasp that sacrifice *of* the god had come after sacrifice *to* the god.[47] At the time his lucidity was unable to discern patterns of the same order in his own formulations. Yet they are apparent the moment that the Maussian model explicitly reveals in diagrammatic form that the *self*-sacrificing god points to the ultimate form of the sacrificial process. We insist on this point. According to the *Essai* of 1899, if sacrifice *to* the god comes first, and if, by virtue of the abnegation found therein, it is the operative principle of the social system by which society forms itself, then the sacrifice *of* the god who sacrifices *himself* defines the highest and, as it were, ideal limit of undivided abnegation.[48] Mauss puts it clearly: "Transformed and sublimated, the sacrifice *of* the god has been retained by Christian theology."[49] Cannot one in fact see, he adds, in the paschal lamb designating Christ even today the usual victim of an agrarian or pastoral sacrifice, the divinized victim, like the bull of Dionysus or another animal symbolizing the "wheat spirit"?[50] But the theory that has led to this endpoint undermines it nonetheless. For, incontestably, if all egotistical purposes seem to have disappeared in the sacrifice *of* the god (while interest and disinterestedness blend in the sacrifice *to* the god),[51] it remains that in the most advanced type of sacrifice the intermediary term, without which there is no sacrificial process in the Maussian model, recedes and vanishes so that the self-sacrificing god is confused with the victim and, in the most extreme case, with the sacrificer.[52] In other words, the analysis of Hubert and Mauss results in an image

of sacrifice that is not bound by the rule of the interplay between sacralization and desacralization, but whose privileged position seems essentially
linked to the extreme renunciation concentrated in the sacrifice of the divine person. The triumph reserved for "abnegation"—so total that it
brings with it the end of the contractual and the communional—would
not be so striking were not the final term in Mauss' theory also a point of
departure: i.e., the only possible locus for a unitary image of sacrifice in a
society in which any question pertaining to religion must necessarily be
posed in the field circumscribed by dominant Christian mentality.[53]

But it is certainly in the work of Emile Durkheim, in *Les formes élémentaires de la vie religieuse* (1910), where in the period between 1880 and
1930 the presuppositions motivating theoretical reflection on the phenomenon of sacrifice are best expressed. In 1910 totemism, in which the
most primitive social order seems to coincide with the most elementary
religious sense, had already begun to be suspect;[54] however, no one at that
time thought of questioning sacrifice. Everyone agreed to recognize it as
a fundamental phenomenon of both religion and society. Some even said
that the instinct for sacrifice is part of human nature.[55] In any case, there
was no doubt that it was the sacred act par excellence, and in a program
to analyze the constitutive elements of religion Alfred Loisy unhesitatingly
gave it first place.[56] No one doubts that sacrifice is a "great religious institution called upon to become one of the foundations of positive cult in
the advanced religions."[57] When Durkheim turns to totemism he well
knows that it is a hybrid, a monster uniting different species, but that it
can be disguised by building it a triple mask, albeit bizarre, with a sexual
totem framed by an individual and then a collective totem. The founder
of modern sociology would not have been so bold had he not been sure
of finding what he sought: a mixture of crude beliefs among which could
be found high peaks meeting at the point where the religions that followed began.[58] To demonstrate that the most primitive religious system
already contained all the essential elements of spiritual thought and life, it
was necessary to take the argument beyond the realm of beliefs to the level
of organized acts and practices into the realm of the cultic, at the very
point where, according to the interpretation originating with Hegel, the
god becomes aware of ego and, reciprocally, ego becomes aware of
the god.[59]

In practice the division is clearcut: the negative on one side, the positive
on the other. And the first precedes and introduces the second. This is
what Durkheim calls the ascetic path: prohibitions, inhibited activities,
the set of practices aiming to impose discomforts, abstinences, privations,

suffering, and renunciation.[60] The way is clearly marked: "Positive cult is possible only if man is trained in renunciation, abnegation, self-detachment and, consequently, suffering."[61] Asceticism is the hypertrophied form of cultic practice negatively denoted. But under the circumstances, the negative is only the obverse of a positivity that, in the Durkheimian argument, takes its force and vigor from it; for even before discovering the positive side of cult we can no longer doubt that "asceticism plays an integral role in all human culture,"[62] and that without disinterest and endurance there is no religion.

After this warning we have only to examine how, in the most primitive religious system—the Arunta, in Durkheim's collection—all the elements of sacrifice are already arranged. We are invited to the spectacle of the *Intichiuma*.[63] We are introduced to the Caterpillar clan. They are important people, no longer a horde or an "unstable mass of individuals" like the Pygmies (concerning whom Durkheim wonders if they possess even one of the attributes determining human society).[64] The Caterpillar clan forms a troupe; it is a society that participates in civilization. It has its banner, an animal emblem, the Caterpillar, with which the clan sentimentally identifies itself. And the Caterpillar clan has its festival, set by the chief. It is marked by two phases. In the first are rites meant to assure the prosperity of the animal species and marked by interdictions and ascetic practices. The people of the clan draw their own blood to revive the virtues of the totem and severely forbid one another to eat representatives of their totem species. The second phase is marked by the lifting of the restrictions. A great harvest of caterpillars takes place, and all eat them in abundance. In the center is the chief's meal, during which he is presented specimens that he solemnly consumes in order to re-create the species.

What are the essential elements of the sacrificial model found in this primitive spectacle? Durkheim pays lengthy homage to Robertson Smith for his insight in having seen, from Aberdeen, Scotland, and without ever attending an *Intichiuma*, an "act of alimentary communion" in the original sacrifice—that is, a meal that permits men to take communion with a divine power through the same flesh and thereby commemorate their natural kinship.[65] Later the discovery of the totemic meal allows this model to be refined by showing that food communion is accomplished through the incorporation of the clan's vital principle, its soul and person. There the sacred being is eaten, immolated by the very people who worship it. But Durkheim goes further.[66] Sacrifice is not only communion; it is also, as its primitive form suggests, renunciation and abnegation. In the *Intichiuma* the decisive action is not the eating but the offering. And the oblation is there for a key reason; the act of offering implies the idea of a moral subject that the offering is meant to satisfy. Thanks to the study of Caterpillar clan, there is no longer any doubt; there can be no communion without renunciation. Even the most crude and primitive of sacrifices is inspired by a moral force.

During the same time many historians of religion, with different intentions, put the sacrament of the Eucharist, in which the Christian eats the body of the Lord and drinks his blood, on a parallel with the ancient practice of the worshipers of Dionysus who tear animals apart to devour them, believing that they are eating the god's flesh. This forced defenders of the Christian faith, such as the Dominican M.-J. Lagrange,[67] to denounce the "aberration of the religious sense in extremely low clans," where "carnal and disgusting" rites were practiced—the Greeks being absolved from this condemnation because they were so sensitive to the horror involved that before taking part in the enactment of the drama of Zagreus-Dionysus, "they covered their faces with plaster, surely to avoid being recognized." All the while the same apologists, in order to show "how humanity left to its own devices comes to profane its most noble tendencies in a degrading manner," bring to light the spiritual nature of the Christian rite, in which one eats *according to the spirit.*

To avoid confusing the crude rites of the "people of nature" with the spiritual mystery of the Eucharist in the one true religion, a division was made within sacrifice—between an instinct that had strayed into the abject practice of devouring bloody flesh and, at the other extreme, the noble tendencies of a purely spiritual relationship where the forms of eating are negligible and whose alimentary aspects are glossed over, as if denied. Catholic exegesis criticized Robertson Smith, in fact, for blurring the line between what Lagrange (among others) calls "mythology," where animism thrives recognizable by its scandalous ways, and religion, which cannot be put on an equal footing with nature—for it appears only at the level of human civilization, with the emergence of moral needs.[68]

Durkheim's analysis follows the same course by showing that the most primitive and thus the simplest offering implies an act of renunciation and postulates a moral subject. However, for Durkheim there is no break but only a difference of degree between the Caterpillar clan, where the most elementary form of society is established, and Catholic, Protestant, or Jewish milieus of high spirituality.[69] At either extreme is the same ethical will, which minimizes alimentary customs as well as the details of the killing and the status of the victim—everything that is not the essence of the sacrificial relationship, in other words, the spirit of sacrifice. "We are in a phase of moral mediocrity."[70] The statement Durkheim makes at the close of *Les formes élémentaires de la vie religieuse* is an underlying motivation for Sociology. Like Tylor's science of civilization,[71] Durkheimian social analysis is animated by a reforming spirit. Sociology, writes Georges Davy, should be the philosophy that will aid in definitively establishing the republic and in inspiring rational reforms at the same time that it endows the nation with a principle of order and a moral doctrine.[72] When in 1916, at the height of World War I, he composed a primary school course on morals, Durkheim applied the same strategy to his reflections on the state in his lessons on socialism.[73] The schools of tomorrow must reestablish moral authority by teaching the child the religion of discipline and showing him "the joy of acting in concert with others and following an impersonal law shared by all."[74] Socialism has as its mission to bring forth a new moral solidarity among men in a state that is first and foremost an organ of reflection—"intelligence put in the place of dark instinct"—where everyone is to varying degrees in service of society, where each individual agrees "to conform to a moral discipline."[75] These words are certainly those of a great priest of humanity, as the philosopher André Lalande respectfully notes in 1906.[76] And if society thwarts our natural appetites (precisely because it has a mission to raise us above ourselves),[77] this is because the social is wholly rooted in the spirit of sacrifice, and society is unthinkable without its intricate relationship to the lofty figure of sacrifice.

After 1800 (the year of the first celebration of July 14—memorable since the young Durkheim, it is said, spent the whole day in the street to be part of the enthusiasm of the crowd[78]) the vocation of sacrifice is to fulfill the major social function: to mobilize mental and moral energies. Without abnegation, the collective forces would be deprived of ideal existence, and the sacred would suffer a great decline.

But between 1880 and 1930 the unitary figure of sacrifice is not confined to the milieu of the sociologists, who did the most to give it the seductive status of a universal form of religion. It also occupies a central place in the thought of a "European" philosopher such as Cassirer, whose *Philosophy of Symbolic Forms*[79] makes the sacrificial act the kernel around which intellectual activity develops and the practice of worship first is organized: a practice ordered by a truth inherent in the so-called higher religions because they seem to lead humanity's spiritual tendency to its conclusion, drawing the forms of worship toward an increasingly developed interiorization. The trajectory of the sacrificial institution is marked by its original form: an innate negativity—what Cassirer calls the limitation of sensate desire—a renunciation that the ego imposes on itself. "It is there we find one of the essential motives of the sacrifice, which from the beginning raises it above the magical vision of the world."[80] The simplest forms of the sacrificial act reveal a new orientation of will in human action. Up to then, that is, in the earlier magical state, the ego still knew no barrier that it could not truly surpass on occasion. With the appearance of sacrifice, everything changes, for the most obscure or even the crudest of sacrificial acts implies something unprecedented: a movement of self-abandon. It is the intuition that any expansion, any increase of the forces of the ego, is tied to a corresponding limitation.[81]

In the conclusion of the *Essai* and in profound agreement with what Cassirer will write twenty years later, Mauss observes that everyone finds an advantage in sacrifice: the collectivity and individuals, the social norm, and above all, civilization.[82] By means of sacrificial activity, the collectivity attains "this good, strong, serious, terrible character" that is one of the essential traits of any social personality. The fatherland, property, work, the human person, all are to be credited to sacrifice as a social phenomenon.[83] The asceticism within this institution enables the individual to discover a fixed center within, a singleness of will when confronted with the multiple and divergent flux of the pulsions of the sensations. The gift, the desire to give, and the oblation all confirm this orientation. It is then that the human being detaches himself to some extent from the objects of immediate desire. And this movement becomes broader and more elevated, from the fundamental forms of totemism to the enactment of animal sacrifice in the religions of the highly developed cultures with, as the ultimate expression giving sacrifice its true significance, the god who sacrifices himself—the figure that joins, for Cassirer as for Mauss, the mythology of the mysteries of Dionysus with the exemplary spirituality of the Christian mystery of the Eucharist.[84] Today, from a distance that is extended even more by the analyses published in this volume, it seems important to say that the notion of sacrifice is indeed a category of the thought of yesterday, conceived of as arbitrarily as totemism—decried earlier by Lévi-Strauss—both because it gathers into one artificial type elements taken from here and there in the symbolic fabric of societies and because it reveals the surprising power of annexation that Christianity still subtly exercises on the thought of these historians and sociologists who were convinced they were inventing a new science.[85]

TWO

At Man's Table:
Hesiod's Foundation Myth of Sacrifice
Jean-Pierre Vernant

TO determine the status of Greek sacrifice we have at our disposal a
mythical account that, if fully analyzed, provides a valuable key to the
mental system to which the ritual refers and the vast network of meanings
that it bears. In an episode of the *Theogony,* some sequences of which are
taken up again in *Works and Days,* Hesiod tells the story of how Prometheus, acting as Zeus' rival, works by fraud, lies, and trickery to achieve
his own aims while thwarting those of the ruler of the gods. Now, the first
result of this battle of wits between Titan and Olympian is the ritual distribution of the pieces of the sacrificed domestic animal (in this case a great
ox led, slaughtered, and carved by Prometheus) to men (the meat and the
entrails laden with fat, everything that can be eaten) and to gods (the bare
bones consumed in the sacrificial fire with some fat and aromatics).[1] Explicitly expressed in lines 556–57, "From this it happens that on earth the
human race burns white bones for the Immortals on altars exuding the
perfume of incense," the etiological value of this sequence of the myth has
been recognized by all commentators. But its significance has been re-
markably reduced. It has almost always been seen as the explanation of a
particular and minor characteristic of the rite, the answer to a kind of
paradox that the blood sacrifice, which is also a meal, would have posed
for the religious conscience of the Greeks because of an incomprehensible
detail. Sacrifice appeared as an offering to the gods to honor them and
encourage their favor. Under these conditions, how can we explain that
instead of setting the best part aside for them, men give the gods the
inedible part of the animal, the scraps, as it were? By restricting the meaning of the first part of the text to this single point, we are forced to consider it more or less gratuitous and to misunderstand the connections with

The first half of this article appeared in a different translation entitled "Sacrificial and Alimentary Codes in Hesiod's Myth of Prometheus," in *Myth, Religion, and Society: Structuralist
Essays by M. Detienne, L. Gernet, J.-P. Vernant and P. Vidal-Naquet.* Ed. R. L. Gordon. (Cambridge University Press–Editions de la Maison des Sciences de l'Homme, 1981).—TRANS.

the following sequences that give the myth its overall import. If this epic presenting the character Prometheus, his rivalry with Zeus, and his final failure, recounted by Hesiod in the long passage of the *Theogony* (507–616) devoted to the descendants of Iapetus, concerns sacrifice only incidentally and by chance, we are then led to concede that Hesiod arbitrarily chose Prometheus to bear the responsibility for sacrificial practice. Hesiod would not reveal the profound significance of this practice by placing it at the nexus of an elaborate theological system but would instead propose a circumstantial explanation by creating a fable as one would concoct a pretext to justify oneself after the fact. From this perspective it would be impossible to see what the relationship could be between the first act of the Promethean drama in the Hesiodic version and what follows—between the carving of the ox and the ritual allocation of its parts on the one hand, and the theft of fire in the second part and the creation of the first woman that concludes this tragedy on the other. Thus Hesiod would have stitched completely disparate elements together in the same text. To the traditional theme of the theft of fire he would have artificially connected an etiological myth intended to account for what he found strange in sacrificial practice and a story entirely of his own invention about the origins of woman that reflected his personal antifeminist "philosophy." It would be as vain, then, to seek a coherent meaning in the myth as to hope to find some enlightenment there concerning the nature and function of sacrifice.

This position can no longer be maintained, not only because it arises from a conception of mythical thought that is now outmoded, but more specifically and also more concretely because the text contradicts it on all points. In his study of the *Theogony*, Hans Schwabl has shown that on the formal level the Promethean episode obeys strict compositional rules that give the entire passage an incontestable unity and make it a rigorously articulated whole.[2] This cohesion is no less strong on the level of the narrative content, since in the linking of the episodes Hesiod emphasizes the perfect continuity of the account and shows very clearly for each sequence its necessary dependence on the preceding one. It is because Zeus never forgets for an instant the trick Prometheus played on him by giving men the meat of the sacrificed animal that he decides henceforth to deny mortals his (heavenly) fire.[3] It is because he sees the fire, secretly stolen by the Titan, burning in the midst of the humans that he counters this new fraudulent gift that men have received by offering them this third and last fraudulent gift, this "opposite of fire," the first woman.[4] The action obeys a flawless logic from beginning to end, following the thread of a drama whose successive stages are rigorously governed by the order of the narrative. Finally, on the semantic level we have shown in a previous study[5] that a very tight network of symbolic correspondences exists, so that if the elements are linked to each other in the linear sequence of the narration, they form together at the end a unique picture in which all the parts echo one another in a highly ordered arrangement.

On the diachronic level, the theft of fire plays a mediating role; by it and through it the link is made between the first act, Prometheus' cunning (*dolos*) in allocating the sacrificial parts, and the last, Zeus' craftiness (*dolos*) in giving men the first woman. This deed also brings about the reversal of the action and respective positions of the actors. In the first part of the story, the initiative and guile belong to Prometheus; Zeus appears to be the dupe.[6] The Titan gives men gifts that delight them. After the theft of fire, everything is inverted. The initiative and cunning pass to the side of Zeus. Now it is he who "gives" to men, but the joy that the humans feel when presented with the divine gift is precisely the snare in which they will be caught and even, broadly speaking, the symbol of the unhappiness of the mortal condition. From this standpoint, the last episode appears not simply as the ineluctable consequence of what preceded it. As if in a mirror, it reflects all the preceding events, puts them into place, and organizes them. Because of it, they illuminate each other and take on their true meaning, which can be revealed only at the end of the whole adventure. It is necessary indeed for the "trap" of woman to have appeared in order for the true nature of the "trap" set for Zeus at the outset by Prometheus, when the Titan "fixes" the portions of the sacrificial victim so that men benefit from all the meat, to be revealed in all its ramifications. The good portion, over which the mortals congratulate themselves (as they do over the "beautiful evil" that Zeus grants them in the person of Woman), is revealed in reality as the bad. The ambush the Titan prepared to outwit Zeus backfires and ultimately redounds to the humans. Even fire, this fire stolen by Prometheus, despite its advantages, is a gift no less ambiguous than the first feminine creature, as it too is well adorned with dangerous seductive powers.[7]

In the texture of the narrative the sequences are too tightly knit, their symbolic values too enmeshed, for it to be possible to isolate them and treat each one separately. The myth must be taken for what it is, not an aggregate of heterogeneous episodes but a single story; and it is necessary to recognize that in this cohesive structure the relationships that unite the blood sacrifice, the Promethean fire, and the creation of woman cannot be the product either of pure chance or the gratuitous fantasy of the author. They respond to a necessary order that is the result of the very content of the myth, of the function that Hesiod assigns it in the context of his *Theogony*. What is at issue in the conflict pitting the Titan's craftiness against the Olympian's faultless intelligence is, in the final analysis, the status of the human condition, the mode of existence characterizing humanity. Sacrificial practice is presented as the first result and most direct expression of the distance created between men and gods on the day that Prometheus started his road to rebellion. The myth connects the ritual of sacrifice to primordial events that have made men what they are, mortal creatures[8] living on earth[9] in the midst of countless ills,[10] eating grain from the fields they have worked,[11] and accompanied by female spouses.[12] In other words, men have become a race of beings completely separated from those to whom at the outset they were very close, living together and sitting at the same tables to share the same meals[13]—the Blessed Immortals, residing in heaven and fed on ambrosia, toward whom now rises the smoke of sacrificial offerings.

The episode concerning the sacrifice is neither secondary nor supplementary. It is at the heart of the myth. It does not aim to explain a strange detail of the ritual, the cremation of the bones. In the distinction between the shares allocated to men and gods in the sacrifice, it stresses the difference that now separates them, their membership in two distinct races. Just as this former proximity was mythically expressed by the image of a community of guests enjoying a banquet together, the eventual separation is reflected in the contrast between two types of eating. The difference between diets found at the very heart of the ritual seeks, however, to establish a kind of contact and communication between the two separated races, a bond that leads, as much as possible, to building a bridge between the earth and heaven.

The issue of food, so pronounced in the myth, has multiple echoes. Sacrifice is presented as a meal in which meat is eaten, but this consumption of fleshly food obeys a whole series of restrictions and constraints. First, it is limited to some animal species and excludes others. Second, the killing, butchering, carving, preparation, and consumption of the meat follow precise rules. Finally, there is a religious intentionality to the meal. It aims to honor the gods by inviting them to take part in a feast that is thereby at least theoretically their own, a *dais theōn*, at which they make themselves present in some manner and the offering of which they can either accept or reject.[14] In this sense as an alimentary rite sacrifice is not limited to establishing the conditions that authorize the slaughter of an animal for food and make it legal or even an act of piety for men to consume its flesh. Because it is directed toward the gods and claims to include them with the group of guests in the solemnity and joy of the celebration, it evokes the memory of the ancient commensality when, seated together, men and gods made merry day after day at shared meals. However, if in its intent sacrifice hearkens back to these far-off times of the golden age when, sharing the same food, men still lived "like gods," far from all evils, work, disease, old age, and women,[15] it is no less true that sacrifice is a reminder that these blessed times when men and gods sat down together to feast are forever ended. The ritual sets the incorruptible bones aside for the gods and sends them, consumed by the flames, on high in the form of fragrant smoke and gives men the meat of an already lifeless animal, a piece of dead flesh, so that they may satisfy for a moment their constantly awakening hunger. Normally, meat cannot be eaten except on the occasion of a sacrifice and by following its rules. The presence of the gods sanctions this feast of fleshly food, but only to the extent that what truly belongs to the gods is set aside for them: the very life of the animal, released from the bones with the soul at the moment the victim falls dead and gushing forth in the blood splattering the altar—in short, those parts of the animal that, like the aromatics with which they are burned, escape the putrefaction of death. By eating the edible pieces men, even as they reinvigorate their failing strength, recognize the inferiority of their mortal condition and confirm their complete submission to the Olympians whom the Titan believed he could dupe with impunity when he established the model of the first sacrifice. The alimentary rite that brings men into contact with the divine underscores the distance that separates them. Communication is established by a religious procedure that in reminding men of the Promethean fault emphasizes the insurmountable distance between men and gods. It is the very function of the myth, as Hesiod tells it, to reveal the origins and dire consequences of this situation.

In this perspective the analysis of the Hesiodic account confirms and extends the conclusions that Jean Casabona, working from a completely different viewpoint, had drawn from his research on the Greek sacrificial vocabulary.[16] Recalling that for us sacrifice and butchering belong to different semantic zones, he noted that among the Greeks matters were completely different. The same vocabulary encompasses the two domains, from Homer to the end of the classical age. Ancient Greek has no other terms to convey the idea of slaughtering an animal to butcher it than those referring to sacrifice or killing for the gods. *Hiereuō* can be translated in the one way as well as the other. In Homer *hiereion* refers to the animal both as "sacrificial victim" and as "animal to be butchered"; in contrast to *sphagion*, *hiereion* conveys the sense of the victim whose flesh will be eaten.

The term simultaneously evokes sacrifice and butchering. Lastly, *thuō*, which eventually prevailed as the general term referring to the totality of the sacrifical ceremony and never ceased to convey the memory of burnt offerings and fragrant smoke, applies both to the rite of slaughtering the animal and the fleshly feast that follows it. It is found associated with terms meaning "to feast, to eat well."

By distinguishing, in the body of the ritually slaughtered animal, between two and only two parts,[17] which are sharply contrasted because they are opposites from the standpoint of their food value—in other words, by treating the sacrifice as a type of eating characteristic of man as distinct from the gods—Hesiod fashions this first sequence of the Promethean myth within the lines of traditional religious thought. Far from innovating on this point by forcing the meanings of the terms or quibbling about widespread notions, his account is firmly supported by the semantic field of the sacrificial vocabulary and can be substantiated by ordinary linguistic usage.

1. The Quarrel over the Portions

Whoever wishes to understand the form of Greek sacrifice that pertains to the consumption of food must therefore take Hesiod's account completely seriously. He must keep to the text as closely as possible, discounting nothing, and examine both the similarities and the differences between the two versions given in the *Theogony* and *Works and Days*.

First of all, how does the Promethean episode fit into each poem? And how may this context clarify the status of the sacrificial rite? In the *Theogony* the situation is clear. The work is entirely devoted to the origins, birth, battles, and victory of Zeus, his achievement of a sovereignty that unlike the preceding reign succeeds in establishing the foundations of a definitively assured, unshakable, and permanent power. Zeus' conquest of the celestial kingship not only means, as the text emphasizes on three occasions, that everything is set in place for the gods with a strict distribution of honors, functions and privileges among them;[18] along with the monarch who has instituted it, the ordered arrangement of the entire cosmos is henceforth maintained as immutable and intangible.

In an account where everything happens on the level of the gods and between gods, there is no place for an anthropogony in the strict sense of the word. We learn how the gods came to be, not men. The *Theogony* does not tell us whether Gaea, the Earth, gave birth to men as she did to the first divine powers, or whether they were created by Zeus and the Immortals, or born from the ashes of the stricken Titans, as the Orphic tradition has it. Men are nonetheless present in the narrative; they suddenly appear in a byway, in an episode that the poet devotes to the offspring of Iapetus, or more precisely his son, Prometheus. Here is no human genesis, as one might expect in a creation poem. The text speaks of humans as if they are beings that were already there, living with the gods and mingling with them.[19] Prometheus' act does not bring men to the existence they already possess but reaffirms the status imparted to them at the heart of an organized universe; it defines their mortal condition in contrast to that of the Blessed Immortals. This positioning of humanity, this delineation of the ways of living that are appropriate to it and make it a separate race occurs by means of an allocation between men and gods of what is due each of them. At Zeus' demand, or at least with his agreement, Prometheus is responsible for bringing about this decisive apportionment; the procedure that he employs to carry out this task is precisely the carving and the distribution of the parts of the sacrificial victim.[20] The division of the ox slaughtered by the son of Iapetus and the creation, by his efforts, of two separate shares intended for gods and men determine the cleavage between the two races. The division of the animal both provokes and reflects the opposition between the two respective parties. The distance separating mortals from Immortals is begun in sacrifice and perpetuated by sacrifice. On the lines separating the different portions taken from the victim is projected the boundary between the immutable youth of the Olympians, masters of heaven, and this ephemeral form of existence that men on earth must assume to become who they are.

Thus humanity was made into what it is following a division analogous to the one over which Zeus presided with respect to the gods after he acceded to the throne, when he established the domain and attributes for each one.[21] But among the gods the division follows two modalities that stand in sharp contrast. In the case of his enemies and rivals for divine sovereignty, the Titans and Typhon, the distribution of honors is governed by violence and coercion.[22] Banished to Tartarus, the defeated gods are thrown out of the game. Shriven of all honor (*atimoi*), they are excluded from the organized world. Among the Olympians and their allies, on the other hand, the allocation is made amid harmony and mutual consent.[23] What of the distribution that gave men their status? It is the result neither of brutal violence nor mutual agreement. It was not imposed by force or decided by common consent. It operates according to a procedure that is fundamentally ambiguous, contradictory, and rigged. On the one hand, violence is concealed by its opposite: smiles, praises, politeness, and feigned reverence;[24] on the other, the contract and the rules of the game

function only as subterfuges that mask the ways the adversary is manipu-
lated in spite of himself. Instead of the open warfare that divided the Titans and Olympians there is a muted conflict, a test of cleverness and du-
plicity, in which the rival is quietly defeated by being caught in his own
trap. Instead of the loyal and trusted agreement that governed the allocation among victorious allies, there is deceit, a double game in which the
words uttered in broad daylight always conceal a treacherous ulterior mo-
tive. This untrustworthy and contorted procedure corresponds to the
equivocal character of the status of men in the relationships which bind
them to the gods even as they separate them. For Zeus, men are not adversaries of such high caliber that it would be necessary to remove them
once and for all by means of an all-out war. Nor are they peers who must
be tactfully managed in an alliance by an equitable sharing of privileges.
Like all mortal creatures, like the animals, they are on a different level from
the gods, at a distance, alien to the divine sphere. But alone among mortal
creatures and unlike the animals, their way of living involves a constant
reference to the supernatural powers, a relationship peculiar to them
alone. No city, no human life exists that is not linked by organized worship to the divine world and does not establish a kind of community with
it. In the divine sphere it is Prometheus who exhibits the ambiguity of the
human condition, as separate as it is close to the divine, both external and
related to it. With respect to Zeus his position is equivocal on all levels.
Though a Titan, he has not gone back to his brothers' clan to fight the
Olympian in the war among the gods. He is not the enemy of Zeus, but
according to Aeschylus by his plotting he himself ensured the Olympian's
triumph. Nor will he be forever banished from the world, consigned at
the end to the depths of Tartarus. For all that, however, he is not a faithful
and reliable ally. At the very heart of the ordered universe over which Zeus
presides, he stands as a rival, embodying even in the circle of the Olympian
divinities an opposing point where is expressed, in the form of a claim or
even rebellion, a sort of complicity with everything that the world contains in contrast to the gods—negative, gratuitous suffering, inexplicable
and arbitrary misfortune. This opposition is all the more dangerous because it takes place on the very ground where Zeus sees himself as unsur-
passable: that of intelligence, cleverness, foresight, of that "knowledge" of
which men, for their part, claim to have their share. Prometheus uses the
resources of a fertile and farseeing mind in order to favor the humans at
the gods' expense. He seeks to remove the ills inseparable from the human
condition and obtain benefits for them that the gods have kept as their
privilege.[25] If he secretly undermines Zeus' plans, including the mission

with which the latter had entrusted him, it is because he aims, by reducing the distance between men and gods as much as possible, to make men into beings that in some way are his equals, truly Promethean creatures who will be neither completely separate, distant, inferior, and subordinate, as Zeus wishes them to be, nor completely identical, near, equal, and gifted, as the Blessed Immortals are among themselves. Men would be situated midway between, in an intermediate position that recalls his own mediating function, his ambiguous role of hostile ally, rival accomplice, freed bondsman, pardoned criminal, reconciled and redeemed rebel.

In the episode of the *Theogony* the Titan Prometheus, close enough to humanity to wish to bring it closer to the gods, represents a subverting of the Olympian order. This order has envisioned for the particular category of beings that is humanity (with whom the Titan is on special terms) fatigue, loss of strength, pain, disease, and death—in other words, all misfortune, which constitutes the radical negation of the divine state. If Prometheus had prevailed in this battle of wits waged to separate men and gods, sacrifice would commemorate men's access to this nonmortal form of existence to which men cannot help but aspire. Prometheus' failure not only makes the sacrificial rite into an act symbolizing the complete segregation of the two races, it gives this rupture the character of an irremediable and justified fall whose justice mortals acknowledge every time they sacrifice according to the Promethean mode and enter into communication with the higher powers.

*

Indeed, the context and some details of the text in Hesiod's account of the series of misfortunes unleashed by Prometheus find their full justification on a theological level. Paradoxically, Prometheus is described as good, benevolent (*eus*).[26] But the benevolence he displays toward men is only the other side, the visible obverse of his secret hostility toward Zeus. The partiality (*heterozēlōs*, 1. 544) he shows in his allocation of the meat reflects his desire to subvert the distributive order embodied by Zeus the sovereign. The plots he contrives in carrying out the arbiter's tasks entrusted to him are the expression of his deep-seated rivalry with Zeus (*erizeto boulas*, 534). Humanity's fall is thus directly connected with competition, jealousy, and quarrelsomeness—in a word, with *eris,* that sinister daughter of Night who, because of Prometheus, has insidiously slipped into the ethereal world of the gods of Olympus. Now in this world *eris* is foreign. More exactly, with Zeus as king, *eris* should have vanished. Although this world was the result of an open battle, the victory of the son of Cronus has not only put an end to conflict but has consigned the period of the conflicts between the gods to a time predating the Olympian order, just as it has banished the enemy powers to a space outside the realm of the Immortals.[27] A passage of the *Theogony* is clear on the subject; if any conflict and discord (*eris kai neikos*) arise among the Blessed Ones, a procedure has been established to dispatch the guilty party without delay or debate to the reaches beyond the divine domain. Deprived of awareness, breath, and life, wrapped in a deathlike sleep, he is excluded from the council and the banquets where the Immortals feast.[28]

As the narrative of an *eris* between a god and Zeus, the entire Promethean episode introduces into the plot of the *Theogony* the tale of a rivalry that is paradoxical, unlike others, and essentially concerning creatures other than the gods. Compared to the quarrel between the Titans and the Olympians, the difference is obvious. Promethean *eris* is not frank hostility or open war. It seeks no power and does not claim to usurp Zeus' place. It does not appear prior to his victory, at the foundation of order, when the honors were distributed. This *eris* does not question the Olympian's sovereignty, but in a surreptitious way attempts to bend it from within. And it does not resemble the other *eris* mentioned in the *Theogony* as occuring among the Immortals, whose rule, already firmly established and organized in divine society, is settled from the first by a quasi-juridical procedure of expelling the guilty one. Promethean *eris* does not appear after the foundation of the order or prior to it. It seems to occur mythically at the same time as the foundation of order, coextensive with the distributive tasks undertaken by Zeus. More exactly, it coincides with a very particular aspect of these tasks, with something that does not fit and raises a problem because it involves equivocal, disconcerting creatures whose status could only be the result of a lopsided compromise—a rough and ready arrangement at the outcome of a contest between divine adversaries who have opposed one another point by point, each blocking the projects of the other in turn until the final result is achieved. Certainly, at the end of the match, Zeus' will triumphs. But to prevail it must follow the path laid out by the conflict with Prometheus, accepting new stakes with each hand and keeping track of the points scored in favor of men by the Titan in his cleverness—points that Zeus, unable to simply make disappear, must turn against men.

This analysis explains the skewed character of the Promethean episode, which forms a parenthesis within the developmental line of the *Theogony*. It is a double parenthesis, which appears first on the level of the genealogical exposition and then on the succession of divine events. In line 337, Hesiod begins to relate the lineage of the Titans, whose names he has already given in the order of their birth running (for the males) from Oceanus to Cronus—from eldest to youngest—by way of Coeus, Crios, Hyperion, and Iapetus. In this way we learn who were the children of Oceanus, Hyperion, Crios, and Coeus. But beginning with line 453, where the lineage of Cronus appears instead of Iapetus', the genealogical account, via Zeus' birth, connects with the account of mythical events forming the second set of legends of divine succession (the first set contained the emasculation of Uranus and the establishment of Cronus as king) and goes into the central theme of the conflicts over the sovereignty of heaven (the struggle between Zeus and Cronus, the Olympians against the Titans). Cronus swallows his children so that none of them will take his place on the throne. Zeus escapes his father's voracity. First he makes Cronus cough up those he has swallowed. Then he delivers the Cyclopes from their bonds, and they give him the instrument of his victory, lightning, "on which Zeus henceforth relies in order to reign over mortals and Immortals" (506). It is at this point that Hesiod interrupts the narrative of Zeus' battles to return to the genealogy with the lineage of Iapetus, which normally should have appeared after those of the Titans older than Cronus. But in reality the primary function of Iapetus' genealogy is to introduce the account of the *eris* that pits Prometheus against Zeus. This *eris* is at the periphery both of the battles for sovereignty (it has nothing to do with the battles of the Titans) and of the organization of the divine world under Zeus' reign (since this reign excludes *eris*). Thus its logical place in the account is neither clearly before nor clearly after Zeus' victory. It is located to the side, at the periphery, just as the status of the human race in the *Theogony* appears external and foreign to the great conflict over the possession of power that split the world of the gods. Indeed there is not the slightest allusion in the poem to human existence under the reign of Cronus. The Promethean sequence precedes the florid narrative of the war against the Titans, the triumph of Zeus, and the distribution of honors. Positioned between the liberation of the Cyclopes and the gift of lightning that precede it, and the liberation of the Hundred Arms signifying the Olympian victory, which immediately follows, this parenthesis appears in a context where Zeus' reign appears assured even before the details of the struggle have been the subject of a real narrative.

The scene takes place in Mecone, the ancient name for Sicyon. Therefore we know the exact earthly and human place that was the arena of the match but not the precise moment it occurred in the the divine chronology. In other words, to the extent that the confrontation between the two divinities concerns the nature of the relations between men and gods instead of divine society itself, Promethean *eris* operates on a temporal axis that does not exactly match that of the gods. The two temporal orders seem to correspond in the account, but exact congruence is impossible. Similarly, Promethean *eris,* unlike the Titans' and the juridical *eris* of the Olympians, brings to the divine sphere a dimension of existence, a quality of being that is too closely linked to the human for it to be perfectly integrated into the hierarchical order of the divine powers.

*

The drama of the *eris,* in the *Theogony* directed toward and finally reaching men by way of the gods, is played out in *Works and Days* on Boeotian soil with no intermediaries between Hesiod and his brother Perses.

The parallels between the contexts of each account are more developed than is first apparent. In the *Theogony,* the Promethean hoax concerning the parts of the sacrificed animal had been introduced by *gar,* "for," which connected the episode that is the source of man's misfortune directly with the preceding line relating Prometheus' *eris* toward Zeus. In *Works and Days,* the version of the Promethean theme also opens with a *gar,* which this time relates to the lesson that Hesiod has just given his brother on the occasion of the *eris* that divides them. Their *klēros,* their family inheritance, has been divided between them. This division is not the result of violence or brute force, as when one makes off with enemy loot in a war. Nor is it the result of an amicable agreement between the two brothers, as it should have been. To get more than his share Perses stirred up quarrels and dissension (*neikea kai dērin*). He brought the affair before the judgment of the kings of Thespiae, who in principle represent the distributive justice of Zeus the sovereign. But bribed by presents, the kings did not decide equitably. They gave a twisted sentence, a biased opinion. Favoring the party in the wrong, they divided the shares unequally, giving to one much of what belonged to the other, in the same spirit of partiality that, ironically, Zeus resented in Prometheus in the *Theogony.* The analogy between the two situations, divine and human, introducing the Promethean myth in each work with the sad consequences involved for mortals, appears obvious. This is not all. Hesiod does not stop with reminding his brother of the quarrel the latter had sought with him and of the fraudulent distribution he was able to obtain at Hesiod's expense. He widens the scope of this private conflict to the dimensions of universal justice and order, and founds on it what can be termed a veritable theology of *eris,* insofar as Night's daughter has stamped all of human existence with her seal. And this theology opens *Works and Days* with an explicit allusion to the *Theogony,* which it takes up and refines in the chapter on *eris.*

From the gods' perspective, in fact, *eris* appeared unique. The only example the Immortals knew was the violent fight during which Zeus triumphed over his rivals; his victory banished it from divine society.[29] But the moment matters are viewed from the human standpoint, the picture changes. Then there is no longer one *eris* but two, and this duplication of the daughter of Night corresponds to the omnipotence she exerts over men's lives, to her constant presence for good as well as for evil. In her contrasted, doubled, and ambiguous form, *eris* is consubstantial to the human condition. The bad *eris* already has two sides, just as there are two sorts of evil disputes among men: war with a foreign enemy on the battlefield, and discord within the community in the public square.[30] The first relies on the force of arms, the second sets tongues wagging and guile in motion.[31] However, whether they utilize force or guile, both have the same goal: to lay a hand on the loot, to take a part of the wealth at another's expense by stripping him of what is rightly his. Ill-gotten gains are short-lived. Zeus himself hastens to award the guilty the hard retribution for their crimes,[32] just as he squelched the brutal force of the Titans and punished the fraudulent ruse of Prometheus. This bad *eris,* extinct among the gods, punished among mortals, is not loved by men. If they honor it, says Hesiod, it is against their will, compelled by the decisions of the Immortals (1.15).

But before giving birth to this divisive *eris,* which the divine will has given man as companion against his will, Night had given birth to another one, similar but with a different nature, whose praises the wise man must sing. This *eris* inspires any man who sees abundance thrive in the fields and house of a neighbor who has worked harder than he to emulate that neighbor. From his luminous ethereal heights Zeus established this competitive *eris,* this zeal for work, as the foundation here below of any fairly-gotten wealth. He buried it deep in the roots of the earth (*gaie*)[33] where men live and from which they draw their subsistence. The son of Cronus wanted men to find the way to wealth by this *eris,* according to the order that he himself established. So there is no way for mortal man to escape *eris,* which completely bounds his life. There is only the choice of the good over the bad. It is not by idling away the hours talking in the agora, meddling in disputes, and avoiding agricultural labor (*ap' ergou*) that Perses can hope to manage his affairs.[34] If he is to have the means to live (*bios*), that is, the fruit of Demeter (*Dēmeteros akte*)[35] that Gaea gives to men in the necessary quantity when the earth is cultivated, he must devote himself to the task—water the furrows with his sweat, and compete with others in the work. How could it be otherwise? On the one hand, Zeus makes men struggle to atone for the gains obtained by violence or deceit, the gains obtained by bad *eris;* on the other hand, he does not want them to acquire the wealth he concedes to them, these riches concealed in the earth that give them life (*bios*), without labor (*kai aergon eonta*),[36] without doing so through the good *eris.*

Once upon a time, however, during the Golden Age, things were different. The earth needed no plowing or sowing for the nourishing grains to sprout with such great bounty that neither destruction by war nor theft by stealth—no *eris* of any kind—had any place here below or in the heavens. People could live and eat without effort.[37] But from the moment Zeus found himself tricked by the wily Prometheus, the gods have hidden men's livelihood from them, burying it in the depths of the soil.[38] Since that time human existence is as we see it today: completely locked into a double struggle. Men are endlessly torn in two directions: mercilessly punished by the gods if they chose the bad *eris* in an attempt to avoid the harsh effort of labor, or shackled by the chain of painful toil if they chose the good one in hopes of peacefully enjoying honestly gotten riches.

*

The two versions of the Promethean fraud echo and illuminate one another—one, located in the *Theogony* within the framework of the divine epic having consequences that concern men only indirectly, and the other in *Works and Days,* directly inspired by Hesiod's own bitter experience of his quarrel with his brother. If men's lives, unlike those of the gods, cannot avoid *eris,* it is because the mortal condition finds its origin and raison d'être in the *eris* that pitted Prometheus against Zeus. Inversely, if Prometheus holds an equivocal position in divine society as the founder of a sacrificial rite whose ultimate consequence is to remove men from the gods and deliver them to Night's progeny, it is because the Titan's affinity with humanity is expressed first of all in the nocturnal *eris* that he stirs up in his rebellion against Zeus even in the luminous world of Olympus. Sacrifice itself, with its delicate equilibrium, is a response to this tension between two competing poles. As the central act of worship it links men with gods, but it does so by separating their respective shares. Men cannot take more than what they were given at the end of the trial in which the two rival divinities confronted each other. By conforming to the ritual order in the fleshly meal, which reflects and recalls this first *eris* between the two powers of the beyond, sacrifice—by the same right as its mythical founder Prometheus and with an ambiguity comparable in all points— takes on a mediating role between gods and men. It serves as an intermediary between the two races. But if sacrifice makes communication between them possible, it is by means of an allocation that sets them against each other. It unites them, not so they may be rejoined (as Prometheus wished, according to the *Theogony;* as was indeed the case in the Golden Age, according to *Works and Days*) but to confirm the necessary distance between them.

2. Ox and Wheat

The comparison of the two accounts is enlightening on yet another point. *Works and Days* does not repeat the first sequence, which the *Theogony* had broadly developed, of the cutting and sham distribution of the pieces of the sacrificial meat. It only mentions it as if it were a well-known fact, with an allusion to Zeus' anger "when Prometheus with his crooked schemes had duped him."[39] Then it immediately proceeds to the second episode of the myth, the theft of fire. Thus we may wonder if the version in *Works and Days,* with its account of the divine rivalry from which the current state of humanity is derived, has dropped the issue of food, which seemed so fundamental in the *Theogony.* As we said, sacrifice, the model for which was established by the Promethean deception, is capable of establishing and expressing the distance between gods and men because it involves completely opposite types of food for each party. Why does Hesiod not refer more explicitly in *Works and Days* to the allocation that by establishing the first sacrifice not only began the whole process of decline but continues, by its twofold nature as religious rite and way of eating, to symbolize the ambiguity of a human condition, a state that finds men connected with the gods by cult and separated from them by everything that their portion of sacrificial meat unfortunately represents?

In reality, the alimentary dimension of the Promethean myth is no less pronounced in *Works and Days* than in the *Theogony.* The theme of a food reserved for man and intimately connected to his specific form of existence is central to each of the two accounts. The theme has only changed its locus. And this shift, which can be explained if we consider the different perspective of each text, sheds light on some of the essential aspects of the myth in its relation to sacrifice. In *Works and Days* the products of the cultivated soil—Demeter's wheat, or grain food—occupy a position analogous to that of the sacrificed ox—pieces of meat, or fleshly food—in the *Theogony.* Indeed, for the author of the *Erga* (i.e., *Works and Days*)[40] man is considered in his capacity as farmer. Therefore he is viewed first of all as someone "who eats bread." For the author of the *Theogony* man, seen from the viewpoint of the divinity, is the one who eats the part of the sacrificial victim offered to the gods that is ritually reserved for him. But in both cases human food bears the same stamp of the Promethean *eris*. Ever since Zeus hid away his food (*bios*), man can eat bread only if he has paid for it with his suffering, earned it with the sweat of his brow. Grain foods, which are accessible only by labor, remind us of the Titan's spirit of rivalry just as the sacrificial animal does. Furthermore, grain was not simply hidden during the conflict with the Olympian. The change of status that made food once freely available to all disappear beneath the earth is Zeus' reply to the Promethean ruse of concealing the edible portions of the animal under its hide to give them to men.[41] The cultivation of grains is thus the counterpart of the sacrificial rite, its reverse. Thanks to Prometheus' deception, mortals henceforth have the flesh of the ox to eat; by Zeus' will the grain that they need in order to live no longer lies within easy reach.

Again, like the sacrificial victim, cereal food is eaten at the culmination of a regulated relation to the gods. The food creates a mode of pious communication between mortals and Immortals at the very moment that it underscores in that very communication the cleavage, distance, and disparity between the status of each side. For Hesiod the cultivation of wheat constitutes a truly cultic act that the peasant must perform for the divine powers.[42] In his eyes work is a daily devotion; each task is assiduously executed at the proper moment out of respect for such sanctified acts. If the peasant, his storehouse full of grain, has enough bread to live comfortably, it is the result of harsh, regimented toil whose exact accomplishment had the ritual virtue of making the performer dear to the Blessed Ones, of making him dear (*philos*) to Demeter.[43] But this divine friendship and proximity, which eliminate want (*limos*), presuppose that the hardworking peasant has recognized and accepted the austere law of the fields[44] imposed by Zeus, a law that with the end of the Golden Age signals that gone are the days when men, ever youthful, lived without work or fatigue, feasting like gods. The significance of grain foods is that to avoid starvation, man, this sad child of *eris*, has no other choice but to devote himself entirely to painful effort, to *ponos*, the other child of *eris*.[45] To escape the misfortune engendered by *eris*, one must take the way of his brother.

There is one last similarity. We have maintained that in the logic of the myth, the comestible parts of the sacrificial victim go to men because these pieces of meat, already deprived of life and endowed with the capacity to satisfy an ever-recurrent hunger or to renew strength that would fail without food, constitute the diet of thoroughly mortal beings. Unlike the vitality of the gods, which is pure of all negative elements, theirs is precarious, unstable, fleeting, and doomed to death from the outset. The very term *bios,* which Hesiod employs to indicate the ear of grain men use as their particular food, underscores a relationship between grains and the vitality peculiar to men, a relationship so intimate that we must speak of consubstantiality. The fabric of human life is cut from the same material that forms the food that sustains it. It is "because they do not eat bread" that the gods are not mortals. Not knowing wheat, fed on ambrosia, they have no blood.[46] Their *ikhōr* knows no declines or eclipses in power—those ups and downs that among men are like the stigmata of an ephemeral existence, the first taste of death that eating can only postpone. Let us recall the formula from the *Iliad* that describes human beings: "At one time they are in the fullness of their ardor, eating the fruit of the cultivated earth, at another lifeless, they are eaten away."[47] To go back to the terms of the *Odyssey,* barley and wheat constitute the *muelos andrōn,* men's marrow, the very substance of their life force.[48]

These relationships and correspondences in the Promethean myth serve to establish a close connection between sacrifice and the cultivation of grain. They appear as two orders of phenomena that are both interrelated and equivalent. Their relationship is seen in the explicit textual references we have mentioned. It is perhaps even more evident in what the text does not say, in its silence. The abrupt and disconcerting allusion to Zeus hiding the *bios* in *Works and Days* would be a foreign, absurd, and incomprehensible element if the text did not presuppose, as part of the framing of the myth, the symmetrical position and complementary status of cereal *bios* and sacrificial victim. Since the sacrificial ritual has the same role in the context of eating meat that the cultivation of grains has in the eating of grains and vegetables, the sequence linking Prometheus' deceit with the need for men to work the fields to obtain the sustaining *bios* is amply justified by its mere presence in the text. Let us add that the ox slain and carved by Prometheus at the first sacrifice is the domestic animal closest to man, the animal best integrated into his sphere of existence, especially when it is harnessed to the plow to open the furrows of the earth. The ox is thus the very opposite of the wild animals that men hunt like enemies rather than sacrifice. In principle, domestic animals are sacrificed with their consent, as beings that can, by their proximity to men, if not represent them directly, at least serve as their delegates. The distance between wild animals and the human sphere is particularly marked in matters of eating. Wild animals eat one another, without any rule or restriction, without setting part of their prey aside for the divine powers. What they take is determined by no law but appetite. Indifferent to justice and piety, the animal meal does not reflect a higher divine order either in technique or execution. It reflects the relationships of brute force in the war that the animals wage against one another for food.[49]

What the ox is to wild animals, wheat is to wild plants. Of all the fruits of the earth, it is the most humanized. Wild plants grow by themselves wherever conditions permit. Wheat is harvested only after being cultivated over a year of careful attention comparable to the education given children to make them men.[50] At harvest time, human effort and divine good will echo one another in a balance of regular exchanges. Noncarnivorous animals find their food growing in uncultivated nature, in the wild grasses and plants that grow away from the fields and orchards worked by human hands, beyond the domestic horizon.[51] Bread belongs only to man. It is a sign and guarantor of civilized life, separating humanity from the animals as well as from the gods. Eating cultivated domestic plants and sacrificed domestic animals are the features of a dietary regimen that serves to place the human race midway between animals and gods—beings both close and far from man—and establishes man in the intermediary status that determines the conditions of his particular existence.[52]

3. Cook the Food, Burn the Dead

Perhaps it is now easier to understand all the implications of the bond in the myth that links the theft of fire to the division of the sacrificial victim on the one hand and to the hiding of grain beneath the earth on the other. According to the *Theogony*, it is because he never forgets the trick Prometheus played by rigging the portions so men got the edible share that Zeus decides from that day forward not to give men (*ouk edidou*, 1. 563) the flame of his celestial fire, the lightning ever-ready in the ash trees that they had enjoyed while they lived and celebrated with the gods. Why this response and what is its significance? Clearly, Zeus wants first of all to prevent men from using the gift they have received as the outcome of this first hand of the game. By depriving them of fire, he forbids them to cook the meat, which they cannot eat raw. Thus, Promethean fire is first of all associated with food; and the Titan's parry when he snatches the flame, hiding it inside a fennel stalk to bring it to men, is intended to give them all that is necessary for sacrificial cooking. But cooking meat before eating it also reinforces the contrast with the animals that feed on raw flesh. So the value of the cooking fire of Hesiod's Prometheus is already far-reaching. It represents culture as opposed to wildness. In this way it prepares the way for the theme of the "civilizing" fire, "master of all arts," that will be developed in Aeschylus' *Prometheus*.[53] But it does so in its own way, with all the complexities and ambiguities brought to the myth by the intermediate status of humanity. Promethean fire is not the fire of the gods, the fire of heaven, the lightning that is all-powerful in the hands of Zeus and like its master, immortal. It is a perishable fire, created, hungry, and precarious, like all mortal creatures. To start it requires a seed of fire, kept beneath the ashes or carried in the hollow of a fennel stalk in the Promethean manner.[54] To keep it alive it must be fed. It dies when it is not nourished.[55] Fire's insatiable voracity, which makes it devour everything in its path, would liken it to a wild animal, as many formulas appearing as early as Homer suggest,[56] if, placed in man's hands to be mastered, it did not appear tame at the same time.

This civilized aspect, which provides a balance to the unleashing of a violent and bestial nature, is seen in the intelligent artifice and subtle invention embodied by the Promethean fire. It is not only the product of a ruse that, escaping Zeus' vigilance, enabled men to appropriate what the god had refused them. It involves a technique of transporting, conserving, and lighting the fire, part of the know-how inseparable from human life. But the *tekhnai* men use are no less equivocal than the Titan who granted them. Fire is a *dolos,* a misleading trick, a trap directed first at Zeus, who let himself be caught, but also effective against men should the occasion warrant—not only because the "ardor of the tireless fire" harbors a power beyond human control, but more precisely because this force carries something mysterious, a supernatural quality called Hephaestus that adds a new dimension to animal savagery and the acquired experience of human culture.[57] On three levels—animal, human, and divine—fire can play a mediating role at the heart of the sacrifice. Lighted on the altar and rising toward the gods to carry the fragrant smoke to them, it is not confined to tracing the path linking earth to heaven. It brings the work of distribution undertaken by Prometheus to its full completion in the cooking process by differentiating what is only roasted or boiled and belongs to men from what is completely consumed and sent to the beyond with the animal's very life. By eating what has not been burned but only cooked—that is, softened and weakened to enable the puny forces of the human body to assimilate it—mortals in some ways have what is left over from the sacrifice. Men eat the remains of a divine meal in which the essential is accessible only through total cremation, leading to the complete disappearance of the victim, devoured in the heat of the flames, from here below.

*

In this respect, the similarities and differences between sacrificial cooking and funeral cremation rites are illuminating. Walter Burkert believed he had found a virtual identity between the structure and function of the two practices.[58] He insisted on the importance of the meal in funerals as well as in the sacrifice. But simply because funerals include a meal does not mean that it is of the same order as the sacrificial meal. For the funeral of Patrocles, Achilles offers a feast near the corpse of the dead man. Bulls, lambs, goats, and pigs are slaughtered, and this flesh is cooked "in the fire of Hephaestus," while the blood of the victims, collected in cups, is poured in libation all around the corpse.[59] In this case, then, the lives of the animals, whose edible parts will be eaten, are offered to the dead man. The sacrificial meal that opens the funeral establishes a kind of communion with him. Yet the fire lighted somewhat later on the pyre to burn the remains[60]—and with them the animals and the Trojans offered as a holocaust—is not a cooking fire: the corpse is not eaten.[61] The body is consumed by flames to open the doors of Hades to the *psukhē* of the dead man,[62] to send him from the visible world, where his earthly remains linger as long as the body has not had its "share of fire," to the invisible realm of the beyond.[63] Here again fire plays a mediating role, making the body disappear from human sight (*ap' ophtalmōn*, 1. 53), its flames devouring the flesh in the manner of a wild animal. The terms Homer uses to designate this fiery funeral feast are *nemomai, esthiō, daptō*.[64] Their connection with eating is strengthened by the relationship Achilles explicitly establishes between the glorious treatment given to Patrocles' remains, given to the flames, and the opposite, ignominious end the hero has in mind for the body of Hector, to be thrown to the dogs.[65] The opposition between honor and dishonor is not the only issue. To be devoured by fire means that the body is entirely consumed in its integral corporeal form, so that it moves as an intact whole into the realm of the beyond. On the other hand, to be devoured by dogs means, as the text clearly indicates, that the flesh is given to "be torn apart raw by the dogs" (*kusin ōma dasasthai*).[66] If Achilles had accomplished his plan, Hector's corpse, torn to pieces in its natural raw state, would be both dishonored in this world and forever deprived in the next of the invisible existence attained by cremation in the fire of the funeral pyre.

Something else must be kept in mind. The part of the human corpse that the flames devour without a trace is the same part of the animal victim that goes to men for their meal: the meat, including the tendons and internal organs, everything that is perishable and would rot after death.[67] But the funeral fire is not allowed to consume the body to the point that it cannot be distinguished from the ashes of the pyre. Wine is poured wherever the flames have reigned.[68] The remains of the dead man, that is, the bones, are then carefully gathered. Specifically these are the white bones, *ostea leuka*,[69] which are clearly visible among the ashes (*tephrē*)[70] where they are easy to spot even if they have been charred.[71] Covered with a double layer of fat,[72] these bones are placed in a vial or small box wrapped with cloth and placed in a grave, the dead man's subterranean abode. In the funeral rite cremation totally consumes the body and sends into the invisible realm what would be the parts reserved in the sacrifice for man's meal; it makes the removal of these "white bones" possible. In the sacrifice these very bones, again covered with fat, constitute the gods' portion—the part that the *mageiros*, who has carved the animal so that the long bones are completely stripped, had set aside in advance to place on the altar to be burned. The two practices are indeed homologous, but since their purposes are different, they work in opposite directions. At the outset of the sacrifice, the incorruptible white bones are set aside and re-served for the gods, who receive them in the form of smoke. In funeral cremation, fire is used to burn the perishable flesh away from the white bones, cleaning them so that men may keep them as an earthly sign of the dead man in his tomb, evidence of his presence in the eyes of his kin. If the essential, the authentic living life of the animal is returned to the gods in the sacrifice with the calcinated bones, while men sustain themselves on the half-raw, half-cooked remains of the divine meal, the funeral uses fire to purify the body of all its corruptible parts, in which life and death are inextricably mixed, and to reduce the remains to the essential—the white bones, the intermediaries that connect living men with the deceased.

*

In *Works and Days,* the episode of the theft of fire is introduced in an allusive, abrupt, and apparently illogical way. "The gods," explains Hesiod to Perses, "have hidden their *bios* (i.e., wheat) from men. Otherwise you could live without doing anything, without working. But Zeus hid your *bios* when he found out that Prometheus had deceived him. From that day on he plotted woes for men; he hid fire from them." We would wonder what fire was doing in this story if we did not already know from the *Theogony* that Zeus' refusal to give fire is motivated by the Promethean trick concerning the parts of the sacrifice. Nonetheless the account still seems completely incoherent. Zeus' anger at being duped by the Titan is invoked to justify the need for agricultural labor. Furious at being taken in, Zeus hides life by burying the grain. His "hiding the fire" appears purely gratuitous in this context, with no discernible relationship with what has gone before it—unless for the archaic Greek hiding the *bios* and hiding the fire had such an intimate and obvious relationship that the one could not appear without the other.

First, let us note that the situation at the beginning is the same for both fire and grain. During the Golden Age before men and gods were separated, before the business at Mecone, barley and flames are both freely and directly accessible to man. They are available to him as "natural" gifts: he has no need to seek them, nor are they the subject of any worry or searching on his part. For the gods, "to hide" grain and fire means concretely that grain must first be buried, hidden in the ground in the form of seed to germinate and then ripen on the surface.[73] As a seed, fire must be buried and hidden in the ashes or a fennel stalk in order to rise and then blaze above the hearth. From a moral or metaphysical standpoint these two benefits, hitherto given naturally for man's free use, must henceforth be acquired, won, and paid for. They can be attained only by penetrating the layer of evils that surrounds them: painful effort, laborious activity, constant and assiduous attention. These difficulties, the requisite counterpart to advantages that were once freely and prodigally dispensed, make barley and fire triumphs of human civilization instead of the natural products they were in the beginning. That is not all. For the Greeks, grains and all cultivated plants in general are to wild plants as the cooked is to the raw.[74] The cooking that distinguishes them is based not only on the fact that the species that lend themselves to cultivation are those in which internal "cooking" is more complete than in wild plants, whose raw humors remain dominant, but also that men's hands, by opening and turning the soil so that the sun penetrates it, contribute to a better, more developed "cooking" of domesticated plants. To these two cooking types, the first spontaneous and the second through agriculture, is then added a third to complete the process. In transforming flour into bread and cakes, the cooking done in the kitchen makes grains fully edible. It severs their last bond to the domain of nature and rawness in which flour is a hybrid, a half-formed thing neither raw nor cooked, wild nor civilized. Taken from the oven, bread has become something else. Henceforth it is *sitos,* human food, in the same way that a piece of raw and bloody meat is transformed into a civilized dish once it is roasted or boiled.[75]

Now, the earth spontaneously offered to men of the Golden Age fruits and grains that in their natural state possessed all the traits and qualities of cultivated plants. These products grew already cooked, as if the soil had been worked and turned by the plow without human labor. Furthermore, they were immediately edible without having to be transformed and humanized by the action of the cooking fire. The Golden Age does not reflect the opposition between a state of nature and civilization; it abolishes any difference between them. It presents civilized food as the spontaneous products of nature that man, without having to do anything, would find already cultivated, harvested, stored, and cooked—ready to eat. In this respect, the harvests of grain the earth brought forth in the Golden Age are like these harvests of meat the fortunate Ethiopians found near the Sun's Table, according to Herodotus. Every morning, the meats were there, scattered about the plain that brought them forth from itself in the night, all carved, divided, and already boiled, so the diners merely had to sit down to eat. They are produced in a naturally cooked state.[76]

*

Thus the end of the Golden Age signals the need for sacrificial fire to cook meat, agricultural labor to cook grains, and the cooking fire to make the grains edible. With one stroke, the angry Zeus hides fire and wheat to make men atone for the meat they received by the grace of Prometheus. If things had stayed this way at Mecone, men would not have been able to eat any more of the fruit of domesticated plants, for it would be raw, just as in the version of the *Theogony* they would not be able to eat the raw meat of domesticated animals.

Promethean trickery not only sets up the rules for sharing the victim once and for all. With the same harshness it brings an equally ineluctable consequence in its wake, the need for work, *ponos*. To eat human food men must devote themselves from that day forward to the cultivation of grains as well as sacrificial cooking.

4. The Titan of Hesiod, the Titans of Orpheus

Before considering the final sequence of the tale, Zeus' creation of the "beautiful evil" that will seal mortals' fate by changing them from the state of *anthrōpoi*, which they had occupied alone up to that point, to that of *andres*,[77] male men faced with female women, the necessary complement to males but also their negation, double, and opposite,[78] we must go back over some textual details to confirm and refine our analysis.

We have seen that the *eris* between Prometheus and Zeus takes place at Mecone. Why there? Hesiod sheds no light on this point, but accounts and allusions found elsewhere lead to three comments.

1. *Mecone* is an ancient name for Sicyon.[79] It is there, recalls Callimachus among others, that the gods had established their seat at the end of the war against the Giants (*hedranon*) when they divided up the honors (*timai*) among themselves using a lottery.[80] An earthly site and abode of the gods, Mecone can represent that place where men and divinities still living side by side used to be seated at the same tables, feasting together at banquets and eating identical food.

On the other hand, the name of this city, which passed for the most ancient in all Greece,[81] remains linked to the memory of the allocation by the Olympians after their victory over their competitors for heavenly sovereignty. The allocation through which Prometheus indicates his will when he carves the sacrificial ox thus is directly in line with the regulated distribution that Zeus inaugurates when he takes the throne and that is the very sign of his supremacy.

2. From Sicyon toward Corinth extends a plain that the ancients named Asopia. Its reputation for fertility was proverbial: all one needed to become rich, it was said, was to own land between Sicyon and Corinth.[82] With its rich plain Mecone evokes a land of felicity, the soil of the golden age when, to borrow Hesiod's formula from the *Works and Days*, "the fertile soil produced a generous and abundant harvest by itself."[83]

3. Not far from Sicyon, at the summit of a small rise along the Asopos river, is a place called Titane, the name for which, according to the locals, comes from the first inhabitant, Titan. A local tradition, undoubtedly, but one from which it is all the more difficult to completely divorce Hesiod's account, because connections can be seen rather clearly between the Titan of Sicyon, the mythical fertility of Asopia, and the primordial allocation at Mecone. With respect to Titan, Pausanias reports that the people of the country have made him a brother of Helios, the Sun; and he interprets this information in the following way: Titan was amazingly clever (*deinos*) at observing the seasons of the year and the moment the Sun makes the cereals and fruits grow by cooking them. For the Periegetae, then, the extreme fertility of the soil of this place, combined with the cooking of the sun's fire to obtain the maximum effect, is based on the exceptional ingenuity of the first inhabitant of the region.[84]

The kinship between this Titan and the Sun recalls a similar legend from Corinth. The Corinthians used to say that at the moment of the allocation, their country had been contested between Poseidon and Helios; each had claimed it for himself. The arbitration of the dispute was entrusted to Briareos, who judged that the isthmus, that is, the lower part, be awarded to Poseidon, and the upper portion above the town be given to Helios, as if dedicating the lower ground to the aquatic elements and the upper to the heavenly fire. Pausanias, once again our witness, observes while reporting the story that this theme of a quarrel between the gods and a judgment awarding a territory is not confined to Corinth.[85] He cites in particular the case of Attica, where, as we know, the history of the city begins with Cecrops, the autochthonous king, a primordial being born of the earth, half-man, half-snake, and sometimes presented as bisexual.

Called upon to resolve matters between Athena and Poseidon, who both claim dominion over the town, Cecrops chooses the goddess. Poseidon takes revenge by flooding the lands of Attica with salt water. Transcending human limitations, Cecrops takes on the functions of a civilizing hero for the Athenians. He wrests the first inhabitants of the country from their still savage existence.

Pausanias also could have mentioned the parallel of Argos, where Phoroneus—the first human king, son of the river god Inachus, whose sovereignty stretched with his waters across the entire Argolid—plays the same role as Cecrops in Athens. As the arbiter of a conflict between Hera and Poseidon who quarrel over the Peloponnesus, he gives preference to the goddess. Again the god takes revenge, but this time by withdrawing all the water sources from the Argolid. Lacking ground water to feed them, rivers and springs—beginning with the Inachus—empty in the summer and dry out as the land is deserted by the water needed to give and sustain life. Phoroneus gathers the scattered men and unites them into one community. In this civilizing action, he approaches Prometheus, even matching him on some essential points. The people of Argos attributed to him and not the son of Iapetus the introduction of fire to human existence and the establishment of the first sacrifice.[86] Phoroneus had a brother, Aigialeus, whose name after his death was given to the Peloponnesus, which became the Aigialaea. Now, before it was called Mecone, Sicyon itself was also called Aigialaea after the name of the autochthonous king Aigialeus, born of this fertile land from which he was the first to emerge.[87]

To the bond that connects Sicyon to the Argolid via Aigialeus, we must add certain significant relationships between Asopia and Attica, especially the plain of Marathon. In his epic poem devoted to the history of Corinth, Eumelus maintained that the country's sole inhabitant at the very beginning was a daughter of Oceanus, Ephyra, followed by Marathon, the great grandson of the Sun and master of the land. After emigrating to Attica toward the plain that bears his name,[88] Marathon gave his kingdom to his two sons, Sicyon and Corinthos. Henceforth Asopia was called Sicyon and Ephyra, Corinth.[89] Now, as scholars have not failed to note,[90] the Titan and the place-name Titane of Asopia correspond in Attica, on the one hand, to the *Titanis gē*, the Titan's land, which in early times would have designated the territory of Athens, and on the other hand, to two characters specifically located on the plain of Marathon. The first of these is Titenius, living near Marathon, who was a Titan but more ancient than the people of the same name. He existed prior to the divinities and was a stranger to their quarrels, since, alone among all the homonyms, he refused to fight on either side in the war between the gods.[91] Then there is Titacus of Aphidna, at a similar distance from Marathon. When evoking these figures Ister, in the *Atthides,* his collection of stories of Attica, implies that these were not Titans in the ordinary sense of the term but rather autochthonous kings like Cecrops, whom they preceded as first inhabitants and rulers of the land.[92] These Titans, neither gods nor men and of a time prior to the disjunction between the two, figure as primordial beings tied to the earth out of which they are born and where they abide, as humans do. But in these creatures the earthly element seems combined with an igneous element. The earth produces them aided by the action of solar heat. Indeed their name evokes calcinated earth, the white ash or quicklime that Greeks call *titanos* without always clearly distinguishing it from gypsum, *gupsos.*[93] Made of a mixture of earth and fire, the first chthonic beings not only arose directly out of the sun-scorched ground with no need for the union of male and female to create them,[94] they are also distinct from men and closer to the gods because of their igneous nature, which preserves them from the rotting and corruption that befall all mortal creatures. If, as Aristotle says, the inhabitants of hot countries live longer than other people "because they have a drier nature, and what is drier is less corruptible and lasts longer, as death is a type of rotting," we understand that the autochthones, like gods, are unacquainted with old age and mortality.[95] What makes Titans unlike humans is what differentiates earth mixed with fire (quicklime or gypsum, *titanos* or *gupsos*) from earth mixed with water (mud or clay, *pēlos*).[96]

In the *Theogony* Hesiod is silent about how the human race, the *génos anthrōpōn,* made its appearance on earth in the days when it was living side by side with the gods in Mecone. Not a word appears, either, about the material out of which men are made. On the other hand, in the case of the "beautiful evil" from which the race of women, the *genos gunaikōn,* is issued, we know that Hephaestus "forms it with earth into the likeness of a chaste virgin according to the wishes of the son of Cronus" (572). The formula is repeated almost word for word in line 71 of *Works and Days.* But this time Hesiod is more explicit about the meaning of this "formation" with or from earth. Indeed Zeus orders Hephaestus "to moisten the earth with some water"[97] to give it "the lovely form of a virgin in the likeness of the immortal goddesses." In the *parthenos,* henceforth associated with man, the face, *eidos,* is that of a goddess, but the substance, a mixture of earth and water, is mud or clay, *pēlos.*[98] Now in the most widespread Greek tradition—which Hesiod could not fail to know since it is already expressed in a passage in Homer (Menelaus takes aside the

Achaians, who hesitate to face Hector in man-to-man combat, and says to them, "All of you here, be earth and water once more," [*hudōr kai gaia*])—it is not only women but the entire human race that is made of mud or formed out of clay.[99] If Aeschylus closely follows Hesiod when he evokes in Pandora "the mortal woman, issued from fashioned clay,"[100] Aristophanes gives the formula its full breadth when he uses it to contrast male men, *andres*, these *plasmata pēlou*, these beings "formed of clay," with aerial and celestial beings, the immortal gods.[101] In the same way, to describe man Callimachus uses the expression, *ho pēlos ho Promētheios*, "Promethean clay," the value of which is made clear in another passage: "If Prometheus made you, you are born from clay and nothing else."[102] To be born of clay does not mean just that one will once again become clay, that one will perish; born from a prosaic and common material, one is doomed to obscurity, impotence, and insubstantiality. "Aware of who he is and what clay he is made from," is what Battaros, the seller of girls, will say of his adversary to discredit him before the judges in one of the *Mimes* of Herondas.[103]

Hesiod's silence on the origin of the *anthrōpoi*—before Prometheus' deception results in their condition as *andres*, associated with women and therefore facing the double fate of procreation and death—is perhaps explained by the fact that he found it impossible to accept either of the solutions offered by the representation of earthly creatures made of earth and fire or earth and water. In the first case, the humans of Mecone, like the primordial autochthones of Sicyon, Argos, and Athens, would be too close to the gods to ever become what they must inevitably be: poor perishable creatures. In the second, humanity "formed from clay" would be doomed from the outset to all weaknesses and ills that the creation of Woman must introduce into existence: hunger, fatigue, work, sickness, old age, and death.

With Hesiod the myth of the Promethean sacrifice is intended to justify a religion that places man midway between animals and gods and that bars all possibility either of identifying him with one or the other or of completely dissociating him from them. Mud and clay would reduce man to the condition of animals; quicklime and gypsum would lift him toward identification with the divine.

When she emerges from the hands of Hephaestus, Pandora's likeness to the gods—her external appearance, her beautiful face that will ensnare male desire (*kalon eidos epēraton*)[104]—is only a pretense. Within she is endowed with the spirit of a bitch, *kuneos noos*, which reflects her deep-seated animality. What she shares with the *andres* and makes her "human" (*anthrōpou*, in line 61) is only strength (*sthenos*) and articulated speech (*audē,*

61–62 or *phōnē*, 79). Nothing about her suggests the presence of a divine element, the breath or fire introduced into the clay from outside to "animate" the product of Hephaestus' art in order to grant it, along with life, a status other than that of simple earth moistened with water.

What, then, sets man apart from animals shaped from clay like himself? What puts him in his own particular intermediary position, separated as much from the gods as the animals, to be sure, but tied to both nonetheless? In the interplay of the three elements, earth, water, and fire, that cause generation in the model we have noted, one solution emerges. All that was needed was for man to embody all three elements at once, for him to be their point of intersection. It is this figure that Ovid depicts with great clarity when he outlines the genesis and appearance of man in the first book of the *Metamorphoses*. The elements are differentiated and established. Animals already inhabit the earth. Only one is lacking, nobler than the others. The earth, which has just separated from the burning ether, still contains in her breast the seeds of heaven. It is this soil sown by fire that Prometheus, who had mixed it with the waters of a river, shapes in the image of the gods.[105] In other versions such as that of Servius in his commentary on Virgil, Prometheus makes man out of mud, then, rising with Athena's help to heaven, he touches the Sun's wheel with his fennel stalk and steals a seed of fire, which he introduces into man's breast to bring his work to life.[106]

This sort of conception is alien to Hesiod, not only because it presupposes a notion of the elements and how they combine that came after him as an outgrowth of Ionian philosophy, but also for intrinsic reasons concerning the way he views the problems of man in relation to animals and gods. If Hesiod does not express man's "intermediate" condition via traditional images contrasting man, made of earth and water, with luminous and celestial beings such as the Olympian gods, or with beings made of earth and fire such as the autochthones, it is because in his view man's humanity does not reside either in a particular "nature" linked to the elements that form him or in an origin peculiar to him alone. Man's true nature arises from the position that he occupies in the midst of a whole, from his status in a hierarchy of functions, prerogatives, and honors. Of course flesh-and-blood men are not made of the same material as the Immortals. Nor did they come to be at the same time or in the same manner as the gods. Their genealogy follows a completely different course. The Titans are the sons of Uranus, the sons of the Heaven. Their progeny, particularly the children of Cronus, i.e., the Olympians, also belong to an Uranian lineage. But Uranus himself was born of Gaea, the Earth, who bore all beings, whoever they are, except for Chaos. In this way, if one goes all the way back to the very beginning, gods and men have a common origin: Gaea, the Earth-Mother, from whom also derives the fire of heaven as well as the waters of Oceanus, Pontos, and all the rivers. So Hesiod is not contradicting himself in *Works and Days* when he introduces the creation of the different races of men who have appeared on the surface of the earth with counsel addressed to Perses, "And bear in mind that gods and mortal men have the same origin,"[107] and then goes on to say that the first two are produced (*poiēsan*, 110 and 128) by the immortal inhabitants of Olympus, the following two by Zeus (*poiēse*, 144 and 158), and the last appear without any indication of the producer.

The variations between one race of men and another, like the distance that separates the human race in general from gods and animals, are not put in terms of the differences between the elements from which they all are issued and to which they are linked (golden, silver, or bronze men are not made of these metals, any more than Hesiod and his contemporaries are or believe themselves to be made of iron). The divergences correspond to contrasting types of life, conduct, and behavior. Each race is defined by the functions it assumes, the activities to which it is devoted. What does it do, and above all, how? Does it observe Justice, the daughter of Zeus, venerated by the gods, or give itself over to Hubris?

What brings men close to the gods, then, is not the more or less hidden presence of a portion of the divine but the observance, out of a respect for Justice, of rules that govern the relations of mortals among one another and with the higher powers. By fully submitting to these norms, men institute a type of communication with the gods that establishes their exact place and at the same time makes them fully men, i.e., miserable, weak, and mortal creatures whose hearts are inhabited by Shame and Fear, *Aidōs* and *Nemesis*, and whose minds are capable of recognizing Justice.[108]

For Hesiod no other kinship between men and gods exists besides the one constituted through cultic acts and maintained by the scrupulous execution of rites—whence, from his standpoint, the importance and breadth of the foundation myth of sacrifice. For Hesiod, revealing man's condition does not consist in defining a "human nature" about which he has no idea but in uncovering, by means of the account of the foundation of the sacrifice, all the implications, narrow and broad, of the cultic procedure with respect to the status of humans and their assigned place in an order based and affirmed far away in Zeus.

Thus, any eschatological dimension, any opening onto a realm beyond earthly existence, is from the outset excluded from Hesiod's vision of humankind. Piety is not supposed to develop the part of our being shared with the gods to raise us to their level but rather to establish the type of relationship with the divine that puts us in our place. Death does not separate the part of us made of and belonging to earth from the part that comes from above and rejoins its place of origin. Like hunger, sickness, and old age, death is one of the constitutive marks of human existence, one of the characteristics that is proof of the unbridgeable abyss that separates the ever-youthful Immortals from the ephemeral creatures who are doomed, at the end of a life in which no good appears without evil, no light without shadow, to disappear into the anonymous darkness of Hades.

On this level, the connections and dissimilarities with what we can learn of the Orphic anthropogony appear with more clarity. As Marcel Detienne has demonstrated,[109] the status of humans in this anthropogony has its basis and explanation in a myth of sacrifice—this time an impious, monstrous sacrifice, for it concerns the death of the child Dionysus and his dismemberment and consumption at the hands of the Titans. Unlike those of the *Theogony,* the Titans of this account are not the first royal gods, the children of Uranus fighting under the leadership of their brother Cronos against the younger divinities warring for the power that Zeus wishes to command. They are the ancestors of humanity, and beneath the layer of gypsum they have put on to outwit the small god/child, they seem very close to the Titans of Sicyon and Marathon, those autochthonous beings that emerged from the sun-scorched earth.

The fable of the criminal Titans cutting Dionysus apart in order to devour him is not the aberrant and gratuitous invention of late Hellenism. It is based on the local legends that Hesiod had already used—as the allusion to Mecone attests—extensively reworking them himself. The reference to an initial sacrifice that is the basis for the human condition, which is common to both Hesiod's and the Orphic versions, shows that it is not possible to separate the two mythical accounts, despite their differences; they complement one another. On several points their differences correspond and reinforce each other, which makes the fundamental divergences in religious orientation more apparent. Each one must be studied in the context of the other, which illuminates it by contrast.

For Hesiod the justification of blood sacrifice is intimately linked to man's acceptance of his mortal status with all its particularities, as well as to the observance of a religious practice requiring that the distance between gods and earthly creatures be recognized, respected, and sanctified in every act of worship and throughout the course of daily life, in order to establish communication with the divine. Among the Orphics the radical condemnation of sacrifice, which is tied to the sacrilegious murder the Titans committed in the beginning, entails both an entirely different status for man and the rejection of the official religion. Engorged with the flesh of Dionysus, whose body they devoured piece by piece except for the heart, the Titans are struck by Zeus' lightning and reduced to ashes. From this calcinated dust men are born.[110] Made of the same burnt matter as the beings from which they are issued, humans, because of their Titanic heredity, bear the weight of the criminal fault that stamped their origin and dooms them to a life of expiation. But they also partake of Dionysus, whose flesh was assimilated by the ancestors who had eaten part of it.[111] Instead of locking men in an immutable position between animals and gods, the myth assigns them a trajectory leading from the scattered ashes of the Titans, where they begin, to Dionysus, who has been wholly reconstituted from his preserved heart by the gods.[112] Piety no longer means keeping an equal distance from each of the two poles between which man is located but leading a kind of life that raises man toward the higher of the two. By consenting to sacrifice a living animal to the gods in the Promethean manner, as official worship requires, men only repeat the Titans' crime indefinitely. By refusing this sacrifice, by forbidding the bloodshed of any animal, by turning away from fleshly food to dedicate themselves to a totally "pure" ascetic life—a life also completely alien to the social and religious norms of the city—men would shed all the Titanic elements of their nature. In Dionysus they would be able to restore that part of themselves that is divine. By returning to the god in this way each would accomplish, on the human level and within the framework of individual existence, this same movement of reunification that Dionysus himself knew[113] as a god during the torment in which he was first dismembered and then reconstituted. This is the same movement that the Orphic theogonies celebrate in the cosmic realm when they sing of the return of the world at the sixth divine generation—that of Dionysus, to be exact—to its original total unity from a dispersed and differentiated state.

5. The Perils of Mediation

In the logic of these two equally consistent theological systems, the characters responsible for the introduction of the human race do not have the same status and functions in both versions. Once their crime is committed, the Orphic Titans disappear from the scene, giving way to those born from their ashes, men. They survive only in the trace left at the very heart of humanity in the form of the Titanic fault inherited by each individual in his own unique existence, a fault that the Orphic way of life should abolish, as the Titans themselves were blasted from the surface of the earth by Zeus' lightning. Because the religious drama played out within each human creature follows the same model and course as the cosmic and divine drama—from unity lost to unity regained—the Titans have no other function than to join anthropogony to theogony. They are not to serve as intermediaries between men and gods; on the contrary, they represent the part of man that he must root out if he is to identify with the divinity through expiation, paying the price for the ancient murder.[114]

For Hesiod, Prometheus belongs to the divine world. He is an Immortal. But his unfortunate encounters with Zeus give him a marginal place in the society of the Olympian gods; even when he is pardoned and admitted to heaven, he remains apart. It is precisely the somewhat strange and equivocal character of his position in the divine universe that gives him the vocation of mediator for those earthly and mortal creatures whose own intermediary status both sets them apart and brings them close to the gods in a relationship that is never free from ambiguity. Prometheus can no more vanish from the divine scene—like the other Hesiodic Titans who were expelled from the cosmos and shut away in the Night of Tartarus where they lie forever in chains—than men can escape their "mediate" position. The existence of a sacrificial rite among men, which completely separates them from the gods in order to unite them, is based on the correlative presence in the divine realm of a being who combines in his person two opposing figures: the rebel, chastised and rebuked; and the benefactor, the civilizer, at last unbound from his chains, welcomed and redeemed.

More details can perhaps be determined about this "complicity" between Prometheus and the human race as it appears at the end of the duel between Zeus and the son of Iapetus in Mecone. All the benefits men owe to the Titan are also revealed as misfortunes and punishment, for them as well as for him. And the moral of the mythical account, "Thus, it is not possible to hide from or elude the mind of Zeus" (*Theogony*, 613), is intended for men; but it comes to them via the example of the "beneficent Prometheus who, despite all his skills," suffered because of them (614–616). From their unlucky benefactor men have inherited characteristics that in some respects make them Promethean creatures. First of all, know-how and a form of intelligence that gives them access to an orderly, reasoned, and civilized life—on the condition, however, that they do not claim to compete with the wisdom of Zeus, as Prometheus thought he could. His failure reveals, both to men and to himself, the limits of Promethean intelligence. Here cleverness and foresight are always joined by foolishness and improvidence. Prometheus and Epimetheus, the two brothers, form a single and unique figure of which one side, the Promethean, is closer to the gods and the other, the Epimethean, closer to men. With this symbiosis of two opposite figures, every ingenious project one undertakes is realized by the other in the form of an unexpected disaster.

The Titan's revolt against Zeus brought men a life completely devoted to rivalry and struggle. Whether it is a good thing—emulation of work—or evil—war and discord—the same *eris* holds us that pushed Prometheus to rebel against the decisions of Zeus. Again, the Titan's failure offers an unforgettable lesson to those who have inherited his fighting spirit. Rooted by Zeus on earth, *Eris* extends its power to all realms of human life except the relationships with the heavenly gods. Men can indeed compete with one another for everything; but they can never compete with the Immortals, claim to equal them in any fashion, nor attempt to approach the divine state. To perform the blood sacrifice according to the Promethean model is to commemorate the Titan's *eris* and its consequences, and thus to engage in a relationship of complete submission to the gods precluding the slightest impulse toward *eris*. In the sacrificial ceremony the festive side of joyous communion with the gods can never be separated from the other aspect of the ritual—recognized and proclaimed subordination to the gods, the resigned acceptance of the mortal condition, and the permanent abdication of all claims to what lies beyond the human. All participants in the sacrifice wear a crown, a symbol of accomplishment, victory, and consecration. But this auspicious festival adornment recalls the memory of the founder of the sacrifice; it is the "crown of Prometheus," the one the Titan had to consent to wear always, as a price for his reconciliation with Zeus in exchange for the chains from which he had been freed.[115] On the heads of those who approach the gods to have communion with them through sacrifice, the crown of consecration, this "Promethean bond," also represents the chains that bound the rebel Titan to punish him for his "partiality" toward the human race.

Even in his punishment, Prometheus appears in a mediating position, torn between gods and men. In the spectacle of his torment, the Titans and Typhon are hurled into Tartarus, as far below Earth as the Earth is below heaven, beyond the abode of Night in that deep world guarded by Prometheus' brother Atlas, also in punishment, "holding up the vast heavens, with his head and arms,"[116] like an immense column or cosmic pillar. Prometheus, for his part, is bound to the summit of a high mountain, in the air, between heaven and earth. Hesiod notes that to bind him Zeus had wound his chains "halfway up a column."[117] The image of a heavenly column, *kiōn ourania,* is all the more familiar because Typhon is sometimes represented, not bound halfway up the column like the son of Iapetus but lying under it, crushed beneath the earth by its massive weight.[118]

Prometheus brought fire down from heaven, where it belonged, and placed it on earth, unbeknownst to Zeus. In this transfer from above to below, Prometheus is the flame-bearer, the *purphoros.* What Zeus hurls at him in punishment in the form of the royal or wild eagle, equivalent to lightning, is his own kingly flame-bearer,[119] the flying winged arrow that, on his orders, draws a trail of fire between heaven and earth.[120] To punish the guilty Titan for the theft of fire and the deception at Mecone, this lightning-bird, this flame-bird, becomes a ravening animal, a voracious dog. It comes like a vulture, uninvited and insatiable, to the feast where Prometheus appears no longer as the founder of the sacrifice or designated distributor of the portions but as the victim condemned to offer his body as the choice morsel of food. Greek tradition is unanimous concerning the organ that the eagle sent by Zeus devours: "The eagle ate his immortal liver,"[121] writes Hesiod. In the tragedy of Aeschylus, Hermes speaking in Zeus' name announces to Prometheus what lies ahead of him in these terms: "Then Zeus' winged dog, the wild eagle, will voraciously carve into pieces a large strip from your body . . . he will feed until the black food of your liver is gone."[122] Why the liver? Perhaps we have the right to venture some hypotheses on this point deriving on the one hand from the status of the liver in the sacrifice and, on the other, its place and functions among living creatures, particularly man. In sacrificial cuisine the liver plays a special role among the *splankhna* that represent, by the way they are cooked and eaten, those pieces where the shares of gods and men tend, if not to overlap, at least to be as close as possible. It is the organ that the sacrificer first reaches for to examine when the animal has been cut open.[123] Its configuration, sheen, grain, and color tell whether the victim may be accepted or not,[124] whether the animal's life is suitable for ensuring communication between earth and heaven. The liver, along with the other *splankhna,* is more than one of the "vital" parts connected with the blood of the sacrificed animal. Hidden inside the animal, it seems to be turned toward the divine world because of its divinatory role. In it are reflected, down in the entrails of the victim, the dispositions of the divinities with respect to mortal beings and their consent or refusal to come into contact with them by the path of the sacrificial ritual.

Surprisingly, Plato assigns the liver an analogous mediating function in the human body.[125] This is most startling because this organ, localized in the lower abdomen below the diaphragm and laden with food, is the seat of the inferior part of the soul, concupiscence or *epithumia*. The soul, we know, has three parts. Between the immortal part and the *epithumia*, as between the head and the belly, the intermediary role should be reserved for the part of the soul designated by its medial position (between the "wall" of the diaphragm and the "isthmus" of the neck) and role as intercessor (the soul forcefully rules desire with the commandments of reason) to ensure the joining of the extreme elements and thereby submit the whole body to its best part. This mediating soul is *thumos*, courage, located in the thorax, seated in the heart, and thereby placed "at the watchman's post" to send blood, as if from a spring, through all the vessels to wherever reason demands obedience from the body.

Plato presents the liver as a "manger" (*phatnē*), to which the part of the soul that has the appetite for food and drink is tied like a wild animal (*hōs thremma agrion*) that must be fed while bound. Roped forever to this rack where it finds its sustenance, the hungry soul has been confined "as far away as possible from the part that deliberates, bringing it the least possible trouble and noise, so that it may leave this master part to deliberate in peace over everything concerning the good of the whole or the parts of the body."[126]

Thus the maximum distance separates the liver and the intellect, so that the dichotomy of functions and the opposition between mortal and immortal will be respected. However, as if Plato the physiologist could not completely forget what the languages of religion and myth say about the liver, this distance is paradoxically matched by a peculiar closeness. The liver is a manger, but its structure is such that, in its place in the abdominal cavity, it functions as a mirror reflecting the thoughts directly projected there by the power of the intellect in the form of images. In a kind of emanation, the *nous* may frighten the liver by drawing fearful visions on its surface or calm it with light and gentle figures, making it the organ of divination during sleep.

In man the liver represents the wildness of the appetite for food bound with the need to eat. But in the reflections that form on its surface this organ possesses the capacity to be "impressed" by what lies beyond it, surpasses it, and belongs to another domain of reality. Down in the manger of the liver, the immortal and divine element contained in the human soul can, outside all reason and bypassing the intermediary of the heart, be manifested in some way in the phantasms that haunt the dreams of the sleeper.

Prometheus' liver is a "mediator" from yet another standpoint. As is normal for a divine being, his liver is immortal, *hēpar athanaton,* as Hesiod insists in line 524. But its nonmortality is not the constant plenitude, the immutable youth enjoyed by the Blessed Ones. It is an immortality of eclipses, a regular cycle of disappearance and rebirth whose phases alternate, just as night and day endlessly follow each other on the surface of the earth. In the day the eagle devours the liver down to the last bite. "He will feed until the black food of your liver is gone," proclaimed the Hermes of *Prometheus Bound.* Hesiod is more specific: "The eagle ate the immortal liver, but it grew back again at night to be in all ways the equal of what, during the day, the eagle with open wings had devoured."[127]

Midway between human life, which inexorably moves from birth toward death where it is annihilated, and divine life, with its complete permanence and stability, the immortality of the Promethean liver corresponds to the mode of existence of these natural phemonena that, without ever disappearing, nonetheless survive only because they are periodically renewed.[128] Once eaten, the liver grows back, and it grows back in order to be devoured once more. The nightly growth is matched by the ever-renewed hunger of Zeus' winged dog, a guest whose hunger, like that of men, is born again each morning in search of new food.

Along with the fire he gave them, Prometheus determined the type of food fit for mortal men: meat from sacrificed domestic animals and wheat from cultivated fields. The other side of these benefits was that men would need absolutely to eat in order to live, because they would be inhabited by a hunger that no meal could sate forever but only appease for a short while. Like the Titan's immortal liver, the hunger of mortal men grows back during the day to its original size, making it imperative for the foods that sustain men in their precarious and brief life to be ceaselessly renewed. The irony of the punishment inflicted on the son of Iapetus is that the founder of the sacrifice is made into the victim of insatiable hunger, transformed through his liver into a meal readied daily, into a portion of meat that is indefinitely restored with no hope of ever satisfying the immortal appetite that Zeus has set against him. His suffering is both the expiation for and mockery of the diet that men owe to him, in which eating no longer appears without two sinister companions, both Night's progeny, Hunger and Death.[129]

One detail should be emphasized at this point. To say that Prometheus' liver "grew back" during the night, Hesiod uses the term *aexeto,* which literally means, "it grew," and whose value in this passage becomes more specific if we observe that Hesiod uses it on two other highly significant occasions. It appears in *Works and Days* (394) regarding the fruits of Demeter, the grain plants that, if the farmer has carried out his labors on time as he should have, "each grow in their time (*hekasta hōri' aexētai*)" and keep the peasant from having to beg for bread. In the *Theogony* (444) the poet pays homage to Hecate who, with Hermes, knows how "in the stables to make the animals grow (*en stathmoisi . . . lēid' aexein*)." Devoured every day, Prometheus' liver grows back every night, just as two types of "cultivated" foods grow in seasonal rhythm and with the help of the gods and human labor, foods that since the drama at Mecone have become the specific diet of the human race—the products of grain cultivation and the meat of domesticated animals.[130]

6. A Story of Stomachs

Let us now look at the way Prometheus goes about rigging the two portions of the victim that he gives Zeus to choose from. The portions are to be arranged in such a way that each appears to be the opposite of what it truly is. The one that is good to eat must seem inedible and repugnant, while the one that cannot be eaten must seem appetizing. Thus, Prometheus "hides" the actual contents of each ration in a deceptive wrapping. Split into an exterior and interior that contradict each other, the shares are a lie, a perfidious ruse. They are *doloi*, "traps." But what exactly is the structure of these traps, and what do they correspond to in the overall foundation myth of sacrifice? For the portion Zeus keeps, there is no problem. Prometheus gathers in a heap the white bones, stripped completely of flesh; then he disguises it all with a layer of white fat. Thus prepared, this share essentially corresponds to what in the rite is indeed placed on the altar to be burned for the gods: the bones covered with fat.[131] And the second portion? It contains the flesh and the entrails (with both viscera and intestines) laden with fat: that is, all the edible parts of the animal. First wrapped in an ox-hide, the edibles are hidden in the animal's stomach, *gastēr*. The use of the hide is understandable: completely inedible, it is all the better adapted to its role of "concealing" the edible internal parts because it already covers them on the living animal. Moreover, in the sacrifice the hide, even though uneaten, in fact returns to men. It is not burned as an offering to the gods with the bones on the flames of the altar. Whatever its purpose—as the priest's share, which can be sold to collect the revenue of the *dermatikon*, as an exhibit commemorating the completed sacrifice (*endrata*), or for use in making a stuffed ox as in the Bouphonia—the hide is what remains here below of the victim when its bones have been burned (for the gods) and its flesh eaten (by men). It recalls both the living animal and the ritual act that immolated the animal, consecrating its life to the divinity. In the *Odyssey*[132] Odysseus' companions, wracked with hunger, slaughter the oxen of the Sun, the god's property forbidden to humans in an impious parody of sacrifice. The slaughtered animals were skinned, carved, and the pieces put to cook on the spit. But this divine, immortal herd, not subject to "growth" or generation, is not of the comestible type. The sacrilegious sacrifice was carried out; the sacrilege remains and will be punished. But the sacrifice cannot really have taken place. On the skewers the raw and cooked flesh lows with the powerful voices of the oxen. The skins move all by themselves, as if the external wrapping, despite being emptied of flesh and bones, is nonetheless still inhabited by the living animal.

So in all respects the hide is suited to its role of wrapping the share that will fall to men. But why "conceal" this package with an additional disguise by stuffing it in the stomach? This is a detail that is all the more surprising—and consequently all the more meaningful for the interpreter—because the stomach, unlike the skin, is an "internal" part of the animal. First, the *gastēr* is of a repellent aspect; the Greeks do not eat it. Between a portion of tempting white fat and a fibrous stomach, we understand why Zeus, invited to choose first, shows no hesitation. Moreover, the shape and solidity of the *gastēr* evoke a receptacle used to cook meat. The part of the tripod placed on the fire, the cooking pot, is called *gastrē*, the belly or the paunch of the tripod.[133] Describing the forms of sacrifice among the Scythians, Herodotus brings us information about the *gastēr* that perhaps is more revealing of the Greek imagination on the subject than of the customs of the Scythians.[134] The victims having been flayed, he says, the flesh is stripped from the bones and thrown into the lebes, caldrons, of the country, which resemble the craters of Lesbos. But if the Scythians, as it sometimes happens, have no lebes, "they put all the flesh of the sacrificed animals in the stomachs (*es tas gasteras*) mixing it with water" to boil them there. Herodotus adds, "The *gastēr* easily contains the flesh removed from the bones." We need also recall that, again according to our author, the Scythians, even less well provided with wood than kettles, use the animals' bones as fuel, "which burns quite well under the stomach." In this way, "an ox is cooked by itself and the other victims as well, each one cooking itself." Did Herodotus remember, while "describing" the Scythian sacrifice, which is as impious (the bones of the victim are not offered to the gods) as it is ingenious and economical, the Greek recipe of which an early example is found in Homer? In chant 38 of the *Odyssey*, Antinous gives the claimants the menu for which the two palace beggars, Iros and the disguised Odysseus, are ready to fight one another: "We have on the fire," he says, "goat stomachs (*gasteres aigōn*) stuffed with fat and blood."[135]

So the *gastēr* could sometimes be used the way we would use intestines today to make blood sausage, as a receptacle in which to cook the animal's blood and fat[136]—a minor culinary custom that certainly does not reveal the essential. On the contrary, in the very passage of the *Odyssey* we have just mentioned, the real reason is clearly revealed for the role that Hesiod assigns to the *gastēr* by making it the wrapping where the part of the victim is hidden, as if in a sack, that will fall to the humans and decide their condition. The goats' stomachs are on the fire; the meal is ready. Odysseus, who plays the weakened old man exhausted from misery, must find a reason to explain why an old man like himself accepts the risk of confronting someone younger and stronger. He has no desire to expose himself to blows, "But," says he, "the evil *gastēr* is urging me."[137] *Gastēr kakoergos*, the ill-doing belly, *gastēr stugerē*, the odious belly, *gastēr lugrē*, the contemptible belly, *gastēr oulomenē*, the deadly belly, the belly that "gives so much pain," that brings "so many painful cares to mortals,"— this theme returns with an obsessive force in the *Odyssey* to denounce the curse of the "belly," the frightful need man suffers to eat in order to live, and in order to eat, to have what is necessary.[138] Man is a "belly" or "slave of the belly" when, possessed by hunger, he can think only of ways of satisfying it. Jesper Svenbro has noted certain social implications of the "belly" in Homer and Hesiod.[139] For example, the poet who depends on others—on his audience—for his subsistence, for want of sufficient resources at home to protect him from hunger, is necessarily reduced to the state of a belly; it is the *gastēr* in some way that commands his song.

However, the term seems to us to have a more general value. It indicates the human condition in its totality. As Pindar says, "Each one makes an effort to keep pernicious hunger away from his *gastēr*."[140] The *gastēr* represents the ardent, bestial, and wild element in man, that internal animality that chains us to the need for food. The formula in the *Odyssey* (7.216), "Is there nothing more like a dog (*kunteron*) than the odious belly," is echoed by Epimenides' epithet for the Cretans, those liars, "evil wild beasts, lazy bellies (*kaka thēria, gasteres argai*)."[141] Just as *gastrizō* means to fill one's paunch, to feast, and as *gastrimargia* refers to the gluttony that

Plato will say in the *Timaeus* makes the human species "a stranger to philosophy and the muses (*aphilosophon kai amouson*),"[142] and *gastris*, potbellied, evokes the glutton, the term *gastēr* is used throughout a long textual tradition to represent the one who, dominated by his appetite for food, has no other horizon or mainspring than his belly. This voracious sensuality, this gluttonous greed is often found associated with sloth and lewdness, as if, according to the expression that Xenophon puts in the mouth of Socrates, one were slave all at once to "the belly, sleep, and dissipation."[143] This is why the same Xenophon, in the choice of a wife, requires a well brought up woman, *amphi gastera,* just as he will only accept as a housekeeper the one of his women servants who seems to him to be the least inclined "to the *gastēr,* to wine, to sleep, and to union with men."[144] A precept from the *Golden Verses* (9–10) recommends: "Master first of all the *gastēr,* and sleep, luxury, and anger." In his commentary, Hierocles explains the priority of the *gastēr* in the cohort of vices: "The *gastēr,* when it is too full, provokes a surplus of sleep and these two excesses together . . . incite one beyond measure to the pleasures of Aphrodite."

In Hesiod, as we will see, the idle and lewd aspect of the *gastēr* is found particularly projected on women. To be sure, the feminine *gastēr* is not unacquainted—far from it—with gluttony. It is even less exempt from this defect in Hesiod's picture because, since women do not work, they represent not the producer in the couple but the consumer. When gorging themselves at their husband's table, women stuff their stomachs with food the poor fellow had to accumulate painfully by the sweat of his brow.[145] However, in the case of female creatures, the appetite for food seems easily to lead to sexual appetite. This connection is explained by the fact that with reference to women the term *gastēr* designates the stomach, as it does for men, but also the womb, the "breast" where the child is conceived and fed.

At Mecone, when Prometheus presents the two shares of the victim to the assembled gods and humans, there were no women yet; their belly will appear later on. Wrapping men's share in the ox's *gastēr* means first of all, of course, giving it the most repugnant appearance in hopes of tricking Zeus. Then and above all it means, from Hesiod's standpoint, emphasizing that when he set all the meat aside for the mortals, Prometheus made them a fool's bargain. To keep in the sacrificed animal all of what can be eaten implies that one becomes a *gastēr* oneself, that one begins an existence in which life can only be sustained or strength restored by stuffing one's paunch, ever and again, just as the flesh and entrails of the ox are stuffed in the *gastēr*. The most tragic part is that, thanks to the Titan, humans are led to assume this status of "belly" within the very framework of the ritual that unites them, to the extent it is possible in their new state, with Immortals who live on ambrosia. It is by eating, by the indirect means of the meal, by becoming in some way a meat sack, that the mortal creature normally communicates (i.e., by sacrifice) with the gods.

Undoubtedly, for some "divine men" like Hesiod, there are other paths.[146] In the beginning of the *Theogony* the poet tells how the Muses have singled him out and inspired him while he was pasturing his flocks, as shepherds do, at the foot of Mt. Helicon. They taught him the beautiful song that they themselves used on Olympus to charm the ears of Zeus.[147] By telling of everything that was from the beginning, everything that is, and everything that will be—about the gods that came first, the birth of the son of Cronus, his struggles, his victory, his reign, and about Prometheus as well, with his race of men—this chant celebrates the glory of the sovereign who dominates the world. It distinguishes his power and order with the brilliance of praise and the radiance of the sung word.[148] By repeating this truthful song on earth, by joining his human voice in unison with those of the daughters of Zeus to sound the great epic of the Olympian among mortal creatures, the inspired poet contributes here below, among humans, to this glorification needed to ensure the permanence of the divine order.[149] In this manner he takes a mediating role between earth and heaven analogous to that of the king of Justice, the nursling of Zeus, that the Muses must also inspire.[150] Since the separation from the gods was accomplished, human life has been devoted to *eris* and unhappiness. With soft words the king knows how to calm quarrels; with the sweetness of song, the poet knows how to lull sorrow to sleep.[151] One works by justice, the other by poetry to create a bridge between mortal existence and the universe of the gods. They establish a link that bypasses the Promethean sacrifice, one that does not go through the belly. When the Muses spoke to Hesiod, they first addressed him in the plural, failing to recognize him in the crowd of shepherds like him. They said, "Herdsmen abiding in the fields, sad shameful people, who are nothing but bellies (*gasteres oion*)."[152] But in granting him the privilege to proclaim, as they do, not fictions but truths (*alēthea*),[153] and to sing of the genesis of the gods and the world, Zeus' distribution of honors, Prometheus' fault, the sacrificial allocation, and man's ambiguous status, the Muses make the inspired poet one who, although establishing the inevitable place of the *gastēr* in the sacrifice, no longer is likened only to a belly in his relationship with the gods.

7. A Beautiful Evil, Fire's Counterpart

We have to come to the last act of the myth, woman. By creating her
(*teuxen, Theogony* 570 and 585), Zeus pulls off his master coup. He ends
the game with Prometheus. The Titan can no longer respond. He has been
checkmated. The trap closes on the *anthrōpoi*, who are forced into an on-
going confrontation and need to live with this "half" of themselves created for them with the intention of making them what they are, *andres;*
but they do not recognize themselves in her. Their indispensable complement, whom they cannot live with or without, presents the dual aspect of
unhappiness and attraction. In the eyes of humans, once only males,
women are strange beings.[154]

Every trick employed by the cunning, deceitful, and thieving Prometheus in preparing the sacrificial portions and stealing fire is turned against
the humans by Zeus when he creates the "beautiful evil" (*kalon kakon*)
intended for them.[155] This gift is also a "trap," which suddenly springs
shut and permits no escape (*dolon aipún, amēkhanon anthrōpoisi*).[156] She
has the appearance of a chaste virgin, like the immortal goddesses in every
way.[157] Her divine beauty, her white robe, the multicolored veil that covers
her, the crowns of flowers, the diadem, the engraved jewelry that adorn
her make her into an astonishing marvel to behold (*thauma idesthai*),[158] a
being haloed with a radiant charm[159] whose appearance incites desire.[160]
One cannot see her without loving her;[161] but behind this irresistible attraction, this almost supernatural grace (*kharis*), what is there? What does
the *kalon* conceal? Prometheus had hidden bones beneath the brilliant
white of the fat; inside the green freshness of a stalk of fennel, he had
hidden the glowing embers. Beneath the beauty of woman is not only this
mixture of earth and water of which she is made. Inside her Zeus hides
the spirit of a bitch and the temperament of a thief (*kuneon te noon kai
epiklopon ēthos*), which Hermes, acting on his orders, puts into the mud
along with lies and deceitful words (*pseudea th' haimulious te logous*).[162]

In the versions in both the *Theogony* and *Works and Days,* the creation
of woman, whether she is the one out of whom issues the race of female
women (*Theogony* 590–91) or bears the name of Pandora (*Works* 80–82),
follows the second round of the game between Zeus and Prometheus. It
is when he sees the flames of the heavenly fire burning on earth, the fire
that he had resolved always to keep from humans to prevent them from
cooking meat, that Zeus gives way to his rage and decides to deal the final
blow.[163]

Also, in both versions the text gives equal emphasis to the idea that this
creation of a being, heretofore nonexistent, constitutes the reply to Pro-

metheus' theft. Woman, this evil, *kakon*, is sent into the world *anti puros*, as a counterpart to fire (*Theogony* 570; *Works* 57). What does this mean? The simplest solution is to suppose that since Prometheus had offered men a good thing in the form of fire, Zeus in revenge restored the balance with the gift of an evil. This interpretation would seem all the more justified because the *kakon* is not only described as *anti puros*, the counterpart to fire, but on two occasions (*Theogony* 585 and 602), as *ant' agathoio*, the "counterpart of a benefit," or "in place of a good." Consequently it is tempting simply to identify the fire with a good and see in the expressions *anti puros* and *ant' agathoio* two equivalent formulas. However, this reading is not possible. It has the defect not only of smoothing over the text by ignoring its complexities but of rendering the *ant' agathoio* of line 602 incomprehensible. How does it do so? Fire, at least the fire that men have at their disposal through the theft committed by Prometheus, is undoubtedly a good, but it is not a "pure and simple" good. It is an ambiguous gift, like the meat of the victim and, we have already had occasion to stress, has dangerous and worrisome aspects. To be sure, after his thievery Prometheus is glad to have stolen the fire and tricked Zeus, but his adversary immediately puts things in their place: "You rejoice," he says to the Titan, "over what, for you and for the men to come, is a great misfortune, *mega pēma*."[164] Conversely, if woman is incontestably a misfortune, it is still necessary to add that this evil has the appearance of a good. Woman is beauty; now, for the Greeks, the beautiful is not possible without the good. On the one hand, Prometheus takes delight in fire as if it were a good, while it is also a great misfortune. On the other hand, men, before the misfortune that is woman, "will rejoice in the depths of their hearts to surround her with love,"[165] as if their misfortune were also a good.

Furthermore, all women are not equally bad. There is one *genos gunaikōn*, one race of women, but several *phula*, in the plural, different tribes of these women.[166] After all, Hesiod admits that one can chance upon a good and wise wife, who pleases your heart;[167] she will give you what is one of the greatest "goods" in life, one that only a woman, even the worst of them, can procure for a man: a son like his father, who will continue the line after his death. Woman is not entirely bad, any more than fire is entirely good. What is still true, however, is that even if she is among the best, even if her heart is in agreement with yours, she was made by Zeus as a feminine woman in such a way that all through life, in her and by her, misfortune will come to balance out the good (*kakon esthlōi antipherizei, Theogony* 609).

Thus the *anti* of *ant' agathoio* works on two levels. Woman, this misfortune, is with respect to fire the counterpart of a good; but with respect to herself, in her own feminine nature, this misfortune is like the obverse of a good. We will note in this respect that not once does Hesiod simply say *kakon ant' agathoio,* a misfortune in the place of a good. When he uses this expression in the first passage,[168] it is to emphasize from the outset that, because of her beauty, this misfortune contains a positive aspect. Indeed, he writes *kalon kakon ant' agathoio,* which from this standpoint can be translated, to bring out the nuance, "A beautiful misfortune, the reverse of a good."

The second use of the phrase is even more instructive.[169] Hesiod has just likened the presence of women in the midst of the *andres* to that of the drones acting as parasites among bees. "Evil works" and "hard works" are associated both with women in the home and drones in the hives.[170] Thus it is indeed in the form of a misfortune that Zeus has placed women in human dwellings. But before telling of the consequences of this misfortune, Hesiod adds that Zeus has thereby procured for mortal men *heteron kakon ant' agathoio.* What does this *héteron* mean? Unlike *allos,* which indicates difference in general, *heteros* refers to one out of two, an other, but in cases where it can be a matter of only one or the other. *Heteron kakon* means "one of the two misfortunes," "a second evil with respect to the first." In what way would woman be "another" misfortune or second evil in this precise meaning of the word, if the good to which she is the counterpart is fire? The sentence would be meaningless. This is why M. L. West comments on the first *ant' agathoio,* in line 585, by saying, "The *agathon* is fire; cf. 570: *anti puros teuxen kakon.* The words *kakon ant' agathoio* are repeated in line 602"; and then goes on to note at line 602, "*Kakon ant' agathoio* is repeated from 585; the *agathon,* in this case, is celibacy (Guyet)."[171] To avoid having to make this jump from fire to celibacy while elucidating a formula that is presented as a repetition, it is necessary to view the problem as a whole. In this passage to say that the good is celibacy is insufficient. If a woman is an evil, celibacy, the lack of a woman is necessarily a good. The interest of the formula and the use of *heteron* (*kakon*) results from the effect of a reversal that they produce, the oscillation between a good and a misfortune, which are as connected as they are contrasted with the *anti* that links them in the text. The dilemma woman–absence-of-woman (marriage-celibacy) does not correspond to a simple choice between evil on the one hand and good on the other (as would have to be the case if we grant that woman is all evil, fire all good). Woman, an evil, contains a good; the absence of woman, a good, contains another evil, *heteron kakon.* Hesiod's text is perfectly clear in this respect.

Ever since Zeus created the race of women to live with men, the *andres* are stuck with a choice between two and only two solutions. They may decide to shun the feminine "evil" and refuse to marry. Then for the rest of their lives they spend their days without care or misery; they will have bread for as long as they live, since woman, that drone, that parasite, will not eat theirs.[172] But because of the lack of sons to continue their lineage and carry on their place in the house, the wealth they have been able to accumulate during their lives because of their celibacy is dispersed among distant kin after their death.[173] The status of woman is such that her absence (the refusal of marriage) entails another evil that replaces the first, taking its place like an only son, who is opposite the father from a generational standpoint but his equivalent from the standpoint of the *oikos* and who is the successor when his old man is gone.[174]

The second alternative is as follows. One gets married. Then one will have children, either one son, "to feed the paternal holdings—so the wealth of houses grows,"[175] or several, who can also "bring an immense fortune."[176] On this level, then, everything is for the best. But this happiness must be paid for. Most often it is bought by a life of hell with the drone, a pain for which there is no cure, in the person of the wife one had lodged in one's own house. And if one has the rare good luck to encounter a woman who resembles the worker bee more than the drone—even with her, inexorably, "the bad will offset the good."[177]

Thus each alternative is presented either as a good balanced out by an evil or an evil balanced out by a good. Ever since the creation of the *genos gunaikōn,* the *andres* struggle in vain. With a woman or without one, they will always be faced with a *kakon ant' agathoio.* If they claim to avoid the one, they run into the other (*heteron*). As a snare handed to men, woman is truly a twofold creature: through her, good and evil are combined in human existence like the two inseparable sides of the same reality. We understand why Zeus bursts out laughing at the idea of the *kalon kakon* that he is going to have fashioned for the humans. With this evil whose beauty makes men love her as a good, the good itself can only appear as the reverse of another evil.

These remarks enable us to understand the full significance of the expression *anti puros.* First of all, woman is the countergift to fire in the banal sense that, if Zeus brought her to men, it is to make them pay for the fire that Prometheus had stolen from him as a gift to them. However, once again, *anti* does not only mean "in exchange," "in return," but also "equal to." The epithet that describes an Amazon as *antianeira* presents her both as an enemy of men—against them—and the same as men—

equal to them. Woman can compensate for fire and provide the balance because she herself is a kind of fire, which will burn men alive by consuming their strength day by day. The fire stolen by the Titan is echoed by this other type of fire, this thieving fire that Zeus creates as the instrument of his revenge placed among mortals forever.

But in what way, it will be asked, do women in Hesiod's eyes "roast" (*optan*) their husbands, in what way do they put them "on the grill" (*statheuein*), to borrow the expressions that Aristophanes uses in *Lysistrata*? [178] In two ways, according to the Boeotian poet: first of all by their appetite for food and then by their hunger for sex. And this double need, which makes the woman an insatiable *gastēr,* corresponds to both the misfortunes that stalk the male, depending on whether he marries or stays single. In the first place, woman is a ravenous belly that cannot adjust to the frugal regimen of poverty but wishes to be able to eat until sated or surfeited (*koros, Theogony* 593); when she smiles at a man she is already eyeing his storehouse like a thief toward taking the contents for herself.[179] When she moves into a man's house, it is to store up the fruit of the labors of others in her *gastēr,* like a drone.[180] All day long worker bees toil outside to store honey that the drones, like thieves, will feed on in the shelter of the hives. All day long human men, too, toil in the fields, parched by their labor (*ponos*) to harvest the grain that the women—with their thieves' temperament (*epiklopon ēthos, Works* 67 and 78)—will eat. Because she is *deipnolokhēs* (*Works* 74), ever on the lookout for a feast, always ready to sit down to a meal, woman, writes Hesiod, "no matter how vigorous her husband, grills him over the fire, dries him out without a torch (*heuei ater daloio*), and sends him into premature old age."[181] With her insatiable appetite the wife is like an incarnation of Hunger, *Limos,* the progeny of *Eris* that the daughter of Night bore when she gave gave birth to *Ponos* (hard labor). Hesiod makes Hunger the companion of the *anēr aergos,*[182] the man who refuses to work and who thereby himself becomes, like a woman, similar to a stingless drone among the bees.[183] What Hunger is to the idle man, a wife is to the hardworking man: a hunger settled in like a companion under his roof, a burning hunger, ablaze, *limos aithōn,*[184] which burns like the flaming fire, *aithomenos pur.*[185] Need we recall that, according to a Hesiodic fragment, Erysichthon, the man Demeter afflicted with a devouring hunger in punishment, is named precisely because of his insatiable appetite, *Aithōn,* the Burning One?[186]

The ardor of the woman's belly for food, an ardor that absorbs the vigor that the males have expended in agricultural labor along with the grain products, forms one aspect of this *kuneos noos* (*Works* 67), that doglike spirit that, by Zeus' orders, inhabits women. "Is there anything more like a dog (*kunteron*) than the odious belly?" exclaimed Odysseus, wracked with hunger, in the *Odyssey*?[187] Narrating the crime of Clytemnestra (the "bitch face," *kunōpis*), Agamemnon repeats the formula word for word, replacing "belly" with woman, "Is there anything more like a dog than a woman?"[188] and the same terms are found, following Clement of Alexandria, in the Orphic precept according to which "there is nothing more like a dog than a woman."[189] However, this feminine *gastēr* that sweeps up the foods of life for its own benefit, who gulps them down into her depths at the male's expense, is the same belly who bears and nourishes in her breast a child to give to her husband. Since the time when, thanks to Prometheus, grains no longer grow by themselves, it has been necessary to bury seeds in the belly of the earth and then watch them disappear in the form of *sitos*, grain food, into the bellies of women. From the day that Zeus' will determined the existence of women, men, like wheat, no longer grow by themselves out of the ground. Men must put their seed in the belly of their wives so that it may germinate; and when the time comes, legitimate children who can extend their father's lineage will emerge from it. However, even on this level, where the woman's belly appears beneficial, the woman takes on the role of *anti puros*, the opposite of fire. Henceforth the procreation of children will result from sexual union. And in this area even the best of women, the most chaste of wives, are liable, when Sirius approaches the earth and consumes it with his fire, to be transformed into lascivious and lewd creatures who draw from their laboring husbands the little bit of moisture they maintain during that burning season. For at the hottest time of the summer, women, made of water and clay, feel their own immodest ardors rise within (*makhlotatai*, *Works* 586); men, by contrast of a less humid temperament, with their skin dried out and their head and knees[190] burned by Sirius the burning Dog (*Works* 587–88), are already so weakened by natural dryness (*aphaurotatoi*, *Works* 586) that they do not wish to see their wives, bitchlike in this season, add their erotic heat to that of the Dog Days.[191]

By her double voraciousness for both food and sex, the shameless feminine *gastēr* consumes the male's energy and dispatches him from the greenness of youth to a desiccated old age. In this sense Hesiod's text, in a series of concordant references, indeed presents the woman as a fire created by Zeus as a counterpart to the fire stolen by Prometheus to give to humans. To the modern commentators who, finding this analysis too subtle or forced, remain skeptical, and to those who have given their irony free rein concerning this point, we will only observe that the Greeks, who were no less capable of understanding Hesiod than they are, read him in this manner. This reading does not, as some who have challenged it have written,[192] date from the sixth century A.D. but from the fifth century B.C., since it is already found in Euripides in a fragment of the *First Hippolytus,* where, according to the poet, women were created as a counterpart to fire (*anti puros*), like another fire that is stronger (*allo pur meizon*) and more difficult to fight.[193] In the same vein, two texts from Palladas of Alexandria provide the best commentary on the interpretation that we believe can be offered. They appear in book 9 of the *Palatine Anthology,* numbers 165 and 167, and their discovery seems to us to confirm a reading that the text of Hesiod had originally suggested to us by itself. According to the first passage, "Zeus, for the ransom of the fire (*anti puros*), gave us the gift of another fire, women. Would it please the gods that neither woman nor fire appeared! At least fire can be quickly extinguished, but woman is an inextinguishable fire, full of ardor, who always bursts into flame." The second is more specific in its reference to Hesiod: "Woman is Zeus' anger; she was given to us to avenge fire (*anti puros*), a fatal gift that is the countergift of fire (*dōron aniēron tou puros antidoton*). For she burns the man with cares, she consumes him (*andra gar ekkaiei tais phrontisin ēde marainei*), she transforms his youth into premature old age."

8. To Marry the Worker Bee or the Drone?

In addition to the wife, *Works and Days* mentions other types of women. There is, for example, the woman that the peasant must first obtain along with his house and a working ox if he wishes to begin work with some hope of profit, a servant woman that Hesiod describes as "bought, not married."[194] Also there is the maiden, the *parthenos* with delicate skin, ignorant of the works of Aphrodite, typically depicted cozily in her house with her mother in deepest winter, bathing her tender body and rubbing it with rich oil before stretching out in the warmth.[195] On the other hand, in the versions of the Promethean myth in the *Theogony* and *Works and Days,* in the third and final act of the drama, after the allocation of the sacrificial parts and the theft of fire, the woman who, by order of Zeus, emerges fashioned by divine hands has no other form than that of the wife. To be sure, it is in the form of a *parthenos* that Hephaestus models the clay into a feminine creature;[196] but the product of his art is completely different from the sweet young maiden of the genre we mentioned, who, ignorant of the works of Aphrodite, remains at her tender mother's side in her own home.[197] The *parthenos* that Zeus intends for the *andres* emanates seduction. She provokes men's desire, knows it, and plays upon it.

She is the young maiden already a woman (*gunē parthenos*, as the *Theogony* says in 713–14), good and ready to marry, about to leave for the house where she will be the spouse. The fashioning done by Hephaestus is a prelude to the "outer" preparations of which Athena is in charge, either by herself or aided by the Charites, the Hours, and Peitho, and to the "inner" wiles that Hermes will place in the creature's heart. Athena garbs her in a white robe; she ties her belt (which the husband will untie); she drapes over her forehead the veil that covers her face; and she crowns her with a diadem, exactly as one prepares the *numphē*, the veiled bride, on the day of her wedding.

It is indeed as a wife that Pandora, conducted by Hermes, who is well-suited to lead this nuptial procession, is sent to Epimetheus. A gift (*dōron*) sent by all of Olympus to earth, she constitutes, as a spouse accepted in the husband's house for regulated cohabitation, the (poisoned) present from all the gods "to men who eat bread."[198] Prometheus, the Fore-sighted, warned his brother Epimetheus, the After-thinker, never to accept any "gift" from Zeus, but if he received one, to send it back whence it came immediately. Epimetheus, as he must, forgets the advice. He opens his door, welcomes the gift, the misfortune (*pēma*)—Pandora, "gift of all the gods."[199] He understands the evil, *kakon*, that the race of mortals will inherit with him only when the wife has taken up her abode in his house.[200]

This version of the myth, where the first woman is called Pandora and is the wife of Epimetheus, appears in *Works and Days*. The *Theogony* nei-ther tells the tale nor mentions her name. What then does Hephaestus create on Zeus' orders in the corresponding sequence of the *Theogony*? An evil (*kakon*, 570), a beautiful evil (*kalon kakon*, 585), a trap (*dolos*, 589), in the likeness of a chaste virgin (*parthenōi aidoiēi ikelon*, 572); and it is from this "she" (*ek tēs*, 590; *tēs gar*, 591), from the feminine that is never named or directly designated but simply evoked in the mode (neuter or mascu-line) of what it will represent for the males, that the race of women issues, described as a terrible scourge (*pēma mega*) because they live with mortal men (*thnētoisi met' andrasi naietaousin*).[201] The signs are already clear; woman is seen in her status as wife who has come to share the house of her husband. This is why the theogonic version of the creation of woman reaches its natural conclusion in the recognition of man's inescapable di-lemma: to flee marriage (*gamon pheugōn*, 603) or to accept it as his fate (*gamou meta moira*, 607). That is not all. If Pandora and Epimetheus are not explicitly referred to as the first married couple, this is because, in the economy of the theogonic account, the case of the brothers of Prometheus in general and Epimetheus in particular has already been decided in a preceding passage introducing the Promethean myth (507–519). Now, in this preamble, the few lines devoted to Epimetheus (511–14) refer to him unequivocally as the husband of this first woman, whose fashioning by Zeus (to win victory over Prometheus) Hesiod is about to recount. Epimetheus is described in the following way, "Epimetheus, the clumsy one, who from the beginning (*ex arkhēs*) brought misfortune to men who eat bread;[202] for Epimetheus was the first to welcome under his roof (*hupedekto*) the *gunē parthenos,* the virgin woman shaped by Zeus."[203] Thus in the context of our myth it is the first marriage that is represented by the creation of woman. As a human institution inaugurating conjugal life, with the foundation of the blood sacrifice, the fire stolen by the Titan, the cultivation of grain, and the institution of labor, this marriage acts to determine man's condition since that time in Mecone when, because of Prometheus, the apportionment between gods and mortals was made under the sign of *Eris.*

It seems to us that the matrimonial implications of this last sequence of the myth shed some light on the significance of the comparison between women and drones and account for its apparently paradoxical aspects. How is the account presented? Hephaestus and Athena have finished their work. Zeus parades the "beautiful evil," a deep, inescapable trap intended to be the human lot, before both Immortals and mortals, still united and equally amazed. It is from this creature, continues the text, that the cursed race and tribes of women spring forth, a terrible scourge living with mortal men and making themselves their companions not in the bane of poverty but only in satiety. That is all on the subject of women; nothing more is said about them. Then a comparison begins introduced by *hōs,*[204] "in this way," and leading six lines later to a return to women by means of a *hōs d' autōs,*[205] "likewise in this way," permitting without further ado the conclusion that it is indeed for the great unhappiness of mortal males that Zeus founded the race of women. Therefore the whole weight of the text is a result of the likeness it establishes between drones among the worker bees and women among men.

What do drones represent with respect to worker bees? Three characteristics stand out. First, cohabitation: living "in vaulted hives"[206] they share the house of the workers where they are established as if at home. Then, inactivity: they live without doing anything, without taking part in the labor of their hosts; while the latter busy themselves all day long outside the hive, the drones remain "inside," sheltered under the roof of the hives.[207] Finally, the *gastēr:* in the hollow space of the dwelling where they lodge, the drones form many other hollows within the greater one; they are mouths to feed, bellies to fill; the only activity of these inactive ones is to "store" in the base of their *gastēr* what the bees harvest outside so it may be stored on the honeycombs.[208] And in this way, for those who must feed them, the drones, the *aergoi* or idle ones, are very much like the *kaka erga*,[209] the works of evil. If the same complicity between the "works of evil" can describe the position of women among men,[210] it is because of their conjugal status. In the eyes of the Greeks they appear to be dwelling in the house of their husband, confined to the domestic space and excluded from all outside work, which, whether agriculture, pastoral activities, or maritime enterprises, is reserved for males. The creatures dedicated to living "inside" and depending on their husbands for food are also "bellies" who, by ingesting the harvests with which they have had nothing to do, empty the storehouses where the peasant locks up the fruits of his labor. The comparison is valid in all respects. Moreover, it sheds some light on the tie that in the myth links the "gift" of woman to man's new condition: since Zeus hid the wheat the male must toil greatly to feed himself. But this is not all. In addition to his own *gastēr,* which he must fill every day if he wishes to survive personally, he is again compelled, if he wants a son to survive him after his death, to satisfy the voracious *gastēr* of his feminine half. And this increase in effort, expended without respite, dries him up the way a fire would.

However, this extensive comparison between women and drones has something wrong with it, which is related to a point that is central enough that it first seems to affect the entire force of the comparison. The analogy between the human and insect worlds is indeed intended to clarify the status of women with respect to men. Yet sexually, the terms have been reversed. In the insect world, the parasites are males (*hoi kēphēnes*), and the workers, the feeders, are female (*hai melissai*). Among humans, the males are in the position of female, worker bees, and the women created by Zeus are in that of male drones. This contradiction did not escape Hesiod, who explicitly stresses it. He develops his comparison in six lines; the first two pose the general relation between worker bees and drones, the former "feeding" the latter.[211] The next four lines are divided into two equal parts: first concerning the worker bees and then concerning the drones. And each of these parts, introduced by *hai men* ("*they* [fem.]," on the one hand) and *hoi de* ("but *they* [masc.]," on the other), clearly contrasts the behaviors by denoting them as feminine or masculine. Furthermore, as we have already indicated, the same comparison in *Works and Days* (303–306) this time likens the drones not to women but to the *aergos anēr,* the male who refuses to work.

What then does this disparity, which Hesiod did not seek to minimize (since, to the contrary, the text of the *Theogony* emphasizes it), mean for the status of the two sexes? Let us first note a detail in *Works and Days* that gives the idle male, by his likeness to drones, a feminine connotation. Drones are described as *kothouroi,* stingless.[212] Since this adjective, close to *kolouros,* also evokes what is mutilated, cut off, and, more specifically, what has its tail cut off, we will accept all the more easily that the term for the drone, *kēphēn,* is itself related to *kōphos,* "dulled," "weakened." Plato will express the contrast between the stingless drone and the stinging insect in terms of the difference between that which is less virile and that which is very much so (*anandroteron/andreiotaton*).[213] The pairing of *kothouros* to *kēphēn* when referring to a male shifts the idle man to the realm of the effeminate if not to that of women—women who by their very nature, in the logic of the myth, embody nonparticipation in manly work.

Having clarified that point, let us move on to the essential. Two arguments can explain this reversal of the status of the sexes when we move from humans to insects. Let us begin with the least important. The Promethean version of the sacrificial myth told by Hesiod presents humans in a position midway between animals and gods. The differentiation of the sexes and its correlatives—sexual union, birth from procreation, aging, and death—are characteristics shared by humans and animals. However, monogamous marriage, fitting for civilized humanity and more a contractual matter than a natural bond, grants the married woman and her relations with her male mate a different character from that of the female animal living in generalized sexual promiscuity that, like omophagia and allelophagia (the eating of raw food and all forms of cannibalism), determine for the Greeks a state of savagery or bestiality. The full implications of the presence of woman are understood only in the framework of the Promethean adventure, in connection with the characteristic eating habits of the human species, with the mastery of fire and the hardworking life that are the lot of mortals since their separation from the gods. The human wife is not a "natural" being but the sophisticated product of the *mētis* of the sovereign of the gods, Zeus' reply to the tricks of Prometheus. A comparison with animals that permits women to be condemned as an "evil," with its reversal of male and female, underscores the distance between animals and men at the very point where it seems they must be completely identified. Her origins, her functions, and her meaning in human life differentiate woman from the female animal. The text proves it in the very example chosen to show the likeness between them. The model that most clearly reveals the status of the wife at home is the beehive. But in the hive it is the male who holds the role that Zeus has assigned to the human woman.

The second reason is more basic and more clearly reveals the wifely value of the feminine creature created by Zeus. As Marcel Detienne has shown, in Greek tradition a model animal for the human wife exists, a symbol of conjugal virtues such as fidelity, decency and reserve, moderation of the appetites and sensuality, the diligent care brought to domestic interests, and the steward's vigilant attention to preserve the wealth accumulated in the household by the male.[214] The qualities of the legitimate wife are emblematically expressed, in the ritual of the Thesmophoria as well as in literature and myth, in the image of the bee—chaste, pure, laborious, a stranger to all the deceits of seduction. In this respect the text of Hesiod has an ironic and polemical meaning. The tone is mocking. No, woman is not a bee. She has nothing of this modest and chaste creature that Xenophon, following Semonides, represents as innocent of all gluttony, drunkenness, and amorous license so she may dedicate herself completely to household work. In the hive she is a famished belly that demands satisfaction, the drone. In the married couple it is the male who plays the role of the bee, in expiation for the Titan's revolt.

Even in marriage, which distances man from the animals and connects him with the gods, negativity and unhappiness take the form of the wife so that men are reminded of their sorry state. The wonder (*thauma*), the gift that the gods sent to humans to live with them in their homes, the fine present that they fashioned for them with their hands "in the likeness of goddesses," is a snare, like the portions of the sacrificial victim, an ardor that burns like the fire stolen by Prometheus, a trap that makes them rejoice, to be sure, and which they will never be able to do without, but in which they are lost with no hope of escape.

9. Full and Empty: Pandora's Jar

After the twists and turns of the route we have taken sometimes a bit slowly to explore some of the secret contours of the text, we can say that in the continuous series of disasters unleashed by the Titan's transgression in the allocation at Mecone, married life, like the cultivation of grain, seems linked to sacrificial cooking. If bread is to vegetable food as the cooked meat of the sacrificial victim is to fleshly food, union with a married woman, a *gunē gametē,* is to sexual union what bread and cooked meat are to the consumption of food.

Sacrifice, agriculture, and marriage are the three inseparable factors of the human condition since the *anthrōpoi,* cut off from the Blessed Immortals, became both *andres,* male men, and poor mortals. Perishable creatures but once very close to the gods, they can only sustain their lives as individuals or perpetuate them in the family group by acts in which biological necessities are conjoined with religious needs. The satisfaction of vital needs is then carried out by means of cult practices that bring about a delicate balance, an uneasy compromise between the mode of existence shared by all mortal animals and the status reserved for the divine. Like animals, men must kill, eat, and procreate in order to survive. But in these three activities rigorous prohibitions circumscribe the domain of what is possible for humans, actions that must be both licit and pious with respect to the gods. One cannot kill just any living creature, eat just any kind of food, or couple with whomever one pleases.[215] The slaughter of animals, the eating of food—both animal and plant—and sexual union obey strict rules. Carried out according to ritual, these activities are not only under the patronage and warranty of the gods, they constitute religious procedures by which men and gods are joined, united, and enter into common fellowship. It is by sacrificing a victim and eating of its flesh, by working the soil as is fitting, and leading one's spouse home according to rite, that a man establishes and maintains contact with the divine; by these very acts he places himself within the boundaries of the human realm. The drama, which the foundation myth of sacrifice accounts for in its fashion, is that the union with the gods also constitutes the distance, barriers, and renunciation of that state of quasi-divine felicity humanity once knew and sacrificial ceremony evokes—at the very moment that it consecrates and justifies its disappearance.

This polarity that myth places at the heart of the sacrifice extends to the whole of human life in man's own torn condition. As sacrifice both brings men and gods together and separates them, both likens men to animals and brings out the distance between them, it puts humanity in a state of being that is fundamentally ambiguous and marked by dualities and contradictions. Henceforth everything will contain its opposite, its nocturnal side. No more abundance without painful effort, no more men without women, no more birth without death, no more good without the counterbalancing of an evil. The Promethean part in us, which raises us above the animals, is not without its opposite, that of Epimetheus, who brings about the break with the earlier beatitude when man was close to the gods, and with it the fall into an inferior existence doomed to unhappiness and discord.

A philosopher might describe such an existence by saying that being is entwined with nonbeing, plenitude with privation. Hesiod is no philosopher. As we read his tale this form of existence that is now ours emerges as a crucible, a mixture of interlocking goods and evils that can never be separated, a tension that is constantly maintained, and an oscillation between contrasting and similar poles, opposed and inseparable sides.

Undoubtedly, it is in this context that we must view the episode of the jar of evils opened by Pandora—an episode that serves as a conclusion to the Promethean myth in *Works and Days*.[216] This passage poses several problems, which the text is unable to resolve and which are, moreover, secondary to its interpretation. We do not know exactly where this jar comes from, who gave it, or received it—whether Epimetheus or Pandora, since the jar is found at their house. According to the scholia, Prometheus, after receiving it from the Satyrs, gave it to his brother to keep so that it would remain forever unopened. One thing is certain: by opening the jar the woman, that beautiful evil, that trap set by Zeus under Epimetheus' roof, carries out her office as instrument of divine punishment. When Pandora "lifts the great lid of the *pithos* with her hands,"[217] her action recalls and avenges the offense made against the sovereign of the gods when, "lifting the white fat with his hands" and finding the bare bones,[218] Zeus knew he had been duped by Prometheus. Moreover, "the painful cares" (*kēdea lugra*) that the woman envisions for humans by acting as she does are the very ones that Zeus, in the beginning of the acount, already envisioned for them in his fury at being the dupe of the rascally Titan.[219]

How is this story of the jar presented? Hesiod has just explained that the thoughtless Epimetheus understood only later after the fact the blunder that he committed by welcoming into his house the gods' gift, a misfortune that will be with him evermore.

This evil, this *kakon*, is the very subject of the rest of the tale. "For beforehand" (*Prin men gar*), continues the text—in other words, referring to the times before Pandora and the incident at Mecone—the tribe of humans lived on earth in a state comparable to that of the men of the golden race: "separated and far from all misfortunes"[220]—painful work, sickness, old age, and death. These are the evils, *kaka*, that Pandora, by removing the lid, scatters throughout the world, "filling"[221] the earth and sea with their wandering presence. In these unhappy surroundings, men henceforth have myriads of ills at their side: never leaving them day or night, the *nousoi*, "sicknesses," cling fast to ruin and destroy them "by bringing them pains," *kaka*.[222] The situation surpasses the punishment of Prometheus: holding fast to the Titan, the eagle tears off pieces of his liver during the day; but at least during the night the bird leaves him in peace, and the liver can take advantage of this respite and entirely regain its shape. Moreover, the pain (*nousos*) that gnaws away at Prometheus' body is a single event; Hercules, driving off the eagle with Zeus' consent, forever liberates Prometheus from the cruel malady (*kakēn nouson*)[223] that the Olympian had set upon Prometheus to torture him.

This "plenitude" of ills in the sphere of human life recalls the fate of another of the races Hesiod describes in the series after the Promethean myth. It is the last of races, that of the men of iron who live "now" and of which Hesiod and his contemporaries are part—in other words, humanity in its present state. These men, we are told, "never cease suffering miseries and fatigues during the day, nor cease being consumed by them at night; the gods will give them the gift of painful cares."[224] However, Hesiod immediately goes on to add, "for the latter as well, good will still be mixed with misfortune."[225] The present mix of good and evil contrasts on the one hand with the golden race in which men enjoy all good without knowing any ill, and on the other hand with the apocalyptic view the poet expresses—of a humanity adrift, cut off from all its connections with the divine and having no respect for justice or fear of the gods anymore, living like wild animals, given over to bad *Eris*—when there will be no remedy for evil and humans will be left with nothing but those painful sufferings (*algea lugra*, 200) that Zeus and Pandora had envisioned for mortals (*kēdea lugra*, 49 and 95) and that the woman had freed from the jar to occupy the inhabited world (*muria lugra*, 100).

But what is the exact form of this "melange" of good and ill that characterizes the humanity of today? To answer this question requires examining the relationship between the "evil" introduced by Zeus among men in the person of Pandora and the "evils" introduced by Pandora among the same men when, on Zeus' order, she opens the jar. Between the first evil and the evils released from the jar there is first of all a homology, if not a redundancy. In some ways, the episode of the jar only repeats the theme developed on another level that the creation of Pandora and her coming to Epimetheus had already established: the intrusion of evil in its varied guises in the life of mortals.[226] However, the two stories do not repeat one another; in many respects concerning the mixture of good and evil the second story fills out and completes the one that precedes it.

In Pandora good and evil are connected in two ways. The first relationship is that of exterior to interior. The evil is disguised inside Pandora beneath a seductive exterior. And this seduction entices the eyes—with the deceptive charm of her beauty—as well as the ears—with the misleading attractiveness of her speech, her *phōnē*.[227] In this respect woman is indeed a trap (*dolos*): the evil she conceals is seen and heard in the guise of a good. Good and evil are joined together like the two sides of a coin. Woman is an evil, but without this evil the corresponding good is lacking. It is impossible to have one without the other.

What about the evils that escape from the jar? In the beginning they are hidden within it. As long as they remain there, they are harmless. It is when they move from the inside to the outside that humans are assailed with misfortunes. This unhappiness does not have Pandora's ambiguity: fatigue, suffering, disease, and death have nothing seductive about them. If we could avoid them, we would not fail to do so. Still, it would be necessary to be able to assess them and recognize them. Now, no matter what we do, they strike at any time, as if they were produced by spontaneous generation (*automatoi*), in the same way that in the golden age of yore the food of life (*bios*) grew all by itself, independently of men and their efforts. Misfortunes can no more be seen ahead of time than heard. They move forward silently and invisibly. Zeus has denied them the *phōnē* with which he endowed women to dupe men.[228]

So, the situation is this: The evil that can be seen and heard is hidden in the seductive form of a desirable good. Once hidden in the jar but today scattered outside it, the evils that cannot be taken for a good remain hidden and overtake us by surprise. In both cases man can neither foresee nor avoid the evil. When he sees it, he mistakes it for a good; and even when he does see it and recognizes its true nature, this evil remains invisible until it has befallen him.

Let us go one step further. The evils were lodged inside the jar as if in a house (*en domoisin*, "in their lodging," in 96; *thuraze*, "beyond the doors," in 97)[229] or inside a belly (*hupo kheilesin*, "below the lips," in 97). What is a jar, for Hesiod; what normally contains this domestic "belly" in the house, and what does opening it normally mean? In *Works and Days*, in addition to the episode of Pandora, we find three cases where a *pithos* is involved, and in all three it is precisely a question of opening it (*oigō* in 819, *arkhomai* in 815 and 368).[230] To open a jar is to begin using provisions, the "reserves stored in the house," as Hesiod says (*to g' ein oikōi katakeimenon*, 364). Since wheat no longer grows by itself, man can no longer live in idleness, sure of finding food every day without having to worry about the morrow. Just as he must work the soil so that the wheat ripens, he must store up the grain after the harvest in the cellar, in the *pithoi* that he will open on the suitable dates (not all days are good for this),[231] depending on the resources that he has been able to husband for himself.

In this respect the representation of the jar in the text is related to Pandora; it too has something deceptive about it. When a peasant stores a closed *pithos* in his house, this jar hides within it the *bios* the household will live on. The day it is open is like a holiday; the peasant drops his miserliness and for once gives himself over to satiety (*arkhomenou de pithou . . . koresasthai*).[232] Pandora's jar, then, is a double deception. It does not contain, as it should, *bios*, life food; it is full of all the evils that grind man down and consume his life. Moreover, the woman has barely opened the lid when all the evils fly outside at once (*exiptamai*, 98) and are scattered (*skedannumi*, 95) around the world, over land and sea—rather than moving slowly in a measured way without leaving the domestic enclosure, as the *bios* moves from the belly of the jar to those of the members of the family. When full Pandora's jar must always remain closed; the moment it is opened it is empty, at least of what a *pithos* is supposed to contain, the *bios*. Yet unlike the *kaka*, something has not passed the lips of the jar. It remains inside (*endon emimne*, 97)[233] like the drone in the hive, like Pandora in the house, and does not fly away (*oude thuraze exeptē*, 98). It is *Elpis* (Expectation), which, by the will of Zeus, the woman shutting the lid gave no time to leave.

10. Elpis *Remains inside the House*

Before examining the meaning that should be given to *Elpis* and its status in the account (is it an evil, a good, or both? does its presence in the jar mean it is within men's reach or does it remove it from their life?), we must further clarify the relations between the *bios*, customarily stored in the peasant's *pithoi*, and the *kaka* enclosed in Pandora's *pithos*. To put it clearly, the "evils" that escape from the jar essentially are the counterpart or reverse of the *bios*; they are the price that mortals must henceforth pay to eat the food that enables them to live. The evils once enclosed in the *pithos* and now wandering throughout the world are of two types: painful work (*khalepos ponos*) and painful diseases (*argaleai nousoi*), which bring males death (if we read *kēras* in line 92) or old age (if we read *gēras*). Death or old age. In either case the term *nousos* must be taken in the broad sense: everything that harms men's health, everything that destroys their vital integrity.[234] That is what is clearly stated in line 93, borrowed from the

Odyssey but entirely fitting in this context: "For mortals age quickly in the state of misery (*en kakotēti*)." The gods' inalterable youth and their immortality are only the other half of their status as Blessed Ones (*Makares*) who know no work, fatigue, or painful cares. As long as humans lived in the felicity of the golden age, without doing anything, far from "labors and suffering" (*ater te ponōn kai oizuos*, 113), they too did not grow old; never wearing down, they remained forever as they always were.[235] What in the iron age, on the other hand, is the source of their loss and leads to their destruction (*phtheiromenoi*, 178) is "fatigue and suffering" (*kamatou kai oizuos*, 177),[236] to which the gods add the gift of "painful cares" (*khalepas merimnas*, 178).

Thus on the one hand there is the *bios*, the cereal food belonging to men "who eat bread," a food with which their energy is restored, that makes them survive and is, we have seen, like the fabric of their lives. On the other are the *kaka*—labor, the fatigue from work, the suffering associated with them, and last, disease (*ponos, kamatos, oizus, nousoi*)—everything that saps the strength of mortals, ruins their vitality, and makes them age and die (as woman does likewise). However, if the myth of Prometheus teaches us anything, it is that Zeus, hiding the *bios* from men, makes it available to them only through a series of misfortunes he has concocted for them, misfortunes closely related to *Eris* in the catalogue of the Children of Night. To fill the jars with *bios* and ensure an adequate supply of the food of life, it is necessary for the male to spare no pain, fatigue, or suffering; he must exhaust his strength, little by little ruin his health, and spend his youth in hard labor.

We can go further. By opening the jar, Pandora, following Zeus, envisions the *kēdea lugra*, for men the sad cares (just as the gods offer painful worries to the men of iron). But when the harvest has been plentiful and the jars are full of wheat, man is no longer anxious about the *bios* for the time being; he lives without worrying about the morrow, in the manner of the men of the golden race his heart free of care (*akēdea thumon*).[237] Hesiod is extremely clear on this point. If by slow accumulation one creates reserves, one's soul will be in peace. It is good (*esthlon*),[238] he says, to take from what one has. There is nothing better than finding everything at home, for "it is not what one stores at home that gives man care (*anera kēdei*, 364–66)." What puts suffering in the heart (*pēma de thumōi*, 366)[239] is, on the contrary, needing what one does not have (*khrēizein apeontos*, 367), being a man in a state of indigence (*anēr kekhrēmenos*, 478). The "care" is related to the lack, the emptiness, the absence of the *bios*. But who among mortals "lacks bread" (*khrēizōn biotoio*, 499)? Whose "life is

not assured," not "sheltered from care" (*tōi mē bios arkios eiē,* 501)?[240] And
who in this way finds himself the prey of cruel anxiety or the dupe of a
vain hope (*keneēn epi elpida,* 498)? It is the *aergos anēr,* the man who does
not work, the drone. His companion is not only Hunger (302), but also
the Hope that is not good (*elpis d' ouk agathē,* 500), the bad *Elpis.* The
idle man is contrasted with the one who has understood the lesson of the
Promethean misfortunes and who devotes his life to work. Demeter fills
his storehouse full of the life-giving wheat (*biotou,* 301): he can "clear the
spider webs from his pots (*ek d' angeōn*)";[241] for, the moment the thresh-
ing is over, he will have put all his *bios* in his pots (*en angesin*), measuring
and storing it inside his house (*endothi oikou*).[242] Since the *pithoi* of this
peasant are full of *bios,* for him hope is not empty, either. Hesiod deems
this man worthy of having good hope (*eolpa,* 475) because he will have
the joy of taking the *biotos* from the stores he has gathered and living in
plenty until spring, without looking to his neighbor; on the contrary, it is
he that the stranger will need.[243] Of course, this happy lack of care had to
be acquired, to be bought by always having in mind at the proper moments the "care" that is the task at hand. *Meletē*—care, diligence, the ardor
for work (443), the attention to each task (457), the zeal for work (380,
412), the recourse to work to watch over the bread (*meletais biou,* 316),
the constant preoccupation with work (*memēlota erga,* 231)—this is what
secures a man a moment of respite, a share of good in the midst of the
evils and sad torments that Zeus has prepared for mortals. Here again the
good, the *esthla,* appears inseparably blended with the evils, the *kaka.*[244] It
is by thinking of the *bios,* by caring for it during the whole cycle of agricultural activities from sowing to harvest, that one is freed from the "painful cares" and vain hope that accompany those who, because of culpable
lack of care for their work,[245] are seized with anxiety or sustained by deceptive illusions at the sight of empty jars.

   Our comments thus far give an idea of the interpretation of *Elpis* that
emerges from our reading of Hesiod's account. Without going into the
details of the controversies generated by this sequence of the myth, we
must address two objections that are likely to be raised. First of all,
shouldn't we recognize that, since *Elpis* is enclosed with the ills in the
pithos, that Hesiod too saw it as an evil? And doesn't this lead to a contradiction—if the evils must escape from the jar in order to enter human
lives, isn't *Elpis,* by remaining inside, removed from human existence and
forever out of reach? If we accept the two parts to this conclusion, which
seem founded on sound logic, we make of *Elpis* not Hope, or expectation
in general, but the expectation of misfortunes, a kind of negative foresight.

Then its continued presence inside the jar is interpreted as the course Zeus must have taken at the last moment in order to keep human existence from being absolutely intolerable. That there are evils, it has been observed, is still tolerable; but if men knew by *elpis kakōn* all the catastrophes that would befall them, how would they find the strength to live?

The key issue revolves around whether the logic supporting this interpretation is indeed that of the text. Let us begin with the term *elpis*. In order to defend the idea that the Hesiodic *Elpis* refers exclusively to the expectation of misfortunes, we consult a passage from the *Leges* (644 c–d) where Plato makes a distinction between two forms of human opinions concerning the future. All opinions relating to the future (*doxai mellontōn*) bear the common name *elpis*; but when it is a question of the *elpis* of a coming pain, it is called *phobos*, fear, and in the opposite case, *tharros*, confidence. *Elpis*, then, has the general meaning not of hope, which implies the prospect of a good, but of expectation. What this text proves is that *elpis*, when neither specified as fear or confidence, is neutral; it can refer to a good or an evil. This raises a question: if Hesiod, by placing *Elpis* in the jar along with the misfortunes, was classing it as something bad and making it exclusively the anxious expectation of misfortune, wouldn't he have called it *Phobos* rather than *Elpis* to avoid all ambiguity? There is a more serious matter. The moment that *Elpis* is made into the expectation of misfortunes, it can be seen as the "ultimate evil," "the worst of all." More terrible than the misfortune itself is this foreknowledge of evils to come; its presence dwells in man's mind even before any actual misfortune befalls him.

Now, to us *Elpis* contains a fundamental dimension of uncertainty. It may be the expectation of an evil or a good; it is never firm or assured. It does not have the value of *pronoia*, prescience. Since it is on the order of conjecture, always implying some credulity,[246] it wavers between the dreams of the presumptuous and the terrors of the fearful.[247] With regard to Hesiod we will say that *Elpis* is no less foreign to *promētheia*, foresight, than it is to *epimētheia*, understanding after the fact. By his *mētis* Prometheus represents, in the misfortunes that strike him, the prescient hero: "I know beforehand precisely all the events to come; for me, no sorrow (*pēma*) will arrive unforeseen."[248] The complete certainty that the Titan possesses concerning his foreordained suffering is in a way the opposite of the uncertainty of the *Elpis* that is the human lot. Pindar will be able to contrast, in the case of the men to whom Zeus "has refused all clear indications of the future," *elpis*, on the one hand, with *promētheia*, foresight, on the other.[249]

This same opposition between *elpis* and the foresight of misfortune can be seen in a passage in *Prometheus Bound* in which it appears to us that Aeschylus is recalling Hesiod. The Titan enumerates the benefits he has showered on men: "I delivered mortals," he proclaims, "from the fore-knowledge of death (*thnētous g'epausa mē proderkesthai moron*)." "What cure have you found for this ill (*nosos*)," asks the chorus. "I have given them endless blind hope (*tuphlas en autois elpidas katōikisa*),"[250] replies Prometheus. Here it is not the foresight of evil or foreknowledge of death that is called *elpis;* on the contrary, the *elpis* permanently placed (*katoikizō*) in men, as Pandora is placed among them, constitutes *in its blindness* the antidote to foresight. It is not a cure for death, which has none, since death is inscribed, no matter what one does, in the course of human life. However, lodged in the innermost hearts of mortals, *elpis* can counterbalance their consciousness of mortality with their ignorance of the moment and manner in which death will take them.[251]

Next, how could Hesiod by depicting *Elpis* enclosed in the jar convey the idea that, unlike the evils, *Elpis* is at least set aside, away from contact with men? It is impossible to make such a claim unless the Promethean myth is taken out of the context of *Works and Days*. Furthermore, it would be necessary to view the *Elpis* remaining in Pandora's jar as having no connection either with the *elpis* that to Hesiod is related to the *anēr aergos* or with the other *elpis* that Hesiod on two occasions claims for himself,[252] first when he counts on an abundance of *bios* for the man who has worked and then when he is hopeful that Zeus will not leave crimes unpunished or allow the unjust to triumph. Let us even admit for a moment that the *Elpis* of the jar is not neutral (the expectation of either an evil or a good) or ambiguous (now good now bad); let us posit that it is categorized solely as an evil. Even in this case, the reference to a bad *elpis*, which is associated with a refusal to work, forces the interpreter either to recognize that for Hesiod men actually possess *elpis*, that they use it and too often, alas, misuse it, or else to maintain that the *elpis* of the idle man, which is explicitly qualified as bad, is however something completely different from this *Elpis* in the jar, also characterized by its malignity.

If we take all the passages in which *elpis* is mentioned into consideration, something becomes very clear. In *Works and Days*, *Elpis* occupies a niche that is comparable on all points to that of the other "polar" notions that offer both positive and negative aspects: *Eris, Zēlos, Aidōs,* and *Nemesis*. To speak, as Hesiod does, of *Elpis ouk agathē*,[253] presupposes that there also exists a good *Elpis*. The parallels between the bad *Aidōs* and the bad *Elpis* are complete, moreover; the same formula is used to describe both of them. It is a bad shame that clings to the indigent in line 316; it is a bad *elpis* that clings to the indigent in line 500. That bad *Aidōs* exists does not in any way keep it from being indispensable to men's life nor from characterizing the condition of their existence wherein evil is mixed with good and righteousness still counterbalances the spirit of immoderation (*Hubris*) and discord (*Zēlos* or *Eris*). But the day that *Aidōs*, with *Nemesis* (equally ambivalent because she figures among the children of Night while playing a benevolent role), "will leave" the humans among whom she has sojourned to rise to rejoin the Immortals, there will no longer be "any remedy for evil."[254]

Things are no different for *Elpis*. The departure of *Aidōs* for heaven, which Hesiod fears, echoes the cynical remark of Theognis: "All conscience (*Aidōs*) is ever afterwards dead among men."[255] And the poet adds elsewhere in the same spirit: "*Elpis* is the only good divinity that has remained among men (*en anthrōpoisin . . . enestin*); all the others have abandoned them to go back to Olympus."[256] In this human world—where happiness and misfortune are inextricably mixed, where there is no possibility of foreseeing either one with complete certainty, where men's minds, scrutinizing the future, oscillate between the exact foresight of Prometheus and his brother's total blindness—it is in the ambiguous form of *elpis*—of expectation, whether vain or well founded, good or bad—that the horizon of the future is laid out for mortals.

Two questions remain. First, why, if it is not entirely bad, is *Elpis* found mixed with the evils in the jar? To a large extent P. Mazon has provided the answer: "Because," he writes, "if hope is not an evil, it only can accompany evils—it is the daughter of unhappiness; it could not exist in Good Fortune."[257] Let us simply add, in pure good fortune. The gods, the men of the golden race, the *andres* of our myth before the drama at Mecone, cannot know *elpis*. They have nothing to desire; all good things are theirs, and they have nothing to fear; all evils are far from them. Introducing evils into the human universe to mix them with what is good automatically means giving *Elpis* a permanent home there, making it, for better or worse, the inseparable "companion" of humans.

There is a second question: Why does *Elpis*, unlike the evils, remain in the jar? If *Elpis* is not purely bad, if there is a good side or a good use to it, and if, moreover, its enclosure in the jar does not mean that it is placed outside of human reach—what exactly does the difference between the freeing of the evils and the enclosing of *Elpis* mean? We can propose several related ideas. Just as men leave the house and bees fly out of the hive, the evils flee from the jar. Filling up land and sea, they occupy the entire exterior world where virile activities, the *erga* of the males, normally take place. Like Pandora, *Elpis* remains inside, in the domestic space at the bottom of the empty jar. This contrast is reinforced by another character- istic of the evils released from the jar: their incessant motion, their contin- ual wandering (*alalētai,* 100). They move about here and there striking men, sometimes one, sometimes another, in their random peregrinations over land and sea. When the *nousoi* do not reach their victims by day, they come to visit them at home at night. They visit them (*phoitōsi,* 103) like a passing stranger who comes to the house but does not intend to stay there. *Elpis,* on the other hand, does not leave the house. It lives permanently with humans, all share it equally; whereas misfortune encounters certain men on certain days, as it goes around the world. In their unforeseeable mobility, the evils act *automatoi:*[258] following their own route, their own movement, they suddenly descend on man, who can do nothing about it. On the contrary *Elpis,* despite being shared, fixed, and constant, still de- pends on human initiative. Whether one is just or injust, pious or impious, hardworking or lazy, the expectation nursed by every man, no matter who, shifts from one side to the other. His *elpis* may be good or bad, taking the form of hollow illusions that lead a man astray from his tasks and doom him to disaster, or of legitimate confidence in the equity of all-seeing Zeus.[259] To the man of merit, who does not spare his sweat on the long and arduous route of effort,[260] the god gives prosperity at last[261]—or at least the share of wealth that the just man still has a right to count on in the midst of innumerable ills.

The *Elpis* of *Works and Days* combines the two sides of the Promethean myth in the framework of this vast poetic exhortation to work. In this context the misery that men owe to the faults of Prometheus is first of all the need for work, work that cannot be avoided if a man wishes to have enough to eat, enough to live on.[262] When the fertile wheat fields, *aroura,* germinated by themselves, unlike today, there was no need for men to have *pithoi* filled with wheat in their lodgings. Nor, for that matter, was there any need for the evils flying out of Pandora's *pithos* or the *Elpis* shut in the bottom of the jar. Now that the evils have escaped, we must fill the bellies of our jars with vital food and carefully measure it out during the course of the year to fill our bellies and those of our wives. The fear of want when the jars are empty, the aspiration to seeing them filled with wheat after the harvest is finished—this is the *Elpis* that inspires the good man to the labor imposed by Zeus and moreover guarantees him plenty, the same *Elpis* that lulls the idle man with an illusory hope and brings him the evil of poverty.

Linked to this first aspect of *Elpis* is another dimension, which could be called anthropological (not to say metaphysical) and was highlighted by the sacrificial myth in the *Theogony*. Zeus' punishment of the Titan's deception is of course hard work without which no well-being is possible for men. It is also in a broader sense the separation from the divine life that we once led in the company of the Blessed Immortals, without need or fatigue, age or death, and without women—a life that knew no "care," no preoccupation with the morrow, and neither anguished nor confident expectation of the future—because at the time no distance separated "now" and "forever" for us any more than it did for the gods. Associated with sacrifice, agriculture, and marriage, *Elpis,* like woman the ambiguous companion of man, puts its imprint on the new condition of mortal existence, halfway between animals and gods, in the mixed human universe that characterizes the age of iron. If, as in the golden age, human life contained only good, if all the evils were still shut up in the jar, there would be no need to hope for anything other than what one has.[264] If life were completely, irremediably given over to evil and unhappiness, again there would be no place for *Elpis*.[265] But since evils are henceforth inextricably bound up with good without our being able to foresee exactly what will happen to us tomorrow, we are always waiting, fearing, and hoping. If men had Zeus' infallible prescience at their disposal, they would have no need for *Elpis*. If they lived bounded by the present, without knowing anything of the future, without the slightest worry about it, again they would not know *Elpis*. But caught between the lucid foresight of Prometheus and the unreflecting blindness of Epimetheus, oscillating between the one and the other without ever being able to separate them, they know in advance that sufferings, sickness, and death are their inevitable lot, and not knowing what form this misfortune will take, they recognize it only too late, once it has already struck.

For immortal beings such as the gods, there is no need of *Elpis*. No *Elpis*, either, for creatures like animals who are unaware they are mortal. If man, mortal like the animals, foresaw the whole future as the gods do, if he were entirely Promethean, he would not have the strength to live, lacking the ability to look his own death in the face. But since he knows himself to be mortal without knowing when or how he will die, since he knows *Elpis*—foresight but blind foresight, a necessary illusion, a good and an evil at the same time—only *Elpis* can enable him to live this ambiguous, dual existence caused by the Promethean fraud when the first sacrificial meal was instituted. Henceforth everything has its opposite: no more contact with the gods that is not also, through sacrifice, the consecration of an unbridgeable gap between mortals and Immortals; no more happiness without unhappiness; birth without death; plenty without suffering and fatigue; food without hunger, decline, old age, and mortality. There are no more men without women, no Prometheus without Epimetheus. There is no more human existence without the twofold *Elpis*, this ambiguous expectation both fearful and hopeful about an uncertain future—*Elpis* in which, as in the best of wives, "bad throughout life comes to offset the good."[266]

THREE

Greek Animals:
Toward a Topology of Edible Bodies
Jean-Louis Durand

all' esatta violenza appartiene un' esatta stenografia
Adriano Spatola, *Il poema Stalin*

F OR the Greeks of the classical age, as for us today, the relationship to
animals is established through use of meat. But the meat of Greek
animals comes via the gods.[1] All edible flesh is treated first of all within
the rite,[2] a religiously determined context, and everything relating to meat
is of importance with respect to this context. From the outset, then, we
are faced with a problem of categories. Butchering, religion, cooking—
the Greeks combine these into what they called *thusia* and we call sacrifice.
This alignment of categories arises out of a different relationship to the
killing of animals and practices utterly different from our own approach,
which until recently was stamped with the theoretical imprint of Christianity. Any look we take at the practice of another is, by virtue of the fact
that we have a point of view, already a "key" to a reading. The perspective
that determines the observations presented in the following pages, and
doubtless the point of view of most readers as well, is the cultural context
of the West, which is informed by practices that are largely Christian. Here
the death of animals, which in other cultures has religious significance, is
radically excluded from the domain of the sacred. Only one sacrifice is
possible, that in which the god is the only victim worthy of himself. As a

This material was analyzed some time ago by my friend Guy Berthiaume in his work on the
status of the *mageiros* (Berthiaume, 122–40). Since considerable progress has been made in
the field studies on which the analysis are based as well as in procedures for pottery interpretation, a new overall view of the data in accord with solutions that have been brought to
light since earlier attempts seemed necessary. I am of course solely responsible for the conclusions offered in these pages. Furthermore, the problem of the economic implications of sacrificial practice, which received special attention in the work of G. Berthiaume, has not been
examined here. We have dealt only with the anthropological side of the questions raised by
the killing and carving of animal victims.

result, the killing of animals does not provide the ground for developing an elaborate network of meanings.

This theological arrogance makes it impossible to see the religious dimension in the death of animals in other cultures. Called sacrifice, this animal death, which is at once sublimated and rejected in the Holy Sacrifice (the one true sacrifice), is considered a lowly, vaguely repugnant practice; yet such a death is scarcely different from the unspeakable practices of our own slaughterhouses.[3] Thus, on matters concerning what we call animal sacrifice we have nothing to say, for our own customs disqualify us. Paradoxically, it is an abuse of language, a truly imperialist extension of our categories—even if they are scientifically produced—that brings us to subsume under this heading the religious forms of the death of animals in different cultures. Ultimately, in our system, sacrifice occupies no more than a blank space, though at that strategic point where, out of contempt and fascination, rejection of the other arises.

So are we truly barred from speaking of the Greek *thusia?* Certainly, unless we attempt to free ourselves from the logic of our own classificatory apparatus so that we may approach that of another. We thought a good technique was to observe living systems, where the frustrations of the historian have no place, systems in which the only vehicle is the spoken language.[4] A "contrastive" anthropology, in the linguist's sense of the term, was required at this point. And in order to drive out the ethnocentrism that is a major epistemological obstacle, it seemed all the more necessary to destroy the analyst's own system of categories, in a temporary effort to negate that system via the understanding of a third logic at work on site. By this circuitous strategy the old comparativism becomes a demand for a concrete understanding of coherent universes of different meanings. The result of this strategy, moreover, was a look at what, in Western cultural systems, displayed features comparable to those found in the religious killing of animals. Thus the death of a pig in rural societies underlies kinship systems and in its own language says something about the bodies of men themselves.[5] This movement back and forth from one logic to another has the potential for illuminating levels of meaning by the discovery of that which differentiates—and equalizes—human societies.

We have chosen to examine the logic of bodies—bodies of dead animals and those of the men around them—as this logic provides a focal point out of which a meaning can arise. We have attempted to grasp this logic as it is seen in its silence in the images on figured vases and by taking as our guide a very lovely Ionian hydria from Caere (figs. 1–4) on which all our classificatory categories blend.[6] Around the shoulder of the vase is a frieze depicting a series of actions and poses related to animals being prepared for consumption. This grouping is utterly exceptional; most often in iconography sacrificial sequences are frozen into distinct moments highlighted by the artist. It is extremely rare to see more than one sequence or perhaps two that echo each other on each side of the vase. This exception in the collection invites us to look at the whole iconic sequence with at least some hope of proposing Greek organizational categories and sacrificial frameworks beyond our categories of butchering and cooking.

All the figures are placed in the same pictorial space and set on the line that separates the images on the shoulder from those on the belly of the vase. The sequential nature of the frieze is indicated graphically by the continuous design of ivy and grapevines entwined above each scene; the trunks grow out of the ground at either end of the sequence, next to the black glazed section underneath the vertical handle. This motif occupies the space above the heads of the figures all the way to the beginning of the neck of the vase and creates a strong sense of temporal and spatial continuity among them.

In the same pictorial mode in this uniform space-time of the sacrifice we see a series of activities that cannot be classified under the headings of butchering, sacrifice, or cooking—headings that are all touched by the hidden theoretical opposition between sacred and profane, lay and religious, that the Western reading of the behavior of others only abandons with great effort. As an ideological category of Judeo-Christian thought on religious fact disguised as an object of scientific study, "sacrifice" is only a word, a lexical illusion. What exists is the *thusia*, and it is to be considered as such in terms of its own organization, territory, and boundaries. To avoid repeating "Greek alimentary blood sacrifice," henceforth we will use the term *thusia*.

Playing a full part in the imagery, plant motifs traditionally serve in the sequence as supports for different elements depicted in the sacrificial space, and it is with the very emergence of the ivy stems at the left of the series that the pictorial sequence begins. A wicker basket with handles hangs from a branch, and an amphora with a base is on the ground against the trunk (fig. 1). These two accessories are indispensable to the sacrificial practice and from the outset place the sequence under the heading of what can be eaten, a dual sign indicating wet and dry. And immediately the preparation of the animal body begins.

The Moment of Truth?

The first scene that we can isolate (fig. 1) represents the actions of two nude men handling a large swine directly beneath them, its back on the ground, legs in the air, and head to our left. The big carcass does not lie completely on the ground. A mass highlighted in white is indicated under the \animal's withers. The head, fallen backwards, does not touch the ground but hangs freely above the stone, displaying in full sight the location on the neck of the exact spot where the blade must enter to slit the animal's throat—that is, to cut at least the two carotid arteries if not the trachea. The tension exerted on the two forelegs by the figure on the right makes the laryngeal zone, which is perfectly exposed in this way, even more accessible. The figure on the left leans over the neck holding a long thin blade. There are no ritual signs near the body. No altar (*bōmos*) or blood vase (*sphageion*) is there as a reminder that the animal's blood flows for the gods.[7] Consequently this cannot be an image representing the pouring of the blood, the actual moment when the animal's throat is slit, *sphazein*. That has been accomplished, and yet close inspection of the vase leaves no room for doubt:[8] from the victim's head a network of fine lines branches out toward the ground; blood is flowing. This is not the blood of the fatal hemorrhage. Even when the precaution has been taken to stun the animal beforehand, a large body does not let life escape so peacefully; and here the carcass is shown with exactness as inert, manipulable, and completely given over to the hands of men. As a matter of fact, once bled, the victim still has some blood in its veins. A certain quantity of blood remains in the veins around the wound, held in the flesh and injured tissues. This will be freed according to a system of rules in which blood is not part of what may be consumed because it is reserved for the divine. Thus the figure on the left holding his blade, *makhaira*, in both hands has the task of incising the mortal wound and loosening the end of the respiratory apparatus from the neck. There is still enough blood for the painter to capture it in the network of signs that he has chosen. Thus, it is possible to eliminate the first temptation to analyze the whole as a chronological sequence of actions beginning with the death of the animal: death, initial treatment of the carcass (butchering), oblation (sacrifice), and cooking (eating). The first scene represents a step in the preparation of the carcass. The actual death is not present; the body is somewhere else than at this difficult and problematic exit from the world of the living about which the Greek images have nothing to say.[9] This absence is indeed a general one. Here between the last and first scenes of the sequence there is a gap, a blackout in the form of the dark glaze. There is nothing beneath the handle. Everything begins after the death. This discretion is something to be examined; nothing is ever revealed of the Greek version of the hemorrhage of the animal to be eaten. The reticence of the vases is never disturbed; without exception death and sacrifice are separated. The act that opens up the passage to the animal's death is never represented. The blade approaches, sometimes very near,[10] but the deed that actually drenches the blade and altar in blood is never pictured. Whenever the throat is shown hewn by the sword, the sacrificial meaning has departed from the image. The gaping throat, then, speaks of nothing more than the fact of the animal's death, a death that is mysterious and incomprehensible and refers only to itself.[11] Or else the officiant's gesture brings the blade toward the animal's throat, which has been exposed by lifting the muzzle by force, and we are no longer witness to a sacrifice by human hands. Nike, mistress of victories, kneels on the animal's back, and it is she who pulls back the head, doing violence to the animal[12]—something men could not permit themselves to examine this closely, with certain exceptions. Paradoxically, Greek figured vases show no repugnance at representing human blood spurting from a slit throat to water the gods' altar in a horrible sacrifice (fig. 8).[13] It is better to show human sacrifice in the realm of the imaginary, just as the cannibalism so close to it is best imagined in the faraway reaches of myth[14] or in the tales of another people. It is the blood of Polyxena that is seen splashing up, not that of pigs or sheep. The black glazed section under the handle of the Ricci vase both reveals and conceals the moment of truth: the blood of animals is outside the human realm. In the sacrifice, where men and gods are joined in their distance, the animal passes without transition from the state of live quadruped to that of a mass of meat to be shaped. From the procession, *pompē,* the moment that takes one to the sacrifice, *thusia,* the moment the blood gushes, belongs to the gods. Men seek no omen in it, no sign. The altar and the ground alone receive the liquid. A special instrument, a vase, the *sphageion,* makes it possible to catch the blood and then pour it properly on the altar, *bōmos.* It will flow over the surfaces made by men[15] to sink into the earth of the divine domain, *hieron,* that supports them. An irrefutable sign of the piety of men and the power of the gods, it perfectly establishes the relationship through distance that men maintain with the gods via animals. The blood is not offered, that is, temporarily presented to the divine powers, but truly abandoned, intended to tie the visible world to the other in the course of the oblation. The ritual time that ensues is that in which the animal, withdrawn from the coherence of the living, enters a different logic, that of human eating. In a completely adequate way, the moment of death as rupture belongs to the gods alone. It lies beyond human grasp, reserved ideally for the divine world. Sometimes mention is made of blood put at man's disposal,[16] but the essential lies elsewhere. The live animal moves from one system to another through death, which disorganizes it to make its reorganization possible.

The Viscera as Center

If the first scene of the Ricci vase indeed represents an initial step in the preparation of the flesh to be eaten, the whole group of scenes, from the first victim up to the altar, revolves around the same ritual problem: to extract the noble viscera, *splankhna,* from the thoracic and abdominal cavities of the carcass to be dressed. The second scene groups three officiants around an animal body (fig. 1). The absence of one of the carving implements, the meat table or *trapeza,* which along with the *makhaira* is quasi-obligatory, does not at all affect the technique being performed. The *trapeza* usually but not always eliminates the need for a third acolyte, but without it a third is required for a technique of carving along the horizontal. Here a large goat is held up by two assistants, its head hanging freely and spine parallel to the ground, which its beard touches. Standing to the left and right of the body the two men pull the fore and hind legs in opposite directions, creating a tension exceeding what is necessary to simply keep the back straight. The thoracic organs are raised and spread open, the abdominals positioned flat against the inside dorsal wall. A third man, his legs directly in front of the animal's hindquarters and the customary *makhaira* in his right hand, stands in front of the animal, bending over the powerful rib cage. With his left hand he grasps the hock of the animal's left foreleg. His position, carefully delineated by the painter, makes any cutting motion impossible. The officiant leans over this area between the forelegs and seems to be regulating the distance between the outspread forelegs. This is the part of the animal where the thoracic cavity, protected by the ribs, borders the soft abdominal mass, separated by the sternum. Here again, and as we will see, not necessarily in chronological order, everything is organized around the *splankhna* and their removal. The consumption of the *splankhna,* the central moment of the sacrifice as religious act, is in some ways a focal point toward which gestures and actions are directed; it organizes their relationship and sequence within the space and time of the rite. And in a way it is of little importance how these acts lead to the consumption of the meat or interconnect. It is necessary and sufficient that the moment the urgency of the central act dominates, everything is ready to make it possible. Between the first moment, the death, and the time of roasting and eating the holy grilled meat, the different concrete processes set in motion can be presented in different ways, from strict order to more or less simultaneous manipulations, marked by differing degrees of autonomy and in extreme cases interchangeable. Because of the considerations of the moment, of emphasizing one particular aspect instead of another, many variations are possible. Any desire to reduce them to uniformity is not only vain but useless, because it is irrelevant. Coherence does not lie in the uniformity of the acts or the unvarying nature of the sequences or even in establishing all the movements. A loose structure may reveal the true constraints operating in the pattern nonetheless.

Thus, once the carcass is ready, the logic of the carving operations can follow different courses. Here the logic of practice is a logic of different possibilities for action. Better, as the second scene of the Ricci vase shows (fig. 1), the body, man's first instrument,[17] conforms its techniques to the practice imposed by the pattern. Here the logic of practice[18] is an arrangement in which material constraints are few in number and infinitely less important than the way in which they are utilized. To eat an animal it is necessary to kill it. Sacrificial practice is concerned primarily with how this is done. The important thing about a practice is the meaning it produces; our task is to decipher it.

The first and second scenes of the Ricci vase are typical of this diversity of possible circuits leading to the same practical objective. The two carcasses discussed above display different graphic treatments of certain details, which it is possible to interpret. The marked presence of animals is not limited to the two bodies still in one piece. A half-carcass hangs by the forelegs among the leaves of an ivy branch. The head of the animal, a ram with curved horns, hangs above the assistant to the right of the carcass on the ground, exactly plumb with the branches. The ram's body is cut in half at the thorax crosswise at the lower ribs; and the first flesh of the inner abdominal wall points downward, exactly vertical, over the right foot of the assistant to the left of the carcass above the ground, who makes an effort, his legs apart, to hold it on the horizontal by pulling on each hind leg, as we have seen. Linking the two scenes organized around the still intact carcasses, the carcass of the ram placed toward the tip of the triangle clearly indicates the goal of the men's actions at the sacrifice—to cut up the bodies of the animals—and displays the interim result.

At this stage, to preserve the integrity of the skin, *derma,* saved especially for the sacrificer[19] or used as a permanent sign of the sacrifice in the temples, it has been necessary to skin the carcass before cutting it into at least two pieces. Three white highlights behind the shoulder convey the

brilliant gleaming of light on freshly skinned flesh. The same white highlights on the thorax of the pig on the ground strive for the identical effect.
As for the ram, the marks start at the shoulder blade and stop above the
flank, the slightly curved strokes perhaps suggesting the last ribs below the
sternum. Thus the pig would already have been skinned, and the white
mass of the abdomen would indicate the mass of digestive organs visible
after the incision in the thin wall of stomach muscle. However, indicated
in color, like the men's hair, the skin still adheres to the neck, and a series
of thin lines marks the dorsal mane of the hairy Greek pigs. Similar
strokes, longer and somewhat parallel, extend below the shoulder blade
and along the spinal column down to the abundant brush of the tail. Here
we will grant that the skin has still not been completely detached from the
body, thereby protecting the flesh from any contact with the ground.

After the operations on the carcass, a few cuts are all that is needed to
completely detach the skin from the body. This technique[20] makes it possible to skin the animal quickly and with relative ease, and once its protective function is accomplished, the skin can be set aside for later treatment,
cleaned on the fleshy and hairy sides, and eventually used. In this fashion,
on a red-figured amphora (fig. 8),[21] an acolyte wearing the traditional
loincloth[22] of those appointed to work with meat, pulls a large hide by its
long brush of a tail—doubtless from a bovine—that he drags on the
ground without other precautions.

If this reading is correct, the goat held above the ground on the Ricci
vase has not yet been skinned (fig. 1). Its neck, like the pig's, shows signs
of hair, while no highlights or brushstrokes indicate the gleaming of flesh.
The stance of the assistant holding the knife remains to be interpreted. We
will attempt this by offering a series of scenes with similar depictions. If
the bearer of the *makhaira* is indeed occupied with the *splankhna,* as we
believe we have been able to determine, he is working on an animal that,
except for its mortal wound, is intact. The tension that pulls the carcass in
both directions, clearly indicated by the length of the legs, results in raising the thorax and lowering the abdomen, separating the viscera from
both ends of the diaphragm. This procedure thus makes particularly accessible this median zone, the decisive place for sacrificial practice, where
the internal organs are found: the spleen, *splēn,* on the left; the liver, *hēpar,*
on the right, protected by the lower ribs in the cavity that the Greeks
specifically call *lagones* and associated more loosely in our own linguistic
habits with the whole of the flanks. The liver is joined to the cardiopulmonary system by the epiphrenic ligament and powerful blood vessels that

crisscross the fine muscle sheet of the diaphragm. Once the skin has been opened at the right place, a simple incision is all that is needed to discon-nect the two organs from the diaphragm without damaging the stomach matter, massive in large and small ruminants and in pigs.[23] The spleen adheres to the stomach, from which it must be detached; the liver can also be removed at this stage, particularly if, as with cattle, it is of large size. Then it is possible to split the sternum from bottom to top starting at the diaphragm, or from top to bottom starting from the neck wound, thereby making the trachea accessible. The figure to the left of the pig in the first scene (fig. 1), working between the abdomen and the mortal wound at the neck, can proceed in either way, once the incision is made in the man-ner we have suggested. The cutting instrument, wielded with both hands, permits the assistant to break the somewhat resistant bone of the sternum, *khelus*. At this point grasping the trachea and bringing out the entire mass of innards (*splankhna*) have become a relatively easy matter. If the liver has not been removed beforehand, a simple incision separates it from the dia-phragm, and in one single pull (for smaller animals at least), the group of the upper *splankhna*—heart, lungs, and liver—is obtained.

It is this moment of the carving that we propose is shown on a small fragment of an Attic pyxis preserved in Bonn (fig. 5).[24] Around the *tra-peza* bearing a goat, its head hanging in the very position of that of the Ricci vase, three acolytes are busy. The extremely small size of this ceramic shard does not make it easy to decipher. However, enlarging the image makes it possible to recognize it without any doubt as a carving scene forming part of a more extended sacrificial sequence with a running figure identifiable next to the break on the right. The *trapeza* and the victim are in front of the bearer of the *makhaira*. The assistant on the right holds the forelegs outstretched by leaning backwards. Unfortunately, the break pre-vents us from understanding the pose of the assistant on the left, who is almost certainly involved with the hind legs, which given the slight curve in the victim's abdomen must be held in the same way, undoubtedly half-bent. We can only see the man's flexed knee. By rare good fortune the part of the image that has been preserved is the richest in information. The officiant's *makhaira* is pointed downward, the thick handle projecting out beyond the right fist that encircles it, thumb up. The knife is sunk halfway down the blade into the thorax, spreading apart the ribs below the shoul-der blade. With his other hand, which appears behind the visible part of the handle, the figure holds a thick forked stick that is lodged between the two forefeet. Using his *makhaira* to spread apart the double row of ribs that the assistant steadies by pulling on the forelegs, he removes through the trachea the group of upper *splankhna*, which we see emerging with the two pulmonary lobes.

To reach the kidneys, *nephros*, the last viscera of the splanchnic series, it is necessary to remove the mass of digestive organs that form a distinct group from the stomach to the intestines surrounded by several folds of membrane. The esophagus, made accessible when the cardiopulmonary organs are withdrawn, will be cut at one end and the rectal muscle removed at the other. This is what the two figures are doing to the left and right of a *trapeza* where the carcass of a ram is being prepared (fig. 9).[25] The animal has been skinned, except at the neck where the rest of its fleece is rendered with white highlights, and displays marks indicating the lower ribs on its right flank. The bearer of the *makhaira* on the left, on the side of the head hanging over the edge of the table in the position we have already noted, moves his left hand around inside the animal's body. At the height of the shoulder blade he grasps the broken ribs, which he holds up, while the visible end of the left foot hangs freely much lower down on the other side. He prepares to make a cut between leg and abdomen, to perform an operation that to date has not been noted anywhere else in similar images. The assistant on the left, clamping the hooves under his right arm, holds the two hind legs together in his right hand. The result of the whole process is that the intestinal organs bulge out, thereby rendering them accessible to the blade of the assistant on the left. The thorax is empty. The figures busy themselves with the abdomen, visibly convex because of the way they hold the carcass, as the drawing shows with care. At the juncture between stomach and intestine, the bearer of the *makhaira* can easily slice the abdominal musculature that has been stretched thin, revealing the intestinal mass that is already shown in the pig on the first sequence of the Ricci vase and indicated, we will recall, with white highlights.

Once the carcass is completely emptied, the kidneys remain joined to the inside wall of the back, *nōtos*, and covered with fat; it is now very easy to remove them. This is what a bearded and crowned figure is doing to the right of a *trapeza* bearing a sheep, its head hanging to the same side (fig. 10).[26] Plunging his right arm up to the elbow in the animal's open breast,[27] he works, bent forward in the attitude of pulling something toward him, his back foot raised, free hand open, fingers tensed. The unseen part of his arm, introduced into the body via the opened sternum, reaches exactly to the kidney, which is extracted with bare hands without the *makhaira*. The young acolyte on the left resists the strong pull by holding the victim's hind legs by the hooves and extending them to their fullest, his arms outstretched and leaning all his weight to the left. The details of the animal's body, finely noted, show that here again the animal has not been completely skinned. The sheepskin covers half the body, from mid-thigh to the head. We can easily see the left leg in the skinned area and the skin folded over the fleece, at the level of the shoulder blade. The fleece itself is suggested by fine lines, which do not appear on the skinned side. This last detail perfectly reveals the urgency involved in maneuvering the entire splanchnic group and how the preparation of the carcass is subordinated to it. Hercules' haste is so great that we can see him alone, cutting up an animal on the ground. There is no *trapeza* where the later sharing of the meat takes place[28]—a detail we know does not concern him. Dressed in his lionskin, he leans over an enormous sheep still completely covered with its fleece; the same tracery marks the skin of the one and the fleece of the other. On the left Hercules holds between his legs the two hind legs of the sheep; its head and neck rest against a female figure on the right. This is probably Athena; her exact pose is hidden because of damage to the painting. A second gap prevents us from seeing the carver's arms. He holds his *makhaira,* apparently in both hands, and pierces with its point the intestinal mass indicated by the white highlighting. Clearly, the harvest of the *splankhna* is already at the abdominal stage, and the drawings show with exactness that the skinning has not even started. Here the haste might no longer be that of the rite but of pure gluttony.

The activity of the men around the *trapeza* represented in the image moves—in the spatial meaning of the term—via the splanchnic center. Whether a matter of making it accessible, operating on it, or extending the visceral harvest to the rest of the body, it is always this zone between belly and neck that holds the painter's attention. For as long as the carcass remains whole in the image, the organization of the series of movements always develops through that space, just as, on the level of the ritual, the series of operations is organized around the consumption of the viscera, which is its first focal point.

This is the splanchnic center, focus of the image and the ritual. The focus of desire and anguish, too, as we can see in the extraordinary text of Euripides' *Electra,* where the full interplay of the ambiguities of life and death, men and beasts, culminates in the death—the sacrificial death—of Aegisthus.[29] The urgency to recover the *splankhna* operates on two levels—and becomes twice as pressing. When provoked by Aegisthus, Orestes and Pylades, passing for Thessalians, make it a point of honor to dress the victim, a large ox that Clytemnestra's husband has just slaughtered, all by themselves. They begin, then, by skinning the animal. "Orestes took in his hands the Dorian knife with the well-honed blade, threw his elegant traveling cloak off his shoulders, and his extended arm unclothed the shining flesh" (819–24).

Then the sacred parts, *hiera*, are drawn out of the cavity, *lagones*. These parts are immediately recognized as *splankhna* and then more precisely as the lobes of the liver, which are subjected to mantic scrutiny. Aegisthus' uneasiness is fed by the contemplation of the horrible aspect of the zones in which meaning can be read: "The liver lacks one lobe; the opening vein and the blood vessels next to the gall bladder display to his eyes troubling protrusions" (826–29).

Thus, of the splanchnic viscera the liver is seen as the preeminent organ, the one in which meaning is inscribed and that is held up as the first thing to be read, so great is the uneasiness that resides within the sacrificer. This central place in the animal is the one in which the mysterious link between the animal as bearer of meaning, the gods who give it to be seen, and the men for whom it is intended, is given material form in the secrets of the now open belly. For someone worried about the future, the anguish pivots on this moment:[30] the gods' initial acceptance or rejection of the whole sacrificial oblation is revealed in the aspect of the sacrificial liver. In turn, this refusal or acceptance is laden with meaning and can be interpreted.

Making fools of the obliging hosts, Orestes, as a Thessalian invited to the sacrifice, receives the confidences of Aegisthus regarding the enemy of his house, the son of Agamemnon, Orestes himself. To banish the king's somber premonitions, Orestes the Foreigner offers as a remedy the prospect of the pleasure of sacred skewers of meat: "Now then, so we may feast on the innards, instead of the Dorian blade bring me a Phthian blade (cutter), and I will open the thorax" (835–37).

To distract Aegisthus, Orestes speaks in terms of a culinary feast, the powerful pleasure of eating. The delight taken in the grilled meats—to feast, *thoinasthai*—is the alternative Orestes proposes to the anguished manipulation of the raw viscera, the other side of the splanchnic moment.[31]

It will be noted that the vases always present hieroscopy, the manipulation and contemplation of the viscera, in a context characterized by uncertainty about the future (fig. 14). The scenes always depict a young hoplite ready to depart being presented with the dark mass of the liver, which he scrutinizes by lifting the lobe or the vesicle with his free hand. This tense hieroscopic scene is counterbalanced, on the vases as in the text of Euripides, by the agreeable side of handling the *splankhna*: the roasting, with the theme, so frequent in the imagery, of the burning altar at which the acolyte grillmaster, the *splankhnoptēs,* cooks the bundle of viscera on the points of long skewers.[32] Three such figures can be seen on the Ricci vase in the fourth scene, after a third scene (fig. 2) in which the priest, the *hiereus,* followed by a flutist, *aulētēs,* and a third vase-bearer, prays with upraised hand before making the libation. On long skewers, *oboloi,* they hold the men's first portion over the flames rising on the very altar where the gods' share has burned.[33] The black color indicates that these are *splankhna;* the other flesh shown later will be touched with white high- lights indicating the mixture of fat and lean. The agreement is obvious between the scenes depicted in the image and the Aristotelian theory that the viscera are condensed blood, different in nature from the flesh of other meats.[34]

The painters know their sacrifice as well as the scholar. Their images are of an anatomical precision that on the whole is rather advanced. Since sacrifice lay at the heart of daily experience, it is not surprising to find the knowledge that it presupposes translated into artistic representations. It is yet more interesting to see theorizing about this knowledge in the erudi- tion of the anatomist and still more so to bring it out into the open as the model for the Aristotelian logic of the body. A practitioner of dissection, Aristotle[35] is also an observer of sacrificial techniques, and the notes ob- tained in hieroscopy[36] are precious to him because they are based on healthy animals slaughtered shortly before they were observed. Further- more, his anatomical descriptions proceed along the path traced by the *makhaira* of the carver of the animals, the *mageiros.* An apparently awk- ward transition is revealing: "After having dealt with the neck, the esoph- agus, and the tracheal artery, then we must speak of the viscera."[37] The order is the very same as is followed in the dressing of the carcass on the *trapeza.* The *splankhna* will be studied one at a time, in the order of their removal: heart, lungs, liver, spleen, and at the end, at the bottom of the list just as it is at the end of the harvest, the kidneys. Here, just as it is under the blade of the *mageiros,* the diaphragm serves to separate the vis- cera into two groups: the cardiopulmonary group, and the liver, spleen, and kidneys (which are indeed far from the diaphragm). This is enough to lead our distinguished anatomist-sacrificer to discuss the diaphragm *after* dealing with the viscera. Afterwards he discusses this muscle from above and from below, in a way that only makes sense if the man or animal is stretched out on the *trapeza* and seen by the carver. This symmetrical model starting with the diaphragm compares what is above it to the noble and what is below to that which is less so[39] and further organizes a similar division from left to right that follows the route of the knife hunting for the viscera.

Aristotle explains that despite appearances the viscera are all double: the kidneys obviously so, the heart in its internal structure, the lungs visibly doubled.[40] Despite legitimate hesitations, he states that the central position, which is filled by the inner organs of the cavity, is itself divided in two.[41] Liver and spleen, viscera of the same sacrificial level, are of the same nature. The spleen is a bastard liver, *nothos,* owing to the left-right symmetry and required by it.[42] Visceral symmetry guides the sacrificial palpation in this strategic zone for splanchnic operations. On a more general level the viscera are that by which the blood vessels are attached to the body, as if anchors;[43] the spleen and liver are like nails whose nature is to attach the great vein. This is meant literally: "Thus, by means of the viscera, the cohesion of the animals is made possible." Aristotle is following the dressing of the carcass on the *trapeza* step by step. Once the body is emptied of what ensures its vital cohesion, the *splankhna,* it breaks down and is disorganized, but by human hands. Definitively located beyond the cohesion of the living, the body enters the networks of distribution as pieces of meat. The anatomy of animals is the space onto which an order of human needs is secretly projected: a typology.

The Dismantled Body

The digestive system must be removed from the body to be carved into meat, *sarx.* Aristotle does not know quite what to make of the other internal parts, the entrails, since for him the internal parts are the *splankhna* in the strict sense of the term. Before discussing the stomach and intestines, also internal parts, he compares the relationship between meat and *splankhna* to that between the outer to the inner. The sacrificial model does not shed much light on the position of the digestive system, the entrails, *entera,* in the system of body parts.[45] The anatomist is silent regarding their status. After stating the opposition between *sarx* and *splankhna,* he goes on to the digestive tract, starting once again at the diaphragm. For him it is an internal part but belonging with meat, and the description follows the pattern of the sacrificial distribution, which is also caught in a contradiction: the *entera* are not cooked on the spit.

Laid out on the *trapeza* the cleaned carcass is reduced to what, according to Aristotle's phrase, serves to "protect the viscera."[46] Exactly as in Aristotle, the first carving separates the upper body from the lower at the level of the lower ribs, as we can see from the half-ram on the Ricci vase (fig. 1). To the right of the half-ram and similarly hanging from an ivy branch is a black form ending in the shape of a hoof acting as a hook; it is the animal's thigh. The painter has carefully shown a hollow in the fleshy part, leaving the place for the femur; as we know, the bones set aside to be burned in offering to the gods must be carefully removed. This explains the pieces of meat, limp—they have been boned—and ending in a hoof, that painters depict being transported by an acolyte or held still by a figure grasping the part containing what remains of the bone. Here the carving proceeds along the skeletal joints. An ancient gloss explains that the term for carver, *artamos,* is used accurately to refer to "the *mageiros,* the one who cuts along the joints, *ho kat' arthra temnōn.*"[47] And in the *Phaedrus* Socrates finds no better comment on the dialectic method:[48] "It is . . . to be able to separate the details according to the natural joints, *diatemnein kat' arthra;* it is to strive not to break any part and avoid the ways of a poor carver, *kakou mageirou.*"

The carving of the dead body of an animal is a curious way to evoke the organic nature of the second part of the dialectician's operation, division. Yet the body that is dismembered according to the strict rules of carving reveals the former cohesion of life in a primary state. The splanchnic order enables the anatomist to arrange his description just as the first carving, by its movement back and forth from life to death, informs the philosopher's images. The secret heart of sacrifice beats deep within the Greek imagination. The body must be dismantled, but according to recognized steps that will gradually transform it into the state of edible food. Thus the carving instrument, the *makhaira,* is used in the first moment as a knife for boning and dressing, not as a breaking instrument of the cleaver type.[49] This difference is particularly important for the joint at the hindquarter, because it is difficult for the carver to separate the flesh from the thigh and reach the epiphysis without causing the havoc condemned by Socrates. However, an image from a vase shows with all the precision of sacrificial know-how (fig. 9)[50] a powerful thigh, painted black, on a *trapeza,* with two spots on the orange background indicating the double head of the femur and a slight curve that outlines the flesh detached at the fold under the groin. The joint of the foreleg does not, strictly speaking, pose a problem. There is no boney socket connecting the shoulder blade to the thoracic cavity; it can be cut without difficulty. A *mageiros* holds a foreleg over the *trapeza,* the *makhaira* hanging from his right hand (fig. 23).[51] At this point, the carcass from head to tail is reduced to what is held by the vertebral column: ribs, the fleshy part of the back, the area of the hindquarters. The head is cut separately. We see a goat's head on the ground in a carving scene (fig. 11),[52] level with the foot of the *mageiros* standing to the left of the *trapeza,* while two soft fleshy thighs, femurs removed, hang in the background. We know nothing or next to nothing about the fate of the thoracic cage. The back, *nōtos,* on the other hand, is mentioned in the cultic statutes. If we follow the Socratic formulation of the joints and Aristotelian anatomy,[53] the back begins where the ribs end. At the lower end it holds the kidneys and in the Greek view makes fat to compensate for the lack of protective flesh, since this entire zone, *osphus,* is a point of flexion and has very little to cushion it. *Osphus*[54] refers to both the lumbar region and the flesh-covered bones of the haunches and is a part of the carcass set aside for the gods, as Prometheus reminds us in Aeschylus' tragedy where the Titan next to the thighbones has the long spine, *makra osphus,* displayed on the altar.[55] When these bones are cremated, omens are read whose interpretation, he says, he has permitted. On the Ricci vase (fig. 2) the curved form of the *osphus* sticks out above the flames. On the crater with the goat's head on the ground (fig. 7), it appears on the altar, where it curves in and out of the fire several times. This portion of the spine is a series of vertebrae of rather extensive length, perhaps the very vertebrae connected by the bone of the haunch between the tail and the back, *nōtos.*

This carving along the joints is not what produces the small pieces of meat that, on the Ricci vase (fig. 2), an acolyte spears into a large caldron set on a tripod, *lebēs,* where they are put to boil. After they are cooked, using his meathook, *kreagra,*[56] he puts them on the meat platter, *kreidokos skaphis,*[57] which he holds with his left hand. Other steps have been necessary to reach the final stage of the cooking. The Greek language lumps them together under the general term, *koptein,* to cut. On the *trapeza* with the giant thigh (fig. 12) we see three large slices carved from the thick flesh after the femur had been removed. The carving stops at the next joint, resulting in the piece hanging in the branches above the scene, the shin. These slices are carved in turn, as can be seen on the lid of a Boeotian dish (fig. 22), where these practices are represented in detail. Three scenes, one set between two columns, are placed in a circle around the cover. At the left of one of the columns, two *mageiroi* hold in their hands a slice of some kind that the figure on the right, seated on a stool, prepares to carve with the *makhaira* he brandishes in his right hand. Between them a short-legged *trapeza* supports five slices of the same type, which appear to be awaiting identical treatment. In the foreground of the next scene to the right is an enormous black glazed mass. Curved lines at approximately equal intervals suggest similar slices. The figure to the right takes one of them in both hands and holds it out above this undifferentiated piece to another figure, who moves forward as if ready to take it.[59] The meat sketched in this way represents the pieces, *krea,* together indistinctly, indicating neither the direction of the fibers nor the relative tenderness of the flesh. In the realm of cooking techniques, the opposition between roasted and boiled[60] in sacrificial cookery strikes an "objective" limitation—at least for people who, like the Greeks, prize tender meat.[61] Tough, freshly-killed meat that has been cut up in such a manner is barely edible if it is not boiled. For the Greeks boiling is the most complete form of cooking. Fresh viscera can be put directly on the flames to roast without a problem. Yet as a social model this way of carving presupposes an isonomic conception in which the equality of each one before the common meat is the very sign of belonging to the egalitarian city.[62] Even Plutarch[63] tells us that the essentially democratic procedure of a lottery was used to ensure the equal distribution of pieces.

On the Boeotian lid (fig. 22), in the background behind the mass of meat cut into regular pieces stands a skewer, *obelos,* loaded up to its point with meat. In the following scene, to the right of the second column, it is again found in the background full of sliced pieces and also on the ground, leaning to the right on a support made of crosspieces. On the right a *mageiros* with his *makhaira* carves a big piece that an acolyte to the left of the *obelos* holds out with both hands. Between the column and the upright skewer is a third figure who runs holding an *obelos* with meat covering a third of its length; this skewer will doubtless be completely filled with the pieces cut by the two others. This process is depicted on the Ricci vase (figs. 3–4). After a scene of ritual ablutions indicating the end of one sequence of the ceremony, two *mageiroi* at the *trapeza,* one on the right and one on the left, skewer small pieces of meat identical to the ones that have been boiled. Each one holds the *obelos* upright in his right hand and with his left loads the remaining pieces from the *trapeza.* The pieces, here smaller than on the Boeotian lid, are slid onto the skewer one by one. The pieces in the scenes on the lid seem to have been wrapped around the metal skewer. In these images the spit is no longer a cooking utensil but serves as a way of setting meat aside for later use, as is sometimes expected.[65] The *obelos* held in reserve appears on the cup (fig. 23) where the *mageiros* on the left holds a shoulder. The one on his right holds out a hand, though not to take the joint. (The red paint has disappeared, leaving traces on the black glaze.) And on the table pieces of meat are distinctly seen,[66] along with the piece held by the bearer of the *obelos.* In the inner medallion of the cup a bearded figure plunges the same pieces, quite visible again, into the large kettle on a tripod, *lebēs.* Whether to be eaten on the spot or carried on the *obelos,* the meat is cut in the same way, into equal pieces.[67]

At this point the animal's body is completely taken apart, as if it has exploded in such a way as to coincide with the very limits of the society of men in the city organized around it. The trajectory assigned to the animal's body, beginning with the splanchnic center, slice after slice, reaches out to the whole social body. The ultimate raison d'être of the edible body is to be blended with the civic space, conforming ultimately to an exact geometry.

In Conclusion: The Route of Human Honor

Between the first center and the equal civic portions, according to good egalitarian logic, room is made for the exception required for honor. The methods of honorific distribution are many; the gratified, numerous. In any sacrificial practice there is at least one exception to the regular provision of the animal body to the group of those who recognize one another as members of the same collectivity, as if the tie of once organically joined flesh periodically assures the cohesiveness of the social body. This essential act in Greek life is a moment when the world is set in place under the eyes of the gods. The relationship to the supernatural must be legitimated; a guarantee must be had of the regularity of the procedures that transform the live body into a body that is eaten by others. This is the function of the priest, *hiereus.* The presence of this person is required for the religious death of animals to be valid within the framework of the city. His supervision at the least puts the totality of men's action directly under the eyes of the gods; he knows their demands. It even happens that he receives what has been placed at the gods' disposal on the *trapeza.* If he is not a substitute for the gods, he extends their presence to men in some way. Shares of meat are placed on the table in oblation to the gods; later the priest disposes of them. Along with the inedible shares that have been completely consumed by the flames, the gods thus receive the shares eaten by the ministers of the cult. The priest has a special relationship to the divine. Like the god who receives the total oblation of the animal with its death, the priest receives the part that made for its wholeness in the beginning, the vital wrapping: the hide, the only evidence of what once was, left at the end of the rite. The status of the *hiereus* is indicated by samples taken from the center out of the men's share, even before the question of finding a place in the animal's body that honors men arises. The priest can receive a share of the *splankhna* as prescribed by the cult statutes without further discussion. Of those organs shown by Aristotle to have a double nature, he alone can receive half of the last one to be harvested: one kidney. A share is thus reserved for the priest from the splanchnic center, which gives him a privileged position without depriving anyone else, because it is unique. He will be the only one to have a *nephros* taken from the collective skewers, a choice morsel that allows him to take part in the center as the sole beneficiary. The meat privilege, *geras,* likewise means being the only one to obtain something without taking anything away from the others. Various parts are then removed from the animal body in anonymous portions; the details of the procedure are difficult to follow, moreover. The essential point with respect to the meat, *krea,* could well be that the priest is offered a part of the body before its transformation into flesh—a part offered as a place and thus relating to its organic function in the sacrificial body. What seems at issue here is the same relationship with the divine as that born of proximity via the substitution of the offerings at the table, the *trapezōmata.*[68] The place on the body reserved for the priest is that which harbored one of the divine portions at the time of the first carving, after the center had been opened up. The most frequent share, which includes the hoof, *skelos,* and thigh, *kōlē,* is the one from which the divine femur has been drawn.[69] Similarly, the *osphus,* the flesh-covered haunch was, in the architecture of the body, considered a continuation of the *osphus,* the backbone burned on the altar. Here the relation to the divine is one of contiguity. The place of honor is that which utters its name in the very first stroke of the carver's knife, a name that places it at the juncture with the separate domain of the supernatural. In the topology of the body the priest is located at the logical place, at the very point of contact between men and gods.

A share, a very small one, is often given to the *hiereus.* It is also given to Hermes in some sacrifices dedicated to him. It is the tongue,[70] given to Hermes, the god of passages, hinterlands, and ambiguous places.[71] Metaphorically the tongue is the locus of communication. Hermes' metaphoric share is given to the priest, who establishes the relation to the divine and brings about the passage from one to the other. Even when it is not offered, the tongue is always cut separately or at least momentarily set aside.[72] Thus before the animal's flesh is transformed into anonymous pieces of meat, the shares of honor utter their names, repeated on the stones bearing the statutory inscriptions. In the context of the anonymity of the dismantled body, privilege consists in obtaining a place that, by its position in the carving, bespeaks the honor of approaching the gods. The places of the body are logical to the very end.

4

5

6

7

8

9

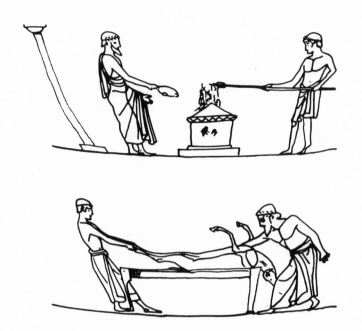

10

11

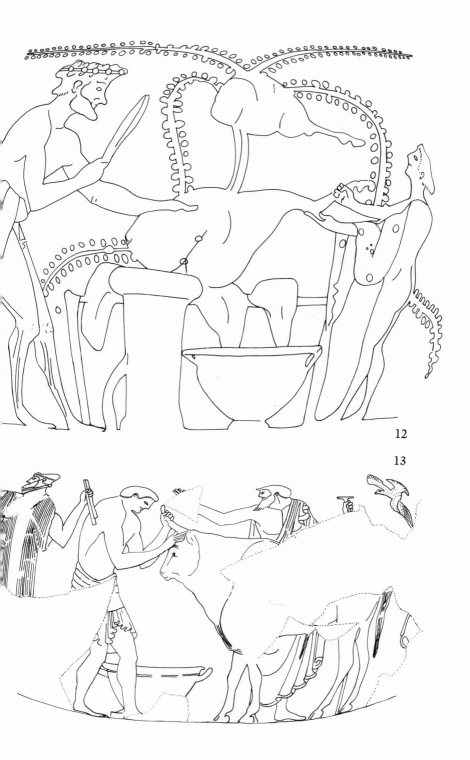

12

13

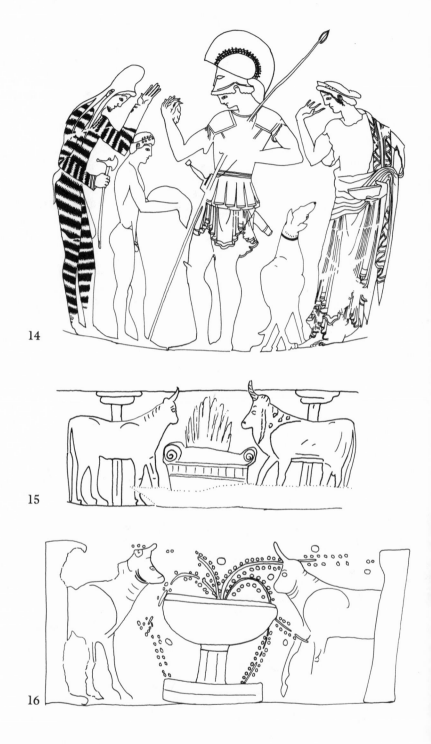

14

15

16

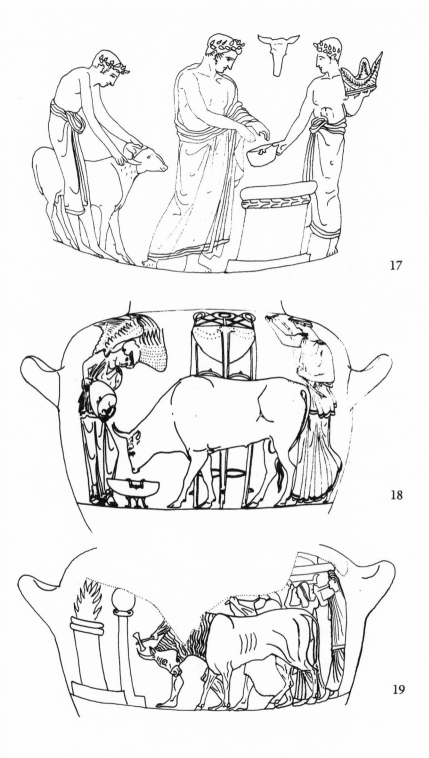

17

18

19

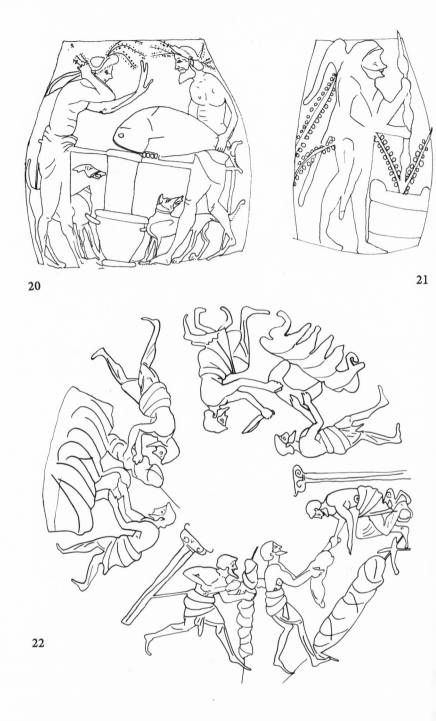

20

21

22

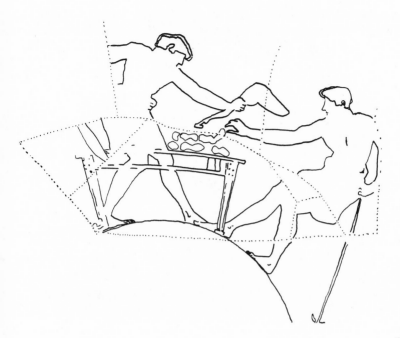

23

I wish to thank the curators of the museums and collections who provided the photographs used by F. Lassarrague to create the sketches illustrating these articles. The original photographs can be found in the photography collection at the Center for Comparative Research on Ancient Societies.

Jean-Louis Durand

Ritual As Instrumentality

Jean-Louis Durand

INSTRUMENTAL, adj. Didact. That which serves as an instrument. The instrumental cause.

Instrumental case: said, in grammatical terms, of a case that, in some languages, serves to express the instrument, the means.

In music, meaning that which is executed, or is to be executed by instruments.

Translated from *Dictionnaire de l'Académie française,*
8th ed. (1935), vol. 2.

To celebrate a rite is to do something. There is nothing more difficult than imagining how something is done without going to see it. The spatial distribution of actors and actions, the layout of the space itself, the unfolding and organization of the series of movements, the atmosphere and geography of the rite—all are critical. In ancient Greece ritualist discourse dealing with sacrifice is rather scarce; it is in ceramic painting that the Greeks present themselves as sacrificers.[1]

But for those who avoid the traps of ethnocentrism[2] and the naive logic of illustration, an image cannot provide a clear reflection of daily life, and so we have used the least restrictive criteria to select the scenes to be discussed. We have retained without any other consideration all representations in which men and animals, either present or suggested by allusion, are gathered in situations where, for example, the death of the latter or the feeding of the former is involved, or both. Thus we obtain a series of images that in essence are articulated around the ritual itself, with relatively few iconic versions of sacrificial myths. An examination of these relationships between rite and image will serve here in lieu of prolegomena.[3]

An earlier version of this study was presented in Italian in the journal *Dialoghi di archeologia* in 1979.

Rite, Space, and Image

Let us start with the idea that an image is a place, a space where signs occur.[4] Positioned according to spatial criteria—left/right, high/low, in front of/behind—signs and elements represented in the image combine with one another. Out of this combination or combinations a meaning is produced. Everything in the image, then, is capable of bearing meaning. The relationships between the representation and what underlies it are not to be excluded from this "economy of meaning," nor are relationships among neighboring images.[5] Furthermore, for the person looking at it, the image generates a discourse, interpretation, about itself that gives rise to polysemy. This extreme complexity is compounded in the case of the Greek images by the fact that they are forever silent. None of our terminology is fit to deal with them; we have no right to such language, lacking as we do the necessary cultural competence.[6] Even the simple anthropological status of the Greek image is not clear. As a consequence we are locked into a silent space lighted by the beacons of the Greek imagemakers, condemned merely to see.

The greater the constraints, the more numerous the levels of definition, the more it is possible to believe that rules can be uncovered. The representations in which the rite is depicted are of this sort. A rite is first of all a matter of movement, and as such it is first influenced by the culture around it, in which it takes place. But the acts of others are ambiguous to us; the rules that govern the poses, inaccessible. The meaning they take on can only be revealed within a clear contextual position. This first, purely anthropological level enables us to assess only the specific form of the stances depicted, not even the economy of their selection.

The ritual itself, like the image, is a silent space, where regularly organized behaviors develop in groups of sequences that are more strict than those governing ordinary movements in which the programs for action are much more open. It is exactly this type of programmatic constraint that enables us to distinguish a rite from what is not a rite. It is impossible to understand the rite if we do not know the names of the actions and the sequences: language is the first interpreter of the real.[7] The path is there to be explored. But the rite maintains relations of a secondary degree with language. Itself a language, rite produces meaning—a meaning that, here again, is dependent upon space. During the unfolding of the ritual process, men are brought into contact with animate and inanimate beings that in some way are already meaningful in themselves. In the relations established by human actions such as postures, movements, or manipulations of animal bodies (here speech is an active type of occurrence or action), the program of action becomes a ritual process; a meaning emerges. Understanding it presupposes considering the status of each of the elements of Greek culture involved in the rite, the system of representation in its totality.[8]

The idea accepted for a long time that ritual, like myth, operates analogously to linguistic events is not completely tenable.[9] There is the problem of time in the ritual; however, there is first of all the matter of space. A mythical account develops in a narrative time in which the before and after are limitations of a linguistic type.[10] In the case of rite, things are different. We have seen that the order in which the actions take place is not always restrictive.[11] The scenes concerning the viscera, *splankhna*, show that temporality is of another order, focal this time. Time from the overall sequence can be reserved for those who are late and be enough to validate the whole ritual act.[12] On the other hand, there are certain focal points that absolutely must be recognized, on pain of disaster. In the sacrifice one cannot reverse with impunity the successive order of the roasted and the boiled; too much is invested there.[13] There is, in short, a culinary temporality. The order in which the diverse elements of a dish are prepared is of little consequence. The important thing is to put it all on to cook in the proper sequence. For example, garlic and onions must not be confused, or carrots and potatoes. Note the temporality of music, if one prefers, of jazz in particular, in which everyone improvises in his own fashion. Within the framework of a given rhythmical program, each interpreter leads with his solo up to a moment of collective creation when all play the chorus together. The Greeks were sensitive to such musical values of the ritual tempo. In Euripides' *Cyclops* Odysseus tells of the final moments of his companions before being devoured by the ogre in a man-eating sacrifice, contradictory in its terms and monstrous:

> When everything was ready, the cursed of the gods, the infernal *mageiros*, grabbed two of my companions at once and slaughtered them not without *rhuthmōi tini*,[14] slaying one on the bronze belly of the caldron, while seizing the other one by the heel, he dashed out his brains on the sharp point of a piece of rock. (396–402)

Polyphemus himself is a good sacrificial interpreter.

In ritual we know that above all it is a matter of instruments.[15] By means of instruments human things come under the eyes of the gods; the whole totality is constructed with them—hence the hypothesis that it is with these objects that the reading of the image can effectively begin. Thus at one time we looked at the arrangement of the images in terms of objects. But the iconic is not the ritual. Men and objects are positioned in the space of the rite *and* in the space of the image, the image being taken from the rite. How do the objects of the rite organize the space of the image, and what is the relationship between the space of the rite and the space of the image? These are the most fruitful questions concerning the scenes of sacrifice depicted on the vases. We have chosen finally to present some sacrificial instruments of the *thusia* type and to examine the space that develops around them.

The Tree Laden with Meat

Two persons (fig. 12) to the left and the right of a table, *trapeza*,[16] the one on the right wearing the crown of the sacrifice, prepare to cut into an enormous thigh. What we take here to be ritual space[17] is arranged around two elements that articulate men's activity on the divine temple ground, *hieron*. The first, placed there by human hands, is the altar, *bōmos*, a dark vertical mass in the foreground. The other, well-rooted, is an immense tree whose branches emerge from the trunk behind and to the left of the altar to spread out over the whole vase and thus give the entire background a certain materiality. The totality of the scene is captured in depth between these two fixed elements, for which the relation to space begins with their relation to the earth.

In this framework are two portable instruments, each of which has a different relationship with the whole arrangement determined by the position they hold. On the exact same plane as the altar is a receptacle of considerable size, a silhouette of a columned crater on the same ground.[18] On a third plane, midway between the *bōmos* and the plant, the long table, *trapeza*, is silhouetted with one leg visible at each end. As they are combined in the whole, the tree sets the stage for the ritual action by situating it in the space in the fresh air of the temple, *hieron*, where the rite takes place. The tree is directly involved in the men's action; it is used to support a quarter of the meat, a shin from which the muscular mass of the thigh has already been removed, as the bone must be extracted and burned in the honor of the gods. Three slices of the carved thigh hang from the table, while the two cutters, *mageiroi*, ready themselves to remove the femur from the piece that is still whole.[19] This enormous thigh is set behind the *bōmos* on the *trapeza;* and the person on the left, between the table and the altar, wields the carving instrument, *makhaira*, ready to make a cut into the mass of the powerful leg. With his left hand he helps steady the entire mass, the other end of which is held between hoof and heel by the beardless and crownless person on the right. In the overall arrangement, the branches of the tree indeed function on the same level as the other instruments. Henceforth, in scenes of sacrifice we can accept the idea that the tree is meaningful because of its instrumental character. Barring inconsistencies accepted in Greek culture, any tree will always have the potential for being a meat-tree.[20] As a result we can combine it with other instrumental elements and assess the homological relations that, because of its rootedness in the earth, it can maintain with other elements of the same type serving to organize the image.

Death-dealing Waters

Facing each other on either side of a flaming altar (fig. 15), two bovines stand in front of two columns.[21] If the fire on the altar replaces the tree of the background (cf. fig. 16), the *hieron* is present in the image by a redundant architectural sign, built like the *bōmos* and with the verticality of the tree—the colonnade in the background. In the image attributed to the same artisan (fig. 16) the space is constructed in a similar fashion around a basin for lustral water, *loutērion*.[22] Going from the *bōmos* to the *loutērion* makes it possible to reestablish the presence of the tree in the background. The permutation of the sign reintroduces the pair—the iconic syntagma—of the tree behind an architectural element of the *hieron*. The reappearance of the tree guarantees the homologous position of the *loutērion* and the *bōmos*. The animals are not there to drink but to be put to death, and the tree laden with meat is there as the mark of their fate in the sacrificial proceedings. *Loutērion*, the water phase, is the first phase of the sacrifice; the tree, the last phase, signifies the moment that the dead body is reduced to meat. The course taken by the sacrifice is completely but obliquely embodied in the image. The *loutērion*, the reservoir of pure water, is at a great distance from blood. It is there to wash the blood away in the post-sacrificial phase. However, the *loutērion*, which is in the contextual position of the altar, remains the spatial center of the sacrifice in the painting, the image of a sacrifice yet to happen, where the animals have yet to come in contact with the water. The pure water that must touch them in the rite is only suggested by the container. Animals and death-dealing water are face to face; nothing has happened yet if everything is still in position.

If there is a maenad mounted on the bovine next to the *loutērion*, this simple addition disrupts the meanings carried by the elements of the image.[23] Relations between men and animals are completely different in the framework of Dionysianism than in the sacrificial space of eating cooked foods. The image is no longer of the ritual, and the mounted bovine is related to that realm apart where the god can miraculously join the human presence.[24] The basin is there to signal the purity of this conjunction.

Set in the ground, the basin of pure water is a sacrificial place by the same token as the altar is. The animals approach the basin in the same way that they move toward the altar; in the space of the rite as in that of the image, altar and basin, as signs of death, are separated like water and blood. Therefore the officiants having any connection with blood are nude or, like those on the oenochoë depicting the giant leg of meat (fig. 12), they wear special cloths or light loincloths (fig. 9).[25] No trace of blood can be seen on the clothing of those who have a part in the blood gushing from the slit throat or any phase of the handling of the meat. In the polarized space of the sacrifice it is important to carry to the animal the water that is needed for the victim to be accepted. It is the hydria that takes this vehicular role. A discreet instrument of sacrifice, it nonetheless occupies an essential place.[26] Without the water it enables one to bring, the sacrifice comes to a halt.[27] But the separation between the place of water and the place of blood is so great that a second relay to the altar is needed. Another instrument, a kind of basin, *khernips,* is used to present water to the officiant, who puts his hands in it, sprinkles the animal, and thus puts it in contact with the drops signifying death (fig. 17).[28]

However, the death-bringing hydria, as depicted on a stamnos (fig. 18),[29] serves in a paradoxical way to water the sacrificial beast, a bovine with horns already draped with streamers. The animal, its muzzle low, goes or comes to drink from a basin on a low tripod. Above this bronze receptacle a winged Nike leans down to pour the hydria, which she holds by its foot and vertical handle. If the test by permutation is accurate, the bronze basin would have nothing in common with a *loutērion.* Surprisingly, at least at first glance, it turns out to be a basin for washing feet, *podaniptēr.*[30] The prize at athletic contests, it is to be seen in connection with a giant tripod, also of bronze, as the obligatory reward for poetic combat. This is not a ritual scene. The reference to the agonistic context suggested by the Nike's presence is absolutely clear in the relationship of the two objects about to be consecrated to the gods. Moreover, the hydria itself is a possible prize in these contests.[31] In combination with the two other objects of consecration, its presence strengthens the agonistic meaning of the ensemble. But if the *podaniptēr* is not a ritually styled water vessel, the hydria remains the bearer of the ceremonial values of animal death. Portable, meant to be carried, it can be used to water the animal selected as a victim outside the sacrificial space. Terribly ambiguous, it remains the attenuated but sure sign of death. The animal is thus peacefully kept alive thanks to the instrument that in the future will bring it to consent to its role as victim. The Nike present in the scene would be enough to pose the problem of the exact relationship between the image and the realities of the cult. It seems possible to envisage a situation of this type enacted by men; religious boutrophia is not unknown in Greek life. But what about presacrificial feeding habits? This scene permits us to suppose that the animal would be watered at least. For the ease of the *mageiros* it is preferable to dress an animal that has not been fed, but it is much more difficult to keep it calm without recourse to violence when it is hungry, especially in the case of powerful or large animals. Yet a slow procession, with the animal peacefully escorted by those who will eat it in the future, is essential to the proper performance of the sacrifice.

Whatever the case, the iconic discourse here is not the ritual itself speaking but rather speaks *about* the ritual. Nike goddess of victories was using one of the prizes to be offered to the gods after the test to feed an animal that has been readied much earlier so that the sacrifice may be consecrated by the victor. Thus, a sacrifice was in view; an iconic procedure may speak with reference to the past, the future, and the future perfect.

The Blood Vase

To the right of the altar in the Boston oenochoë (fig. 12) appears the silhouette of a great columned crater. This vase intended to receive the sacrificial blood is a redundant sign, with the altar, that the blood of animals has flowed for the gods. Mobile and portable like the table, *trapeza,* it can ritually define the space of the image alone or in combination with the table. On the stamnos in the Louvre (fig. 13), two instruments appear in sacrificial combination:[32] the double flute, *aulos,* and the blood vase, *sphageion.* We will not hesitate to include here the flute with the instruments of the rite. In the total silence of the those attending the sacrifice, only its modulations and possibly the cries of the women accompany the exact moment of the slaying. The musician, *aulētēs,* is not playing in this depiction. He holds the instrument in his hand at a moment when, once the procession has broken up, death would in some way be suspended. On the ground a large vase of the skyphos type is placed between a half-nude person, whose loins are tied with the garment required of those assistants connected with blood, and a bovine standing next to the vase with its head extended above the vase as far as its withers. The flute, the ambiguous instrument of sweetness in the procession and violence at the moment of death, does not suggest death by itself; the relationship to

the *sphageion* is what makes it obvious. It is no longer a question of water-
ing the animal at a basin but placing the animal so that the blood that will
gush from the wound can be caught. But the gentle atmosphere still dominates, and above the *sphageion* the assistant connected with blood calms
the animal, his right hand pressed on its forehead, the left holding one of
the horns. It is not a water instrument that organizes the image but a
blood instrument, blood that is imminent but held back for the moment.
It is a time of silence before the first modulations of the killing.

The vase in the position of the *sphageion* is always large, either a crater
or skyphos or a similar formal style. This detail will perhaps enable us to
solve the annoying problem posed by a gap in a processional scene on a
hydria from Caere (fig. 19).[33] Furthermore, this vase leads one to wonder
about the relationship between the meanings expressed by various images
painted on the same object; we can see hunting scenes on one side of the
vase combined with sacrificial scenes on the other. Our concerns here will
narrow to the complex group presented in the sacrificial scene. It is a
procession where the spatial organization creates a difficulty with respect
to the sacrificial instrumentation. Turned toward a flaming altar, the bearer
of an ax for striking cattle, *boutupos,* is shown carrying out his office. The
second figure, mutilated by the gap, poses a problem. The basket-bearer,
kanēphoros, is seen in motion, the basket held at the height of her head.
The flutist plays his instrument. The ritual moment does not correspond
to the position of the figures in the space of the image. Only the *boutupos*
at the head of the procession and the flutist at the rear seem to adequately
confine the animal within the exact space of death. And the other officiants? Despite the formal arrangement of the sequence of figures, it does
not seem to be a funeral here. The basket-bearer is putting down her *kanoun* instead of carrying it, thereby implying that the procession is over.[34]
If the interpretation that this is the space of death is correct, it is no longer
the time when the double ax, *pelekus,*[35] is threatening, or, as K. F. Johansen
thought, to use water or the grains from the *kanoun*. As for the basket,
which is going to be put down, one can imagine that it contains an offering of sacred cakes consistent with the cremation of the bone and aromatics. As to the instruments of the second officiant, something closely related
to the blood spilled after the slaughter with the *pelekus* seems likely. In fact,
one of them seems clearly recognizable to us: a large skyphos, one handle
of which is visible and the other hidden by the left hand of the person
who perhaps holds the handle of the *makhaira,* the blade of which is perhaps pointed upward. In any event, this cannot be a matter of carrying the
instrument of slaughter in procession, for it must remain invisible; rather

the instruments of the bloody death are being set in place. The large sky-phos is indeed a blood vase. In the strictly delimited space of the death, between the one who brings it and the one who sets it to music, the hydria and basin are superfluous. It is that moment in the relationship between man and animal when violence is exactly at the point of meeting gentle-ness. The right hand of the second officiant poised behind the skyphos on the bovine's withers corresponds exactly to the hand that brandishes the *pelekus*. The one reverses the meaning of the other.

The Blood of a Tuna

Strictly speaking, a system of combinations involving only the system of objects without accounting for their placement in the image and the space of the rite would not be possible. During the ritual process, the movement of objects and changes of position establish relations through which a discourse moves. In the image of the rite, the relative place of objects is in fact inseparable from the organization of space. The Boston oenochoë (fig. 12) shows the blood vase to the right of the *bōmos* and on the same plane; except for this detail a closely similar iconic arrangement is found on an olpe in Berlin (fig. 20).[36] *Bōmos, trapeza,* and *sphageion* are in place, but the vase is in front of the altar, not on the same plane, with the altar again in front of the cutting table. The pieces on the table are absent, as well as the tree. It is true that the animal is in one piece and that it is a huge fish, a tuna. It is well known that the quantity of blood in these fish is particularly abundant. Thus with the head of the fish placed exactly above the altar and the receptacle, the hemorrhage caused by the first blow struck by the person on the right brandishing the *makhaira* will be able to reach the *bōmos* as desired and flow into the *sphageion*. The arrangement of elements in the image leaves hardly any room for doubt. The figure on the left grasps the fish by the tail with his left hand and holds it horizontally, by the gills, at the proper height. The fingers visible between the animal and the table make it obvious that the figure holds the fish over the table instead of resting it on top. And since nothing is missing, not even the crowns of the officiants, why not speak of a sacrifice of tuna? There is nothing inconsistent in the image, nothing in Greek culture as a system of representations referred to by the combination of signs. This sacrifice, along with that of the eel, is the only one cited in the framework of the blood ritual of the alimentary type.[37] It has a specific name, *thunnaion*. This moreover poses the problem of the animal's status, given its place in the classification of fish, with respect to species that can be sacrificed. But the image at least shows to what point the blood indispensable in a religious act is central in representing the rite, in which it is always in some way present even if it is never truly shown. It is for this reason that a fish that bleeds is fit to die for the gods.[38]

The Skewers of the Divine Glutton

We will end with a simple remark. Borne by the ritual process, the figurative syntagma is a choice made from among the innumerable possibilities that the continuum of ritual action offers the system of iconic combinations. The strategy is meaningful in itself; and one can wonder about the production of the syntagma of the altar with respect to the *splankhnoptēs*, grillmaster, and about the complete absence in the imagery of eaters of viscera, *splankhna*, for example. Once established, the syntagma can itself become the bearer of meaning through the permutation of one of the elements that compose it. Thus the skewers, *oboloi*, do not have the same meaning when, kept at the altar, they are used to grill the first pieces of the victim *splankhna*, put on to cook, as they do when they are loaded from tip to handle with garlands of pieces set aside for later eating. The grillmaster can always be seen at the altar. At the distribution table, several pieces are skewered along the length of the *oboloi*. Hercules can roast meat at the altar;[39] but when he puts meat on the skewer, he is never at the *trapeza* where the shares are apportioned. He remains at the altar as if, since all the meat is reserved for him (fig. 17), he never took the detour to the table where the pieces for distribution are placed.[40] We can see him with the reserve skewer on a cup in the Louvre which lacks the altar upon which, without exception, the death of the animals must take place.[41] Hercules' lone skewer betrays the hero as divine glutton. His diet reveals how difficult it is for him, at the sacrifice as quite often elsewhere, to behave like a human.

The place of the image in which the ritual is captured remains to be studied in its totality, then. Meaning moves from sign to sign, depending on the multiple possibilities that the combining procedures employed by the interpreter attempt to reveal. It is quite clear that the series are open-ended. Borne by the same culture, referring to the same system of representation, it is a reasonable hope that new images will enrich the analysis which, like the corpus, always remains open. The only certainty required is that the image is a place of coherence.

FIVE

The Violence of Wellborn Ladies: Women in the Thesmophoria

Marcel Detienne

A woman's fate in turn is bounded by two titles, no less noble, wife and mother of a citizen.
Mme de Rémusat, *Essai sur l'éducation des femmes*, 3d ed. (Paris, 1825), 106.

TO determine the status of women in matters of sacrifice is to enter by the back door into the system of ritual acts in which eating behaviors constantly intermingle with political practices—a system in which the proximity of the culinary and the political may lead in some places to a fundamental issue: the division between the feminine and the masculine. No ritual context is more central in showing women in the act of making sacrifices or more helpful in establishing the motivations that lead to their assuredly marginal place than the festival in honor of Demeter Thesmophorus.[1] For women only, and more specifically, for the lawful wives of citizens, the Thesmophoria, from at least the seventh century B.C. to the Hellenistic period, takes on a politico-religious function in the Greek city, which, owing to their physiological nature and privilege of fecundity, directly concerns the "race of women."[2] In the cult of Demeter Thesmophorus, who is often called Legislatrix—she who gives the city its laws—can be seen the contradictions within a society and system of thought that deliberately relegates the female sex to the periphery of the politico-religious space but finds itself led, by certain limitations inherent in its own values, to give women a determining role in the reproduction of the entire system.

Anecdotally, two separate accounts present a strange, exclusively feminine sacrificial activity, which in both cases leads to violence—a generalized violence at that. The first of these stories tells of the misadventure of the king of Cyrene, Battus the Founder.[3] One day, the good king Battus wanted to learn about the mysteries of the Thesmophoria. To satisfy his avid eyes, he resorted to violence (*bia*). The priestesses at first tried to dissuade him and resist his desire. But Battus was not to be moved. The women, however, refused to let the king take part in "what he was forbidden to hear and what it was better not to see."[4] On the other hand, the priestesses did allow him to watch the first part of the ceremonies,[5] the part "that contained nothing out of the ordinary for spectators as well as actors." And this is what Battus saw: "Clothed in their holy garments, and wholly possessed because of their initiation into the mysteries, the female slayers (*sphaktriai*) brandished their naked swords (*xiphē*); their hands and faces were stained with the blood of the victims (*hiereia*)." But the spectacle comes to a sudden halt. "All together, as if in response to an agreed signal (*sunthēma*), they leaped upon Battus, to remove the part of him that made him a male (*anēr*)."[6]

The second narrative, which is less dramatic, belongs to the Messenian tradition.[7] It is an episode from the exploits of Aristomenes, a hero of the resistance to the Spartan aggression against Messenia. At Aegila, in Laconia the women have shut themselves in Demeter's temple on the occasion of a festival that forbids any males to be present. They are easy hostages for Aristomenes and his men.[8] But Pausanias tells of the Messenians' mortification: the women—and here we must undoubtedly see Demeter's work—repel the assailants and wound most of the Messenians by stabbing them with the knives (*makhaira*) that they used to sacrifice their victims and with the skewers (*oheloi*) with which they were preparing to roast the meat (*krea*). The rout was so complete that Aristomenes, the Fox, the elusive, was knocked senseless by the firebrands and captured alive. And if he succeeded nonetheless in escaping at nightfall, it was only with the help of one of Demeter's priestesses who had been his mistress.

These are marginal, dubious stories, particularly since the second tale seems to come from the pages of a Messenian novel and the first is notably outrageous. And doubly so;[9] the majesty and whiteness of the Thesmophorian robes ill become a scene that evokes the frenzy of the Bacchae. Wives, mothers of families, with consecrated virtue, could not commit such an act. As for Battus the founder, his reputation as a wise and pious king is enough to belie such misfortune. Historians consult one another and conclude that "the historic content of the event is highly doubtful."[10] The two stories remain, with their shared Demetrian context in which women together exercise a violence against males with weapons that are the instruments of fleshly sacrifice. Cast-off, discarded stories indeed, but they hold our attention. First, they tell of curious and unusual aspects of the culinary and the sacrificial; but they are also striking when they paradoxically place within the same confines a feminine practice of blood sacrifice in which diet is a motivating force, and a brutal war in which the banished sex is always the more or less pitiful victim. These are tales that lie far outside the mainstream, and their marginality all too consistently imposes on women a position in the sacrificial space that calls for further investigation.

In the Greek city, as is well known, there is no lack of marginal inhabitants. Without making an exhaustive list, we can situate them in the present case between two poles:[11] at one extreme are the renouncers, who choose to reject meat, blood, and the works of sacrifice; at the other are the male citizens, users with full rights in the politico-religious system in which sacrifice has an integral part. Foreigners and half-castes represent two "unfavored" categories. The former may have access to the altars only by the official mediation of a citizen who speaks on their behalf before the gods and the local community.[12] The latter, having no right to make sacrifices themselves, can join the expanded circle of commensals. For example, they are admitted to the division and distribution of the victims at the *Hephaistia* celebrated at Athens for Athena and Hephaestus, the powers jointly governing the activities of artisans.[13] But with respect to sacrifice, it is the female population that forms the most important category of marginals.

As a general rule, by virtue of the homology between political power and sacrificial practice, the place reserved for women perfectly corresponds to the one they occupy—or rather, do not occupy—in the space of the city.[14] Just as women are without the political rights reserved for male citizens, they are kept apart from the altars, meat, and blood. Within the sacrificial sphere itself, participation can occur on three levels, at least: within the broad community of those who are admitted to eat the portions of the victim; within the narrow circle of those who eat the viscera roasted on the spit; and finally, right in the center, the sacrifier-sacrificer, the one who wields the knife to stab the animal offered to the gods by his efforts. When women have access to meat, the rules of the cult are careful to specify the precise terms and conditions. For these things are not self-evident. Thus, at Thasos in the ceremonies celebrated every other year in honor of Athena Patrōa, who is connected with the families of the founders from Paros, "married women also take part in the distribution of the portions."[15] This clause seems only to refer to wives (*gunaikes*) and, undoubtedly, first of all the wives of the citizens who are members of those "countries" that take the place of tribes and phratries. The restriction is more explicit in the oldest Attic statute concerning the orgeones,[16] members of the religious confraternities, wherein the terms of distributing the sacrificial meats are set out: to the orgeones present goes one portion; to their sons, half a portion; and to the wives of the orgeones, the free ones (*eleutherai*), an equal (*isaia*) share; to their daughters, a portion that is not less than half.[17] There is one final detail: the portion meant for the wives is entrusted to the man (*anēr*).[18] Thus, a woman's equality with respect to meat is subject to two conditions that determine the limits of the hidden citizenship of free women who are lawfully wedded wives. They come third in the hierarchy, after the men, fathers and sons; and their husbands play the role of mediator between them and the shared pieces of the victim. Just as women require a representative in court for any legal proceeding[19]—where they are treated no differently from half-castes—they are admitted into the larger circle of commensals only by the intermediary of someone having the right to obtain for them this favored treatment.

At a sacrifice, particularly a blood sacrifice, women cannot function as full adults. It is precluded by the reciprocity established in the city between a meat-eating diet and political practice. There are exceptional cases, of course. Thus, in the calendar of the deme of Erchia in Attica, on the occasion of a sacrifice offered by a priestess to Semele and Dionysus, the parts of the victim, a goat, are distributed among the women and consumed on the spot.[20] This is a sacrifice where the dominance of the feminine element is related to the power of Dionysus, who in this instance is clearly associated with his mother.[21] But another example is found at Olympia in the context of the celebrations for Hera, the *Hēraia*, organized by the college of the Sixteen Women of Elis.[22] In races reserved for girls— divided into three categories according to age[23]—the winner of each race held in the stadium received a crown of olive branches and a portion of the cow sacrificed in Hera's honor.[24] With their hair unbound and their knees and shoulders left bare by a short tunic, the fastest of the adolescent girls of Olympia enjoyed the same privileges as male athletes. Here the right to sacrificial meat is part of the extension of "male" values traditionally associated with tests of speed.

The same transference of virile and warlike values explains the role given to women in the ritual of Tegea.[25] Under the sign of Ares, surnamed *Gunaikothoinas* because on this occasion he presides over the women's banquet, the wives of citizens make a sacrifice to the god of war, whose statue stands in the agora in memory of the victory that women achieved by themselves over the Spartan warriors in days of yore. Therefore, on this day the women of Ares do not give a single portion of meat to the representatives of the male sex. They consign their husbands to the outer fringes of the sacrifice, permitting them only to watch.[26] In this way, once a year and on an ephemeral basis, they reverse the traditional roles. What is explained by reference to virile or warlike virtues in the last two examples can be justified in the first one by Dionysianism alone, by the preeminence of its feminine values that serve, here as elsewhere, a subversive intent.

These are all just so many exceptions that prove the male monopoly in matters of blood sacrifice and everything connected with meat-eating. Kept away from meat, Greek women are totally unqualified to handle the instruments that we would see, in view of their culinary functions, as naturally belonging to the domestic and feminine world. Women have no rights to the kettle, the spit, or the knife.[27] In public sacrifices the skewers are most often in the hands of ephebes; knives and axes are normally entrusted to mature men. And if the caldron in which the pieces of the victim are boiled is often used on a symbolic level to evoke the female belly, on the contrary it by no means involves the presence of one or more women.[28] Meat and blood sacrifice are men's affair.[29] Consequently, for a long time it was thought that only vegetables were offered at the Thesmophoria, not flesh or blood. From Nilsson to Festugière[30] it seemed obvious that the "sacrifice" held on the last day of the festival, once the fasts ended and the piglets rotting in the crevices of the ground had been scooped out, consisted of grains and cakes: barley, wheat (either raw or as gruel), dried figs, oil, wine, honey, cooked sesame seeds, poppy seeds, garlic, and cheese.[31] Among the women of Demeter making their retreat for three full days, a kind of vegetarianism would seem appropriate,[32] particularly since this event luckily coincides with a sowing festival that gives the altar the modest role of a table at which each wife comes to pick up part of the rotten meat gathered by the "scoopers" to mix it with the seeds for the next harvest.[33]

This reading of the Thesmophoria as a festival involving only nauseating seeds and vegetarian matrons dressed in white obscures a whole aspect of the Demetrian ritual in which the role of meat and blood is clearly indicated by the data.[34] These references are scattered but point in the same direction. First, we may cite an aberrant custom, noted by Plutarch in the form of the Greek Question: Why at Eretria do the women at the Thesmophoria cook meat in the sun instead of roasting it on the fire?[35] This first deviation is reinforced by a second: the Eretrian women do not invoke the Beautiful Birth, the power of the third day, *Kalligeneia*. In this instance, there is little significance to the explanation Plutarch offers by telling how these women, prisoners of Agamemnon on his return from Troy, take advantage of the nearby passage of a ship to flee in the middle of the sacrifice without taking the time to roast the flesh of the victims. The mere formulation of the Question bears witness in negative terms to a "Thesmophoric" custom of a blood sacrifice that had undoubtedly taken place after the fast of the second day, when the time came for joyously invoking the Beautiful Birth.[36] The categorical assertion by one of Aristophanes' ancient commentators[37] that the women of the Thesmophoria are carnivorous (*kreophageîn*), that they slaughter pigs (*khoirosphageîn*), is fully confirmed by what we find in the sacred archives at Delos. Between 314 and 166 B.C. the ledgers of the hieropes contain a special category for money for the purchase of animals to serve as victims at the Thesmophoria: a pregnant sow for Demeter, pigs for Demeter Kore and Zeus Eubuleus, as well as to purify the *Thesmophorion*. It is foreseen that the priestesses of Demeter receive a certain sum of money to feed the victims, while they have at their disposal cooking materials, with oil, fruit, and caul sausages, as well as charcoal and wood to cook the meat.[38]

Reexamining all the Delian source materials, Philippe Bruneau has shown that it is necessary to make a distinction between two Thesmophorian ways of using pigs as "sacrificial" victims.[39] In the first, the animal is hurled into crevices in the earth, the *megara*,[40] a ritual gesture that we can see represented on an Athenian lekythos: the woman bends over the ground, and she carries a basket laden with cakes in her left hand, while in her right she holds a piglet by the tail, undoubtedly before dropping it into the abyss.[41] Similarly, several statuettes of women dedicators found in Sicilian temples represent a woman with a torch in her right hand and a little pig dangling head down at the end of her left arm.[42] This type of victim must not be stabbed; it is hurled into the bowels of the earth, where it disappears, like others of its kind from the time of Eubuleus that had been swallowed up in the great rift opened up by the god who ravished Persephone. The animal is left to rot. Its blood flows neither on the ground nor on the altar, and its flesh is withdrawn from the realm of what is eaten as well as from contact with the cooking or destroying fire. In the other case, the victim is prepared in the sacrificial manner and is subject to alimentary acts and practices. It is for this type of victim that all the items noted in the ledger are intended, from cooking utensils to the least of condiments.[43]

To the epigraphic data is added evidence from Aristophanes' play, *Thesmophoriazusae*. Sent by Euripides, who hopes to foil the plans of a group of women determined to ruin him, the obliging Kinsman, who has come to aid the "misogynistic" Poet, finds that he has no other way out of his predicament, once he is unmasked in the middle of the Thesmophoria, than to take as hostage an infant wrested from its mother's arms. He threatens to slit its throat near the victims on the altar: "Right here, on the thighbones (the *mēria* of sacrificed animals), stabbed by this knife (*makhaira*), its spilled blood will drench the altar."[44] And when, crazed, he stabs the poor nursling, which in reality is a wineskin swaddled like a baby, the tearful mother calls for the blood vase (*sphageion*) in order to collect the precious liquid.[45] The scene would have no comic effect if spilled blood were incongruous at the Thesmophoria. The knife, the basin to catch the blood, the altar, the bones reserved for the gods, as well as the hide that must go to the priestess[46] are all marks referring to the blood and food sacrifice inside the framework of the fifth-century Thesmophoria.

At this point the question arises of the character, exceptional or not, of a blood sacrifice undertaken by women practicing commensality in the isolation imposed on them by the prohibition against any male presence.[47] Aren't the mishaps told of Battus or Aristomenes to some point directly linked to the unusual example of an alimentary and fleshly sacrifice carried out by females under circumstances so particular as to intensify the marginality of the female race? Lacking full rights at the "political" banquet, would the feminine race on the occasion of an outrageous ritual be credited with aberrant behavior that puts them in the role of slayers, bloodstained women, killers of men?

Kept at a distance from meat, Greek women are nevertheless not excluded from the domain of sacrifice. In the demes and the cities, priesthoods and ministries are open to them; some are even for women only.[48] Powers such as Aglaurus, Artemis, Athena, or Demeter require priestesses. And in the city, sacerdotal functions that bring with them the rank of "magistrate" involve obligations and duties: managing funds and maintaining relations with the assembly or the magistrates on duty. Thus the priestesses of Athena can file a lawsuit, appear before the Council of the Five Hundred, and obtain certain public honors, as the following two examples demonstrate. In Athens, the wife of the King Archon, the elected guardian of the religious traditions of the city, bears the title of queen, *Basilinna*.[49] She had to be Athenian, be a "virgin" at the time of her marriage, and know no man prior to her royal husband. Attended by fourteen maids of honor, the *Gererai,* on the occasion of the Anthesteria, a springtime festival of renewal, she carried out sacrifices and secret rites for and in the name of the whole city.[50] In Pergea in Pamphylia, in the temple of Artemis *Pergaia,* a "poliad" deity, the priesthood could only be held by a woman, a citizen (*astē*) residing in the town (*astú*), born of a family who had lived in the city for three generations on both paternal and maternal sides.[51] Priestess for life, she is responsible for all private and public sacrifices, and on each new moon she must make a sacrifice for the "health of the city." She receives a choice piece from each victim offered in public sacrifice, "a thigh and the shares given in addition to the thigh." But above all, each year on the twelfth of the month called *Herakleion,* the priestess of Artemis *Pergaia* celebrates the great official sacrifice, for which the prytaneis are responsible but whose execution is entrusted to the wives of the magistrates. The statute calls for an "equal share" (*isomoiros*)[52] for the priestess and for the wives of the prytaneis responsible for the sacrifice. Partaking of equal rights, here women instead of their husbands are in the position of meat-eaters, who at this time of year are citizens endowed with political power. But it is no longer merely a question of having access to meat. The affair is played out on another level: surrounding the priestess of Artemis *Pergaia,* women occupy the entire sacrificial area. This is a *political* sacrifice, connected to the city in three ways: through the "poliad" function of Artemis, participation in the town-city that must extend back for three generations, and the commensality of legitimate wives, assistants of the citizens most intimately associated with the decisions of the city. Indirectly, as a divine power granting privileges to the female sex in the form of priesthood and ritual, female citizenship comes out of its latency to fill the ephemeral moments of a festival—but a collective, public festival embodying the entire political and visible realm of the blood sacrifice.

The case of the Artemis of Pamphylia shows even more clearly than the Athenian Anthesteria that the sacrificial authority of women is given full expression in the order of the city as well as on a political level where the egalitarian right to ritual slaughter and sharing of animal victims is inextricably tied to the exercise of real power in the religious and political affairs of the city—even if this power appears only in the form of an assistantship. Just as under the rule of the Attic orgeones women of free birth only achieve equal rights to meat via the mediation of a hubasnd belonging to the narrow circle of commensals, in the temple of Artemis the women of Pergea exercise authority in sacrificial matters only when the political rights held by the prytaneis husbands are temporarily delegated to them.

The political dimension of women at the sacrifice appears still more clearly in the ritual of the Thesmophoria in several ways: through the status of those admitted to honor Demeter Thesmophorus, as well as according to references to places of power, and above all, in the politico-religious intent that orients the whole ritual. If all men, whoever they are, are excluded from the Thesmophoria, not all women are admitted, either. Female slaves may not enter the temple or see what goes on there.[53] Moreover, a girl (*parthenos*) is not permitted to watch the ceremonies until—as Callimachus puts it—a husband has come to her to achieve nuptial union.[54] As for courtesans, during the classical age it was an outright scandal if their presence was suspected in such an assembly.[55] In the measured vocabulary of the orators, the woman who attends the Thermosphoria has two qualities: she is a citizen (*astē*) and is lawfully married (*enguētē*).[56] Demeter Thesmophorus recruits her faithful from among the elements of the female population who are connected most intimately with the affairs of the city, by birth and by marriage. These are the "Wellborn Ladies" (*eugeneis*) of good lineage and excellent upbringing.[57]

On more than one occasion, male power admits its collusion with the Thesmophoria. This is not only because the magistrates of the city, whether the demarch in Piraeus or the first magistrate, called the demiurge in Arcadia, have the task of enforcing the statutes of the temples.[58] Rather it is because Demeter's domain in some cities is largely hemmed in by politics, to the point of cohabitation, in the literal sense of the term. Thus in Thebes Cadmus the Founder and his descendants were at one time housed in the temple of Demeter Thesmophorus, who was depicted by a statue buried breast deep in the ground, representing the cultivated soil of the royal house of Thebes, out of which grew fruit and youths who would grow into men.[59] Similarly, in Thasos the *Thesmophorion* gathers within its precincts the powers that make up the most political of configurations: Zeus, Artemis, Athena, and the "short-tressed" nymphs, all divinities to whom homage was paid by the great families, the *patrai,* who had earlier come from Paros to colonize the Thracian island under the patronage of Demeter and her clergy.[60]

More generally, it is the very purpose of the ritual of the Thesmophoria to ground it in the center of the city and at the heart of politics.[61] Celebrated in Pyanopsion, in October–November, the time of labor and sowing, Demeter's festival ends under the sign of the Beautiful Birth. Mixed in with the rotting remains of the pigs on the altar, the seeds are made fertile, while women secretly mold stiff dough into figurines in the likeness of serpents and sexual organs, both male and female.[62] An ancient commentator to whom we owe most of our information insists on the twofold intent of the ritual: the birth (*genesis*) of fruit and the seed (*spora*) of men. And this metaphorical inversion shows how much the two levels, plant and human, are interlocked, joined in the Greek word for seed, *sperma.*[63] The women gathered at the Thesmophoria have an essential mission, and this is why in the ritual so much effort goes into distinguishing "legitimate" women from all the rest. With Demeter's aid and using her as a model, and with the wife-mother bringing the relationship with her daughter to the foreground, the "Thesmophoria" must reproduce the city, the whole political body, both in the human species by producing legitimate children and in the cultivated space with fructifying seeds. The Beautiful Birth is an expression of the effective promise that the city have children of good stock and food enough for their keep.[64]

Such an undertaking is not without repercussions for the way women organize themselves during the festival. A whole political vocabulary reveals the details of the social status of the group formed by the citizen-wives, a group that appears endowed with its own autonomy—provisional, to be sure, for it lasts only as long as the festivals, but autonomy nonetheless—since during these three days no male presence, no shadow of a male citizen comes to disturb the society of women. Every year in the demes, women choose[65] from among themselves the ones who will preside over the ceremonies and exercise the power in the Thesmophoria (*arkhein eis ta thesmophoria*).[66] These responsible parties (*arkhousai*)[67] preside over the assembly held on the days established by tradition (*kata ta patria*)[68] and see to it that what is sanctioned by custom (*poiein ta nomizomena*) is carried out.[69] On the functioning of the assembly of women, Aristophanes' account is in agreement with the epigraphic evidence. A cult statute from Mylasa in Caria dating from the third century B.C. recalls that the ceremonies of Demeter Thesmophoros should take place "as the women have decided" (*hōs edoxe tais gunaixi*).[70] This is the classical formula used in a decree, whether it is issued by a council, the assembly, or the people. And in Aristophanes' play *Thesmophoriazusae,* after a solemn prayer that concludes with the formula for imprecations given in public assemblies against those who break the law or betray the country, the action begins at line 372 with a woman-herald reading a proclamation: "The council (*boulē*) of women has decreed the following: Timoklea was president, Lysilla, clerk, Sostrates, orator. An assembly will be held the morning of the middle day of the Thesmophoria, when we have the most leisure, to deliberate above all on the matter of Euripides and the punishment he must suffer, for he has behaved in an unworthy manner, as we are all agreed." This council decree is applied using the customary formula, Who wishes to speak? This is a plenary assembly, where the female race sits, forming a *dēmos* that even in comedy is imagined in the shadow of the "city of Athenians."[71]

When the Thesmophoria call them together, the citizen-women form neither troop, thiasus, nor "sorority" but a society with magistrates, a council, an assembly, and decisions voted by majority rule. On the occasion of Demeter's festival, women govern themselves. They have the right to vote as if back in the days before Erichthonius, when women exercised equal power with men until they made poor use of their right to choose and selected Athena instead of Poseidon.[72] There is a difference, nonetheless: at the Thesmophoria women exercise this right to vote alone, without men. So when they decide to put Euripides, the man they detest, to death,[73] their verdict appears in Aristophanes' work as all the more dangerous, since it is pronounced in silence and in the absence of the male city. For the second festival day that the Council of the Thesmophoria has chosen as a date to meet is a time of no work and of mourning, during which no events or city tribunals are held in the male city.[74] The discretionary power held by the women can lead Euripides to believe he is a dead man, as if the secret assembly of Demeter's faithful conjured up yet another meeting, no less powerfully imaginary, of the women of the island of Lemnos who, incensed at seeing their husbands take beautiful captives for themselves, assembled and unanimously voted for the death of their men and the male race as a whole.[75]

This is an extreme case, but it reveals the difference between what happens in the temple of Artemis Pergea and what goes on within the precincts of the Thesmophoria. At Pergea, women who have the right to sacrifice together and divide the victims up among themselves do so in broad daylight, before the eyes of the assembled city. At the Thesmophoria, no male eyes are tolerated, so that the sacrificial authority the women carry seems to be exercised without outside control, by the sovereignty that the temporary exclusion of men and the city gives them. For three whole days, under the sign of the ancestral tradition (*patria*), the Thesmophoria institute a city of women within the limits of a ritual essential to the reproduction of the city of men. Feminine power wavers between two models: a reduced city shored up by its legitimacy, and a gynocracy where political right to the blood sacrifice is confined to violence directed against the male gender, if not against the "natural" power of the race of men.

With respect to sacrifice, the political dimension of the issue of the women at the Thesmophoria supports the regular and, one might say, orthodox character of the sacrificial cookery that the two narratives about Battus and Aristomenes impute to it. But if the complete absence of any male individual within the arena of the Thesmophoria unambiguously confirms women's political authority in matters of sacrificial practice, on the other hand it leads to questions about one last factor concerning participation in the blood sacrifice. Earlier we noted two such aspects: access to meat, with a further distinction between the two commensal circles; and the qualifications necessary to offer an animal victim to the gods in the name of a group or community.[76] But in the very center, in the shadow of the sacrificer, is found a third mode of participation: the use of the instruments that shed the blood, i.e., the ax and the knife.

Again, a look at the ethnography is necessary in order to recognize the position of the women "slaughterers" of Cyrene and the women converging on Aristomenes with skewers and knives. In all written and pictorial tradition, only two documents make a case for the wielding of sacrificial instruments by female sacrificers. The first case, pictorial in nature, takes us toward one of the frontier zones of the sacrifice, toward the Dionysianism that on occasion favors egalitarian sharing among women without the presence of men. The Ruvo amphora in the Naples museum presents two figures of Dionysus:[77] on the upper level, an ephebe-god bearing the thyrsus and half-reclined among women and satyrs; below, a bearded god in embroidered clothes, standing erect between a table and a sacrificial altar. The second Dionysus, who wears the mask of a cult statue, occupies the center of a ritual arrangement that can be entered from two sides, that of table or that of the altar. Among the officiants, all female, some of whom play cymbals and drum while others wave torches and the thyrsus, two women carry out the tasks of the sacrifice. Different actions are addressed to the same idol. While one of the women places fruit and a basket of cakes on the table as a bloodless offering and flameless sacrifice, the other carries out an animal sacrifice in front of an altar where the sacrificial fire is burning. Her right hand lifts up a knife, the *makhaira,* over the head of a kid (depicted under her left forearm), the victim whose blood will drench the altar. However, the Ruvo slaughterer remains unique, not only in the corpus of sacrificial images from ceramic ware[78] but in the very tradition of Dionysus,[79] where the configuration of political and orthodox sacrifice is constantly subverted on different levels either by the eating of raw foods,[80] the hunt-pursuit,[81] or the intrusion of hybrids like the satyr grillmasters.[82]

With the second document, which dramatizes one of Demeter's rituals[83] at Hermione in Argolis, we remain on the outskirts of the sacrificial system. The festival, called the *Chthonia,* is dominated by a prodigious sacrifice; the largest of the cattle spontaneously come before the altar. This amazing spectacle is described in Aelian's *The Nature of the Animals:*[84] an old woman (*graus*) by herself leads to the altar a "bull" so wild that six men could not control it. And the old woman leads the monster by the ear, which walks beside her like a child led by its mother. The more elaborate version given by Pausanias[85] provides details about the procedures of the sacrifice offered to Demeter to make the land (*klaros*) of Hermione fruitful and abundant. The festival, held every year during the summer, takes place in a temple founded by Chthonia and Clymenus, the two children of Phoroneus, the first man born in the country of Argos. A long procession brings together the priests attending the god, the magistrates on duty, and women and men followed by children dressed in white and crowned with flowers of mourning, known locally as *kosmosandalon*. Bringing up in the rear of the procession are the priests leading the victim: a perfect cow, the finest of the herd but hobbled by cords and trembling with wildness. The animal is driven toward the temple; and while some open the doors, others loosen the animal's bonds, and it leaps through the opening. The doors close on the victim and the four old women who wait for it inside. They are the ones who carry out the "work." The verb *katergazesthai* used by Pausanias evokes both the task that is carried out and the blood that is spilled, an ambiguity inherent in the instrument used for the sacrifice, the sickle (*drepanon*) carried by each of the four old women. The one who reaches the animal first slits its throat.[86] Then the doors are opened, and the same scenario is played out again, until four victims have all been executed in the same way. This sacrifice is all the more amazing, observes Pausanias, because each time the animal falls down on the same side as the first victim. And in front of the temple, next to the statues of Demeter's priestesses, are high raised chairs where the four women sit while waiting for the procession. The execution takes place in secret. Only the old women know what goes on inside the temple. Pausanias insists on it; he saw nothing, nor did anyone else, whether foreigner or citizen of Hermione.

If the two versions are in agreement concerning the strange nature of the sacrifice, they diverge over the means of the killing. The hidden nature of the most important sequence of the ritual perhaps explains that in Aelian's version the sacrificial action is reduced to the spontaneous movement toward the altar of a victim that has abandoned its violence, tamely following a woman sacrificer whose advanced age accentuates her weakness.[87] With its focus on the success of a sacrifice carried out by an old woman, the miraculous draws the reader's attention away from the deviant aspects of the ritual. Moreover, it subdues the violence of the killing, central in Pausanias' complex version, in which crucial relationships between women and a sacrificial instrument come to the fore, while the miraculous shifts to an extreme detail, the side on which the slaughtered animal falls.

Several signs of distortion can be noted in Pausanias' version. First, there is the wildness of the victims, which sets them apart from animals selected for their domestic traits. Instead of being free of all bonds (*apheta*), as is customary, the animals at Hermione are hobbled until they reach the threshold of the temple, where they can finally give way to their violence. There is something of the bullfight in this sacrifice. Then, everything happens inside, in an enclosed space, sheltered from all eyes and the publicity required in community or political sacrifices. As for the instrument chosen to slaughter the victim, it is not a knife, *makhaira*, which given the victim's size and strength should be seconded by an ax, *pelekus*, but a sickle, a tool diverted from its agricultural use and transformed into the weapon of an underhanded war.[88] Lastly and above all, the sacrificers who shed the blood—not on the altar but on the temple floor—are women. The accumulation of so many distortions in one ritual tends to confirm the exceptional status of these priestesses of Demeter who mow down these half-wild cows. The fact that these are old women is certainly not without significance.[89] Because they no longer have an active part in the female biological cycle and the reproduction of the political body, they have greater access to the instruments that concern the slaughtering of sacrificial victims. Old women can shed blood since they are no longer at risk of losing it.

Consequently, after examining the only two data available in an extensive corpus, it appears that the woman-sacrificer holding the instrument of death represents the most extreme case of what is possible in worship. Even in the rituals where the nature of the divine power requires associating female personnel with the practice of particularly cruel sacrifices, it is not ordinarily the priestess who has the task of slitting the victim's throat. In the play of Euripides dominated by the cruelty of Artemis Taurica, Iphigenia explains on two occasions that as priestess she consecrates human victims and pours the lustral water, but that others inside the temple are entrusted with the slaughter (*sphagia*). "It is not she, a female (*thēlus*), who shall kill males (*arsenes*) with the sword (*xiphos*)."[90] Slaughterers are males. They hide within the dwelling place of Artemis. But Iphigenia, who has breasts—that is the meaning of *thēlus*—is content to perform her task of pouring water on the heads of the victims. Her womanly nature designates her as a water bearer, *hydrophorus*,[91] like the woman who opens the sacrificial procession in the ritual of the Bouphonia.[92] And the water can be used to sharpen the ax and the knife, just as the basketful of grain in the hands of the basket-bearers discreetly carries the instrument of the blood sacrifice.[93] But these feminine functions of basket- or water-carrier mark the decent distance separating the participation of women in the sacrifice from the act of shedding blood. Iphigenia is right: in Greek society it is not the woman who can hold the knife. There is not a single example of a *mageiros,* butcher-sacrificer-cook, who is not male. Moreover, the word *mageiros* has no feminine form; it would have to be invented, as Pherecrates, a comic poet of the fourth century B.C., put it.[94]

In other words, the Greek system does not allow any thought of women as butchers and sacrificers. Definitive confirmation of this rule is found in a ritual statute of the Thesmophoria, for it is evidence of a procedure that the city periodically employs in order to reconcile the imperative that a woman cannot strike the mortal blow with the requirement that a blood sacrifice be carried out among women with no men present. In the list of expenses for the Thesmophoria in the archives at Delos, provision is made for the post of butcher-sacrificer-cook, a *mageiros,* hired for the time of the festival for a fee of four obols, at a cost less than the wood needed for the sacrifice.[95] It is unlikely that the mere preparations for a banquet[96] would justify the presence of a *mageiros* of the other sex at the Thesmophoria. There undoubtedly would have to be more serious reasons for a man to penetrate the city forbidden to males: reasons of state, or rather of the city, which good fortune has allowed us to glimpse in the form of an inscription. Coming from a temple dedicated to Demeter at Mylasa in Caria, a statute from the third century B.C.[97] specifies—after recalling that the traditional ceremonies should take place "as the women have decided"—that there must be no male in the ceremonies, and in the subsequent line enjoins the man who slaughters the victims to leave the site as soon as his task is accomplished.[98]

In this instance, the *mageiros* is no longer the vague character who endlessly moves among the three roles of butcher, cook, and sacrificer.[99] The man who slips into the midst of the women has only one act to carry out: to slaughter, to shed blood, to slit the victim's throat with the knife, the *makhaira.* The only male among these women who are jealously intent on protecting their own company is in the literal and technical sense a cutthroat, a *sphageus,* an ephemeral functionary but mentioned in several inscriptions,[100] darting out of the shadows to execute an task that is brief but capital, since it involves the appropriation of the instrumental weapon in the blood sacrifice. Nothing is at stake other than the maintenance of the male privilege to shed blood at a time that it seems most threatened by a ritual order, that of the Thesmophoria, which calls both for the banning of males and the inauguration of a society of women having the high power to sacrifice animal victims.

There is no contradiction between the furtive presence of a slaughterer deputized by the male city to penetrate into the females' fortified camp and the vision of an assembly of furies brandishing knives and skewers, wounding Aristomenes with the best of the Messenians or castrating king Battus. Far from contradicting the stories circulating about the female "slaughterers" of the Thesmophoria, the practice indicated by epigraphic evidence supports them in its way. Each story must be read in the context of the other, as two forms of the same uneasiness that wells up during this month of sowing. The prudence displayed by the city in giving the task of slaughterer only to one of its own, who, moreover, is immediately dismissed, is equalled by the fear of death the cloistered women of the Thesmophoria foster among men.

If we go back to the story of a king overly curious about feminine mysteries, the spectacle that the priestesses reveal to Battus indeed offers nothing mysterious:[101] a commonplace sacrificial scene, as can be seen every day in any Greek city. The discrepancy between Battus' desire and what it cost him to be so mistreated is not innocent. In the temple of the Thesmophoria there are objects forbidden (*arrhēta*) to men, which males cannot see or touch.[102] These are the very objects that, according to Herodotus, Timo, the captive Greek minor priestess of the Demeter of Paros, urges Miltiades to come see and take in his hands if he wishes to overcome the besieged town that resists him. The good king Battus has no access to the intimate mysteries; the crevices in the ground, the sexual organs made of hardened dough, the secret acts remain hidden. On the contrary, instead of glimpsing what the other sex most jealously guards, the master of Cyrene sees a spectacle in which women act like ordinary men. But the ban violated by his mere presence transforms the king with the curious eye into the witness of a more hidden and surely more fascinating violence: a violence marked on Battus' own person, castrated and shorn of the very thing that, in the irony of the account, marked him as the other, apart from the society of women. But in this way, beyond the private misfortune of an indiscreet male, the warlike fury that mysteriously broods in the female race is revealed.

All these narratives about the Thesmophoria only concern establishing the identity of women. Each matron, each wife given to Demeter, is changed into an Amazon, armed in the fortress of the *Thesmophorion*. This mask or role comes from her very resemblance to a masculine world whose political conduct and alimentary practices she imitates in a collegial way. She both resembles the male and is hostile to the male race, according to the double meaning of a Homeric epithet reserved for the Amazons, *antianeirai*.[103] These women are "Demetrian" Amazons, but they are all the more threatening because the political power they hold in the heart of the city puts them in a position to repeat the tyranny of ancient Libya. Instead of waging war against men, the women of the country to which tradition exiles the child Athena, virgin and warrior,[104] had carefully reversed masculine and feminine roles. Keeping the magistratures and administration of common affairs for themselves, they relegate their husbands to domestic tasks such as childcare, without leaving them the right to speak or the slightest political responsibility.[105] For each assembly of women carries the potential for the same danger. Proof of this can be seen in the festival of the *Skira,* from which males are once again banned. We know how the Athenian women take advantage of the situation to decide perfidiously among themselves to decree the takeover of the affairs of the city and impose upon the men constitutional reforms whose advantages are set forth in Aristophanes' *Ecclesiazusae*.[106] In this case the gynocracy arises out of transvestism, which seems to belong to the ritual context of the *Skira:*[107] to act the man effectively one must wear a beard and a cloak.[108] Inversely, at the Thesmophoria, the city of women is set up in the very space where the most specific virtues of the mature female sex are articulated: she is established, rooted in her status of lawful and fertile wife.

For the faithful of Demeter Thesmophorus bear the ritual name of *Melissai,* Bees,[109] after the insect that symbolizes the conjugal virtues. Woman-emblem of the domestic virtues, the bee, faithful to her husband and the mother of legitimate children, rules over the intimate space of the house, taking care of the conjugal wealth without ever abandoning a conduct of reserve and decency (*sōphrosunē* and *aidōs*). In this way she combines the functions of a wife with those of a superintendent who is neither gluttonous nor prone to drinking or sleeping and who obstinately ignores the romantic prattling preferred by womenfolk. Furthermore, the Bee-Woman can be recognized by a pure and chaste life based on a strictly vegetarian diet. She puts the hunt and the carnivorous life behind her with the invention of honey, which wrests humanity from its cannibalistic fate. She rejects all contact with anything that rots, whether meat or spilled blood. Now, these Bee-Women are trained, through the discipline of a ritual, to assume among themselves the entire responsibility for a blood sacrifice of an alimentary type, offering to Battus a spectacle that is both familiar in its similarity to scenes of daily life and disquietingly strange.

For if the woman-sacrificer can appeal to the authority of an institutional model and practice—even if they are subject to certain adjustments—her "slaughterer's" mask transforms the reassuring image of a society of Bee-Women into a hallucinatory vision in which peaceful wives, entrusted by the city with male hopes for reproduction, are suddenly changed into armed furies whose unanimous violence pitilessly confuses edible animal victims with the sexual vigor of the king, the supreme representative of the "other" city. But this is also the phantasm of the male political body; for these are the same celebrants of the Thesmophoria whose purity is praised by the city, whose conjugal virtues are vaunted but whose worst excesses are also feared, since every precaution is taken in statutory practice to forbid female society from taking up the instruments of sacrifice and making them into the weapons of a war that would be waged inevitably against the male sex.

In the same society other mythic configurations, which are not governed by a festival framework, echo the same ambivalent figure of the slaughterer-wife. Two of them in particular reveal a major orientation of the Greek imagination so hounded by the feminine. First are the tales of the Danaids.[110] Traditions from Argos depict the daughters of Danaus in an aquatic setting extending from the waters of the ocean to the new springs that bring fertility to the thirsty soil. This context includes the water of the first sacrifice carried out by the Danaids and their father, a ritual water that douses the initial fire of Phoroneus and prefigures the water of the nuptial bath carried by the same procession of maidens when, according to custom, they open the bloody ceremony of the animal sacrifice. Now, the fate of the Danaids is sealed at the conjunction of two contrasting acts: the slaying of their husbands on their wedding night in the marital bed and, according to Herodotus,[111] the foundation of the ritual of Demeter Thesmophorus in the wake of the ordering of the world of Argos, where the distinction of female status goes along with Hera's double sovereignty over water and marriage.

The other configuration is condensed in the killing of Orpheus, as both shown in vase paintings and narrated in scattered accounts.[112] A man, alone and unarmed, is surrounded by a band of women. The cithara player whose voice calms the fiercest warriors is slain, torn to pieces by women, the whole "female race" led on by the madness of Dionysus or driven into a fury by the disdain of which females are the object, a disdain manifested by the founder of a way of life that rejects both meat and women in order to find the honeyed life of the beginning. And the pure man who shuns blood sacrifices and everything that evokes death and bloodshed is murdered by the "slaughterers" armed with mattocks, earth rammers, and sickles, but also with weapons suitable for political sacrifices: knives, long skewers, and the double ax. Just as the Danaids stained with the blood of their husbands are the founders of the Thesmophoria, the murderesses of Orpheus are, from one standpoint, wives led astray into blood sacrifice.[113]

Finally, if it were necessary to suggest a focal element that would be the most striking or fascinating image from the Greek point of view, it would undoubtedly be a woman covered with blood, like those who have reacted to the male desire to see, so urgent in Battus. The bloodstained woman who causes the blood of others to flow is herself a body that, like a stabbed beast, bleeds. And in Greek culture the comparison is explicit. When Aristotle in the *Historia Animalium* observes that at puberty the flow called the "period" takes place, he goes on to say that the blood then runs "like that of an animal that has just been stabbed" (*neosphakton*).[114] The phenomenon of menstruation is not ignored by the Thesmophoria, which commands Demeter's women to lie for three days on litters woven out of branches of *agnus castus*, a willow-like tree whose virtues are doubly precious because it tempers sexual desire and favors the flowing of the menses,[115] thereby confirming that the body of the legitimate wife is in a state of fecundity—a fecundity that is all the more assured because the female body is kept away from sexual pleasure. In a certain way, even before the sacrifice, blood flows ritually in the Thesmophoria, evoking with the blood shed as the animal is killed the distress at seeing the blood of life that fecundates mix in the same body with the blood of death and war. And this fear, which attributes homicidal—or "androcidal"—projects to the most domestic of women is periodically rekindled. It is reborn in the contradiction manifest in a festival in which women among themselves are assuredly the exemplary "lawful wives" of citizens but in which a city, now the exclusive property of women, at last possesses the weapons of sacrifice and thereby threatens the "other" city—all the more so because the strictly male prerogative to kill and slaughter has fallen into the hands of the best of the race of women.

SIX

The Feast of the Wolves, or the Impossible City

Marcel Detienne and Jesper Svenbro

> Nine wolves and a tenth one slaughtered some sheep. The tenth one
> was greedy . . .; he said: "I will divide them for you. There are nine
> of you, and so one sheep will be your joint share. Therefore, I being
> one, shall take the nine. This shall be my share."
>
> Samuel N. Kramer, *History Begins at Sumer,*
> 2d ed. (London, 1961), 185.

"ODIOUS animal, harmful while alive, useless when dead. . . . In all
manners disagreeable, having a lowly expression, frightful voice, un-
bearable odor, perverse disposition, and ferocious habits. . . ." Clearly, the
author of the article "Wolf" in the *Grand Dictionnaire universel du dix-
neuvième siècle* does not like the carnivore and goes to the point of malign-
ing it even after death. "Its flesh is foul. Only wolves willingly eat wolf
meat"—a statement in which zoological knowledge is distorted by a feel-
ing of reprobation so violent that it seems odd in a society in which the
wolf, driven back and thwarted by the growth of large cities, is already
nothing more than the symbolic animal of nursery stories and Perrault's
fairy tales. But this disdain—if not simply idiosyncratic—may be the sign
of primal fears and terrors belonging to an earlier time.

Surely nothing is more out of place than this estimation in view of the
high esteem in which the Greeks seem to hold the wolf, an animal that
they, unlike the arrogant writer quoted above, knew from long experience
in a society where the urban habitat was a negligible entity amid great
wooded and mountainous regions. There is no Ysengrin, the hoaxed
noble, in the bestiaries and traditional tales giving shape to a history that
remains almost unchanged from the world of Odysseus to the first centuries of the Christian era.[1]

The wolf's canonical virtues are enumerated in Aristotle's zoology: he
is as fierce (*agrios*) as the ox is placid; as cunning (*epiboulos*) as the boar is
stupid; nobly bred (*gennaios*)[2] but not the equal of the lion, who is the
most noble of all beasts.[3] Like the lion, who stands out from all the rest

148

for its courage and generosity, the wolf is an animal-emblem for a world as warlike as it is aristocratic. The war these two animals wage is made up of cynegetic exploits, but while the lion hunts in a solitary manner, the wolf is passionately fond of the collective life.[4] In epic similes, the wolf is almost always mentioned in the plural. Absent from the aristocratic tests in which two champions, each with a lengthy genealogy, confront each other, the wolf is present in the confrontations that hurl Trojans and Achaians together. "Like wolves they sprang upon one another, and each man went after his man."[5] This is the work of war at its best, in which one goes straight for the enemy without thinking of flight, charging like wolves and moving like reapers in a line from one end of the field to the other, making the javelins fall thick and fast.[6] Phalanx against phalanx, troop against troop, wolves travel in bands to hunt and in packs to make war. When Patroclus puts on Achilles' unlucky armor in the light of the flames already devouring the Greek ships, all the men in the contingent prepare to fight: the Myrmidons are likened to "flesh-tearing wolves, their hearts full of a prodigious courage; who in the mountains tear the flesh and then devour a great horned stag. The jowls of every one are red with blood—then they go all in a pack to lap with their lean tongues the surface of the black water that flows from a dark spring, all the while spitting forth the murderers' blood, their bellies weighed down but their hearts always fearless."[7] This has the efficacy of analogy: the Myrmidons have yet to plunge into battle, and already the wolves are sated, gorged with blood; the great torn stag is devoured. The feast is over, and the pack, reddened with blood, takes off again.

But to the wolf's valor are added intelligence and an enterprising spirit.[8] A warrior's virtues, which Xenophon puts forth for a somewhat hesitant cavalry commander to incite him to surprise the enemy, determine his movements and do not allow any opportunity for advantage to pass. Wolves know how to hunt unprotected prey; they furtively make off with things found in shadowy places. If the prey is too well guarded, they "order some members of their troop to fend off the guards while others seize the victim." Or when a dog arrives in pursuit, the wolf attacks if he is the stronger. But if he is not in a position of strength, the wolf retreats after slaying his prey. Such habits prove that plundering wolves are capable of reflection, that they hunt with intelligence.[9] But unlike the fox and the kite, insidious creatures, plunderers who work in darkness, the wolf like the falcon makes his catch in broad daylight; he attacks in the open with the boldness of a brigand.[10] He rushes straight at his enemy, even if afterwards he is able to conceal his tracks in endless twistings and turnings.[11]

Night hunts are the affair of the fox. Wolves on the other hand practice a collective hunt that is so well socialized that more than one narrative endows them with a cynegetic behavior that is eminently cultural, as if they hunted with nets or on the run or led trained hunting dogs.[12] But it is a hunt that runs counter to man's interests, focusing particularly on herds of ruminants: sheep, goats and cattle, in other words, the domestic species whose reproduction has been mastered by humans for their own food supply. Wolves wage a cruel and vicious war against these species that fills the pages of Aesop's fables.[13]

Greek wolves are not only capable of comprehending the relationship between war and hunting, they are also excellent operators in the political arena, or, more precisely, on its outskirts, where warlike behavior and hunting practices crisscross in a hidden tracery resembling the written draft of a social contract. One of Aesop's fables says, "A wolf, having become the general (*stratēgēsas*) of the other wolves, established laws (*nomous etaxe*) for everyone stating that he would place every prize that each one took while hunting in a common lot (*eis meson*) and give each one an equal share (*merida isēn*). In this way, one would never again see wolves reduced to starvation eating each other. But an ass stepped forward and shaking his mane said, 'It's a fine thought that the wolf's heart has inspired in him. But how is it that you yourself have hidden your loot from yesterday in your den? Bring it to the community (*eis meson*) and share it (*apomerisas*).' The wolf, abashed, abolished his laws."[14] Where does this "strategist" turned lawmaker come from? If wolves make war, it is most often by temperament and in a spontaneous way that seals the solidarity of the pack. Another of Aesop's fables contrasts wolves and dogs on this point: dogs are the doubles of wolves, which is all the more haunting because the canine race is in man's camp and entrusted with protecting the coveted herds. "One day hatred broke out between the wolves and the dogs. The dogs elected a Greek dog as their general (*stratēgos*). He was in no hurry to enter into combat, despite the violent threats from the wolves. 'Do you know,' he said to them, 'why I am temporizing? It is because it is always a good idea to think before acting. You others, you are all of the same breed and the same color, but our soldiers have varied customs and each has a homeland he is proud of. Even our color is not one and the same (*mia kai isē*) for all; some are black, others red, others white or grey. How could I lead people to war who are not in agreement and are alike in no way (*mē homoia*)?"[15]

The cultural diversity that afflicts the dogs down to the color of their coats compels them to pick a war chief lucid enough to appreciate the difficulties of the enterprise but doubtless too inclined to take pride in the diversity of canine species to accomplish great victories over such a fearsome adversary. In confrontation the wolves are as one: same breed, same color, alike in all ways; and this uniformity in some way dispenses them from needing a leader to guide them. Their perfect discipline, based on "likeness," is evocative of another one, one revealing the cultural landscape surrounding the assembly of wolves: the formation of the hoplitic type, with its interchangeable units in which everyone is defined as an element like all the others—in equipment, behavior, and even in assigned position.[16] It is "likeness" that provides the framework for the plan for a society laid out by a nomothetic wolf. For the double reference to the *center* as that which is shared and as egalitarian and isonomic distribution defines a social space both circular and central, in which the position of each is reciprocal and reversible with respect to a central point.[17] To place something "in the middle" is the act on which egalitarian practices are based, whose field of application extends in the warriors' world to voting assemblies, the organization of funeral games, and the sharing of loot.[18] The wolf who takes the role of the lawmaker amid his peers at first does nothing other than make explicit, by making it public, a procedure whose efficacity is evidenced by the epic tradition. Wealth to be shared belongs to all and is placed in common by the mere fact of being put "in the middle," in the center of the group of fellows or equals. But the wolf lays this egalitarian practice down as a rule intended to change social relations in a world of predators and flesh-eaters. His statement in Aesop's story alludes most strikingly to the political proclamations that abolished tyranny and called for the foundation of the isonomic city nearly everywhere in the sixth century B.C.

More exactly, the wolf of the fable even in his misfortune evokes the famous attempt of a contemporary of Anaximander, Maeandrius of Samos. At the death of Polycrates, tyrant of the city, Maeandrius called together an assembly of all the citizens to tell them:

> As you know yourselves, I am the one who has received Polycrates' scepter and all his power; and today the time has come to rule over you. But on my part, as much as I can I will avoid doing what I blame others for doing. For Polycrates did not have my approval when he ruled as a despot over men who were his equals (*homoiōn*), and no one else who acts that way will have it either. Now Polycrates has fulfilled his destiny; and I put the power in common (*es meson*) and proclaim equality (*isonomiēn*) for you. However, I deem it fair that I receive some

advantages (*gerea*): let six talents from Polycrates' wealth be set aside for me; and in addition to that, I lay claim for myself and my descendants in perpetuity the priesthood of Zeus the Liberator.

After this fine speech a certain Telesarchus came forward and asked to speak: "You're not worthy of governing us, either, you baseborn plague. You ought instead to account for the money you have had your hands on." And Maeandrius realized that if he surrendered the power, another would become tyrant in his place.[19]

The mishap that befell Polycrates' successor was the same one that struck the nomothetic wolf. He hardly finishes his proclamation when an ass steps forward to ask to speak in the name of the populace he represents in the fable.[20] This industrious private citizen, shaking his mane, denounces the fine legislator who grants himself privileges while announcing the happy arrival of the equal distribution of goods. This confrontation is a strange one, particularly since it takes place on the island of Samos—also familiar to Aesop[21]—but this alone cannot exhaust the symbolism of the wolf longing for the city.

Behind the nomothetic and the strategic sides of the wolf, each equally ephemeral, another side can be seen, one absent in this fable but clearly shown in the bestiaries, along with other fables of Aesop. Whether the spoils of war or the kill from the hunt, there is no difference: the procedure for dividing the bounty does not change. The same isonomic act appears in the alimentary order implied by the practice of hunting in the fable of the wolves and also among human predators when, following the wolves' example, they wage a war of depredation. In the story of the Dioscuri and the Apharetidae, they steal great herds together in Arcadia. The task falls to Idas, one of the sons of Aphareus, to divide the booty among the four plunderers. Immediately he takes an ox, cuts it into four portions, and says that whoever eats the first portion will receive half the spoils and the other half will go to whoever eats the second. Without waiting he eats the portions, gulping down his brothers' share along with his own and then vanishing with the herds. The spoils of war or the hunt are only placed in common through a seemingly egalitarian meal—four shares are foreseen—distorted, however, by the quickness and voracity of the first diner.[22]

The eating of equal portions is the table conduct that the author of the *Sophists at the Dinner Table,* Athenaeus, situates in a history of the human species going from violence toward equality. The first men were rapacious:

"Since they did not have food in abundance, the moment it appeared they all threw themselves upon it together, seized it by force, and took it away from those who had it, so that with the disorder (*akosmia*), murders (*phonoi*) also took place."[23] But from Homer to Plutarch over nearly ten centuries, the egalitarian meal, via sacrifices and public banquets, functions as an institutional practice conjoined with the social relationships that underlie the isonomic figure of the city.[24] In the midst of the group of warriors who are "fellows," as in the shared meals of the Spartans and Cretans, each receives an equal portion of the available food, i.e., the food placed in the center and offered to the community—food that by virtue of having been "put in the middle" is necessarily meant to be equally divided.[25]

By proposing to his fellows that the results of their hunt be shared in common so that each receives an equal part, the wolf-lawmaker is not confusing administrative problems with affairs of state. He knows for a fact that the social contract is first of all a culinary operation. And in this field the wolf is an expert. The information in the bestiary leaves no doubt as to his competence. In another of Aesop's fables, the ass, the eternal partner, has only his wit to thank for keeping him from being the material for the transaction that makes the wolf so fearsome. "An ass, passing by in a field and seeing a wolf approach him, pretended to limp. The wolf, coming closer, asked him why he was limping. He answered that he had stepped on a thorn while stepping over a hedge and asked the wolf to remove it first; afterwards the wolf could eat him without cutting his mouth while chewing. The wolf let himself be persuaded. While he was lifting up the ass' hoof and concentrating on the shoe, the ass knocked his teeth out with a kick in the face. And the wolf said in his pain, 'I deserved it, for why, having learned the butcher's trade (*mageirikēn tekhnēn*) from my father, did I want to try medicine?'"[26] When he says he learned the culinary art from his father, the wolf is being modest, for he is a born chef. Wolves inherit the culinary art from their fathers. Aesop suggests this in another story, this time with a kid replacing the ass. "A kid, fallen behind the flock, was being pursued by a wolf. He turned around and said to him, 'I know very well, wolf, that I am meant to be your supper; but so that I do not die without any glory, take your flute and make me dance.' While the wolf was playing and the kid dancing, the dogs, alerted, ran up and chased the wolf away. The latter, turning around, said to the kid, 'That was well done, for I am the butcher (*makellarios*) and I had no need to play the flute.'"[27] The flute-playing invited by the kid is not inappropriate, for the wolf disguised as a flute player has not left his own realm entirely.

The aulete belongs to the same procession as the *mageiros,* the butcher-sacrificer; he has a part in all blood and food sacrifices. But the wolf's error is to confuse two very distinct, albeit related, arts. And indeed in Sparta, as Herodotus affirms,[28] like the herald, flutists and butcher-sacrificers inherit their role from their fathers, so that the flutist is the son of a flutist and the *mageiros,* the son of a *mageiros.* By letting himself be tempted by the art of the flute, the wolf has put himself in a bad position to fulfill his role as butcher. His supper escapes him, even though he by the grace of nature is the best of chefs and the most skilled of butchers.

The wolf is so skilled for a number of reasons. The first reason—and doubtless the most important for the wolf's career—is that he is not content to kill his prey but bleeds it (*sphazein*).[29] When the wolf takes a sheep, he acts, says Aristotle, with intelligence. Like the weasel, the wolf slits the victim's throat.[30] His powerful jaw acts as a knife. It is the knife that makes the butcher. But the butcher doubles as a cook no less well endowed by nature. The wolf is not only a cutting pair of jaws; his belly has all the properties of a natural caldron and oven. Plutarch's *Quaestiones conviviales* simply had to deal with this subject. Indeed, "why is the flesh of sheep killed by wolves more succulent and why does their wool engender vermin?" Patrocles, one of Plutarch's nephews, had a theory concerning the first question that his uncle considered most apt: "The wild beast's bite tenderizes the meat, for the wolf's vital breath is hot and fiery (*purōdes*) to the point that it softens and dissolves the hardest bones in his stomach (*koilia*). This is also why the corpses of animals killed by wolves rot more quickly than others."[31] What emerges here are three aspects of the wolf's culinary talents: (1) he is a fire-bearing animal, whose igneous virtue is revealed in three ways: the flame that glints from his pupils at night,[32] his affinities with Rage, Lyssa, the violent fire of his fury;[33] and finally, the series of puns on wolf and light that the ancient lexicographers weave; (2) his breath alone tenderizes meat, and with respect to his victim the wolf occupies the same position as the fig tree with respect to sacrificial meats; indeed, the victims hung from the branches of a fig tree rapidly become tender because they receive the benefit of the succulence offered by a botanical species whose internal heat performs the same operation that the wolf performs with his breath;[34] and (3) the fire bearer likewise possesses in the form of a belly a marvelous kettle in which the meats on which he feeds are stewed. His pot is so efficient that it melts even the hardest of bones. In other words, this cook-butcher leaves no leftovers, and he gulps down into his paunch even the long bones, the *mēria* reserved for the gods in men's sacrifices.

There is one final proof of the wolf's mastery of the butcher's art: he possesses the art of carving and apportioning the meat. To wit, when two wolves seize a sheep at the same time, as they are depicted on a Boeotian terra cotta from the sixth century B.C.,[35] and they divide it (*diaireisthai*) with a snap of the jaws, the animal is split into two equal parts (*eis isa*).[36] The wolf's mouth spontaneously carves pieces of the same weight. Its jaws instinctively create equal portions.

It is indubitably this skill, which is part of the wolf's natural vocation in the arts of the butcher and chef, that has opened the doors to a political career for him. A technician at carving meat into equal shares, the wolf, because of his unrivaled mastery of the egalitarian topology, is the bearer of the isonomic model that transforms the community meal into the productive and reproductive act of political equality.

In reality, the legislating wolf is but the double of the butcher, armed with his extraordinary knife. And this double is not without its dark side. For the nomothete presents his plan for an egalitarian community in order to banish the spectre of forced cannibalism. "In this way, one would never again see wolves reduced to starvation eating each other."[37] This is a cannibalism of the time of origins, which wolves would have had in common with the men of Athenaeus' story in whom violence to the point of murder is brought about only by want and scarcity. But in the world of the wolves—and this is already a highly disturbing shadow—the allelophagia is in the present. It is even ritualized in a procedure that strangely recalls the way in which the wolf-nomothete intends to found a new community. The story may come from the Egyptians. The wolves gather in a circle (*es kuklon*) and begin to run. When one of them, dizzy, begins to lose his balance and stumble, the others fall upon him, tear him to pieces, and then eat him.[38] They only act in this way, it is true, during times when game is rare. But this regulated cannibalism takes place in a circular space. And the wolf called upon to provide his fellows with dinner is the one who, leaving the round of animals touching head to tail, goes outside of the circle formed by the egalitarian pack. A kind of lottery tempers and socializes the wolves' cannibalism when they are victims of hunger.

Nonetheless, even if at times they are compelled to eat one another among themselves, wolves have a political bent. Although it does not refer to the Arcadian tradition—wherein Lycaon, the wolf-man, invents the first city, Lycosura, "Wolf Mountain," founds the cult of Zeus, and then devotes himself to strange culinary operations[39]—the story of Athamas confirms the wolves' political vocation. The Boeotian hero had sacrificed the children of his first union and killed Learchus, the son from his second union, with an arrow. Hera's anger plunged him into madness, and the exiled and fugitive Athamas received an order from the Delphic oracle to settle only in a country "where wild animals offer him hospitality." After wandering for a long time, one day "he came upon some wolves that were engaged in dividing up portions of sheep (*probatōn moiras nemomenoi*). When they saw Athamas, they fled, leaving behind what they had been dividing. That is where Athamas settled, giving the country the name of Athamantia."[40] After murders that had banished him from the society of men, Athamas can found a city only on the tracks of wolves and by penetrating the socialized space of the egalitarian feast that the meat-eaters had prepared for him in the deep forest. But the story of Athamas received by ferocious animals whose culinary skills bring him out of the wild state is equally revealing of the limitations of the political ability conceded to the wolves. Outlawed and leading the wandering life of a fugitive, Athamas no longer belongs to the world of men. Hunted down, pursued by his fellow men, he is condemned to a life so wild that the Greeks compare it to that of a wolf.[41] But it is the life of a wolf separated from the pack: the loner more likely to be a man-eater, as Aristotle notes when the *Historia animalium* insists on the asocial character of the wolf in the singular.[42] Athamas, changed into a wolf for killing a man, only recovers his human condition at the wolves' table. The feast of the carnivores dividing up the sheep's flesh according to the rules of the culinary art permits the dehumanized guest to return to the city by crossing the culinary and sacrificial space of an isonomic meal. But the moment Athamas emerges, the wolves disappear; the pack flees and breaks up, abandoning the "table" it had just set to fulfill the oracle. At the height of their social activity, the wolves withdraw before the founder of the city. They return to the wild life that Athamas gives to them at the end of his own life as a wolf. In short, these carnivores, which nature has so well equipped, lack only the table or the know-how to stay there. For the conclusion is the same, in the adventure of Athamas as well as in Aesop's fable: wolves shall not enter the city.

Another part of the tradition explains the wolf's failure to found a city and why he is doomed to remain on the outskirts of the political space. The cannibals of Egyptian history, as well governed as they seem, are sure to recall the cruel figure of the wolf in Plato's *Republic*, when the question of the origin of tyranny is raised at the end of the genealogical history of the "four constitutions."[43] The democratic state precipitates the progress of evil that oligarchical man had been restraining with great difficulty. The people soon choose a "protector." "And how does the protector begin to change into a tyrant? Obviously, isn't it when this fine protector begins to do what is recounted in the legend of the Lycaean Zeus in Arcadia?" And Socrates informs his listener:

> When one has tasted human entrails cut up and mixed with those of other victims, one is inevitably changed into a wolf. . . . Likewise, when the protector of the people, finding the multitude devoted to his orders, can no longer refrain from shedding the blood of the men of his tribe (*emphuliou haimatos*); when, by false accusations, a method cherished by his fellows, he drags them before the tribunals and stains his conscience by having them slain; he tastes with his tongue and impious mouth the blood of his kin (*phonou xungenous*), whom he exiles and kills; and he hints at the abolition of debts and the repartition (*anadasmon*) of lands. From that moment isn't it necessary and like a law of destiny for such a man either to perish at the hands of his enemies or to become a tyrant and be changed into a wolf? [44]

A political reading of the Lycaean ritual: the wolf is the man who tastes human flesh and drinks the blood of his fellows. But regulated cannibalism is no longer appropriate. A wild and unrestrained animal, the wolf-tyrant does not shrink before the horror of any murder (*phonos*) or any food (*brōma*). Isn't he destined to devour his own children? [45] He is an outlaw, and by his bloodthirsty voracity the destroyer of the city. This "tyrannical" wolf is not unknown to the Greek bestiary. He is the antithetical figure of the wolves who live in packs (*agelēdon*) [46] but, for all that, not numbered among the "political" animals such as the bee, the wasp, the ant, the crane, and man. [47] There is an asocial aspect to the wolf [48] that places him alongside birds of prey, for "birds with curved talons never live in flocks." [49] It is perhaps no accident that the wolf-man whose movements are depicted on the medallion of an Etruscan plate is endowed with forelimbs that end in the talons of a bird of prey. [50] But the wolf that serves as example to the tyrant is not only a loner, outside of any society. More than asocial, he is the mortal enemy of any community. A proverbial phrase says it all: "wolf's friendship" means disunity, the negation of all common interest, [51] as if in this animal—otherwise such a remarkable butcher-cook and so clever at dividing up the portions—there were a fault, a secret vice that prevents him from working with his fellows in a common enterprise. [52]

This ambiguity about the wolf can be seen in another proverb that tells of meat and distribution: "The wolf distributes the meat. (This is said) of someone who wants more than his fair share (*pleonektein*) and (who wants to) give." [53] At first this seems a misreading, and one is tempted to correct the text of the proverb by placing a negation in the second clause of the sentence to ascribe to the wolf, desirous of "having more than his share," the intention of *not* giving and thus keeping everything for himself. This certainly is a misreading, for it leaves out what seems paradoxical but is merely the expression of the very contradiction inherent in the wolf functioning as "distributor." If the wolf "distributes the meat," it is in order to give it, as is implied by the function of *kreanomos*, in which the wolf is in the role of the carving master and egalitarian distributor.[54] But the same animal, with a *makhaira* that makes him the technician of the most equitable distribution, suffers from greediness. It is the need to "have more than his fair share," i.e., the *pleonexia*[55] that compromises the plan of Aesop's lawmaker; hasn't he secreted away in his den yesterday's kill, while proposing to all to share the spoils in common in order to give everyone an equal part? The following must also be noted: what the wolf sets aside for himself is not the "choice morsel," the share of honor attributed to the king, the bravest warrior, or the wise man according to the principle of "geometric" (or proportional)[56] equality; it is his own loot that he intends to remove from the isonomic distribution whose gospel he is spreading. Thus it seems that the wolves' spontaneous isonomy is undermined by a congenital "pleonexia." The city that the wolves create each time they begin to move their jaws is doomed from the outset to tyranny and cannibalism.

But it is necessary to take a more careful look at this strange contradiction in the wolf. Dolon the Cunning, clothed in a wolfskin, goes off alone in the night to hunt; he is the *"cutthroat* who slinks ahead" (*pedostibēs sphageus*).[57] For a master of decapitation such as Dolon—who moreover will lose his own head—the technique of the wolf who seizes his prey by the throat is undoubtedly the best. But the cutthroat, or slaughterer, the one who spills the blood, is also the name of a character who at times crosses the sacrificial arena.[58] In truth, he moves furtively; he is only a paid functionary, the quick mask of a *mageiros*-sacrificer when, for an instant, he is identified with the movement of the cutthroat. But however brief his intervention, his name alone is enough to evoke strange fears, which are uttered in the same breath as the cries of civil war and the city torn asunder. The word *sphagē*—a verbal noun[59]—is like a live wound. In the anatomical vocabulary it refers to the throat, but one torn open.[60] And from the time of Solon up to the orators of the fourth century, *sphagē* means above all the blood that flows in fratricidal massacres, in wars between rival factions, in coups d'état, and following "changes in constitution." In the decree of Patroclides referred to by Andocides, *sphageus* is the technical term reserved for someone who commits murder in the course of a civil war. And for the cutthroat who sheds the blood of his own kind, the same decree foresees capital punishment—just as it does for the tyrant, the cutthroat's twin, and the equally bloodthirsty wolf.[61]

The city does not underestimate the threat of confusion between the horrors of civil war and the controlled act that spills the blood of a sacrificial victim. To avert this it seems to have required, in practice, a strict separation of war and sacrifice by banning the presence of arms from the space reserved for the sacrificial ritual, a compelling rule that is singularly dramatized by an episode of the battle of Plataea. Before doing battle, it is customary to sacrifice an animal victim to test the gods' favor on the threshold of the enterprise. The Spartan army, it is well known, never moves without a herd of goats reserved for these tactical sacrifices, which most often take place under the eye of the enemy and to the sound of flutes, which, a moment later if the omens are favorable, will be played by the auletes to accompany the charge of the hoplites.[62] Now, near Plataea, the Lacedaemonians, under the command of Pausanias, launch a maneuver that should enable them to join the forces of the other Greeks; at that moment Mardonius and the Persian army fall upon them. "Seeing what was happening, Pausanias stopped the march and ordered everyone to take his combat post." It was impossible to begin the battle before making a sacrifice. Since he was not obtaining favorable omens,

> Pausanias ordered the Lacedaemonians to put their shields at their feet and hold still, eyes upon him, without defending themselves against any of their enemies, while he himself offered another sacrifice. At that moment, the enemy horsemen charged—their arrows were already arriving and some Spartans were hit. . . . The situation was critical but the soldiers' steadfastness was admirable. They did not try to rebuff the enemy coming upon them. They were waiting for the signal from their deity and their general and allowed themselves to be struck and killed at their posts. According to some writers, the moment that Pausanias sacrificed and was praying somewhat outside the line, a band of Lydians suddenly fell upon him, taking and scattering everything used in the sacrifice. Unarmed, Pausanias and those around him struck them with sticks and whips.[63]

The situation is a difficult: as the soothsayer sacrifices victim after victim, Pausanias in tears implores the gods of Plataea; and the Spartan warriors remain at attention under the blows of the enemy. But what is most surprising is the small circle of men surrounding the soothsayer-sacrificer: when the barbarians come to disturb the progress of the ceremony, Pausanias has no weapon or iron instrument at hand, only the whips and sticks used to lead the herd of goats from which the successive victims are chosen. In the middle of the battlefield and surrounded by all these warriors, the actions of the sacrifice create an "unarmed" space, where the rule forbidding the bearing of weapons is strong enough to be imposed even in such a state of emergency.

It is by relying on respect for the same custom that Polycrates succeeds in taking power on the island of Samos. In the version given by Polyaenus,[64] the coup d'état is prepared under the cover of a procession followed by a sacrifice in honor of Hera.

> While the Samians were preparing a common sacrifice in Hera's temple—on the occasion of which they had the custom of making an armed procession—Polycrates, using the feast as a pretext, gathered as many arms as possible and ordered his brothers Syloson and Pantagnostus to take part in the procession. Afterwards, when the Samians were to make their sacrifice, the majority of them put down their arms to attend the libations and prayers in front of the altars. Syloson, Pantagnostus, and their men, who had kept their arms, began to kill everyone, one after the other, calling out words of encouragement to each other. Having gathered those who in the town were taking part in the coup, Polycrates had the strategic points of the city occupied while he waited for his brothers and their allies with their arms to arrive with all speed from the temple. Reinforcing the acropolis, the 'Astypalaëa'—with a wall, he asked the Naxian tyrant Lygdamis for soldiers and was henceforth tyrant of Samos.

The rule is the same: no arms within the temple precincts. But it is by violating this rule that Polycrates asserts his tyranny even before he exercises it from the height of the acropolis. With a handful of men—"some fifteen hoplites," according to Herodotus[65]—he slaughters his fellow citizens, who had come unarmed to offer a sacrifice on Hera's altar. This is the conduct of a wolf-man, who sheds the "blood of the men of his tribe" and then exiles his brother Syloson, kills his brother Pantagnostus, and thereby sheds the "blood of his kin." On Samos, where Meaendrius has already shown us the nomothetic wolf's need for "having more than his fair share," Polycrates takes on the wolf's guise for his celebratory entrance; but this time it is at the sacrifice. In the middle of the sanctuary, the discreet cutthroat of the sacrificial scene is transformed into a bloody tyrant and instigator of civil war, taking upon himself the two crimes for which the decree of Patroclides will demand the death penalty in the name of the city.

By revealing the fine line that separates sacrifice from murder, Polycrates' "putsch" also poses the question of the status of the *makhaira*, the knife that is the necessary instrument for carrying out a blood sacrifice—a fundamental question that makes the city buzz, especially when voices are raised to denounce the collusion of murderers and sacrificers on all sides. The staging of the feast of the Murder of the Working Ox, the Bouphonia, brings the official response. In the judgment given after the victim's death, the young girls who have brought the water used to sharpen the ax and the knife state that those who have sharpened the instruments are more guilty than they; the latter, in turn, indicate the one who held out the ax; he points to the slayer, who has nothing left to do but charge the *makhaira*, which remains voiceless, and with good reason. The question is resolved: the knife is declared to be guilty and is immediately drowned in the sea, which by swallowing up the instrument of death makes it disappear from the political space.[66]

From this point on, it is settled. The sacrificial knife is no longer a weapon but a simple instrument whose presence the ritual strives to make utterly discreet: it is hidden in the basket amid grains of barley mixed with salt.[67] Man's commensality is bought at a price: speak as little as possible of the ax or the knife. But the city's defense system is even more subtle— until it turns against the city itself. The sacrificial knife, the *makhaira*, cannot be a weapon, since it has no place in the Greek armory.[68] The sword, the *xiphos,* yes, but no Greek fights with a knife. It is the barbarians who do so: Thracians, Persians, Colchidians. Undoubtedly, sometimes a degenerate form of combat takes place, for example, at the pass of Thermopylae, when Leonidas' soldiers waged a desperate battle against the Persians. Their lances had been broken for a long time; they were fighting at close range with swords (*xiphesi*), and then, at the last breath, "with knives (*makhairēisi*), fingernails, and teeth."[69] Georges Roux is perfectly right not to make *makhaira* a synonym for *xiphos.* When knives are drawn, there is no longer combat between warriors but a "battle of wild beasts who claw and bite." Carnage, massacre, a veritable "butchery," as we would say, at the opposite of the Greeks. The *makhaira*, the knife, figures both in war and outside of it. It does not evoke the regular combat of the hoplites confronting one another on a defined field but conjures up pitiless massacres, fratricidal murders, and the blood of civil wars—in other words, everything indicated by the word *sphagē*, slaughter.

And it is here that the tables turn. For can one be sure of making a distinction between the sacrificer holding a knife and the wolf with gaping jaws reddened with blood? If the *makhaira* is not a weapon, then the wolf that enters the precincts of the sacrifice is not breaking the rule the city holds so firmly. And in order to slaughter his kind, Polycrates put on the sacrifier's mask. In short, each knife can conceal a wolf. This is a truth that the city keeps from itself but which bursts forth when there is a murder in a temple. The stories of Neoptolemus[70] and Aesop are more serious than the matter of Polycrates. For this time everything happens at Delphi, in the temple of the "prince of the sacrificers," the god "who sharpens the innumerable cutlasses of Delphi and instructs his servants in this office."[71] And, as a biographer of Aesop remarks, when someone comes to sacrifice to Apollo, the Delphians surround the altar, each one carrying a knife, a *makhaira*, under his garments. Once the priest has spilled the blood, slaughtered the victim, and removed the *splankhna*, all those in the circle— and each according to his strength—throw themselves at the victim to carve themselves a piece, so that often the poor fellow who offered the sacrifice has nothing to chew on.[72] Still he is fortunate if he is spared the fate of Aesop or Neoptolemus, sacrifiers transformed into victims and pilgrims stabbed by cutlass-bearers.

At Apollo's banquet in the Delphian lair, commensality gives way to a rapacity in which the city regresses to a time of disorder (*akosmia*) and murder (*phonoi*), where all "hurl themselves at once on the food and take it by force."[73] The voracious circle presided over by the god, himself armed with a knife, displays the reverse of the figure that the city sees in itself at the end of the Ox Game, when "the descendants of the man who stabbed the victim (*episphazein*) are called *Daitroi*, Distributors, because of the feast that followed the division and sharing (*kreanomia*)."[74] No more peaceful commensals sitting down to feast in a city where blood and murder have almost been forgotten but instead cutthroats armed with *makhairai*, who together, impelled by a unanimous voracity, hurl themselves like a band of ravenous wolves on the victim that the priest's ceremonies seemed to have definitively placed within the civilized confines of sacrificial eating. This is a feast that is elucidated by the genealogy of the murderer of Neoptolemus: Machaireus, the son of Daitas.[75] In other words, the priest—who is master of the banquet rather than an equerry wielding a cutting edge, and who carves up the victim, *daitēs*[76]—engenders and leaves behind him a son called Cutthroat or Cutlass. Under the sign of their lord, Apollo,[77] the wolf pack gathers to form the circle of death and violence that Aesop's nomothete claimed to avert. Is this a detail that would stain the "majesty"[78] of the Delphic site? Rather, in this country-side that is shared because it lies outside every city, it constitutes the other scene, pronouncing the truth of the violence on which politics and the social contract are based.

These are stories of wolves on the outskirts of the city, created around the culinary operation on which different characteristics, more or less elaborated, converge: a certain method of slaughtering the victim evokes the knife that opens the sacrificial field and focuses attention on the political horizon, which further develops the homology between wolf and warrior. They are tales that grip the imagination with the threat they harbor of the confusion between war and blood sacrifice. Other tales speak of it openly: the warriors of the bronze race forged the first *makhaira* and ate the first working ox.[79] The original knife was also a sword,[80] and "impious murders" occur with the wars that follow the tyrannies. Aratus in the *Phaenomena* does not mean, as will be said later on in the seventeenth century, that war presided over the birth of the state and the city,[81] but only seeks to point out the figure that never ceases to haunt the political edifice: a type of man whose trade is death and violence while his dominant behaviors are the basis of social life and its egalitarian rules.

Food in the Countries of the Sun

Jean-Pierre Vernant

IN the first lines of the *Odyssey*[1] the poet evokes the episode that will provide the subject of book 12: the death of Odysseus' companions, victims of their own foolishness for having eaten the cattle of *Hēlios Huperiōn*, the All-High Sun, on the island belonging to the god.[2]

In book 3 of the *Histories*, Herodotus in turn introduces us to another solar country.[3] Before launching the expedition he planned against the long-lived Ethiopians (*Makrobioi*), Cambyses sends a band of Ichthyophagian spies to report on the famous *trapeza Hēliou*, the Table of the Sun, said to exist in the land of the Sun inhabited by the Ethiopians. This land is not, like the country of the All-High Sun, characterized by the star at its zenith and farthest removed from man's habitat but, as Homeric tradition notes,[4] marked by the rising or setting Sun. It is situated at this extreme limit of the world where to the east as well as to the west, the route followed by the star indicates the meeting point of land and sky, the place where man and gods join together to feast.[5]

The comparison of these two texts, which seem at first to be completely different, is not justified only by their common reference to a country of the Sun. It can be shown that they apply the same interpretative framework to situations that are the opposite of one another: a classification of foods that establishes, at the midpoint between the dishes reserved for the gods and the rations for animals, the status of properly human foods.

The theme of food is at the heart of the episode in the *Odyssey*. If Odysseus' crew demands to land on the Sun's island despite the warnings of Tiresias and Circe, it is because, wracked with hunger, they desire to eat the meal that they so desperately need after the ordeal of Charybdis and Scylla.[6] Refusing their request, Odysseus seems "made of iron," as if he did not know the need shared by all mortal creatures to restore eroded

In 1972 this analysis was presented at a meeting of the Association des Etudes grecques. A summary is to be found in *Revue des études grecques* 85 (1972): xiv–xvii.

strength by the daily ingestion of food.[7] At last Odysseus cedes to his companions' objurgations, but he sets the condition that they swear not to "kill" the Sun's cattle.[8] These animals are forbidden to men, who have no right to place them under the yoke or make them work, much less to eat them.[9] Not wild, they are not domesticated, either. Because they belong to the divine realm, they are outside or beyond the two categories. Under the gods' care they, like wild animals, lead a perfectly free and idle existence; but unlike them they do not devour each other, living, rather, in peaceful herds on the lands of the Sun. They have the same exceptional beauty that Herodotus, along with Homer, Pindar, and Skylax, attributes to the Ethiopians of the country of the Sun.[10] Like the men of Hesiod's Golden Age, they are free of the knowledge of birth through procreation, growth, aging, and death.[11] Their number and their age remain constant, as do their strength and beauty. Thus their status appears identical to that of Apollo's herd from which, according to Homer's *Hymn,* Hermes steals fifty cows: divine and immortal animals[12] free from the yoke,[13] living in the open[14] as they please, in a pasture never mowed or touched by human hands.[15] With his theft, Hermes takes these cows from the divine world where they belong to the world of men, where they acquire domestic status. According to the terms of the pact that the young god concludes with his elder, Apollo, to settle the quarrel provoked by the theft, Hermes is officially made patron of the herdsman's activity, reigning, whip in hand,[16] over animals that will thereafter be placed in stables[17] and, by reproducing,[18] will expand the herd that had until then remained constant in size. At the same time that he is *Nomios,* head herdsman, the god is *Bouphonos* and *Mageiros,* killer and cook of cattle. By slaying two animals from the herd and cutting up their flesh, he establishes the first sacrifice.

But what the young god can achieve in his intermediary role as a master of exchanges, ordinary mortals have much less right to attempt, since Hermes is careful not to eat the meat he has prepared. If he tasted it, he would become a man; he hangs it from the stable ceiling without touching it.[19] Odysseus' companions, on the contrary, will feast on animals that remain the property of the gods and in no wise have been granted to them.

Homer contrasts this forbidden meat with two types of authorized eating. First, there is the food that defines man's very condition in double opposition to the immortal gods on the one hand[20] and to wild animals, which devour each other raw, on the other[21]—that food being bread and wine.[22] Cultivated products and the fruits of labor are two types of "cooked"[23] food equally distant from raw grasses, that is, animal food and the dried aromatics burned for the gods.[24] Moreover, they form the reserves of foodstuffs the crew has at its disposal, the truly human *biotos*.[25] Second, there are the products of hunting and fishing, the war against animals. Their stores of bread and wine exhausted, the Greeks must resort to this war in order to obtain not terrestrial quadrupeds like cattle but winged airborne creatures and waterborne fish.[26] Up to this point, all is well; the men are within their rights. But with Odysseus away on a walk Eurymachus proposes that in order to avoid the worst of deaths, starvation,[27] they "sacrifice" the cows in a vast hecatomb.[28] From the very outset this sacrifice is void of all religious meaning. Its only end are the victuals. And, instead of being led in procession to the altar and ritually slaughtered as if by their own accord, the cattle are chased, rounded up, and massacred as if they were wild animals.[29] This mingling of sacrifice and hunting, of domestic animals and ferocious beasts, leads to a travesty, a subversion of the sacrifice. Homer employs the ordinary sacrificial vocabulary but stresses the double anomaly that, with the reversal of the values of the rite, makes the cooking a sacrilege and its products uneatable. The crew have no more grains, neither barley nor wheat flour. Lacking these, they use leaves of an oak, a tree that for the Greeks symbolizes the "wild life" in contrast to the cultivated life, which they call the "life of milled grain."[30] Lacking wine for their libations, they make do with simple fresh water.[31] Then they feast. But since the rules of the alimentary game have not been respected, confusion spreads, and marvels take place. The "dead" animals do not cease to be alive. Their hides, the special part neither eaten by men nor burned for the gods but often given to the priest or exposed as a *sēma* of the sacrificial act, continue to move as if the slain animals were still alive.[32] The pieces of flesh on the skewers low, whether they are roasted or still raw, as if the distinction between raw and cooked disappears along with the line between living and dead, when the opposition between wild and domesticated, sacrifice and hunt, is not respected.[33] "A voice was heard, like that of cattle."[34] The *phōnē*, an expression of life, perpetuates the existence of the herd, which by means of this acoustic phantom, this sonic *eidōlon*, continues from beyond the frontier of death to echo on the Sun's island, as it did earlier when they were living.[35] The end is not long in coming. Like the birds and fish they once sought, Odysseus' companions perish by a wild death and disappear without burial beneath the bitter waves.[36]

*

In Herodotus' account the situation is reversed, but the issue of food remains central. Odysseus' crew, debarking at the Sun's island, came to the gods without being invited; and they took what the gods reserved for

themselves. The emphasis was placed on barriers and prohibitions between mortals and Immortals. In the land of the Ethiopians, it is the gods
who come to men to feast with them; the emphasis is on commensality, a
community of food that has not yet been disrupted.[37] Like the Sun's cattle,
Herodotus' Ethiopians live near the gods by virtue of their solar habitat,
their beauty, their justice, and their long life. This quasi-divine status,
which links them with the men of the Golden Age, grants them the "natural" enjoyment of products that the Persians know only through the con-
tortions of a false and refined art.[38] To seduce the Ethiopians and reduce
them to slavery, Cambyses has gifts delivered whose precious character is
also a deception.[39] First of all, he sends cloths dyed purple; but the Ethiopians' skin, burned by the Sun's heat, glows naturally with the dark brilliance of fire.[40] Then there are perfumes; but the Ethiopians, at the opposite
pole of what is rotten, like the gods, exude their own fragrance, the *euōdia*.[41] Last, there are jewels made of gold; but gold, the solar metal, incorruptible in its perfection, is the most common thing in the land of
Hēlios; it is bronze that is lacking.[42] This natural contiguity with the gods
is marked in the Ethiopians' diet. The fable of the Table of the Sun repeats
in another form the Homeric theme of the gods feasting with the flawless
Ethiopians and the Hesiodic myth of the golden race, at the time when
gods and men, still living together, sat at the same tables to partake of
shared banquets before the foundation of the blood sacrifice came to sanc-
tion their separation and difference in diet.[43] It is truly meat that the
Ethiopians eat, but a meat spontaneously produced by the earth in a
meadow, just as barley and grapes were brought forth in the fields during
the Golden Age.[44] In this framework the consumption of the meat excludes the blood sacrifice instead of implying it. The Ethiopians do not
have to slaughter, carve, and cook the animal whose flesh they eat. All
quadrupeds, both wild and domestic, are graciously offered them every
morning in the form of immediately edible food. This food is not only
completely cooked but laid before them in a state of most perfect, complete cooking: fully boiled with nothing raw about it, inside or out.[45]

Forbidden to men, the Sun's cattle were still raw even though they had
been cooked; even though they had been massacred they were still alive;
and their slaughter, compared to the sacrificial rite, was a like a hunt for
wild animals. The quadrupeds of the Table of the Sun are edible without
the need either to sacrifice them, as is done with domestic animals, or to
hunt them, like wild animals. Born out of the earth in the form of fully
prepared food, they are dead, boiled, and cooked at the quick and natural
stage. Instead of lowering the partakers of this meal to a quasi-bestial state,

this confusion between dead and living, cooked and raw, domestic and wild, raises them to the quasi-divine standing of *makrobioi*.[46] To eat the Sun's cattle was to regress to a state below that of normal sacrifice; to eat at the Table of the Sun is to transcend it. But in both cases bread and wine, specifically human foods, are excluded. In the case of Odysseus' companions, it is because they have none: because they lack bread and wine, they come to eating the cattle. With the Ethiopians, it is because they have no need of it; they have free access to a food furnished by the gods that has almost "ambrosian" virtues.[47]

For these eaters of naturally boiled meat, grains, which for ordinary mortals represent the model of dried and cooked vegetables, appear to be a putrid grass, a kind of dung. Whoever eats it must die young.[48] Wine is a different case. A cultivated product like wheat, it is seen, unlike wheat, as a drink made of fire and related to the Sun. Undoubtedly the Homeric epithet for wine, *aithops*, has contributed to this interpretation with its resemblance to the Ethiopians' own name.[49] Without wine, the Persians— and the common run of men—would not be able to *anapherein*, recover their strength, and their existence would be even more ephemeral.[50] But the Ethiopians do not need this fiery liquid with its invigorating properties. They have a water that has naturally the same powers of rejuvenation and longevity as the cultivated fruit of the vine. It is a water of life, a veritable fountain of youth, that they use for all purposes[51] and in which can be easily recognized those ambrosian springs that some traditions situate at the outermost reaches of the world near the river Oceanus. A fragment of Aeschylus describes it in this way: "near Oceanus, the calm water of the Ethiopians, its surface with its bronze gleams, nourisher of all things, where the Sun who sees all eternally restores his immortal body and relieves his steeds' fatigue in the gentle waves of the river's warm mouth."[52]

Soon after their sacrilege, Odysseus' companions perish like animals, dying without funeral rites and leaving no traces, not even a stele. At the end of a long existence, the Ethiopians in death appear exactly as they did while alive, with nothing nauseating or repulsive about them.[53] When the corpse is dry, it is covered with a layer of gypsum (i.e., for the Greeks, calcinated earth) on which the person's appearance is faithfully reproduced. Then the body is placed not underground but inside a funerary stele. This stele is made of stone but not the normal dark and opaque type that is erected over tombs; this stele is made of transparent stone. Light enters and plays freely within; inside it the body is visible as if in daylight, so it offers to the eye the exact resemblance of the dead person.[54] Kept in the houses of their relatives near the town, the dead continue mixing with the living in the form of a palpable image, just as the Sun's cattle continue to haunt their island in the form of an audible *phōnē*. For the *Makrobioi*, as distant from the rotten and the dark as terrestrial creatures can be, the world of death cannot be marked by decomposition and shadow. Even as corpses, the Ethiopians are close to the dry, the burnt, and the luminous. For them as for the Sun's herds, the boundary between life and death is more uncertain, less clearly drawn than it is for ordinary perishable creatures.

One final remark confirms the presence of an alimentary code underlying both the text of Herodotus and the account in the *Odyssey*. In the military expedition that Cambyses in his impious hubris launches against the Ethiopians to enslave them, his soldiers approaching the forbidden country of the Sun regress under the influence of hunger from the human condition to the state of animals.[55] And each stage of this decline is marked by a change in diet. First, like the companions of Odysseus, they take their meals from their stored "victuals" (*sitia*); then they slaughter the beasts of burden that accompany them (*hupozugia*) for food;[56] when none of these remain, they eat grass (*trophē ek gēs*), like animals;[57] finally, like wild animals, they devour one another.[58]

By eschewing civilized food in this radical way, they, like Odysseus' crew, cut the last ties that bind them to the divine world. To eat another to satisfy one's hunger is an act that is no less horrible, no less terrifying in its impiety, than eating the Sun's cattle.[59] In both cases, one ceases to be human.

Self-cooking Beef and the Drinks of Ares

François Hartog

W HAT gods do the Scythians have? What are their relations with them? Or, to put it differently, how do nomads communicate with their gods? The Scythians implicitly and insistently pose the question for the Greeks, "But how can one be a nomad?"* It can be suggested by way of a hypothesis that, in one way or another, the nomadic way of life must leave traces in the divine space, that this way of life must somehow color the relations of the Scythians with their gods. For example, sacrifice: blood sacrifice is fundamental to the city. Through the slaughtering of the animal and the commensality founded upon it, the city recognizes itself as a community of meat-eaters. If sacrifice is linked to the political order of the *polis,* which it both supports and expresses, if it is indeed this "key piece of the religion of the city,"[1] what can sacrifice be among nomads? Seen in this perspective, sacrificial practices thus become a way of inquiring into human groups, of marking distances and suggesting otherness.

But before applying this question to the two chapters Herodotus devotes to sacrifices among the Scythians,[2] let us look at their pantheon. "The only divinities that they consider auspicious (*hilaskontai*) are the following: Hestia in first place, then Zeus and Earth (they think, *nomizontes,* that Earth is the wife of Zeus), then Apollo, Aphrodite Urania, Heracles and Ares. These divinities are recognized (*nenomikasi*) by all Scythians; those called royal Scythians also sacrifice to Poseidon."[3] This pantheon is striking first of all in its poverty; it contains only seven names (eight in the case of the royal Scythians). All barbarian pantheons except that of the Egyptians moreover contain only a small number of divinities.[4] As for the numerous other gods venerated by the Greeks, Herodotus does not specify whether the Scythians are completely unaware of them. At any rate,

---

*The question is a paraphrase of the famous remark from Montesquieu's *Lettres persanes* (1721), "But how can one be a Persian?"—TRANS.

the Scythians do not "consider them auspicious," i.e., they make no sacrifices to them. Only the case of Dionysus is clear; Skyles' history teaches us that the Scythians absolutely denied him. In addition, the pantheon is strangely composed. The divine hierarchy as conceived by the Scythians only marginally corresponds to the most common theogonies in the Greek world—those of Homer and, above all, Hesiod. Hestia, usually considered the daughter of Rhea and Cronus, and thus Zeus' sister, here is in the position of a primordial divinity.[5] Elsewhere I have attempted to account for her strange presence among the nomads by linking Hestia's centrality with that of the royal power.[6] But the most surprising combination is that of Earth and Zeus, who normally do not belong to the same generation: the generation of Cronus comes between Earth, born from Chaos, and Zeus. The historian, fully aware of the "heretical" character of this statement, interrupts his account to clarify for his listeners that the mistake is not his and that there is a logic to the Scythian "error": "They believe that Earth is the wife of Zeus." With that the Scythian notion takes on some consistency; and no longer in danger of being considered insane, it simply becomes erroneous and thus explainable as a consequence of ignorance.

Their pantheon, then, is characterized by poverty and confusion; they had no Homer or Hesiod to establish a theogony and delineate the figures of the gods.[7] Indeed, the Pelasgians, the ancestors of the Greeks, did not know until recently—until yesterday, one might say[8]—which gods were born from which or if they all existed at the same time or what their attributes were, just as the Scythians thought that Hestia comes before Earth, who is Zeus' wife. However, unlike the Pelasgians who, before learning about the gods from the Egyptians, did not know their "names" (*ounomata*), the Scythians knew what to call them.[9]

The Scythians prayed to their gods by offering them sacrifices, but this cult involved neither the making of statues (*agalmata*), the use of altars (*bōmous*), or the building of temples (*nēous*).[10] Thus there were no places especially for addressing the gods. What can this absence mean? The narrator does not say. However, the appearance of this same triad—statues, temples, and altars—elsewhere in the *Histories* perhaps suggests a key. The Persians likewise did not have the custom of raising statues, temples, and altars. Now, here the narrator intervenes to add that not only do they fail to do this, but they believe it is "foolishness" (*mōriē*) to do so. "The reason for this, in my opinion," adds Herodotus, "is that they have never thought as the Greeks do, that gods are made like men (*anthrōpophueas*)."[11] But although this explanation is valid for the Greeks, and for the Persians, who sacrifice to the sun, moon, fire, etc., it does not hold for the Scythians, who seek to reconcile Hestia, Zeus, Apollo, etc.

At some distance to the north from the Scythians are the Budini, who live in a town completely made of wood. The walls, houses, and also the temples are made of wood, "for in this place are temples of Greek gods (*Hellēnikōn theōn*), containing in the Hellenic way (*Hellēnikōs*) statues, altars, and temples made of wood."[12] In other words, temples, statues, and altars are signs of Greekness and can serve as a criterion for Greekness. Moreover, if the Budini are acquainted with their use, it is no accident because once they were Greeks. Thus these three elements serve as distinguishing features. The lack of specific cultic sites indeed serves to indicate the otherness of Scythian cultic practices.

The same triad appears again, but this time in the mouths of Egyptian priests; the priests of Heliopolis explain to Herodotus that the Egyptians are the first to give names to the twelve gods and the first to have "assigned the gods altars, statues, and temples."[13] These are Egyptian inventions taken over by the Greeks, and to be unacquainted with them is to live in some way in an earlier age. So the difference is termed "primitivism." The Scythians do not seem to have known what the Greeks have learned from the Egyptians. I write "seem," for one encounters the exception of Ares, to whom it is the custom to build temples and who is normally represented by an *agalma*.[14] In his myth Protagoras goes even further:[15] not to build temples or make representations of the gods is not only to live in a time "prior" to this Egyptian invention but to live outside humanity. "Because man partook of a share of the divine, first he was the only one of the animals to honor the gods, and he began to build altars and make divine images." Whoever does not honor the gods denies that divine *moira* that is man's nature.

*

A people of the distant borders, the Scythians nevertheless make sacrifices; their remoteness does not secure them any particular proximity to the gods in return. They are not like Homer's Ethiopians, commensals with the gods, nor are they like Herodotus' long-lived Ethiopians—they have no Table of the Sun that gives them boiled meat every day.[16] Nor do they have a nature like the Cyclopes that allows them not to have to care about Zeus or the other gods and to be oblivious of sacrificial practices. Simple mortals and meat-eaters, such are the Scythians.

The narrator's first comment concerns the uniformity of their sacrifices. All Scythians sacrifice to all gods (except Ares) using the same ritual.[17]

The same formula is used concerning Egyptian sacrifice: all the Egyptians act in the same way with the heads of the sacrificed animals, and all practice the same libations of wine; but the diversity among sacrifices is visible in the removal of the entrails and the cooking.[18] Herodotus gives the example of the ritual in honor "of the divinity they hold to be the most great" (*daimona megistēn*). In other words, the ritual varies according to the god invoked. What does this uniformity suggest in the case of the Scythians? A certain ignorance, perhaps, of the demands pertaining to each god and a certain lack of differentiation within their pantheon?

Since the Scythians build neither temples nor altars, no sacrificial space is laid out. Indeed, apparently every space in their territory is equivalent.[19] The victim is led in (how we do not know) to begin the ceremony. "The victim is standing, its forelegs bound. The sacrifier, standing behind the animal, pulls the end of the rope and pulls him down. When the victim falls, he invokes the god to whom he is sacrificing. Afterwards he puts a noose around the creature's neck, slides a short stick into it that he twists and chokes the animal without lighting a fire, consecrating the victim, or pouring libations."[20]

In this first phase of the killing of the animal, the narrator explicitly points out three missing elements, indicated by the repetition of the word *oute:* absence of fire, absence of first fruits, and absence of libations reveal a threefold difference from the civil sacrifice. When Herodotus describes other sacrificial practices, the appearance of these three points, together or separately, reveals that indeed in his eyes they are criteria of difference. The Persians do not "light a fire before proceeding to the sacrifice,"[21] either. This detail, then, refers to the fire that is lighted on the altar before the victim is slaughtered. The libations, absent from the Scythian ritual, are probably libations of wine that can have already occurred before the killing.[22] The Egyptians, for example, not only build altars and light fires but also "close against the altar . . . pour libations of wine on the victim . . . and slay it."[23] Furthermore, and strangest of all, although the Scythians do not use libations for other gods, they do practice them in honor of Ares; they pour wine on the victim's head before slaying it, but it is a human victim.[24] The last relevant detail in the commentary is the absence of *katarkhesthai*. Legrand translates, "without consecrating first fruits," as if Herodotus had written *aparkhesthai*. On several occasions *aparkhesthai* appears in the *Histories* with the specific meaning of first fruits: once the meat is cooked and before beginning the meal, the Scythians set aside a piece as a first fruit.[25] Before slaughtering the victim, the Libyans cut off a piece of the ear as a first fruit.[26] What does *katarkhesthai* mean if it is not a doublet for *aparkhesthai*? In addition to the above example, Herodotus uses the word two other times: when the Tauri sacrifice prisoners, they begin by "consecrating" (*katarxamenoi*) them before striking them down.[27] Likewise, Heracles, on the point of being sacrificed, had been "consecrated." "Heracles had come to Egypt. Having crowned him, the Egyptians led him in a procession (*pompē*) to sacrifice him to Zeus. Up to that moment he was calm. But once near the altar, as they set about his consecration (*katarkhonto*), he resorted to force and massacred everyone."[28] Heracles rebels at the moment he can no longer doubt that he is not the hero of the feast but the victim designated for the sacrifice. The coronation and procession might be ambiguous, but with the "consecration" the ambiguity vanishes. If the consecration reveals to Heracles his true situation, how is it enacted? When Nestor offers a sacrifice to Athena, he begins by *pouring* the lustral water and barley (*katērkheto*); then he makes a long prayer to Pallas; finally he removes several hairs from the victim's head and throws them into the fire (*aparkhomenos*).[29] Thus, *katarkhesthai* means "to consecrate," i.e., to pour out the lustral water and the barley; and *aparkhesthai*, which comes shortly thereafter, means the removal of the few hairs that will be burned. The Scythians, then, are unaware of the "consecration," and the significance of this ignorance is great. Indeed, the sprinkling of water and the shower of grains on the victim are intended to obtain its consent; shaking its head from right to left, the animal accepts the sacrifice. In this way the ritual removes the violence, and the participants are exculpated in advance of any accusation of murder.[30] Thus the presence or absence of a "consecration" signals the complete distinction between a "nonviolent" and a "violent" sacrifice. The Scythian sacrifice is a violent sacrifice.

The absence of "consecration" means yet something else and repeats on another level the atypicality of the Scythians: they are not farmers. Now, as Jean-Pierre Vernant writes, "sacrificial practice underscores this interdependence between sacrificial animals and cultivated plants by associating barley and wine with the procedures of slaughter and burning of the ritually slaughtered animal."[31] This absence, then, is also the mark of the nomadic life of the Scythians. How could they have barley, they who neither sow nor reap?

In sacrifice the Greeks associate cultivated plants and domestic animals. The Scythians have no knowledge of cultivated plants, yet they sacrifice domestic animals; they do not go so far as to sacrifice wild animals. Of the two, cultivated plants and domestic animals, they keep the second. Indeed, Herodotus is clear: they sacrifice oxen and smaller animals (*próbata*), but also horses. The presence of this third animal once again differentiates their practice from that of the Greeks, who do not commonly sacrifice horses and in any event never do so in a blood sacrifice of the alimentary type. For the Scythians, on the other hand, oxen, smaller animals, and horses seem to be equivalent and can be substituted for one another.[32] Other than the Scythians, the only people in the *Histories* who sacrifice horses are the Massagetae. They sacrifice horses to the sun.[33] Pausanias attributes the same practice to the Sauromates who, he says, kill mares and eat them.[34] It is one thing to sacrifice horses, but to eat their flesh is an aberration.

The animal is slaughtered by surprise, without its consent being sought. It stands with forelegs bound, and the sacrifier stands invisible behind it. He "pulls the end of the cord and pulls him down. When the victim falls, he invokes the god to whom he is sacrificing. Afterwards he puts a noose around the creature's neck, slides a short stick into it that he twists, and chokes the animal. . . ."[35] Thus, instead of the *pelekus,* the ax used to break the animal's neck,[36] and the *makhaira,* the knife with which the animal's throat is slit, the Scythians use a piece of wood and a rope, a lasso (*brokhos*) with which they make a noose. For, and this is the major scandal in the sacrifice, the animal's throat is not cut and its blood does not flow; it is choked. Greek alimentary sacrifice is bloody; the Scythian sacrifice is indeed of an alimentary type, since it ends with the consumption of meat, but it is not bloody.

What does this aberrant killing mean? Not only is strangulation not a frequent sacrificial procedure among the Greeks, it is not even a common form of execution. It is indeed practiced on occasion by the Egyptians,[37] the Babylonians,[38] and by one of the Battiadae:[39] in other words, by non-Greeks, in special circumstances, and by a "tyrant." In the catalogue of Xerxes' army, Herodotus mentions a people, the Sagartians, who in combat use not arms of iron or bronze but the lasso. Nevertheless, they do not strangle their human or animal quarry but simply immobilize it to kill it afterwards with a dagger. However, it is noted—and this is not without importance—that these people are nomads.[40] In other texts, strangulation and hanging represent the worst death; it is the punishment meted out to Odysseus' unfaithful servants; Telemachus promises them a death that will not be an "honorable" (*katharos*) one. "Thus, their heads lined up and the noose passed around all their necks, the young women underwent the most horrible death, and their feet moved an instant, but a very short time."[41] In tragedy, this death (*angkhonē*) is charged with the greatest horror. Andromache, for example, ready to die to save her son, cries out, "You

have me in your hands to stab me, kill me, bind me, hang me."[42] Oedipus
says to the leader of the chorus that he has committed "crimes more heinous than those for which one is hanged" (or for which the guilty party
is strangled?).[43] Strangulation, then, seems to be a particularly "violent"
form of killing.

The Scythians not only fail to avoid sacrificial violence; they emphasize
it all the more by the way in which they slaughter the victim. What about
the lack of blood? Is it possible to assign a precise meaning to this absence?[44] Probably not. If we look at the other non-Greek sacrificial practices Herodotus mentions, it appears that the Egyptians "stab" (*sphazousi*)
their victims after lighting a fire and pouring libations; the Scythians
strangle theirs, but light no fire nor pour any libation.[45] The Libyans
"wring the victim's neck" (*apostrephousi ton aukhena*)[46]—in order to choke
it by crushing the cervical vertebrae? The text is silent concerning the preparations for the Libyan sacrifice: Are there libations? Is a fire lighted? Herodotus states only that as a first fruit they cut a piece of the animal's ear
instead of some hairs pulled from the animal's forehead; and this is thrown
over the shoulder[47] instead of being thrown onto the fire, as is customary.
Such acts would suggest that there is no fire. But above all, this mode of
killing is the work of nomadic Libyans, that is, of people who have the
same way of life as the Scythians. Unfortunately, this evidence is too ten-
uous to permit us to connect sacrifice by strangulation with a nomadic
way of life and thereby provide the meaning of this absence of blood. As
for the Persians, the last people whose sacrificial customs are mentioned
in the narrative, nothing is said about how the victim is killed. However,
it is clearly stated that the Persians light no fire and pour no libations.[48]

After the slaughter comes the carving and the cooking. "Once the victim
has been strangled and skinned, they set about cooking it. . . . When the
victims have been skinned, they separate the flesh from the bones, which
they strip completely bare."[49] After skinning the animal, immediately after
the animal's death, they (we do not know who) divide the animal into two
parts: flesh, *krea*, on one side, and bones, *ostea*, on the other. Thus the only
relevant distinction is between *ostea* and *krea*. Furthermore, these *ostea* will
serve as fuel; they will be used to cook the animal. The aberrations in this
ritual are obvious. First the sacrifice makes no provision for the gods'
share, the *mēria*, the thighbones surrounded by fat that the Greeks burn
on the altar.[50] However, in addition, far from being burned on the altar
for the gods, the bones are burned underneath the victim as fuel. Here is
a scandal that we can find indirectly confirmed by the narrator's rationalization, Toynbeean in inspiration, that explains it: Scythia is poor in wood,

so the Scythians have "invented" (*exeurētai*) using the bones of the sacrificed animals. The scandal of their conduct in the eyes of the Greeks is made comprehensible, if not acceptable. The fact that it is a rationalization can be seen in the hesitations evident in the account regarding the amount of wood in Scythia. If the land as a whole is barren of trees, there nonetheless exists a region, Hylaea, completely covered with forests.[51] The temples to Ares are entirely made of wood and are in the form of squares three stadia long and three stadia wide.[52] Lastly, to punish false soothsayers they are placed on a cart that is filled with wood and set afire.[53]

Along with the *mēria* something else is missing, as implied by the division of the animal into only *ostea* and *krea*—the *splankhna*, or viscera. "The consumption of the viscera necessarily constitutes the first phase of the sacrifice."[54] The entrails are put on skewers to roast while the *mēria* on the altar are consumed in flames. Recalling the example of Telemachus arriving at Pylos, Detienne shows that two circles of eaters are involved in the sacrifice. The first, the "eaters of the *splankhna*," is restricted; the second, larger and more loose, comprises the participants in the sacrificial meal. But it is surely the consumption of the *splankhna* that ensures "maximal participation" in the sacrifice. This necessary phase is completely absent from the Scythian ritual; this strong commensality among the eaters of the *splankhna* does not exist, and the sacrifier appears as a lone individual.

No *splankhna*, no skewers, no roasted meat. It seems that the sacrificial model is defined in negative terms and a completely impoverished ritual is being enacted. Indeed, the phase of roasting, which normally precedes the boiling, does not exist here at all; the only form of cooking practiced by the Scythians is boiling (*hepsēsis*).[55] "They put the flesh into the caldrons of the land, if any happen to be at hand. These caldrons look just like the craters of Lesbos, except that they are much bigger. They put the meat in and cook it (*hepsousi*) by burning the bones of the victims beneath them."[56] Here then at last is the first true sacrificial instrument, the caldron in which the meat is stewed—even if the pot resembles more a large mixing bowl. But once more the familiar ground quickly gives way. Indeed, "if they have no caldron," continues Herodotus, "they put *all* the flesh into the victim's paunch, adding water, and they burn the bones beneath it. These bones burn quite well. The paunch (*gastēr*) easily holds the flesh once the bones have been removed; thus an ox can cook by itself (*heauton*), and the other victims, too, each one."[57] When a character in Menander's *Dyskolos* who is about to sacrifice a sheep notices that he forgot the caldron, after vainly trying to procure one, he decides to roast all the meat.[58] But faced with the same absence, the Scythians, ignorant of roast meat, use the animal's stomach as a *lebēs*. The use of the *gastēr* as a pot is obviously quite surprising. Certainly, Prometheus does cover the flesh and entrails laden with fat with the ox's stomach,[59] but this is a trick to present as inedible what in fact is the best share. If it functions here as a container, the *gastēr* is by no means a substitute for the *lebēs*. To present the Scythian practice, the historian resorts to a rationalization of the same type used earlier: since they have no wood, they burn bones; since they have no caldron, they use the animal's paunch. But why don't they have a caldron, if there are caldrons among them and they are a sacrificial instrument? Here we have a way to limit the profound strangeness of this type of cooking. Once the caldron has disappeared we are left with this startling image of an ox cooking itself, "cooked in itself."

Once the meat is cooked, the last phase of the sacrifice can begin, the meal, about which Herodotus says nothing. "When the flesh has cooked, the sacrifier sets aside as first fruits a share of the flesh and entrails, which he throws before him."[60] We know nothing of the feast. Is the meat divided up? By whom? Among whom? How? In the city it is fundamental that "everyone taste of the animal."[61] Here it is possible to wonder if there even is a shared meal. Indeed, if, as the account of the Bouphonia indicates, sacrifice for the Greeks is political, then whoever is ignorant of the *polis* is also unacquainted with the sacrificial meal, and nomads more than anyone else. I believe, then, that here the silence reflects a lack: neither egalitarian division, nor commensality, nor even true community. Even the sacrifier's action is problematic. To place some food before one is customary,[62] but the composition of the first fruits is surprising: flesh (*krea*) and viscera (*splankhna*). Cooked flesh, so be it; but the viscera? Normally by this time in the ceremony, they would have been eaten by the "*splankhna*-eaters" while the meat was stewing. Moreover, it was clearly stated that the Scythians divided the animal into two parts, bones and flesh. Nothing was said about the viscera—their removal, cooking, or consumption. Must we then admit that these *splankhna* have been treated like meat, that is, boiled as meat is? This is yet another aberration. The final appearance of the *splankhna* thus again adds to the confusion over the ritual. If indeed there is a consecration of a part of the viscera, it can take place only at the beginning of the sacrifice, at the time of their removal even before the victim is skinned, and not at the end when the larger meal begins. The Scythians do not make a distinction between the *splankhna* phase and the *krea* phase of the sacrifice.

All things considered, the Scythian ritual is marked by several lacks. There is no sacrificial space, no preparatory phase (fire, first fruits, or libations), and no blood. The gods' share (*mēria*) plays no part in it, nor does the *splankhna;* and the ritual does not ultimately result in the distribution of the meat or a feast. It lacks the indispensable instruments of sacrifice, which are inseparable from the Greek identity: knife, skewers, and caldron (which it may use but can do without).[63] It is a violent sacrifice. The animal, whose consent is not asked, is furthermore choked to death. Seen in contrast to the Greek model of alimentary sacrifice, this ritual appears impoverished and confused. Overall, it ensures neither mediation between gods and men nor communication among men. It is not possible to assign an unequivocal meaning to each one of these absences, but together they at least suggest that the Scythians have no agriculture and do not truly form a community. Thus it is all the more interesting to note that throughout these chapters Herodotus is in fact speaking only of the sacrifice of oxen. Doubtless the Scythians also sacrificed smaller domestic animals and horses, but Herodotus deals only with oxen. The choice of this animal proves two things: the point of reference, constantly present, is that of the Greek civil sacrifice; and to depict the Scythians as sacrificing oxen is to set them at the greatest distance from the Greeks, for this is precisely the animal they sacrifice the least often. Indeed, if oxen and *polis* go together, then whoever is *apolis* must not sacrifice oxen. Under these conditions, to choose to represent the Scythians sacrificing an ox is to make the aberrations of their practices, culminating in the image of the "beef cooked in itself," all the clearer.

Such is the sacrificial ritual that, by the time it is over, has involved a ceremony that for a Greek is hardly a sacrifice at all; but when seen in the context of the image of the Scythians as "warrior beings," it can appear all too sacrificial. Indeed, when they make their entrance in the *Histories* as master hunters, following Cyaxares, king of Media, they do not hesitate to avenge themselves of an insult by serving up one of the children in their care dressed as meat and "prepared like game."[64] And further, when Astyages, also in revenge, kills Harpagus' son, he treats the body as a sacrificial animal, carving it and cooking it and then serving it to the boy's father.[65] Two cannibalistic meals: in one a human sacrificial victim is eaten and in the other, "game." The Scythians, seeming to know only the hunt and thus wild animals, are ignorant of sacrificial procedures. For Lucian, if the Scythians are not unfamiliar with sacrifices, in any case they reject them all, considering them as "unworthy" or "vile" (*tapeinas*) acts, preferring to "offer humans to Artemis, whom they think to please by acting in this way."[66] Violent, warlike people, they are depicted in the process of offering or sacrificing human beings. For Herodotus, as well, in addition to their animal sacrifices there is a god to which they offer human victims. It is not, as for Lucian, Artemis (who does not even appear in their pantheon), but Ares. To Ares, indeed, they sacrifice (*thuousi*) prisoners of war.

Ares' singularity is evident the moment Herodotus mentions him in the Scythian pantheon. The narrator gives the "Scythian" translation of the names of the different gods, except for Ares. If Ares has no Scythian equivalent, would it be because his name is not "Greek"? A whole tradition, beginning with the *Iliad*, connects him with Thrace: he goes to Thrace, returns there, or he is established there.[67] Further northwest, he is associated with the Amazons, of whom he is the father.[68] His presence in the *Histories* is unobtrusive. He is worshiped in Thrace, where he even takes first place ahead of Dionysus and Artemis.[69] Otherwise he is firmly established in Egypt in the town of Papremis, where celebrations are organized in his honor. In addition to sacrifices, the ceremony includes a strange battle with clubs where more than one of the protagonists, Herodotus reckons, must meet his death.[70] In the Greek world, on the contrary, he appears only in two oracles, in reference to combat: "impetuous Ares mounted in a Syrian chariot," and "Ares who dyed the sea red with blood."[71]

In Scythia he is honored in two ways. Like other gods, he is offered animal victims, but Herodotus does not state whether, as in the case of the other gods, these victims are strangled.[72] We only know that sacrifices of smaller domestic animals and horses are made to him—in other words, no oxen. But he alone among the gods has a right to something else and holds a special place. "In each nome of their kingdoms a temple to Ares is built: bundles of sticks are piled evenly to a length and width of three stadia, lower in height. On this stack is placed a square platform; three sides are steep, and only one can be climbed. Every year one hundred and fifty more cartloads of branches are piled on it, for the stack settles as a result of the weather. In each district an old iron saber (*akinakēs*) is placed on this mound, and that is the representation (*agalma*) of Ares."[73] With Ares we move from undifferentiated space to organized, geometrical, and administered space. While no sacrificial space exists for other gods, Ares possesses a temple in each "province." These *marae*, where he is grandly installed, settle the question of wood.[74] For the other gods, there is no wood at all, so bones must be used as fuel; but Ares benefits from immense wood piles. This is one of the reasons Dumézil, inspired by the example of Batraz of the Ossetes, saw in him a "bully."[75] With him a temporality also appears; time is regulated and counted: "every year" his habitations must be repaired, and "each year" animal sacrifices are offered to him, while for other gods nothing of such periodicity of offerings is known. Moreover, his temple metonymically represents Scythian space. Scythia forms a square; the royal tomb is dug in a square; and Ares' temple is built as a square.[76] Finally, as a last mark of singularity, he has the right to a concrete representation (*agalma*); indeed, he is present on the terrace of his temple in the form of an "ancient iron saber" (*akinakēs*).[77] This *agalma*, however, is only a saber, nothing but a saber, while ordinarily (notably in the *Histories*) the gods' *agalmata* are statues. For example, the same Ares has an *agalma* in Papremis in the form of a statue.[78] Does this difference in divine representation indicate yet another difference between the Scythians and others? If the absence of a temple and plastic representation reflects a certain "primitivism," Ares is revealed to be the least "primitive" of the Scythian gods, he who could be taken for one of the most primitive in Greece among Greek gods. He appears as the god of organized space, he who is commonly associated with the furious melee involving Phobos and Deimos, his children. From the Scythians he receives particular honors, he whom Sophocles described as "with no share of honor" (*apotimos en theois theos*) among the gods.[79] But lastly, this Scythian Ares, a person of order, appears in a larger context that gives him meaning. Indeed he is related to matters of war and thus to the figure of the king whom I have attempted to show as occupying a central place in this nomadic world where the center must otherwise be empty.[80]

In addition to animal victims, he alone of all the Scythian gods has a right to human victims: "Of all the enemies they capture alive, they sacrifice (*thuousi*) one out of a hundred, not the same way they sacrifice animals, but differently."[81] Aside from the Scythians, the only peoples in the *Histories* to sacrifice prisoners are the Tauri and the Apsinthian Thracians. The Tauri sacrifice shipwrecked sailors to Iphigenia and Greeks taken prisoner at sea.[82] The Thracians offer the Persian Oeobazus, among others, to Pleistorus (*theos epikhōrios*).[83] Thus it is a rare and definitely non-Greek practice. Outside of the *Histories,* Ducrey concludes that this act is rare, even if it has been noted.

The sacrifice to the other gods is free of all libation; the sacrifice offered to Ares includes a libation of wine over the victim's head. While the other ritual is characterized by a curious lack of blood, this one involves stabbing (*aposphazein*) the victim.[85] "They are stabbed over a vase. The vase is then carried to the top of the pile of wood and the blood is poured (*katakheousi*) on the saber." No blood and no libation on the one hand, blood and libation on the other. The two acts seem to belong together. As Ares "drinks" this blood, the victims' bodies undergo another violence, mutilation. The right shoulders and arms are cut off and then thrown in the air. "Then when they are finished (*aperxantes*) with the other victims, they leave. The arm lies where it fell and the body where it lay."[86] After this sort of *maskhalismos*, a final outrage is reserved for these tortured bodies: the lack of a funeral. They rot there in pieces, unburied, and therefore, in the eyes of a Greek, without the power to truly attain the status of the dead.[87] This, then, is the sacrifice that conforms to the image of the Scythians as a people of war. By the same token, just as a Scythian warrior drinks the blood of his first enemy victim and then each year thereafter drinks wine according to the arithmetic of the *aristeia* of the nomarch, so Ares in each nome "drinks" prisoners' blood.

Is Ares a figure of order or disorder? Indeed, if Ares is capable of occupying a central place in the Scythian space, it is because he is marginal in Greece. Thus when Athenian youths swear an oath, they invoke Ares (among other powers); when young Spartans go fight at the Platanistes, they sacrifice a dog to Ares Enyalius by night. He is the father of the Amazons; and Lucian calls him the "god of women" (*theos gunaikōn*), even though women normally are forbidden to fight. In Tegea, women alone sacrifice to an Ares called *gunaikothoinas*, an Ares of the banquet. In Sparta once again, according to Apollodorus of Athens, a man is sacrificed to him. The same marginality is found in his personal behavior; adultery does not frighten him, perhaps not even incest.[88] Marginal: this is exactly what Sophocles means when he calls him "the god with no share of honor," lacking in *timē*.

NINE

Sanctified Slaughter in Modern Greece: The "Kourbánia" of the Saints

Stella Georgoudi

Sacrifice in the Land of Orthodoxy?

The Hellenist ventures into modern Greece. Nothing new about that, but this time the route takes some surprising turns. The expectation is not to find something in today's or yesterday's landscape that would illuminate a heretofore dark corner where ancient practices have miraculously been maintained. The Hellenist does not go of his own accord but is led by the folklorist.

To a considerable extent the oddity is on the modern side. Peasant-sacrificers, village feasts around caldrons in which meat for the saint has stewed, and a village priest blessing it all—truly this is something that the full array of ancient sacrifice can serve to explain. There seems to be a kind of exoticism within Greek consciousness that chooses certain ritual details and explains the meaning of peasant sacrificial practice in terms of their survival from ancient times. Antiquity alive in orthodoxy—the prospect evokes a mixture of horror and fascination.

However, by actually comparing the sacrifices of today's village communities with the model of ancient practices, the following pages reveal several important points and provide the final stop in the territory covered by this book. Yes, sacrificial practice among Greek peasants of today truly exists. Yes, the coherence of these rites seems to engender a distinct meaning, a lofty significance that is comparable to the learned constructions of academic theology. This coherence alone makes it possible to explain what takes place around the meat stewing in the caldrons under the trees in a square before a church. That a different path, Judeo-Christian in this instance, has been pro-

A version of this study was initially presented in Marcel Detienne's seminar in the Fifth Section of the Ecole pratique des Hautes Etudes and at the colloquium "Sacrifice" organized by the Centre Thomas More (L'Arbresle, 23–30 April, 1978). I would like to express my thanks here to Jeannie Carlier and Jean-Louis Durand. Without their friendly and constant help, support, and suggestions, these pages could not have been written.

posed to outline the genesis of these practices changes nothing of the fact that they are organized from within. Thus Christianity contains a sacrificial place, revealed at the heart of Orthodoxy, a place worthy of further study. So we end with the question raised by these pages: Why in Orthodox provinces and not elsewhere? It is not the Hellenist who can answer that.

Jean-Louis Durand

The public killing of a domestic animal followed by the eating of its meat according to rules, within the framework of popular Orthodox worship, is an apparently strange rite that nonetheless takes place today—although much more rarely than before—in some villages of modern Greece. From the very outset, the Hellenist who would like to explore this set of cultic acts encounters a major obstacle resulting from the gaps in our documentation. Today, for many reasons, the ritual is distorted, deprived of certain elements that had once been central and meaningful. The moment we deal with a custom that is slowly deteriorating and dying out, we run the risk of error if we base our argument for a particular interpretation on the absence of an element in a particular place in the ritual; thus older sources must be consulted. Now, the conditions under which our documents were collected are deceptive; we have relied principally on the reports of Greek folklorists.[1] Incomplete, linear, repetitive, and lacking for the most part any truly anthropological and historical perspective, these descriptions clean up, schematize, and leave out "details" that are nonetheless meaningful and consistent (words, prayers, actions, specific remarks concerning times, places, objects used, and types of cooking). They inexorably lead to interpretation according to the theory of "survivals"— a theory that is exactly what we propose to examine here. Once this preliminary obstacle has been taken into account, we can nevertheless recognize the general outline of this ritual, look into some of its particulars, assess its functions, and, finally, propose an interpretation of the whole.[2]

The model that we can construct in broad terms from our documents has not entirely escaped some schematization. The public *kourbáni*[3]—to give it the popular name it has just about everywhere and that refers both to the sacrificial victim and to the act[4]—is the blood sacrifice of a domestic animal offered, as the peasants themselves put it, "to the saint, for the whole village." "To the saint": the sacrifice takes place on certain Orthodox religious feast days in honor of a saint (male or female), an apparently minor figure in official religions but a benevolent tutelary power of primary importance for the village, who lends an ear to the hopes and fears of the individual or the community. However, sometimes the sacrifice is addressed to the Holy Trinity, or sometimes to the Virgin, the mediator par excellence between men and God in the Orthodox faith. God himself, or Christ, can be involved in the sacrificial act by means of prayers that ask them to watch over "this sacrifice (*thusía*) with a calm look and joyful face" and to "accept the sacrifice of [their] servant."[5] "For the whole village": the sacrifice calls the whole village community together, and most often it is celebrated at its expense and always in its name and for its benefit.

*

The victim is a domestic animal slaughtered outside the church, generally during or after mass or, in some villages, the night before the feast day before or during vespers. The sacrificial space opens onto the outdoors: the area extending in front of the village church, or before the country chapel or the small building, often on the outskirts of the community lands, that is just big enough to house the icon of a saint, right next to a "miraculous" spring with "sacred" water endowed with therapeutic properties (*hagiásmata*). This natural milieu, sometimes divided in a rudimentary way and almost always shaded by trees, is also the preferred place, strongly humanized and socialized, for any *panigíri*, any religious festivity of the neo-Greek village.[6] Century-old oaks, walnut, or plane trees have a part in the ritual decor: their trunks make it possible to tie the victim before slaughtering it; their roots sometimes receive the animal's blood; their branches are used to hang the animal while it is being skinned; and their foliage shades men's meals, games, and dances.

However, the fact that the killing most often takes place in open air does not indicate a radical division between indoors and outdoors, for the enclosed space, the interior of the church, incontestably plays a complementary role in the ritual.[7] Not only do the times of the mass and the slaughter coincide or follow each other immediately, but sometimes the victim is led into the church to be presented before the icon of the saint; it is even left inside overnight to sleep on the night before the feast day;[8] or it is led over the threshold to "hear" before its death the prayer offered by the priest in the narthex, which is also the place where the first dish of boiled meat is sometimes brought before the start of the common meal for the priest to bless it.[9]

The conditions under which the festival is held undoubtedly explain its uneven distribution throughout the calendar year. Most of the *kourbánia*, and the most important, are spread out over the period from April to October. A festival celebrated in the open air in a space intended for the *panigíri*, where at times hundreds of people gather, some coming from far away, to pray, eat, sleep, and have fun, often for two to three days at a time—such a festival is the most important event of the year in some villages and is a source of prestige and economic advantage for the community and its church.[10] Such an event requires favorable weather and can be held in winter only with difficulty.[11] Therefore, if the religious feast day falls in that season, the sacrifice will sometimes be moved to a more favorable time. The Akindinoi saints are honored twice in Mistegna on Lesbos: November 2, their feast day (no sacrifice), and on one of the Sundays after Easter, when their *kourbáni* are slaughtered. On the same island, the famous bull sacrifice in honor of Saint Charalambos is set for a Sunday in May, while "the Church celebrates his memory in the deepest winter, on February 10, at a time when it is not convenient to go to his chapel," located on the hillside of Mount Taurus, outside the village of Saint Paraskevi.[12]

*

Looking at the list of the recipients of sacrifice, we quickly note that there are preferred saints who are offered more sacrifices than others. But if we seek an explanation for this, we notice that there cannot be one single answer. Can we find it in the "Saints' Lives" and advance the theory that saints to whom hagiography has attributed pastoral or agricultural functions are naturally the ones who are offered most of the domestic animals, while "military" saints, for example, are less favored? A rapid examination of the "Synaxaries" (collections of saints' lives) shows the fragile nature of this hypothesis. We may consider, for example, Saint Modestus, martyr, and Saint Mamas—two saints whose close relationship to the world of flocks of animals is clearly attested, not only by accounts of their lives but by prayers that bear their name. The first of these, shepherd and above all cowherd, was the supreme protector of working oxen. He healed animals, even brought them back to life, thanks to the powers God had given him. Now, his feast day takes place on December 18 and unambiguously exhibits the functions as a protector of livestock so vividly stressed in his biography. This "feast of oxen," when laborers in some regions give their animals cooked wheat blessed beforehand by the priest is not accompanied by any sacrifice.[13] Saint Mamas is also a great protector of flocks and a pastor if ever there was one, as his biographies and iconography indisputably reveal. Furthermore, as we shall see, he is connected with the foundation myth of neo-Greek sacrifice: but only rarely does he appear on the list of saints who receive sacrifices in their honor.[14]

Saint George provides the complementary proof. Everywhere in the Greek world he is one of the most important beneficiaries of sacrificial victims, notably those offered by shepherds and stockbreeders. Doubtless on occasion he revived animals: for example, an ox belonging to a poor pagan laborer who had converted, and those victims sacrificed by Theopistus, a laborer from Cappadocia.[15] But far from being the exploits that characterize him as a protector of livestock, these miraculous acts appear as minor and insignificant episodes in the career of a figure presented to us above all as a military saint, victorious horseman, killer of dragons, and liberator of prisoners. If this soldier has become a protective power to whom shepherds offer sacrifices, it is, it seems to us, less due to some minor episodes in his biography than because of the date of his feast: April 23 is the day when the most important half of the pastoral year begins. It is the day that the transhumant shepherds leave for the mountain pasturelands; and according to that date, by convention, an entire series of important activities in the world of animal breeding is regulated.[16]

There is another way to approach the question of the preferential treatment some saints receive with respect to sacrifice. One of the benefits expected of the *kourbánia* clearly is protection against the two scourges, natural calamity and disease, both of man and animals. The prayers leave no doubt concerning the second point; in them the word *hugieía*, "health," recurs as a leitmotiv: "we sacrifice for health," "we perform the *kourbáni* for health." We can hypothesize that a certain correlation exists between the quantity of *kourbánia* offered to a saint and the power recognized in him, for various reasons, in one of the two areas: preventing natural calamities and granting or restoring good health. For example, Saint Elias, who enjoyed a great reputation, firmly anchored in biblical tradition,[17] as a rainmaker and regulator of atmospheric phenomena, is with George and Athanasius[18] one of the three saints richest in sacrificial victims. Ordinarily these are offered to him on his feast day, July 20, around his chapels, which are almost always located on mountaintops. But sometimes the need for rain is so great that one of the fundamental rules of the *kourbáni*, its calendrical regularity, is broken, and the sacrifice is held outside of the normal day. Thus Greek peasants in northern Thrace used to slaughter ten to fifteen sheep for Saint Elias on days other than his feast day when drought threatened their fields.[19] As for disease, all the saints who receive *kourbánia* are qualified to combat it,[20] but Saint Paraskevi is one of the few women honored by *kourbánia*. Given the number of private and public victims she was still receiving not long ago in different regions of Greece, she has no reason to envy her male rivals; and she undoubtedly owes her status to her great reputation as a heavenly "doctor," capable of healing all ailments, particularly those afflicting the eyes.[21]

Is it possible to establish a correlation between the saint-recipient and the sacrificial victim—its sex, age, and species? The data, often confused and imprecise, do not permit it. Without a doubt, some victims are more prestigious than others: a vigorous bull is expensive and does honor to the one who pays for him, whether an individual[22] or a community. To substitute another victim, for reasons of economy or anything else, we are sometimes told, is to run the risk of serious calamities for the village.[23] Even then it is not a matter of a special relationship between the saint who receives the sacrifice and the bull, for our sources provide no confirmation for such a connection. So there is no reason to invoke Dionysus, the Bouphonia, or totemic cults.[24] Instead, this refusal to substitute one victim for another reflects the constant care about offering a quality animal and the apprehension about any change in the ritual, as well as the desire to respect the terms of a kind of contract; something promised is something owed. And *táma*, the noun that is used in several cases to refer to the victim, means exactly that, the "thing promised."

The criteria determining the selection of the victim vary, it appears, from one locale to another. If it is a calf, a fat calf with a shiny coat will be chosen. If it is a sheep, it will be all white or all black,[25] and well fattened, too. In some regions males are preferred to females. Beyond possible economic considerations, it seems that the undervaluation of the female sex extends to the animal kingdom as well. Males are sacrificed, it is sometimes said, "because the female is the Devil's creature,"[26] like the wife or daughter a calamity for the family, a dead weight to be gotten rid of by marriage; and even for that a dowry must be paid. Elsewhere the choice pertains not to the sex but the species. Sheep are preferred to goats, which are cursed, according to the popular explanation, for having betrayed Jesus and denounced him to the Jews.[27] The preference for sheep is less obvious when young animals are involved. Shepherds sacrifice lambs and kids to Saint George, but the favored victim remains the lamb, sometimes consecrated ahead of time; it is the *hagiōrgítēs* lamb, which "belongs to Saint George."[28] Obviously the number of participants in the feast determines, if not the species, at least the number of victims. The *kourbáni* of Our Lady of Euboea at Cyme used to attract up to five hundred people, and ten to fifteen well-fed cattle were needed to feed them.[29]

Sometimes the sacrificial victim is provided by a generous donor in the form of a *táma*, or it can be bought with church funds (from the church treasury).[30] But most often it is the community that officially provides the victims or organizes the effort to raise not only the money for the purchase but everything necessary for the common meal as well: wood, vegetables,

grains, salt, and the ground red pepper indispensable for seasoning.[31] In
some cases the effort is solemnly announced by the mayor and local authorities and is addressed not only to the inhabitants of the village but to
all those born there, even if they are far away.[32] Everyone proclaims his
consent and participation in the sacrificial practice by a concrete contri-
bution; and well before the sacrifice the fundraising effort creates bonds
among the participants that will be confirmed by the common meal.
Sometimes the animal is bought several months ahead of time and fed
until it is ready to be slaughtered.[33] These animals intended for sacrifice
enjoy special favor, all sorts of care surrounds them. Wolves do not dare
approach them, it is thought. They are allowed to graze where they will,
even in planted fields.[34] Thus in the village of Mega Monastiri, in northeastern Thrace, the community used to buy the most robust calves and
feed them for the village *kourbánia*. These potential sacrificial victims were
never used for agricultural or domestic labor.[35] In that way the sacrifice
takes on another temporal dimension; it is not limited to the specific day
of the feast but involves the community over a long period of preparation
and waiting.

When the day has come, the victim is led to slaughter without any particular preparation or ceremony. Frequently all the villagers do is attach
lighted candles to the horns of the animal about to die, in the same way
that they light candles at the bedside of the dead. However, in some large
panigíria things are different: bathed, adorned with flowers, ribbons, or
multicolored pearls, its horns gilt or decorated with strips of gold foil, the
victim does honor to the community or the donor. Sometimes the tail,
flanks or forehead of a white sheep may be dyed red: a meaningful gesture,
for after slitting the animal's throat, the participants will be stained with
red, but this time with the blood of the victim.[36] In some cases, a solemn
procession leads the animal to its death. Decked out, accompanied by the
churchwardens or horsemen on decorated mounts, the victim is led
through all the streets and alleyways to the joyous sound of drums, pipes,
and violins. At Saint Paraskevi (on Lesbos) women throw silk cloths,
tablecloths, and embroidered caps on the bull, as if to add to its splendor,
so the victim itself carries these precious gifts to the church.[37] But these
displays are not the rule. Therefore, here again, the reference to ancient
sacrifice is not relevant.

It is basically the village priest who performs a certain number of rites
intended to complete the consecration of the victim before the killing. But
the killing, butchering, preparation, and distribution of the meat are car-

ried out by people who are completely interchangeable: donors of victims, churchwardens, villagers named by the church or who have volunteered for the task.[38]

The slaughter does not have the solemn aspect we find in ancient Greek sacrifice. It happens, albeit rarely, that the actual killing is almost swept under the table, dissociated from the mass, and connected more with butchering than sacrifice. However, some optional gestures serve as reminders that the operation takes place in a ritual framework. The victim's head is turned toward the east, the orientation of the altar in the churches. It is marked with a knife. In some villages people watch attentively for the blood to flow into a ditch, where all the inedible parts (tail, ears, horns, bile, etc.) will also be buried, so "that they are not eaten or scattered by the dogs," for this is the *kourbáni*.[39] This is apparently because the victim, reserved only for humans, must not be touched by any animal; and it is necessary to avoid the dogs in particular, for they are the image of the wicked, to whom, says the Sermon on the Mount, you must not give "what is holy."[40] It must be emphasized that these customs contrast with those of ordinary butchering, which leaves to the village dogs whatever men do not eat. Similar precautions are taken with the bones of the victim after the sacrificial meal. They are thrown on the roofs, where they will be safe from dogs but accessible to the birds, the noble creatures of God.[41]

Of major importance in neo-Greek sacrifice, the blood that gushes from the victim's neck has a universally strong positive value for the faithful. Its flow inspires no revulsion; its contact has a beneficial effect on men and animals. Everyone dips a finger in it to make the sign of the cross on his or her forehead or to leave a fingerprint, "to be in good health," "to make the *kourbáni* safe and sound next year." A guarantor and dispenser of health, the victim's blood also possesses fecundating virtues. The sign of the cross marked with a wad of cotton dipped in this red liquid on the forehead of stallions and mares promises foals for the coming year.[42]

But all these ritual acts seem only the preliminaries to the heart and essence of the festival: the distribution of food and the shared meal. This final phase generally takes place in two parts, clearly demarcated by the action of the priest: the preparation of the food and the banquet itself. Out under the trees in the open area around the church, large, newly started caldrons are bubbling with meat, spices, grains and vegetables, including rice, wheat or gruel, garbanzo beans, onions, garlic, and tomatoes.[43] When it is an important meal and several caldrons are boiling side by side,[44] many people—both men and women—are needed to prepare the food under the supervision of the churchwardens. If the sacrifice was made on the eve of the feast, the meat and grain will cook all night to make a kind of homogeneous gruel that will be ladled out to the participants.[45]

But for the meal to begin, the priest must bless the prepared food so it can be distributed. This ceremony, which is never omitted, separates the act of eating from all that preceded it and makes it something distinct. It is said that the priest "reads the boiled dish," and this concise statement, which reveals the predominant mode of cooking, evokes a solemn scene, where the priest reads the prayer over the caldrons.[46]

The feast may then begin. Gathered around a common table or seated on the grass in groups under the trees, villagers and strangers eat the blessed food, which has been distributed in equal parts. Each one in turn raises his glass and makes toasts for health, prosperity, and happiness. Ordinarily, the priest joins his flock for the feast. According to some sources, honored pieces are given to him (the thigh, shoulder, feet, or head) and sometimes the animal's hide as well, when it is not given to the church or auctioned for the benefit of the ecclesiastical coffers.[47] In some villages where patriarchal power and the distinctions of age and sex completely dominate all realms of life, this social structure is clearly represented in the common meals. For example, in Aïvlassis (northeastern Thrace), according to a witness in 1909, women were completely excluded, not only from the meal but from the whole sacrificial proceeding—an extremely rare happening, but one that speaks eloquently. In Mega Monastiri in the same region, the meals of the village *kourbánia* once were the scene of great gatherings of lineages, each of which maintained its own stone table in the church yard, always reserving the place of honor—to the east—for the oldest man, who presided over the feast. Furthermore, the participants raised their glasses in an order determined by rank and age, following a strict social hierarchy.[48] If there was no common meal, which would be the exception, each took his portion of prepared food home after tasting it at the church; later he would take part in a kind of common meal "in miniature" within the restricted circle of the family.[49] Or again, even more rarely, the raw meat would be divided up into shares for each family in the village, and the mistress of the house would prepare the exceptional dish to mark, at home, the end of the sacrificial proceeding.[50] But we find different combinations. Thus, when the common meal takes place without participation of the whole village, part of the meat is cooked to be eaten on the spot, and the rest is distributed raw, with careful accounts kept of the lots given to each family so that possible inequities may be remedied the following year.[51] It is precisely these last variations, in which the distribution of the shares is more or less disconnected from the common meal and to a certain degree autonomous, that most clearly reveal the importance of this distribution, a process solemnly announced by the tolling of all the churchbells.[52]

Above all, the *kourbáni* is a festival, and of the entire ceremony it is the festive aspect that is the best preserved, even where the sacrificial act has been weakened. It is significant that in some villages the festivities truly begin only after the rapid execution of the victims, or even after the meat has been cooked. Only then does mass begin, and people leave their houses at the sound of the church bells to come to the common meal.[53] The *kourbáni* is really a village festival, a noisy and joyful event where everyone gathers, not only to eat and drink together but also to laugh, sing, and dance to folk music,[54] to fire guns in the air or compete in contests (horseraces, as on Lesbos, or fighting games, tests of courage but once also a display of ethnic rivalry,[55] the prize for which was a lamb, like the sacrificial victim bathed, adorned, and called the *kourbáni*)[56]—in short, to escape their monotonous and regulated everyday life for a few hours or even a few days.

*

For Greek ethnographers and folklorists, the complex problems posed by the interpretation of the *kourbáni,* particularly its interconnection with Orthodox religion, are in some ways solved in advance. Neo-Greek sacrifice is a survival of ancient sacrifice; such a conclusion is related to the idea, widespread in the nineteenth century, that all elements within a religious or social system (notably in civilized Europe) found to be aberrant, heterogeneous, and "wild" are explainable only as residues of an earlier time, survivals that are preserved and fossilized within a more evolved state but immediately discernible the moment they are compared to what is observed elsewhere (outside of Europe) in peoples who have remained at a more archaic degree of evolution.[57] Greek folklorists have no need, however, to resort to "exotic" peoples: ancient Greece provides on the spot an inexhaustible reservoir of usages and customs ready to be transformed into "survivals" to explain certain ambiguous manifestations that correlate poorly with normative practices of Christianity. For them, everything comes from ancient Greece and is perpetuated as a result of the miraculous transformation of the Olympian gods into Christian saints: Saint George replaces Dionysus; Saint Mamas, Attis; Saint Elias, Zeus; Saint Michael, Apollo; and so forth, with each writer creating such "pairs" in line with his personal preferences.[58] In the same way that they unwittingly honor Greek gods under Christian names, the "simple folk" continue by "force of habit" to perform certain acts, which they invest with a new content, having "forgotten or never known" their "true" meaning—the meaning these acts had in antiquity.[59] Proceeding point by point, without ever considering the *kourbáni* as a whole or comparing it as such to the other cohesive whole that is ancient Greek sacrifice, these folklorists connect one detail of the ritual to an ancient antecedent and then base their argument on a disparate series of formal resemblances in order to conclude that a direct line, even an identity of meaning, links the two practices.[60]

This explanatory model of the folklorists, which is connected by its logic to the whole ideological current fed by different theories of the "uninterrupted continuity," "purity," and "eternal nature" of the Greek race,[61] offers a ready-made interpretation: sacrificial ritual only interests us as a vehicle for ancient "survivals."[62] But this explanation, used as a master key, avoids some questions that inevitably arise the moment one takes issue with the preconceived notion of "survivals." Why and how did Orthodoxy—unlike the Catholic church, which has relentlessly banished anything that would contaminate the Eucharist, the "true" Christian sacrifice—adopt a more supple attitude toward the *kourbáni*? Why did it succeed in making a compromise between complete integration and total rejection? How can we explain the homogeneous and consistent quality this ritual has for the village community per se, as well as for each of its members? What meaning does this practice have within the social and religious life of the neo-Greek village? Why does this ritual still form one of the axes of village life, especially where traditional community structures have not completely disintegrated?

*

The Orthodox church is often involved, directly or indirectly, in the sacrificial process. Despite the criticisms and openly hostile attitude of some purists among the high clergy,[63] the bishop himself sometimes honors the festival with his presence,[64] which was much more common at a time when the *kourbáni* was still at the center of the social and religious life of some villages. Often the lower clergy are more kindly disposed toward the sacrificial festival, and the village priest plays an incontestable role. If he is not the one who actually makes the sacrifice (although in some documents allusion is made to this),[65] he takes an active part in the events pertaining to it: he collects contributions for the common meal;[66] he leads the dance at the time of the celebration. And surely the priest's presence cannot be entirely dissociated from the conviction, solidly entrenched among all kourbanists, that to sacrifice an animal in a saint's honor is to do good Christian work and that, inversely, to refrain from doing so would provoke anger from on high and lead to catastrophe for the entire community.[67] Hadn't Saint Charalambos pitilessly struck down in his sleep the man who claimed that the *kourbánia* were "pagan works"?[68] And at the end of the eighteenth century it was the village priests who accused of heresy the monk Nicodemus, an intransigeant purist who vainly attempted to stop the *kourbánia*—a "barbaric custom" and "vestige of ancient pagan error."[69]

The sure economic advantages that the church, monastery, and priests drew from the sacrifices—hides sold to benefit the church coffers, numerous *támata* promised to the saints, some of which provided food for pilgrims but most of which increased the flocks of the monasteries, and sacrificial shares set aside for the priests[70]—all are not enough to explain Orthodoxy's tolerance for this apparently aberrant practice. It is possible to assert that Orthodoxy is a religion "more popular than other Christian confessions, which have more theoretical tendencies."[71] But the problem can be stated in more precise terms by examining the relationship that the *kourbáni* might have with Hebrew sacrifice in the Old Testament.[72]

Undoubtedly, Christian religions are placed under the sign of the New Covenant. But we must emphasize that the New Testament contains no absolute condemnation of blood sacrifice. "We never see Jesus declare the Jewish sacrifice devoid of meaning. . . . Only, for him it belongs to the order of the Old Covenant."[73] What Jesus condemns in the scribes and Pharisees is their conviction that they have discharged their duty to God by spilling the blood of their victims without giving a thought to "justice, mercy, and faith" (Matt. 23:23). This condemnation is already found explicit in the words of 1 Samuel ("Obedience is better than sacrifice, / submissiveness better than the fat of rams" 15:22), and in the prophets.[74] Saint Paul, on the other hand, does not condemn Hebrew sacrifice outright as a cultic practice, even if he stresses the ineffectiveness and temporary character of the sacrifices of the Old Covenant compared to the "true" sacrifice and sole efficacy of Christ, the "spotless victim" (Hebrews 9:11 ff.). Moreover, it is significant that the apostle, writing to the Athenians as a true Jew, essentially denounces not sacrificial practice but the cult of idols (Acts 17:16 ff.), and what he condemns in pagan sacrifice is not the sacrificial act itself, but the intended recipient: whatever pagans immolate in sacrifice, *"they sacrifice to demons who are not God,"* and consequently, Christians who eat meat immolated to idols risk entering into communion with these demons. By partaking in this way "both at the table of the Lord and at the table of demons," they will provoke the Lord's jealousy.[75]

To examine the relationships of the *kourbáni* with Old Testament sacrifice, two types of documents will be considered: Church canons and the prayers that accompany the execution of the animals even today. Even though they condemn certain cultic practices—forbidding laymen or ministers of the faith to bring animals into the church or cook meat there or to distribute the shoulder, brisket, or hide of beef and sheep to the priests within the church—several apostolic canons and conciliaries regard these practices as Jewish rather than Greek. This is reflected most notably in the vocabulary used in these materials, which is directly borrowed from the Septuagint. In the same sense, some commentaries by historians and canonists explain how the Apostles have forbidden the blood sacrifices of the *old* (Mosaic) *law* as well as customs considered Greek *and Jewish*.[76] Similarly, Canon 99 of the Sixth Ecumenical Council (691), which it is necessary to cite even though it refers to Armenian Christians, forbids the faithful to cook meat in the sanctuary and give the priests certain pieces according to *Jewish* custom. But this text also gives commentators the opportunity to bring up the foundation of the blood sacrifice among the Israelites as well as some of the practices involved in this cultic act, such as the Jewish habit of leaving the priests "parts of the sacrificed animal"—practices that are of course "forbidden" to Christians, since "animal sacrifice has been abolished." However, the same canon, in a spirit that seems less severe when compared to the zeal of later commentaries, permits the faithful to bring pieces of meat to the priests, but "outside of the church."[77]

Sacrifice undoubtedly helps ensure the living of the lower clergy, mostly rural, who used to depend in large part on gifts in kind brought by the faithful, as ecclesiastical tradition indicates.[78] A twelfth-century document, canonical responses of Nikitas, archbishop of Salonika, to questions asked by different archpriests, is of interest for several reasons. First he indicates that blood sacrifices were indeed in use in twelfth-century Macedonia and that shared (nonsacrificial) meals among priests and laity were common and permitted. Then he proposes a compromise between the demands of reality—economic, social, and religious—and theoretical requirements: blood sacrifice is condemned, but it is an act of piety to offer priests animals, alive or slaughtered, on the condition that the animals are not brought into the church. And he advises the faithful to bring their offerings according to their means; if they cannot offer a whole ox or part of the animal (the brisket, for example), or even only the hide, then let them give a pigeon or fowl from the barnyard. Moreover, village priests are permitted to bless sheep and oxen. Last, we find there an explicit reference to the Old Testament. Sacrifice as a Jewish and Greek custom is condemned, and the archbishop states at the end that "the Mosaic law is not completely abolished but transformed into something better and more lofty."[79]

Interpreting the *kourbáni* as a vestige of ancient sacrifice, folklorists encounter the obstacle of the prayers, incontestably Christian, that accompany it. A little too often their solution is purely and simply to neglect these prayers, seeing them as "foreign elements," or later additions,[80] which is to arbitrarily dissociate speech from action.

Now, the words pronounced over the victim by the Orthodox priest are part of a very long and ancient tradition. The prayers for the sacrifice of animals, gathered in the euchologion and transmitted through manuscripts dating from the eighth to the sixteenth centuries, are extremely significant, as much for the diachronic study of blood sacrifice in the Eastern church—a subject that extends beyond the limits of this work—as for their incontestable relationship with Hebraic sacrifice. Their headings, which are revealing,[81] as well as their contents, attest that the blood sacrifice is not utterly foreign to longstanding Christian religious practice.[82] Without being able to weigh all the terms and study all the nuances here, we can point out that comparable formulas are used to pray God to bless and accept the victim about to be sacrificed in memory of "your saint," exactly as he accepted the gifts of Abel,[83] the ram of the patriarch Abraham "instead of Isaac whom you loved," the pacifying sacrifices of Samuel, the incense of Zachary, and the burnt offerings of Saint Elias.

In addition to these frequent references to the Old Testament, sometimes whole sentences, slightly modified, are borrowed from the Septuagint: for example, the sacrificial prayer that, echoing Jeremiah, speaks of the abundance of harvests and flocks granted by the Lord to his people and his priests.[84]

Another explicit biblical reference is provided by the "salt vow," which today's priest sometimes utters while blessing the victim. This vow refers to the purification of the waters of Jericho by Elisha, who threw salt in them.[85] Rather than explaining the presence of this prayer by appealing to ancient sacrifice, the popular worship of the Middle Ages, or the eucharistic offering,[86] it might well be necessary to bring up the importance of salt in Hebrew worship, as well as the multiple links between salt and domestic animals in everyday reality, as well as on the level of belief.[87] Finally, when the village priest "reads the boiled dish," he uses a prayer from the Paschal rite, the "prayer to bless the fleshly food of Holy Easter Sunday." It is no accident that this prayer is said at this very moment, before the distribution of food for the common meal. God is not asked, as in the preceding prayers, to accept the sacrifice but to sanctify the meat just as he sanctifies, among other things, the fatted calf that the father kills for his lost and returned son, so that the faithful can, too, "enjoy things sanctified by you and blessed for the nourishment of all of us."[88]

*

The mistake of systematically failing to recognize the Christian context in the interpretation of the *kourbáni* becomes more obvious in the matter of what could be called the "foundation myth of neo-Greek sacrifice." According to different local traditions, every year on a certain feast day, God or the saint being honored would send a stag to the church to be killed and given as food to the participants. But one day the animal was late, and when it arrived, running and lathered, it was hurriedly slaughtered by the faithful (or the priest or the churchwardens, in some versions) without giving the creature time to rest. Henceforth, God (or the saint), angered by this brutal conduct, sent no more stags for the sacrifice; and since that time the faithful sacrifice a bull, cow, or sheep.[89] Here again, in order to try to explain the different sequences of the myth, all the resources of ancient traditions, including those of the Orient, are used. With the help of Mannhardt, the stag becomes a vegetation demon, a bringer of fecundity, seen in relation to the "universal goddess"—Artemis, *potnia thērōn*, Mâ, or Anaïtis, honored by the "deer immolations" offered to her by hunters—as well as to Acteon, Iphigenia, Zeus Icmaeus, or Aristaeus.[90] This is to completely fail to recognize the rich emblematic meaning of the stag in Christian symbolism.[91] As the devil's implacable enemy, the saints' messenger, the image of the catechumen, the soul athirst, or the Apostles or even Christ himself, the stag is fully "the soul rejoicing" in the faithful gathered at a common meal "to the glory" of God or the saints.

Two local traditions closely drawn from the legend of the stag enable us to be more specific about its meaning. On Cyprus every year, Saint Mamas, who, we are told, lived on doe's milk,[92] chose goats from his wild flock to send to men "so that the poor may eat during the *panígiri*."[93] A Thracian legend explicitly combines this illustration of supernatural generosity with the biblical model of Isaac's sacrifice. On the feast of Saint Thomas every year, a ram was found caught in a bush, an animal that "God sent as a *kourbáni*, as he had sent it for Abraham's sacrifice." After prayers were said and the animal killed, the meat was distributed among the poor. This practice continued until, having killed the ram without giving it the time to catch its breath and thus provoking divine wrath with its familiar result, men began to sacrifice sheep for the meal for the poor.[94]

In all three instances God or the saints generously provide for the fleshly meal of the faithful, particularly the poorest among them. But the other theme also seen in the myth of the foundation of the sacrifice is that of the error that ends this divine generosity. The fault is not in the slaughter itself, which is willed by God, but in man's impatience and lack of respect toward the divine gift: in short, the excess of violence. Hurriedly killing the animal, taking it as if it were prey, men did not allow it to approach them as if by its own volition, so that divine will would be carried out according to the rules.[95] They displayed greed and gluttony;[96] they lacked the friendship and love they owe to all God's creatures. By contrast, in contemporary practice the faithful treat the victims with gentleness and without violence, making sure that they arrive well rested and going so far as to pet them, calling them "my sons," "my boys," "my brave ones"—a behavior that reveals not guilt over a "murder" but the ties of profound amity that bind the Greek peasant to domestic animals, which are considered "members of the family."[97]

*

If the close relationship between the ritual killing of an animal and Hebrew sacrifice has continued to be noted over the centuries by the very people who proscribe it, it is no less true that this ritual killing was criticized by some Christian scholars anxious to purify Orthodoxy of any practice suggestive of ancient Greece, any holdover of ancient paganism. On this point the modern folklorists have predecessors. Thus, in the eighteenth century the monk Theophiles of Campania (Macedonia), a learned bishop, violently attacked the *koubanistaí* people who celebrate the *kourbánia,* for being continuators and imitators of the "vain Hellenes," impious people daring to bring their cooked *kourbáni* into the church, even filling "God's temple" with the odor of meat. He wished to flee to the mountains and deserts so as not to see and hear "these Greek things" tolerated—which was the worst part—by "several archpriests, spiritual fathers, hieromonks, and masters."[98]

But these scholars (better versed, perhaps, in matters of antiquity than in popular religion of their own time), who sometimes quote lines from Homer or texts by Greek authors concerning sacrifice in order to condemn the *kourbáni* as a pagan form of communication with God—a communication that in sacramental Christianity is supposed to be ensured only through Communion—are mistaken, it seems to us, in viewing the two practices as identical. A more careful analysis of the elements of the ritual makes it possible to note at least some fundamental differences that should orient the interpretation differently.

To be sure, the *kourbáni* establishes a communication between men on the one hand and God and his saints on the other. But it operates on its own terms, which are different from those of ancient sacrifice. The fire of the *kourbáni* is purely profane, a cooking fire; no part of the victim burns there for God or the saint receiving the sacrifice.[99] Further, no portion of the boiled or roasted meat is set aside as a symbolic offering to the saint, although such a custom should not in any way shock the Orthodox faithful, who under other circumstances set aside part of the cake or bread for the saint being honored. Thus, if it is true that the victim is indeed slaughtered in honor of a saint or the Virgin, to solicit powerful mediation in obtaining the protection and benefits requested of God in the village priest's prayers, the relation to the supernatural sphere remains somewhat fluid, in that it is maintained on a verbal level and not explicitly expressed in ritual acts. The dominant element, which gives neo-Greek sacrifice its own physiognomy, is displayed instead in the communication among men established by the common meal, in the strong bonds created by the "common table" among the diners, whether they belong to one or several communities. Their equal sharing of the same blessed fleshly food makes all of them equally the beneficiaries of the boons requested in the prayers.[100] The importance of this element emerges in the cooking of the meat and the ways it is distributed.

*

In neo-Greek sacrifice, food that has been boiled has far more value than food that has been roasted, and nearly everywhere one finds caldrons and ladles carefully kept from one year to the next.[101] The proverb, "To eat out of the same caldron," aptly expresses this close communication, this common fate. "To boil in the same caldron," a widespread metaphor, also refers to people who share the same destiny. Boiling, which creates a mixture of meat, broth, vegetables, and grains, permits a more equitable distribution of food, with the help of large spoons used for measuring it out.[102] Moreover, by combining meat with vegetable food, the boiled dish not only provides a more abundant meal but above all gives the meal another dimension, mixing in the same caldron and the same spoon the two major products of the peasants' activities.[103]

Roasted meat, although less prominent, is not excluded from the sacrificial scene;[104] and its importance is considerable, to the degree that, when it is mentioned, it is nearly always in conjunction with the great springtime feast of Saint George on April 23. Then the sacrificed sheep are roasted or boiled,[105] but the lambs, the favored offering of shepherds and stockbreeders, are always put on a spit. The choice of roasting the victims can be partly explained here by their age,[106] but also by association with the paschal lamb, which is always roasted, as part of the Judeo-Christian tradition.[107] Two documents on the feast of Saint George in Macedonia show us a combination of roasted and boiled: they speak of a common meal in the central square of the village, where "lambs are roasted and the finest ram is *sacrificed* in the saint's honor." On the basis of that phrase it could be suggested that boiling is reserved for the true sacrificial victim, the ram, while the lambs, *not sacrificed,* are put on the spit to make the meal more plentiful.[108]

The picture would be incomplete if we didn't leave a little room for raw meat, the presence of which, however limited, has not ceased to provide arguments for champions of the notion of ancient "survivals," Dionysiac, in this instance. In the sacrificial ritual of the *Anastenária* (see above, note 38), the flesh of the sacrificed bull is cut up and distributed to the families, sometimes with a strip of the animal's hide.[109] Here we must see, we are told, a "survival of the cult of Dionysus *Isodaítēs,* who was torn apart by the Titans and returned to life more alive than ever."[110] But a whole series of ritual facts weakens this interpretation. According to some folklorists the bull would justify the reference to Dionysus, who is associated with this animal in antiquity; but it is not the only sacrificial victim of the *Anastenária.*[111] Further, very often part of the victim is boiled for the meal of the *Anastenárides* for other participants in the feast.[112] Above all, two other important points must be emphasized. On the one hand, if portions of raw meat are frequently distributed at the *Anastenária,* it is doubtless because in this ritual framework the main function of the fire is not to cook the victim's flesh. It is primarily used to form the layer of burning coals on which the *Anasterárides* walk or dance barefoot, performing a rite that, as opposed to the sacrificial content, is the predominant element, the central part of the whole ceremony. On the other hand, the distribution of portions of raw meat to the village families after the sacrifice so that each may boil it at home[113] is not a practice peculiar to the *Anastenária.* We have encountered it in other sacrifices (see above), where, because of local conditions, there is no shared preparation or meal. Here again, instead of seeking the explanation for this custom in antiquity, it would be more prudent to examine its meaning in the context of Christian religious reality.

Now, in the Orthodox view the distribution of meat appears as an element meaningful in itself, even outside the sacrificial framework. To slaughter one's ox and distribute the meat to the poor is an exemplary act of Christian charity, an act so important that tradition naturally employs it to convey a man's progress toward holiness. Thus, Saint Philip, who had distributed the meat from his ox to the poor, was rewarded: the following morning he found another live ox in his stable, sent to him by God.[114] On the other hand, the importance of the distribution of free meat, especially to the poor, is so pronounced in some private sacrifices that the killing of the animal promised to the saint, even when performed in a highly solemn fashion, appears merely as a simple prelude to the distribution of the fleshly food, which alone, in the final analysis, enables the devout Christian to be acquitted of his debt to the saint.[115] It is in the same spirit that the richest villagers of the province of Saranta Ecclíssia (eastern Thrace) used to offer at sacrifices sheep or heifers with which to prepare a large common meal or at least to provide all the inhabitants with generous portions of meat.[116] Sometimes it is the church that takes on this "good deed," proposing a free meat dinner to all the pilgrims who flock there for a festival.[117] And the fact that the distribution takes place even with no preliminary sacrifice is enough to reveal this as the important dimension of this work of charity in Orthodox religion.

If church canons did not truly succeed in establishing a distinction between the *gifts* offered to the church and clergy, which were permitted and even recommended, and *sacrifices*, which were constantly forbidden, it is undoubtedly because these things were organically linked in everyday practice. And neo-Greek sacrifice cannot be understood without referring to the larger context involving gifts or, to be more exact, vows: as we have seen, *táma*, from *tázein*, to promise, is the thing promised in a sort of contractual engagement between God or the saint and his worshiper, in exchange for a good that has been requested or already received. *Támata* can be acts that one performs (fasting during the saint's feast, having mass said in his or her honor, giving alms, etc.), offerings (oil, incense, wax, fruit, wheat, etc.), or even an animal that one promises to slaughter in the saint's honor on his or her feast day. So it is not possible to separate the killing of the animal from the larger category of *támata*, of which it is a part. It will be objected that the nature of the *táma* is markedly individual; it is limited to establishing a bipolar relationship between giver and receiver, and in this way it is the opposite of the sacrifice, which is eminently collective. But within the framework of sacrifice, the *táma* confuses the boundaries between collective and individual. Even when the animal is slaughtered at home—as often happens in a private sacrifice—things are managed so that the largest possible number of people outside the limited family circle eat some of it. And very often animals killed in a public sacrifice are the *támata* regularly provided on the saint's annual feast day by private individuals or different families. In this case, the individual *táma* loses the chance aspect it usually has, acquires a regular rhythm, and combines with other *támata* to truly become the affair of the collectivity, erasing at the same time the boundary between private and public sacrifices.

The engagement binding the faithful to the saint cannot be revoked or even altered on pain of serious punishment. "Since you promised blood, the saint wants blood to flow," and the saint will not be satisfied with oil, candles, or money. It is also impossible to replace the promised victim with another one, even of more value.[118] The displeased saint not only punishes but seeks his or her due; or rather it is the victim that comes to the saint of his own accord. And the poor worshiper, powerless, thus watches his living *támata* head toward the church on the feast day, unable to stop their ineluctable progress (Cretan tradition).[119]

Interconnected with the exchange system that governs the *támata*, the blood sacrifice of domestic animals becomes more intelligible if it is associated with a more extensive phenomenon, the important place of domestic animals in popular worship, which contains multiple practices aimed at protecting flocks and herds and making them prosper. Hagiographic tradition counts a number of saints who are protectors of animals; during their feasts and sometimes outside them, animals are offered bread that has been blessed at the church. Wool is consecrated to a protector saint, incense is burned in a saint's chapel, and a saint is asked to find lost animals.[120] To prevent or cure epizootic disease, village priests or peasants sprinkle stables and animals with water from a sacred spring; and, as a general rule, they make a cross over the door to the house or stable, sometimes using manure, "to keep evil spirits from entering and protect our animals from diseases."[121] Special masses exist for "any sickness of cattle, sheep, and goats," as well as special prayers in which God is implored to bless the animals as he blessed the flocks of Abraham and Isaac, Jacob and David, to free suffering or dying animals from the Devil's oppression and tyranny, and to make them healthy and robust by having angels protect them. For it is God who gave man animals to serve him.[122] Saint Modestus and Saint Mamas are given as the authors of prayers addressed to God and Christ, which were said, according to one of the titles, "for each mortal sickness and injury of cattle, horses, donkeys, mules, sheep, goats, bees, and other animals."[123] To imagine the ritual context in which these prayers are said, one can resort to the instructions, which are somewhat vague, accompanying a mass for sick sheep to Saint Mamas. It appears that the bell of the lead animal is placed in the center of the church amid the animals, which have evidently been gathered there. After the mass, the priest reads the saint's prayer standing over this bell, which he then uses to sprinkle salt water over the sheep, using the bell instead of a cross. Last, the priest throws the bell among the animals, and as reward for his trouble, he takes the sheep struck by that instrument, while the shepherd leads away his flock, which has been blessed.[124] The presence of animals inside the church is not impossible.[125] Some popular religious practices show us that the village church can be a place open to domestic animals. And it is in this general context that the introduction of sacrificial victims into the institutional space of official religion is best understood.

In attempting to analyze some essential aspects forming the phenomenon of neo-Greek blood sacrifice, we do not claim to have made a complete study of an institution that seems, in its complexity, to be a specific fact of neo-Greek reality. Nor was our goal to venture into the distant past in a compulsory search for its "origins," "fabricating" them if that task proved unsuccessful; we did not organize our observations according to a preconceived scheme. Instead of speculating on weak and risky hypotheses and possibly losing sight of the concrete object—as is often the case in this type of exploration, which is characterized in reality by a tendency toward generalization and an ahistorical outlook—we believed it more interesting to see how the rite of popular worship interconnects with religious and social life within the context of a traditional peasant civilization and to comprehend, beyond its functionality, the values it carries for the culture in which it is alive.

TEN

A Bibliography of Greek Sacrifice
Jesper Svenbro

Preliminary Note

The bibliography presented here was conceived of primarily as a tool. Therefore it does not represent an effort to compile a complete bibliography of Greek sacrifice nor to provide the reader with the components of a history of modern research in this field. The goal was more modest: to gather titles that would be useful in future studies on Greek sacrifice. From this standpoint, it could even appear to be too extensive; however, great care was taken not to eliminate entries that pertain to important work in the area of *realia* even if they perhaps present results no longer valid today.

Consequently, the titles included in this bibliography are of very unequal value. For example, along with basic works such as those by Stengel, Rudhardt, and Casabona are articles of marginal importance but that seemed useful to the pursuit of one or two specific points. Never was one theoretical viewpoint given priority over another. Thus, within the framework of the present volume this theoretically heterogeneous bibliography does not form any sort of scientific "list of allies."

Obviously, this diversity presents problems when attempting to classify the works cited. Instead of a simple alphabetical or chronological presentation, a list of headings was chosen to make consultation easier. Descriptive rather than analytical, the headings are the result of exclusively functional considerations, which do not in any way pertain to an implicit theory of Greek sacrifice but instead are imposed by the practical intent of this bibliography.

1. General Works

Burkert, W. *Griechische Religion der archaischen und klassischen Epoche.* Die Religionen der Menschheit, 15. Stuttgart-Berlin-Cologne-Mainz, 1977.

Corbett, P. E. "Greek Temples and Greek Worshippers: The Literary and Archaeological Evidence." *Bulletin of the Institute of Classical Studies of the University of London* 17 (1970): 149–58.

Deubner, L. *Attische Feste.* 3d ed. Hildesheim, 1966.

Donaldson, J. "On the Expiatory and Substitutionary Sacrifices of the Greeks." *Transactions of the Royal Society of Edinburgh* 27 (1876): 427–65.

Eitrem, S. *Opferritus und Voropfer der Griechen und Römer.* Videnskapsselskapets Skrifter 1914, 2:1. Christiania, 1915.

—— *Beiträge zur griechischen Religionsgeschichte.* Vol. 3. Videnskapsselskapets Skrifter 1919, 2:2. Christiania, 1919.

Garcia Lopez, J. *Sacrificio y sacerdocio en las religiones micenica y homerica.* Manuales y Anejos de "Emerita" 26. Madrid, 1970.

Harrison, J. E. *Themis: A Study of the Social Origins of Greek Religion.* Cambridge, 1912.

Hewitt, J. W. "On the Development of the Thank-offering among the Greeks." *Transactions of the American Philological Association* 43 (1912): 95–111.

James, E. O. *Sacrifice and Sacrament.* London, 1962.

Kérényi, K. *La Religion antique. Ses lignes fondamentales.* Translated by Y. Le Lay. Review by the author and augmented with an unpublished chapter. Geneva, 1957. (Originally published as *Die antike Religion.* 2d ed. Cologne, 1952.)

Legrand, Ph.-E. "Sacrificium." *Dictionnaire des antiquités grecques et romaines* 4, 2 (Paris, 1909): 956–73.

Loisy, A. *Essai historique sur le sacrifice.* Paris, 1920.

Nilsson, M. P. *Griechische Feste von religiöser Bedeutung mit Ausschluss der Attischen.* Leipzig, 1906.

——— *Geschichte der griechischen Religion.* 3d ed. Vol. 1. Handbuch der Altertumswissenschaft 5, 2, 1. Munich, 1967. Vol. 2 (5, 2, 2). Munich, 1974.

Nock, A. D. "The Cult of Heroes." *Harvard Theological Review* 37 (1944): 141–74. (Reprinted in *Essays on Religions and the Ancient World,* 2:575–602. Oxford, 1972.)

Rudhardt, J. *Notions fondamentales de la pensée religieuse et actes constitutifs du culte dans la Grèce ancienne.* Geneva, 1958.

Stengel, P. *Quaestiones sacrificales.* Berlin, 1879.

——— *Opferbräuche der Griechen.* Leipzig-Berlin, 1910.

——— *Die griechischen Kultusaltertümer.* 3d ed. Handbuch der klassischen Altertumswissenschaft 5, 3. Munich, 1920.

Tresp, A. *Die Fragmente der griechischen Kultschriftsteller.* Religionsgeschichtliche Versuche und Vorarbeiten 15, 1. Giessen, 1915.

Yerkes, R. K. *Sacrifice in Greek and Roman Religions and in Early Judaism.* New York, 1952.

Ziehen, L. "Opfer." *Paulys Real-Encyclopädie der classischen Altertumswissenschaft* 18, 1. Stuttgart, 1939, 579–627.

2. Theories of Sacrifice

Bertholet, A. *Der Sinn des kultischen Opfers.* Abhandlungen der Preussischen Akademie der Wissenschaften. Philosphisch-historische Klasse, 1942, 2. Berlin, 1972.

Burkert, W. *Homo Necans. Interpretationen altgriechischer Opferriten und Mythen.* Religionsgeschichtliche Versuche und Vorarbeiten 32. Berlin, 1972.

——— "Opfertypen und antike Gesellschaftsstruktur." *Der Religionswandel unserer Zeit im Spiegel der Religionswissenschaft.* Ed. G. Stephenson. Darmstadt, 1976, 168–87.

Detienne, M. "La cuisine de Pythagore." *Archives de sociologie des religions* 29 (1970): 141–62. (Reprinted in slightly different form in *Les Jardins d'Adonis.* Paris, 1972, 76–114.)

——— *Dionysos mis à mort.* Paris, 1977.

Festugière, A.-J. "Une nouvelle théorie du sacrifice chez les Grecs." *Revue des études grecques* 59–60 (1946–47): 447–55. (Reprinted in *Etudes d'histoire et de philologie*. Paris, 1975, 37–45.) (Regarding the article of K. Meuli cited below.)

Girard, R. *La Violence et le Sacré*. Paris, 1972.

Gusdorf, G. *L'Expérience humaine du sacrifice*. Paris, 1948.

Hubert, H., and Mauss, M. "Essai sur la nature et la fonction du sacrifice," (1899). (Reprinted in M. Mauss, *Oeuvres*. Vol. 1, "Les fonctions sociales du sacré." Paris, 1968, 193–307.)

Laum, B. *Heiliges Geld. Eine historische Untersuchung über den sakralen Ursprung des Geldes*. Tübingen, 1924.

Leeuw, G. van der. "Die Do-ut-des-Formel in der Opfertheorie." *Archiv für Religionswissenschaft* 20 (1920–21): 241–53.

Lefèvre, E. "Die Lehre von der Entstehung des Tieropfers in Ovids Fasten 1.335–456." *Rheinisches Museum* 119 (1976): 39–64.

Loisy, A. "Le régime du sacrifice dans les différentes religions." *Revue bleue. Revue politique et littéraire* 52 (1914): 161–66. (Opening lecture of the course on history of religions at the Collège de France.)

Mauss, M. See Hubert, H., and Mauss, M., above.

Meuli, K. "Griechische Opferbräuche." *Phyllobolia für Peter von der Mühll*. Basel, 1946, 185–288.

Sabbatucci, D. *Saggio sul misticismo greco*. Rome, 1965.

Schwenn, F. *Gebet und Opfer*. Heidelberg, 1927.

Toutain, J. "Sur quelques textes relatifs à la signification du sacrifice chez les peuples de l'Antiquité." *Revue de l'histoire des religions* 83 (1921): 109–119.

Turner, V. "Sacrifice as Quintessential Process." *History of Religions* 16 (1977): 189–215.

Vernant, J.-P. *Leçon inaugurale au Collège de France*. Paris, 1976. (= *Religion grecque, religions antiques*. Paris, 1976. Or "Grèce ancienne et étude comparée des religions." *Archives de sciences sociales des religions* 41 (1976): 5–24.)

Yavis, C. G. "The Central Devotional Act in the Ritual of Sacrifice." Paper summarized in *American Journal of Archaeology* 55 (1951): 152–53.

3. Collections of Inscriptions

Herzog, R. *Heilige Gesetze von Kos*. Abhandlungen der Preussischen Akademie der Wissenschaften. Philologisch-historische Klasse 6. Berlin, 1928.

Prott, I. (H.) von, and Zeihen, L. *Leges Graecorum sacrae e titulis collectae*. Leipzig, 1896–1906.

Rougemont, G. "Lois sacrées et règlements religieux." *Corpus des inscriptions de Delphes*. Vol. 1, Ecole française d'Athènes. Paris, 1977.

Sokolowski, F. *Lois sacrées de l'Asie Mineure*. Ecole française d'Athènes. Travaux et mémoires des anciens membres étrangers de l'Ecole et de divers savants, 9. Paris, 1955.

——— *Lois sacrées des cités grecques. Supplément*. Ecole française d'Athènes. Travaux et mémoires . . . 11. Paris, 1962.

——— *Lois sacrées des cités grecques*. Ecole française d'Athènes. Travaux et mémoires . . . 18. Paris, 1969.

4. Sacrificial Terms

Beer, H.᾽Απαρχή *und verwandte Ausdrücke in griechischen Weihinschriften.* Doctoral diss. Wurzburg, 1914.

Benveniste, E. *Vocabulaire des institutions indo-européennes.* Vols. 1–2. Paris, 1969.

Casabona, J. *Recherches sur le vocabulaire des sacrifices en grec, des origines à la fin de l'époque classique.* Publications des Annales de la faculté des lettres et sciences humaines d'Aix, n.s. 56. Aix-en-Provence, 1966.

Festugière, A.-J. "Omophagion emballein." *Classica et Medievalia* 17 (1956): 31–34. (Reprinted in *Etudes de religion grecque et hellénistique.* Paris, 1972, 110–13.)

Fritze, H. von. "Οὐλαί." *Hermes* 32 (1897): 235–50.

―――― "Zum griechischen Opferritual. Αἴρεσθαι und καταστρέφειν." *Jahrbuch des Deutschen Archäologischen Instituts* 18 (1903): 58–67.

Gill, D. "*Trapezomata:* A Neglected Aspect of Greek Sacrifice." *Harvard Theological Review* 67 (1974): 117–37.

Institut Fernand Courby. "Les mots grecs." *Index du Bulletin épigraphique de J. et L. Robert, 1938–1965.* Vol. 1. Paris, 1972.

Laum, B. "Das Amt der Kolakreten." *Archiv für Religionswissenschaft* 25 (1927): 213–16. (Response to article by E. Maas cited under "Altars and Tables," below.)

Legrand, Ph.-E. "Questions oraculaires. 1. La promanteia." *Revue des études grecques* 13 (1900): 281–301. (Esp. 290–93.)

Merkelbach, R. "Βόλιμον." *Zeitschrift für Papyrologie und Epigraphik* 4 (1969): 203–204.

Paley, F. A. "Upon the Sacrificial Sense of μηροί and μηρία." *Transactions of the Cambridge Philological Society* 1 (1872–80): 202–203.

Platt, A. "Iphigenia and ἑκατόμβη." *Journal of Philology* 22 (1894): 43–48.

Robert, L. *Hellenica* 11–12. Paris, 1960. Chap. 10, "Παρ άστασις ἱερῶν." 126–31.

Roscher, W. H. "Zu den griechischen Religionsaltertümern." *Archiv für Religionswissenschaft* 6 (1903): 62–69. (Zu Hesychios s.v. 1. ὀγδόδιον. 2. βοῦς ῟εβδομος.)

―――― "Über Ursprung und Bedeutung des βοῦς ἕβδομος. Eine Verteidigung." *Archiv für Religionswissenschaft* 7 (1904): 419–36.

Scheller, M. "τρίττοια βόαρχος." *Zeitschrift für vergleichende Sprachforschung* 74 (1956): 233–35.

Sokolowski, F. "On the New Pergamene Lex Sacra." *Greek, Roman and Byzantine Studies* 14 (1973): 407–13. (Περιθύειν, "sacrifice regularly.")

Stengel, P. "Θυσίαι ἄσπονδοι." *Hermes* 22 (1887): 645–48.

―――― "Σπλάγχνα." *Jahrbuch des Deutschen Archäologischen Instituts* 9 (1894): 114–17.

―――― "Zu den griechischen Sakralaltertümern." *Hermes* 39 (1904): 611–17. (1. Δαρτά. 2. Θυηλαί-θυλήματα. 3. ᾽Αναλίσκειν. 4. Theophrastus, *Characters* 22.)

―――― "Κόπτειν." *Berliner philologische Wochenschriften* (1908): 927.

―――― *Opferbräuche der Griechen.* Leipzig-Berlin, 1910.

208   Jesper Svenbro

—— "Σφάγια." *Archiv für Religionswissenschaft* 13 (1910): 85–91.
—— "Zu den griechischen Schwuropfern. Τόμια. Ἱερὰ τέλεια." *Hermes* 49 (1914): 90–101.
—— "Ἐντέμνειν, ἀνατέμνειν." *Hermes* 49 (1914): 320.
—— "Λουτρά, χέρνιβες." *Hermes* 50 (1915): 630–35.
—— "Ἔνδορα." *Hermes* 54 (1919): 208–11.
—— "Zu den griechischen Sakralaltertümern." *Hermes* 59 (1924): 307–321. (1. Aristophanes *Peace* 955 ff.; 2. τέμνειν and ἐντέμνειν.)
Ziehen, L. "Εὐστόν." *Mitteilungen des Deutschen Archäologischen Instituts. Athenische Abteilung* 24 (1899): 267–74.
—— "Οὐλοχύται." *Hermes* 37 (1902): 391–400.
—— "Die Bedeutung von προθύειν." *Rheinisches Museum* 59 (1904): 391–406.
—— "Σφάγια." *Paulys Real-Encyclopädie der classischen Altertumwissenschaft* 2, 3, 2. Stuttgart, 1929, 1669–79.
—— "Zum Opferritus." *Hermes* 66 (1931): 227–34. (Αἴρεσθαι τούς βοῦς.)

5. *Priests and the Priesthood*

Bischoff, E. F. "Kauf und Verkauf von Priesterthümern bei den Griechen." *Rheinisches Museum* 54 (1899): 9–17.
Doermer, G. (Dörmer, W.) *De Graecorum sacrificulis qui ἱεροποιοί dicuntur.* Dissertationes philologicae Argentoratenses selectae 8, 1 (1885): 1–75. Thesis. Strasburg, 1883.
Ghinati, F. "Sacerdozi greci eponimi nella Sicilia romana." *Memorie dell'Accademia Patavina. Classe di Scienze morali, Lettere ed Arti* 77 (1964–65): 331–56. (Ἱεροθύτης ἀμφίπολος.)
Herbrecht, H. *De sacerdotii apud Graecos emptione venditione.* Thesis. Strassburg, 1885.
Lehmann, B. *Quaestiones sacerdotales. 1. De titulis ad sacerdotiorum apud Graecos venditionem pertinentibus.* Thesis. Königsberg, 1888.
Le Roy, C. "Λακωνικά." *Bulletin de correspondance hellénique* 85 (1961): 206–35, esp. 228–34.
Martha, J. *Les Sacerdoces athéniens.* Thesis. Paris, 1881.
Otto, W. "Kauf und Verkauf von Priestertümern bei den Griechen." *Hermes* 44(1909): 594–99.
Piccaluga, G. "Myc. *i-je-re-u:* osservazioni sul ruolo sacrale." *Atti e Memorie del Iº Congresso Internazionale di Micenologia.* Vol. 2. Incunabula Graeca 25, 2. Rome, 1968, 1046–56.
Segre, M. "Osservazioni epigrafiche sulla vendita di sacerdozio." *Rendiconti del r. Istituto Lombardo di Scienze e Lettere* 69 (1936): 811–30, and 70 (1937): 83–105.
Smith, D. R. "The Functions and Origins of Hieropoioi." Ph.D. diss., University of Pennsylvania, 1968. See also *Dissertation Abstracts* 39 (1969) 3593 A–3594A.
—— "Hieropoioi and Hierothytai on Rhodes." *L'Antiquité classique* 41 (1972): 532–39.

Sokolowski, F. "Ventes des prêtrises d'Erythrae." *Bulletin de correspondance hellénique* 70 (1946): 548–51.
——— "Fees and Taxes in the Greek Cults." *Harvard Theological Review* 47 (1954): 153–64.
Ziehen, L. "Die panathenäischen und eleusinischen ἱεροποιοί." *Rheinisches Museum* 51 (1896): 211–25.
——— "Hiereis." *Paulys Real-Encyclopädie der classischen Altertumswissenschaft* 8, 1. Stuttgart, 1913, 1411–24.

6. Butchering, Cooking, and Cooking Equipment

Amyx, D. A. "The Attic Stelai. Part 3: Vases and Other Containers." *Hesperia* 27 (1958): 163–307.
Berthiaume, G. *Les Rôles du mageiros. Étude sur la boucherie, la cuisine et le sacrifice dans la Grèce ancienne* (Mnemosyne. Supplementa 70). Leyden, 1982. (Thesis. University of Paris 8, 1976.)
Blatter, R. "Herakles beim Gelage." *Archäologische Anzeiger* 91 (1976): 49–52. (*Makhaira.*)
Borthwick, E. K. "Two Scenes of Combat in Euripides." *Journal of Hellenic Studies* 90 (1970): 15–21. (Esp. 15–17 on Euripides *Andromache* 1129–34.)
Bruns, G. *Küchenwesen und Mahlzeiten.* Archaeologica Homerica. Die Denkmäler und das frühgriechische Epos 2 Q. Göttingen, 1970.
Delcourt, M. *Pyrrhos et Pyrrha. Recherches sur les valeurs du feu dans les légendes helléniques.* Bibliothèque de la faculté de philosophie et lettres de l'université de Liège 174. Paris, 1965. (Esp. 39–40, on the *makhaira.*)
Dohm, H. *Mageiros. Die Rolle des Kochs in der griechisch-römischen Komödie.* Zetemata 32. Munich, 1964.
Festugière, A.-J. "Omophagion emballein." *Classica et Mediaevalia* 17 (1956): 31–34. (Reprinted in *Etudes de religion grecque et hellénistique.* Paris, 1972, 110–113.) (*Kanoun.*)
Giannini, A. "La figura del cuoco nella commedia greca." *Acme* 13 (1960): 135–216.
Goettling, C. *Commentatio de machaera delphica.* Jena, 1856.
Herrmann, H. V. "Kesselattaschen und Reliefuntersätze." *Die Kessel der orientalisierenden Zeit* 1. Olympische Forschungen 6. Berlin, 1966.
Humborg. "Κανοῦν." *Paulys Real-Encyclopädie der classischen Altertumswissenschaft. Supplementband* 4. Stuttgart, 1924, 867–75.
Kron, U. "Zum Hypogäum von Paestum." *Jahrbuch des Deutschen Archäologischen Instituts* 86 (1971): 117–48. (*Oboloi.*)
Latte, K. "Μάγειρος." *Paulys Real-Encyclopädie der classischen Altertumswissenschaft* 14, 1. Stuttgart, 1928, 393–95.
Laum, B. *Heiliges Geld. Eine historische Untersuchung über den sakralen Ursprung des Geldes.* Tübingen, 1924. (*Oboloi.*)
Masson, O. "Kypriaka. 2. Recherches sur les antiquités de la région de Pyla." *Bulletin de correspondance hellénique* 90 (1966): 1–21. (Two statues of *mageiroi* in the temple of Apollo *Mageirios.*)
Orlandini, P. "Lo scavo del Thesmophorion di Bitalemi e il culto delle divinità ctonie a Gela." *Kokalos* 12 (1966): 8–35. (*Makhaira.*)

Parise, N. "Per un'introduzione allo studio dei Vsegni premonetari' nella Grecia antica." *Annali dell'Istituto Italico di Numismatica.* 1979: 51–74. (*Obeloi.*)

Rankin, E. M. *The Role of the* Μάγειροι *in the Life of the Ancient Greeks.* Chicago, 1907.

Reinach, A. "Veru, verutum, vericulum." *Dictionnaire des antiquités grecques et romaines* 5, 1. (Paris, 1912): 739–41.

Reinach, S. "Culter." *Dictionnaire des antiquités grecques et romaines* 1, 2. Paris, 1887, 1582–87.

Rolley, Cl. *Les Trépieds à cuve clouée.* Ecole française d'Athènes. Fouilles de Delphes 5, 3. Paris, 1977.

Roux, G. "Meurtre dans un sanctuaire sur l'amphore de Panagurište." *Antike Kunst* 7 (1964): 30–41. (*Mákhaira.*)

Schelp, J. *Das Kanoun. Der griechische Opferkorb.* Beiträge zur Archäologie 8. Würzburg, 1975.

Sparkes, B. A. "The Greek Kitchen." *Journal of Hellenic Studies* 82 (1962): 121–37, pl. 4–8.

——— "The Greek Kitchen: Addenda." *Journal of Hellenic Studies* 85 (1965): 162–63.

Svoronos-Hadjimichalis, V. "Fosses à rôtir dans des demeures helléniques du 4ᵉ siècle av. J.-C." *L'Hellénisme contemporain* 10 (1956): 106–24. (Esp. 111–16 on the *obeloi.*)

7. Altars and Tables

Blümner, H. "Die Speisetische der Griechen." *Archäologische Zeitung* 42 (1884): 179–92 and 285.

——— "Nachtrag." *Archäologische Zeitung* 43 (1885): 287–90.

Demangel, R. "Sur l'autel creux." *Revue des études anciennes* 42. Mélanges G. Radet. 1940, 102–105.

Deonna, W. *Le Mobilier délien.* Ecole française d'Athènes. Exploration archéologique de Délos 18. Paris, 1938.

——— "Les cornes gauches des autels de Dréros et de Délos." *Revue des études anciennes* 42. Mélanges G. Radet. 1940, 111–26.

Dow, S., and Gill, D. H. "The Greek Cult Table." *American Journal of Archaeology* 69 (1965): 103–14.

Eitrem, S. "Miscellanea." *Classical Review* 35 (1921): 20–23. (Esp. 20–21 on the sacrificial table [*mensam evertere*].)

Gill, D. H. "The Classical Greek Cult Table." Thesis summarized in *Harvard Studies in Classical Philology* 70 (1965): 265–69.

Goudineau, Ch. "Ἱεραὶ τράπεζαι." *Mélanges d'archéologie et d'histoire de l'Ecole française de Rome* 79 (1967): 77–134.

Hoffmann, H. "Foreign Influence and Native Invention in Archaic Greek Altars." *American Journal of Archaeology* 57 (1953): 189–95.

Hooker, E. M. "The Significance of Altars in Greek Religion." Paper summarized in *Proceedings of the Classical Association* 47 (1950): 31.

Jameson, M. H. "The Prehistory of Greek Sacrifice." Paper summarized in *American Journal of Archaeology* 62 (1958): 223.

Kruse. "Mensa (τράπεζα)." *Paulys Real-Encyclopädie der klassischen Altertumswissenschaft* 15, 1. Stuttgart, 1931, 937–48.

Maas, E. "Bomos un Verwandtes." *Archiv für Religionswissenschaft* 23 (1925): 221–28. (Κωλακρέται. "Zerschneider des Opfertieres" (κείρω); *contra* B. Laum: see above, under "Sacrificial Terms.")

Mare, W. H. "A Study of the Greek βωμός in Classical Greek Literature." Ph.D. diss., University of Pennsylvania, 1961. (See also *Dissertation Abstracts* 23 [1962]: 1011–12.)

Mischkowski, H. *Die heiligen Tische im Götterkultus der Griechen und Römer.* Thesis. Königsberg, 1917.

Nilsson, M. P. "Griechische Hausaltäre." *Neue Beiträge zur klassischen Altertumswissenschaft. Festschrift zum 60. Geburtstag von B. Schweizer.* Stuttgart, 1954, 218–21.

Puchstein, O. "Über Brandopferaltäre." Paper summarized in *Berliner philologische Wochenschriften* 13 (1893): 290–99 and 319–20.

Ridder, A. de. "Mensa, Τράπεζα, table." *Dictionnaire des antiquités grecques et romaines.* 3, 2. (Paris, 1904): 1720–26.

Roux, G. "A propos d'un livre nouveau (S. Dow and R. F. Healey, *A Sacred Calendar of Eleusis.* Harvard Theological Studies 21. Cambridge, Ma., 1965). Le calendrier d'Éleusis et l'offrande pour la table sacrée dans le culte d'Apollon Pythien." *L'Antiquité classique* 35 (1966): 562–73.

Welter, G. "Aeginetica." *Archäologischer Anzeiger* (1938): 1–33. (Esp. 19–30.)

Yavis, C. G. *Greek Altars. Origins and Typology. An Archaeological Study in the History of Religion.* St. Louis University Studies. Monograph Series, Humanities 1. St. Louis, 1949.

8. Sacrificial Oblations

8.1. ANIMALS

Baranski, A. *Geschichte der Thierzucht und Thiermedicin im Altertum.* Vienna, 1886. (Reprinted Hildesheim, 1971.)

Brendel, O. *Die Schafzucht im alten Griechenland.* Thesis (Giessen). Würzburg, 1934.

Capozza, M. "Spartaco e il sacrificio del cavallo (Plut., *Crassus.* 11.8–9)." *Critica storica* 2 (1963): 251–93.

Cirilli, R. "Le sacrifice du chien." *Revue anthropologique* 22 (1912): 325–34.

Cumont, F. "Le coq blanc des Mazdéens et les Pythagoriciens." *Comptes rendus de l'Académie des inscriptions et belles-lettres* (1924): 284–300.

Daly, L. W. "The Cow in Greek Art and Cult." Paper summarized in *American Journal of Archaeology* 54 (1950): 261.

Deubner, L. "Lupercalia." *Archiv für Religionswissenschaft* 13 (1910): 481–508. (Esp. 503 ff. on dog sacrifices.)

Dierauer, U. *Tier und Mensch im Denken der Antike.* Studien zur antiken Philosophie 6. Amsterdam, 1977.

Fraenkel, M. "Epigraphische Miscellen. 1. Die Inschrift der Kamo." *Mitteilungen des Deutschen Archäologischen Instituts. Athenische Abteilung* 21 (1896): 440–43. (Pig sacrifices)

Hoorn, G. van. "Kynika." *Studies Presented to D. M. Robinson*. Vol. 2. St. Louis, 1953, 106–110.

Koppers, W. "Pferdeopfer und Pferdekult der Indogermanen." *Wiener Beiträge zur Kulturgeschichte und Linguistik* 4 (1936): 279–411.

Malten, L. "Der Stier in Kult und mythischem Bild." *Jahrbuch des Deutschen Archäologischen Instituts* 43 (1928): 90–139.

Mayrhofer-Passler, E. "Haustieropfer bei den Indoiraniern und den anderen indogermanischen Völkern." *Archiv Orientální* 21 (1953): 182–205.

Olivieri, A. "Sacrifizio del gallo." *Rivista Indo-Greca-Italica di filologia, lingua, antichità* 8 (1924): 135–37.

Russell, H. L. "Dog-Slaying at the Argive Sheep Festival." *Classical Bulletin* 31 (1955): 61–62.

Scheller, M. "Rinder mit vergoldeten Hörnern." *Zeitschrift für vergleichende Sprachforschung* 72 (1955): 227–28.

Scholz, H. *Der Hund in der griechisch-römischen Magie und Religion*. Thesis. Berlin, 1937.

Stengel, P. "Pferdeopfer der Griechen." *Philologus* 39 (1880): 182–85.

8.2. OTHERS

Amandry, P. *La Mantique apollinienne à Delphes*. Bibliothèque des Ecoles françaises d'Athènes et de Rome 170. Paris. 1950. (Chapter 8 is devoted to the *pelanos*.)

Brelich, A. "Offerte e interdizioni alimentari nel culto della Magna Mater a Roma." *Studi e Materiali di Storia delle Religioni* 36 (1965): 27–42.

Fritze, H. von. *De libatione veterum Graecorum*. Thesis. Berlin, 1893.

——— *Die Rauchopfer bei den Griechen*. Berlin. 1894.

Guérinot, A. "Des sacrifices ignés non sanglants dans l'Antiquité romaine, grecque et hindoue." *Revue de linguistique et de philologie comparée* 33 (1900): 240–63.

Jameson, M. H. "The Vowing of a Pelanos." *American Journal of Philology* 77 (1956): 55–60.

Mayer, Cl. *Das Öl im Kultus der Griechen*. Thesis (Heidelberg). Würzburg, 1917.

Merentitis, K. I. "Αἱ ἀναίμακτοι προσφοραὶ τῶν ἀρχαίων Ἑλλήνων." *Platon* 4 (1952): 199–222.

Pfister, F. "Rauchopfer." *Paulys Real-Encyclopädie der klassischen Altertumswissenschaft*. 2,1, 1. Stuttgart, 1914, 267–86.

Stengel, P. "Käseopfer." *Neue Jahrbücher für Philologie* 125 (1882): 672.

——— "Opferspenden." *Hermes* 57 (1922): 535–50.

Weinreich, O. "Haaropfer an Helios." *Hermes* 55 (1920): 326–28.

9. Modern Exegeses Concerning Various Points of Sacrificial Practice

Kircher, K. *Die sakrale Bedeutung des Weines im Altertum*. Religionsgeschichtliche Versuche und Vorarbeiten 9, 2. Giessen, 1910.

Radke, G. *Die Bedeutung der weissen und der schwarzen Farbe in Kult und Brauch der Griechen und Römer*. Thesis (Berlin). Jena, 1936. (Esp. 23 ff. on the color of the sacrificial animal.)

Rüsche, F. *Blut, Leben und Seele. Ihr Verhältnis nach Auffassung der griechischen und hellenistischen Antike, der Bibel und der alten Alexandrinischen Theologen. Eine*

Vorarbeit zur Religionsgeschichte des Opfers. Studien zur Geschichte und Kulten des Altertums. Ergänzungsband 5. Paderborn, 1930.

Stengel, P. "Die Zunge der Opfertiere." *Jahrbücher für Philologie* 119 (1879): 687–92.

——— "Opferblut und Opfergerste." *Hermes* 41 (1906): 230–46.

Wächter, Th. *Reinheitsvorschriften im griechischen Kult.* Religionsgeschichtliche Versuche und Vorarbeiten 9, 1. Giessen, 1910.

Wunderlich, E. *Die Bedeutung der roten Farbe im Kultus der Griechen und Römer.* Religionsgeschictliche Versuche und Vorarbeiten 20, 1. Giessen, 1925.

10. Divination

Bäckström, A. "Ieroskopia." *Žurnal ministerstva narodnago prosveščenija* (Journal of the Ministry of Public Instruction) 26 (1910): 151–209. (In Russian.)

Bouché-Leclerq, A. *Histoire de la divination dans l'Antiquité.* Vols. 1–4. Paris, 1879–82.

Halliday, W. R. *Greek Divination: A Study of its Methods and Principles.* London, 1913.

Stengel, P. "Prophezeiung aus den σφάγια." *Hermes* 31 (1896): 478–80.

——— "Vogelflug." *Hermes* 37 (1902): 486–87.

11. Division and Distribution

Berthiaume, G. *Les Rôles du mageiros. Étude sur la boucherie, la cuisine et le sacrifice dans la Grèce ancienne.* (Mnemosyne. Supplementa 70). Leyden, 1982. (Thesis. University of Paris 8, 1976.)

Borecký, B. "The Primitive Origin of the Greek Conception of Equality." *ΓΕΡΑΣ: Studies Presented to George Thomson on the Occasion of his Sixtieth Birthday.* Acta Universitatis Carolinae 1963. Philosophica et historica 1. Graecolatina pragensia 2. Prague, 1963, 41–60.

——— *Survivals of Some Tribal Ideas in Classical Greek: The Use and the Meaning of* λαγχάνω, δατέομαι *and the Origin of* ἴσον ἔχειν, ἴσον νέμειν, *and Related Idioms.* Acta Universitatis Carolinae. Philosophica et historica monographica 10. Prague, 1965.

Isenberg, M. "The Sale of Sacrificial Meat." *Classical Philology* 70 (1975): 271–73.

Launey, M. "Le verger d'Héraklès à Thasos." *Bulletin de correspondance hellénique* 61 (1937): 380–409.

Le Guen, B. "La Part du prêtre dans le sacrifice en Grèce ancienne." Unpublished ms. Paris, 1977.

Poland, F. *Geschichte des griechischen Vereinswesens.* Leipzig, 1909.

Puttkammer, F. *Quo modo Graeci victimarum carnes distribuerint.* Thesis. Königsberg, 1912.

Robert, L. *Le Sanctuaire de Sinuri près de Mylasa. 1. Les Inscriptions grecques.* Mémoires de l'Institut français d'archéologie de Stamboul 7. Paris, 1945.

12. Particular Cults and Rites

Balland, S. "Un taureau dans un arbre." *Mélanges de philosophie, de littérature et d'histoire ancienne offerts à P. Boyancé.* Collection de l'Ecole française de Rome 22. Rome, 1974, 39–56.

Besques, S. "L'Apollon Μαγείριος de Chypres." *Revue archéologique* 8 (1936): 3–11.

Blinkenberg, Ch. "Règlements de sacrifices rhodiens." *ΔΡΑΓΜΑ M. P. Nilsson dedicatum.* Acta Instituti Romani Regni Sueciae 2, 1. Lund, 1939, 96–113.

Burkert, W. "Buzyge und Palladion. Gewalt und Gericht im altgriechischen Ritual." *Zeitschrift für Religions- und Geistesgeschichte* 22 (1970): 356–68.

Daux, G. "Un règlement cultuel d'Andros." *Hesperia* 18 (1949): 58–72.

——— "La grande démarchie: Un nouveau calendrier sacrificiel d'Attique (Erchia)." *Bulletin de correspondance hellénique* 87 (1963): 603–38.

——— "Notes de lecture." *Bulletin de correspondance hellénique* 88 (1964): 676–79.

Dow, S. "The Law Codes of Athens." *Proceedings of the Massachusetts Historical Society* 71 (1953–57): 3–36.

——— "The Athenian Calendar of Sacrifices: The Chronology of Nikomakhos' Second Term." *Historia* 9 (1960): 270–93.

——— "The Greater Demarkhia of Erkhia." *Bulletin de correspondance hellénique* 89 (1965): 180–213.

Eitrem, S. "Die Labyaden und die Buzyga." *Eranos* 20 (1922): 91–121.

——— "Les Thesmophoria, les Skirophoria et les Arrhétophoria." *Symbolae Osloenses* 23 (1944): 32–45.

——— "A Purificatory Rite and Some Allied 'Rites de Passage.'" *Symbolae Osloenses* 25 (1947): 36–53.

Feyel, M. "La fête d'Apollon Tarsenos." *Revue des études anciennes* 42. Mélanges G. Radet. 1940, 137–41.

Fontenrose, J. "The Festival Called Boegia at Didyma." *University of California Publications in Classical Archaeology* 1, 11 (Berkeley, 1944): 291–304.

Healey, R. F. "Eleusinian Sacrifices in the Athenian Law Code." Thesis summarized in *Harvard Studies in Classical Philology* 66 (1962): 256–59.

——— "A Sacrifice without Deity in the Athenian State Calendar." *Harvard Theological Review* 57 (1964): 153–59.

Hiller von Gaertringen, F. "Opferinschrift aus Netteia." *Archiv für Religionswissenschaft* 19 (1916–19): 281–85.

Jameson, M. H. "Notes on the Sacrificial Calendar from Erchia." *Bulletin de correspondance hellénique* 89 (1965): 154–72.

Labarbe, J. "L'âge correspondant au sacrifice du κούρειον et les données historiques du sixième discours d'Isée." *Bulletin de la classe des lettres de l'Académie royale de Belgique* 39 (1953): 358–94.

Lawler, L. B. "Three Cakes for the Dogs." *Classical Bulletin* 30 (1954): 25–28.

Pestalozza, U. "Le origini delle Buphonia ateniesi." *Rendiconti dell'Istituto Lombardo. Classe di Lettere, Scienze morali et storiche* 89–90 (1956): 433–54. (Reprinted in *Nuovi saggi di religione mediterranea.* Florence, 1964, 203–223.)

Pfister, F. "Zalmoxis." *Studies Presented to D. M. Robinson.* Vol. 2. St. Louis, 1953, 1112–23.

Pouilloux, J. "Héraclès thasien." *Revue des études anciennes* 76 (1974): 305–316.

Prott, H. von. "Buphonien." *Rheinisches Museum* 52 (1897): 187–204.

Roux, G. "La consultation solennelle des Labyades à Delphes." *Revue archéologique* 26 (1973): 59–78.

Segre, M. "Rituali rodii di sacrifici." *Parola del passato* 6 (1951): 139–53. (Cf. the article by Blinkenberg cited above.)

Visscher, F. de. *Heracles Epitrapezios.* Paris, 1962.

Weniger, L. "Die monatliche Opferung in Olympia. 1. Die Opferordnung." *Klio* 9 (1909): 291–303.

——— "Die monatliche Opferung in Olympia. 2. Die Prozession." *Klio* 14 (1914–15): 398–446.

——— "Die monatliche Opferung in Olympia. 3. Die heilige Handlung." *Klio* 16 (1920): 1–39.

Wünsch, R. "Ein Dankopfer an Asklepios." *Archiv für Religionswissenschaft* 7 (1904): 95–116.

13. Human Sacrifice

Brelich, A. "Symbol of a Symbol." *Myths and Symbols: Studies in Honor of Mircea Eliade.* Chicago, 1969, 195–207.

Clement, P. "New Evidence for the Origin of the Iphigenia Legend." *L'Antiquité classique* 3 (1934): 393–409.

Fontinoy, C. "Le sacrifice nuptial de Polyxène." *L'Antiquité classique* 19 (1950): 383–96.

Griffiths, J. G. "Human Sacrifices in Egypt: The Classical Evidence." *Annales du Service des Antiquités d'Egypte* 48 (1948): 409–23. (1. The Story of Busiris. 2. The Alleged Sacrifice of the 'Typhonian' Men. 3. General Statements.)

Malten, L. "Leichenspiel und Totenkult." *Mitteilungen des Deutschen Archäologischen Instituts. Römische Abteilung* 38–39 (1923–24): 300–40.

Piccaluga, G. *Lykaon. Un tema mitico.* Quaderni di Studi et Materialia di Storia delle Religioni 5. Rome, 1968.

Platt, A. "Iphigenia and ἑκατόμβη." *Journal of Philology* 22 (1894): 43–48.

Schwenn, F. *Die Menschenopfer bei den Griechen und Römern.* Religionsgeschichtliche Versuch und Vorarbeiten 15, 3. Giessen, 1915.

Strachan, J. C. G. "Iphigenia and Human Sacrifice in Euripides' *Iphigenia Taurica.*" *Classical Philology* 71 (1976): 131–40.

Vermeule, E., and Chapman, S. "A Protoattic Human Sacrifice?" *American Journal of Archaeology* 75 (1971): 285–93.

14. War and Sacrifice

Eitrem, S. "Mantis and σφάγια." *Symbolae Osloenses* 18 (1938): 9–30.

Popp, H. *Die Einwirkung von Vorzeichen, Opfern und Festen auf die Kriegführung der Griechen im 5. und 4. Jahrhundert v. Chr.* Thesis (Erlangen). Wurzburg, 1959.

Szymanski, T. *Sacrificia Graecorum in bellis militaria.* Thesis. Marburg, 1909.

15. Representations of Sacrifice in Myths and Texts

Burkert, W. "Greek Tragedy and Sacrificial Ritual." *Greek, Roman and Byzantine Studies* 7 (1966): 87–121.

Durand, J.-L. "Le corps du délit." *Communications* 26 (1977): 46–61.

——— "Le rituel du meurtre du boeuf laboureur et les mythes du premier sacrifice animal en Attique." *Il mito greco. Atti del convegno internazionale. (Urbino 7–12 maggio 1973.)* Rome, 1977, 121–34.

Kahn (Kahn-Lyotard), L. "Le récit d'un passage et ses points nodaux. Le vol et le sacrifice des boeufs d'Apollon par Hermès." *Il mito greco. Atti del convegno internazionale. (Urbino 7–12 maggio 1973.)* Rome, 1977, 107–117.

—— *Hermès passe, ou les ambiguïtés de la communication.* Paris, 1978.

Kérényi, K. "Un sacrificio dionisiaco (Conferenza letta all'Università di Roma nel dicembre del 1950)." *Dionisio* 14 (1951): 139–56.

Rudhardt, J. "Les mythes grecs relatifs à l'instauration du sacrifice. Les rôles corrélatifs de Prométhée and de son fils Deucalion." *Museum Helveticum* 27 (1970): 1–15.

Segal, Ch. "Mariage et sacrifice dans les *Trachiniennes* de Sophocle." *L'Antiquité classique* 44 (1975): 30–53.

Thomsen, A. "Der Trug des Prometheus." *Archiv für Religionswissenschaft* 12 (1909): 460–90.

Vernant, J.-P. "Les troupeaux du Soleil et la Table du Soleil (*Odyssée* 12.260 ff.; Hérodote 3.17–26)." Paper summarized in *Revue des études grecques* 85 (1972): 14–17, and developed in "Food in the Countries of the Sun," above, chapter 7.

—— *Mythe et société en Grèce ancienne.* Paris, 1974. (Esp. 177–94 on the myth of Prometheus.)

Vidal-Naquet, P. "Chasse et sacrifice dans l' *Orestie* d'Eschyle." *Parola del passato* 129 (1969): 401–25. (Reprinted in J.-P. Vernant and P. Vidal-Naquet, *Mythe et tragédie en Grèce ancienne.* Paris, 1972, 133–158.)

—— "Valeurs religieuses et mythiques de la terre et du sacrifice dans l'*Odyssée*." *Annales. Economie, sociétés, civilisations* 25 (1970): 1278–97. (Reprinted in *Problèmes de la terre en Grèce ancienne.* Ed. M. I. Finley. Paris-The Hague, 1973, 269–92.)

Vincent, A. "Essai sur le sacrifice de communion des rois atlantes." *Mémorial Lagrange.* Paris, 1940, 81–96. (Plato *Critias* 119 c 5–120 c 4.)

Zeitlin, F. I. "The Motif of the Corrupted Sacrifice in Aeschylus' *Oresteia*." *Transactions and Proceedings of the American Philological Association* 96 (1965): 463–508.

—— "Postscript to Sacrificial Imagery in the *Oresteia* (*Agamemnon* 1235–37)." *Transactions and Proceedings of the American Philological Association* 97 (1966): 645–53.

16. Pictorial Documentation

Amyx, D. A. "A New Pelike by the Geras Painter." *American Journal of Archaeology* 49 (1945): 508–18.

Blatter, R. "Herakles beim Gelage." *Archäologischer Anzeiger* 91 (1976): 49–52.

Bulard, M. *Description des revêtements peints à sujet religieux.* Ecole française d'Athènes. Exploration archéologique de Délos 9. Paris, 1926. (Italian colony of Delos.)

—— "Un vase grec à figures rouges découvert en Lorraine." *Bulletin de correspondance hellénique* 70 (1946): 42–50. (also *ARV²* 1190, 26.)

Eitrem, S. "Opferaufzug und Opfermusik auf korintischem Amphoriskos." 'Αρχαιολογικὴ Ἐφημερίς, 92–93 (1953–54): vol 1, 25–34. (Ethnographic Museum of Oslo, inv. no. 6909, 5.)

Friis Johansen, K. "Eine neue caeretaner Hydria." *Opuscula romana* 4. Acta Instituti Romani Regni Sueciae, Series in 4°, 22. Lund, 1962. (Copenhagen inv. no. 13567.)

Lehnstaedt, K. *Prozessionsdarstellungen auf attischen Vasen.* Thesis. Munich, 1971.

Masson, O. "Kypriaka. 2. Recherches sur les antiquités de la région de Pyla." *Bulletin de correspondance hellénique* 90 (1966): 1–21. (Two statues of *mageiroi* in the temple of Apollo *Mageirios*.)

Metzger, H. *Recherches sur l'imagerie athénienne.* Publications de la bibliothèque Salomon Reinach 2. Paris, 1965.

Ricci, G. "Una hydria ionica da Caere." *Annuario della R. Scuola Archeologica di Atene* 24–26, n.s. 8–10 (1946–48): 47–57.

Rizza, G. "Una nuova pelike a figure rosse e lo 'splanchnoptes' di Styppax." *Annuario della Scuola Archeologica di Atene* 37–38, n.s. 21–22 (1959–60): 321–45.

Roux, G. "Meurtre dans un sanctuaire sur l'amphore de Panagurišté." *Antike Kunst* 7 (1964): 30–41.

Rumpf, A. *Die Religion der Griechen.* Bilderatlas zur Religionsgeschichte 13–14. Leipzig, 1928.

Simon, E. *Opfernde Götter.* Berlin, 1953. (Self-libations.)

Webster, T. B. L. *Potter and Patron in Classical Athens.* London, 1972. (See index s.v. *cult*, 308.)

Abbreviations

1. Journals, Collections, etc.

ABV	J. D. Beazley. *Attic Black-Figure Vase Painters*. Oxford, 1956.
Annales E.S.C.	*Annales. Economie, sociétés, civilisations.*
ArThTh	*Archeion tou Thrakikou Laographikou kai Glossikou Thisavrou.*
*ARV*²	J. D. Beazley. *Attic Red-Figure Vase Painters*. 2d ed. Oxford, 1963.
ASAA	*Annuario della [R.] Scuola Archeologica di Atene.*
BCH	*Bulletin de correspondance hellénique.*
EKEL	*Epetiris tou Kentrou Erevnis tis hellinikis Laographias.*
ELA	*Epetiris tou Laographikou Archeiou.*
FGrHist.	F. Jacoby. *Fragmente der griechischen Historiker*. Berlin, 1923. Reprinted 1957.
JDAI	*Jahrbuch des Deutschen Archäologischen Instituts.*
Laogr.	*Laographia.*
LSA	F. Sokolowski. *Lois sacrées de l'Asie Mineure*. Paris, 1955.
LSG	——— *Lois sacrées des cités grecques*. Paris, 1969.
LSG Suppl.	——— *Lois sacrées des cités grecques. Supplément.* Paris, 1962.
L.S.J.	Liddell, Scott, Jones. *A Greek-English Lexicon.*
Mes. Gram.	*Mesaionika Grammata.*
O.F. . . . Kern	O. Kern. *Orphicorum Fragmenta*. Berlin, 1922. Reprinted 1963.
R.E.	*Paulys Real-Encyclopädie der klassischen Altertumswissenschaft.*
Thr.	*Thrakika.*

2. Authors

Berthiaume	Berthiaume, G. *Viandes grecques. Le status social et religieux du cuisiner-sacrificateur (mágeiros) en Grèce ancienne*. Thesis. University of Paris, 1976.
Bruneau	Bruneau, Ph. *Recherches sur les cultes de Délos à l'époque hellénistique et à l'époque impériale*. Paris, 1970.
Burkert 1972	Burkert, W. *Homo Necans. Interpretationen altgriechischer Opferriten und Mythen*. Religionsgeschichtliche Versuche und Vorarbeiten 32. Berlin and New York, 1972.

219

Burkert 1977   ——— *Griechische Religion der archäischen und klassischen*
                        Epoche. Die Religionen der Menschheit 15. Stuttgart, Ber-
                        lin, Cologne, Mainz, 1977.
Casabona   Casabona, J. *Recherches sur le vocabulaire des sacrifices en grec,*
                        des origines à la fin de l'époque classique. Aix-en-Provence,
                        1966.
Cassirer   Cassirer, E. *Philosophie des formes symboliques*. Vol. 2. *La pen-*
                        sée mythique [1924]. French ed. 1972. (All page references
                        are to this edition.)
Chantraine   Chantraine, P. *Dictionnaire étymologique de la langue grec-*
                        que. Paris, 1974.
Detienne 1972   Detienne, M. *Les jardins d'Adonis. La mythologie des aro-*
                        mates en Grèce. Paris, 1972.
Detienne 1977   ——— *Dionysus mis à mort*. Paris, 1977.
Durand 1977   Durand, J.-L. "Le corps du délit." *Communications* 26
                        (1977): 46–61.
Durkheim *Formes*   Durkheim, E. *Formes élémentaires de la pensée religieuse*.
                        Paris, 1910.
Durkheim *Textes*   ——— *Textes*. Vols. 2–3. Ed. V. Karady. Paris, 1975.
Roux   Roux, G. "Meurtre dans un sanctuaire sur l'amphore de
                        Panagurišté." *Antike Kunst* 7 (1964): 30–41.
Rudhardt   Rudhardt, J. *Notions fondamentales de la pensée religieuse et*
                        actes constitutifs du culte dans la Grèce classique. Geneva,
                        1958.
Vernant 1974   Vernant, J.-P. *Mythe et société en Grèce ancienne*. Paris, 1974.

Notes

Chapter 1. Culinary Practices and the Spirit of Sacrifice

1. *O.F.,* 34–36, 209–214, Kern. The case is presented by I. M. Linforth, *The Arts of Orpheus* (Berkeley, 1941), 307–64. Interpretations and models are found in Detienne 1977, 161–217.

2. Detienne 1977, 166.

3. 6.5, ed. G. Heuten, 55–57 (*Commentaire* [Brussels, 1938], 152–56).

4. Berkeley, 1950, 277–78.

5. See the comments on *The Golden Bough:* "In truth, Frazer's explanations could not be explanations in any way if they did not in the final analysis appeal to an inclination within ourselves" (French trans., J. Lacoste, in *Actes de la recherche en sciences sociales* 16 [1977]: 37).

6. Detienne 1977, 171ff.

7. *Histories* 2.41.

8. The problem of fish and its importance in the Greek system of foods still remains. See D. Bohlen, *Die Bedeutung der Fischerei für die antike Wirtschaft. Ein Beitrag zur Geschichte der antiken Fischerei,* thesis (Hamburg, 1937). With the exception of the tuna (the only fish that bleeds) offered to Poseidon under exceptional circumstances, fish is never sacrificed before being eaten. In the speech "On the Mother of the Gods" (17), Julian gives two reasons for this. On the one hand, they are not domesticated animals; we do not lead them to pasture, nor do we control their reproduction. Moreover, down in the depths of the ocean, they are in some ways more "chthonian" than grains.

9. Aristotle *Constitution of the Athenians* 57. On the city as an *Opfergemeinschaft,* cf. Burkert 1977, 382–85.

10. Dinarchus *Contra Aristogiton* 9–10. Cf. U. E. Paoli, "Pouvoirs du magistrat de police dans le droit attique," *Revue internationale des droits de l'Antiquité,* 3d ser., 4 (Brussels, 1957): 155.

11. Aristophanes *Birds* 43–45, 356–60, 387–91.

12. 1.25.4.

13. J. Bousquet, "Convention entre Myania et Hypnia," *BCH* 89 (1965): 665–81.

14. Ph. Gauthier, *Symbola: Les étrangers et la justice dans les cités grecques* (Nancy, 1972), 45–47.

15. The concept comes from the Indianists, first Louis Dumont, *Homo hierarchicus: An Essay on the Caste System,* pp. 146–51; and then M. Biardeau and Ch. Malamoud, *Le Sacrifice dans l'Inde ancienne* (Paris, 1976).

16. See "La cuisine de Pythagore," *Archives de sociologie des religions* 29 (1970): 141–62; Detienne 1972, 71–114.

17. Detienne 1977, 163–217.

18. Eudoxus of Cnidus, in Porphyry *Life of Pythagoras* 7.

222   *Notes to Pages 9–15*

19. Detienne 1977, 140–42; Urs Dierauer, *Tier und Mensch im Denken der Antike* (Amsterdam, 1977), 100–161.
20. Plutarch *De defectu oraculorum* 437 b.
21. Plutarch *Quaestiones conviviales* 729 f ff.
22. For example, Pausanias 4.13.1.
23. *LSG*, no. 151, 1ff. For the different meanings see L.S.J., s.v.
24. Plato *Critias* 119 d; *Protagoras* 320 a; Aeschylus *Prometheus* 666; Hesychius, s.v. *anemōtas*.
25. Humborg, s.v. *kanoûn*. *R.E. Suppl.* B. 4 (1924), c. 867–75; Rudhar⸝., 259–61; J. Schelp, *Das Kanoûn. Der griechische Opferkorb* (Wurzburg, 1975), 23–25.
26. Plutarch *Greek Questions* 24.296 f–297 a.
27. On this point, cf. the work of Guy Berthiaume, as well as the comments of J.-L. Durand, this volume, 100–104.
28. Detienne 1977, 174–82.
29. See again the work of G. Berthiaume.
30. See the comments of J.-L. Durand, "Greek Animals," chapter 3 of this volume, section entitled "The Dismantled Body"; in the images "the deed that actually drenches the blade and altar in blood is never pictured."
31. *Sphageus* is, for example, the technical term on Cos (*LSG* 15, 40–41), reserved for the one of the heralds, *kērukes*, who is chosen to stab the ox. Casabona (174–80) has called attention to the political connotations of *sphagē*—a massacre provoked by civil wars.
32. Homer, *Hymn to Apollo* 510–35.
33. Burkert 1972, 136; G. Roux, *Delphes. Son oracle et ses dieux* (Paris, 1976), 88–89; and, above all, Gr. Nagy, *The Best of the Achaeans* (Baltimore, 1981), chap. 7, "The Death of Pyrrhos." Cf. the last pages of chapter 6, this volume.
34. S. Besques, "L'Apollon *Mageiros* de Chypre," *Revue archéologique* 8 (1936): 3–11; O. Masson, "Kypriaka," *BCH* 90 (1966): 1, 10–24.
35. Plato *Phaedrus* 265 e; *Politics* 287 c.
36. B. Borecky, *Survivals of Some Tribal Ideas in Classical Greek* (Prague, 1965), 9–30.
37. L. Robert, *Le Sanctuaire de Sinuri* (Paris, 1945), 49–50, and the work of G. Berthiaume.
38. Plutarch *Quaestiones conviviales* 2.10.642 f–643 e, and the analyses of Laurence Kahn, *Hermès passe ou les ambiguïtés de la communication* (Paris, 1978).
39. L. Gernet, *Anthropologie de la Grèce antique* (Paris, 1968), 382–402.
40. Published in 1899 in the second volume of *L'année sociologique* but reprinted in M. Mauss, *Oeuvres*, vol. 1, *Les fonctions sociales du sacré*, ed. V. Karady (Paris, 1968), 193–307.
41. Rudhardt, 295–96.
42. Lévi-Strauss, *Le Totémisme aujourd'hui* (Paris, 1962), 3–4.
43. J.-Fr. Lafitau, *Les Moeurs des sauvages américains comparées aux moeurs des premiers temps* (Paris, 1724), 1:163. Moreover, sacrifice always concerns animals and plants that men use for food and that are useful to them in some way. "One always sacrificed what was most precious." Christian sacrifice can even be discovered in the religion of the brahmans: the remains of the sacrifice and "the rice that is distributed in the Temples among the Indians has the name of *Prajadam*. This Indian word means 'divine grace' in our language and is what we express by the term *Eucharist*" (2:126).
44. *Lectures on the Religion of the Semites,* 2d ed. (Edinburgh, 1894), 226ff.
45. S. Reinach, *Cultes, mythes et religions*, vol. 1 (Paris, 1905), 103; vol. 3, (Paris, 1908), 36; and other works.
46. Text reprinted in M. Mauss, *Oeuvres,* 1:12.
47. Ibid., 12–15.
48. Ibid., 283–307.

49. Ibid., 300.

50. Ibid., 288.

51. Ibid., 304–305.

52. Ibid., 305.

53. Before concluding, the *Essai* (300) has the sentence, "The Christian imagination has built according to ancient blueprints." This is true, but it is no less true that the imagination of the sociologists, and others, has built according to Christian blueprints.

54. It was also the year when A. A. Goldenweiser published "Totemism: An Analytical Study," *Journal of American Folklore* 23. Cf. Lévi-Strauss, *Le Totémisme aujourd'hui* 6.

55. H. H. Pinard de la Boullaye, *L'Etude comparée des religions*, vol. 2 (Paris, 1925), 199.

56. Inaugural lecture for the chair in the history of religions at the Collège de France, May 3, 1909; *Essai historique sur le sacrifice* (Paris, 1920).

57. Durkheim, *Formes*, 480.

58. Ibid., 422.

59. See Cassirer, 259.

60. Durkheim, *Formes*, 427–64.

61. Ibid., 451.

62. Ibid., 452.

63. Ibid., 465.

64. *L'Année sociologique* (1913): 52–53.

65. Durkheim, *Formes*, 480–86.

66. Ibid., 486–91.

67. M.-J. Lagrange, *Introduction à l'étude du Nouveau Testament*, vol. 4; *Critique historique*, vol. 1; *Les mystères: Porphisme* (Paris, 1937), 207–210.

68. M.-J. Lagrange, *Etudes sur les religions sémitiques*, 2d ed. (Paris, 1905), 2–40.

69. An inadmissible position for a Kantian philosopher such as J. Lachelier, according to whom the true religion, Protestantism or Catholicism, can only be an inner effort and consequently, a solitary one, leading to the isolated state of our inner being and detachment from all else (discussion at the *Société française de Philosophie* (1913), reproduced in Durkheim, *Textes*, 2: 53–59).

70. Durkheim, *Formes*, 610.

71. "The science of civilization . . . is essentially the science of reformers," E. B. Tylor, *La Civilisation primitive*, 2d ed. (1873), French ed., P. Bruet and Ed. Barbier (Paris, 1876), 2:581.

72. G. Davy, "E. Durkheim: l'homme," *Revue de métaphysique et de morale* 26 (1919): 188.

73. *Revue française de sociologie* 17(2) (1976): *A propos de Durkheim* (particularly the articles by B. Lacrois and P. Birnbaum).

74. Text published under the title, "La grandeur morale de la France," January 8, 1916, in the *Manuel général de l'instruction primaire. Journal hebdomadaire des instituteurs et des institutrices* 83 (17), 217–18 (reproduced in the *Revue française de sociologie* 17(2) (1976): 193–95.

75. Durkheim, *Textes*, 3: 174.

76. Regarding a lecture in 1906 (in Durkheim, *Textes*, 2:12, n. 2). Cf. the comments of J.-Cl. Filloux, "Il ne faut pas oublier que je suis fils de rabbin," *Revue française de sociologie* 17(2) (1976): 259–66.

77. Durkheim, *Formes*, 452.

78. Account by G. Davy, cited by B. Lacroix, "La vocation originelle d'Emile Durkheim," *Revue française de sociologie* 17(2) (1976): 218.

79. Cassirer, 257–71: "Cult and Sacrifice."

80. Cassirer, 260.

81. Ibid., 261.
82. M. Mauss, *Oeuvres,* 1:16–17.
83. Ibid., 1:306–307.
84. Cassirer, 222–23, 270; M. Mauss,*Oeuvres,* 1:296–300.
85. With the essay by René Girard (*La Violence et le Sacré* [Paris, 1972], extended and clarified in *Des choses cachées depuis la fondation du monde* [Paris, 1978]), the Christian origins of the model of sacrifice are integrated into a total anthropological project that aims both to "explain" the founding principle of any culture and comprehend the unleashing of violence in the contemporary world. Rehabilitating one of the great factors in Frazerian analysis but generalizing it into a single and essential mechanism, Girard discovers in the "scapegoat"— that is, in the kernel of the sacrificial violence—the principle that accounts for cultural order and symbolic thought. Not only is the unity of all rites embodied in the cosmic figure of sacrifice, but our entire history can be deciphered through the sacrificial mechanism. In the form of a thoroughly sociological explanation—"Society begins . . . with the religious, as Durkheim has seen . . . but the religious is one and the same as the scapegoat" (*La Violence et le Sacré,* 426)—Girard's enterprise is located exactly where the author situates it, in broad daylight: "*Truth comes from the Jews*" (italicized by Girard in the discussion published in *Esprit* [1973]: 556), more exactly, from the Judeo-Christians. Our entire history takes place between two *real* events: the primary lynching (*La Violence et le sacré,* 437), which sets up a single victim in place of the community threatened by destructive violence; and the sacrifice of Jesus Christ who by his death puts an end to the violence at the basis of society, summoning us to understand the new need for nonviolence and giving us in addition the key to our past and our future.

Chapter 2. At Man's Table

1. In his role as founder of the first sacrifice, Prometheus is not presented as the one who kills the animal but the one who leads it into place and then disposes of the parts before lighting the fire on the altar, according to procedures evoked by a quasi-technical vocabulary (*ostea leuka boos . . . euthetisas katethēke kalupsas argeti dēmōi* [*Theogony* 540–41]). Above all, he is the one entrusted with distributing among the assistants the pieces of the sacrificial victim: *dassamenos* in line 537, *diedassao moiras* in line 544. This distributive function, although less spectacular, is nonetheless essential in the ritual of the sacrifice and is highlighted within the particular context of the *Theogony.*

2. *Hesiods Theogonie. Eine unitarische Analyse* (Vienna, 1966), 73–85.

3. *Theogony* 562.

4. Ibid., 569.

5. J.-P. Vernant, "Le mythe prométhéen chez Hésiode," in *Mythe et société en Grèce ancienne* (Paris, 1974), 177–94.

6. Zeus *seems* tricked, since in the perspective of the Hesiodic *Theogony,* everything realized in the universe ultimately corresponds to the will of the sovereign god, to his plan or *boulē.* Thus in a certain manner the trickery of Prometheus is part of the plan, already envisioned by Zeus, to give humans the sad fate that is their own. Therefore, the moment the Titan gives him the shares doctored so that he chooses the one that will go to the gods, the text is quick to indicate that "Zeus of the eternal counsels understood the ruse and did not fail to recognize it. But already he was plotting in his heart how he was indeed to bring about the mortals' misfortune" (551–52). Is this to say that everything is decided in advance and that in this duel, the outcome of which is in some way predetermined, there is no place for true confrontation or initiative, much less for Promethean success, even a temporary one? This would be misreading the logic of a text that, while affirming Zeus' infallibility as a truth in principle, stresses meticulously in the action what is due to Prometheus, the successes he attains, and Zeus' discomfiture, his anger at seeing himself first countered, then tricked by

the Titan (cf. *Theogony* 533: *khōomenos;* 554: *khōsato, kholos;* 568: *ekholōse; Works* 53: *kholōsamenos*). The text of *Works and Days* specifies that this anger is in response to Prometheus' theft of the fire *lathōn Dia* (52) behind Zeus' back. Zeus speaks to the Titan in these terms, "You laugh for having stolen the fire and deceiving my spirits (*emas phrenas ēperopeusas* [55])." If we must state that Zeus foresaw everything, we must immediately add that according to this foresight, Prometheus would take the initiative to compete with him, that he would succeed in tricking him, that the king of the gods would be furious about it, and that he would bring about men's unhappiness, not directly but by means of the very advantages that their defender would have gained against him. For anyone inclined to find this interpretation too "sophisticated" (despite the fact it is called for by the text), it could be recalled that Christian theology affirms God's omnipotence and omniscience and humanity's free will, which implies the undetermined character of human decisions. Suffice it to indicate, keeping with Hesiod, that if in the *Theogony* Cronus swallows his first children, it is because he has learned from Gaea and Uranus that his destiny had been set: his fate is to succumb some day to his own son "by the will of the great Zeus" (465). Now, Zeus has not yet been born. Thus events will unfold according to the plans of Zeus, *Dios . . . dia boulas,* even before Zeus, making his entrance into the universe of the gods, could have thought of these plans.

7. The tale as a whole conveys this seesaw effect; it is only at the end of the contest, when the game is over, that it is borne out that everything always happened according to Zeus' *boulē.* This does not mean that Prometheus has not scored any points during the confrontation, nor does the fact that the outcome of the war between Titans and Olympians is predetermined (Cronus' fate is to be defeated by his son) prevent the combat between the two sides from being real and even uncertain for ten full years (637–38). The narrative device, which consists of establishing from the outset a completely omniscient Zeus in order to then show him surprised and deceived on two occasions prior to his victorious counterattack, gradually reveals throughout the dramatic form of the tale the deceptive character of the Promethean gifts, whose ambiguous advantages always end up working against their beneficiaries.

8. *Theogony* 535, 552, 564, 588, 592, 600; *Works* 92, 103.

9. *Epi khthoni* (*Theogony* 556, 564; *Works* 90; see also 101).

10. *Kakon* or *kaka* (*Theogony* 512, 551–52, 595, 600, 602, 609, 612); *Kēdea lugra* (*Works* 49, 95, 100), *pēma* (*Works* 56); *kakon* or *kaka* (*Works* 58, 88, 91, 101).

11. *Alphēstēs:* who eats wheat (*Theogony* 512 and *Works* 82). These are the only two examples in the *Theogony* and *Works and Days* of the term to describe men (in addition, see fr. 73.5 Merkelbach-West, where Atalanta wishes to flee marriage to the *andrōn alphēstaōn,* and *Scutum* 29, where the adjective distinguishes the gods from the men who follow Alcmenes' husband). In the first two cases, the adjective applies to men in the context of the reception of Pandora, the first human wife. On this level the connection between grain cultivation and marriage is already evident. As P. Vidal-Naquet has noted following Chantraine (*Annales E.S.C.* 25 [1970]:1280, n. 3), *alphēstēs,* the bread-eater, is constructed on the root *ed-od,* "to eat," which is parallel though opposed in meaning to *ōmēstēs,* "eater of raw meat."

12. *Theogony* 513–14, 592, 600–601, 603–612; *Works* 80–82, 94 ff.

13. See fr. 1 Merkelbach-West = 82 Rzach: "For the meals at that time were in common, and common were the seats for the Immortals and mortal men."

14. See *Odyssey* 3, 44, 336, 420; *Iliad* 24, 69. The expression *dais theou* or *theōn* underscores the division in the sacrificial meal between men on the one hand and gods and men on the other. On the aspect of the gift, see Plato, *Euthyphro* 14 c. 8–9: "Is not sacrificing offering gifts to the gods?"

15. *Works* 112 ff. Under the reign of Cronus, the men of the golden age lived *hōs theoi,* like gods: always young, sheltered from pain, misery, work, and old age; far from all evils, *kakōn ektosthen hapantōn,* all goods were theirs, *esthla de panta toisin eēn.* They spent their

time making merry in feasts spontaneously provided by the furrows of a generously fertile earth (*zeidōros aroura automatē*), dispensing them from all labor.

16. Casabona (1966).

17. Hesiod's text does not mention the *splankhna*, the viscera. Given the religious importance of these organs and their ritual consumption, this cannot be a simple omission. The poet deliberately lets it pass; he wishes to consider only the two parts of the victim that, by their different allocation and treatment, unequivocally convey the contrast between the race of gods "who live forever" and that of mortal men, who in order to survive are subjected to the necessity of eating a certain type of food. Although food for humans, the *splankhna*, organs filled with blood, roasted directly over the flames of the altar, have a status that puts them more on the side of the gods and makes the gap separating the two forms of existence less acute (see Detienne 1977, 174–79). This is why Hesiod uses the term *enkata*, entrails, to evoke the internal parts of the animal that are next to the flesh that surrounds them (*sarkes*). The *enkata* also include the *entera*, the intestines, as well as the viscera strictly speaking, that is, the organs of digestion as well as the blood organs (see Berthiaume). By placing flesh and entrails on the same level (*sarkas te kai enkata piona dēmōi* [538]), as parts that are equally edible and reserved for men, in opposition to the *ostea leuka* (540) intended for the gods, Hesiod in some way banishes the problem of the *splankhna*, which men eat but which are kept from being completely confused with the *krea* or *sarkes* because of their sacrificial status. The ambiguity of the term *enkata* that applies, depending on the context, to the intestines (*Odyssey* 9.293) or the viscera (*Odyssey* 12.363–64) makes it possible for him to lump together everything that is not *ostea leuka* without committing himself.

18. *Theogony* 74; 112: *hōs t'aphenos dassanto kai hōs timas dielonto;* 885: *ho de toisin heas diedassato timas.*

19. Ibid. 535: "It was a time when gods and mortal men became separate from each other (*ekrinonto*) at Mecone."

20. Ibid. 537: *dassamenos:* 544: *diedassao moiras.*

21. Compare *Theogony* 535: *ekrinonto;* 537 and 544: *diedassao* (Prometheus, in the conflict between men and gods) with *Theogony* 882: *krinanto* and 885: *diedassato* (Zeus, in the conflict between Titans and Olympians).

22. *Theogony* 882: *timaōn krinanto biēphi.*

23. See *Theogony* 392–96 and 423–28, which give details concerning the meaning and modalities of the *dasmos* over which Zeus presides for the gods (885).

24. Prometheus, speaking to Zeus: *Zeu kudiste megiste theōn* (*Theogony* 548). Zeus speaking to Prometheus: *pantōn arideiket' anaktōn* (*Theogony* 543). Especially to be noted is Zeus' use of the term *pepon* (544 and 560), which, in referring to what is well cooked, soft, or gentle, is not without humor under the circumstances. In this entire passage of the *Theogony*, Hesiod describes Zeus as *aphthita mēdea eidōs* (545, 550, 561); and at the height of his rage the god refers to Prometheus as *pantōn peri mēdea eidōs*, "you who know more about it than anyone in the world," attributing to his rival the description that applies to himself. Throughout the confrontation between the two protagonists, they not only never abandon their mutual politeness, but smilingly meet their adversary, hiding their hostility and giving the aggression the form of mockery. If in *Works and Days* an angry Zeus (*kholōsamenos*, [53]) bursts out laughing (*egelasse* [59]), in the *Theogony* Zeus' mockery (*kertomeōn* [545]) provokes the slight smile of the Titan (*epimeidēsas* [547]), plotting his perfidious ruse (*doliē tekhnē*) and calibrating his deception (*exapatēsen,* [565]). Thus the *eris* between the two divinities uses the sweet and misleading seductions of speech, charm, and persuasion, not the violence of force. It is an *eris* that is played out in the sphere where Aphrodite, associated with Eros and Himerus, usually operates. For indeed the lot of the goddess is, along with gentleness and sweet pleasure, the talk of young women, smiles (*meidēmata*), and deceptions (*exapatas*) (*Theogony* 205). But it must be added that in his way of dividing the sacrifice,

Prometheus feigns the manners of the good king who, in Zeus' name, gives what is due in straightforward sentences, *diakrinonta themistas itheiēsi dikēisin* (85–86). To settle a quarrel (87), the king, inspired by the Muses, uses not force but persuasive charm, courteous gentleness, and the tender pleasure of honeyed words. The musical virtue of his pronouncements of justice has the power of creating an amicable settlement by giving the injured party compensation that reestablishes the correct equilibrium but does so without coercion or violence in a gentle manner: *metatropa erga teleusi rhēidiōs* (89–90). Far from reestablishing the equilibrium, Prometheus disrupts it by dividing the shares in a partial manner; see 544: *heterozēlōs diedassao moiras.*

25. Compare to *Theogony* 657: Cottus greets in Zeus the one who has "spared" the Immortals the shuddering evil (*alktēr*), and 614: *akakēta Promētheus,* Prometheus the benefactor (with respect to men).

26. *Theogony* 565; *Works* 50.

27. See *Theogony* 386ff. In the divine world under Zeus' dominion, Zelus no longer acts as an element of confrontation and dissociation. By the same right as his brother and sister, Cratus and Bia, who continually frame the person of Zeus and accompany him wherever he goes, Zelus acts as the guarantor of the supremacy of the new king of the gods. Closely associated with Nike, with whom he is paired, he immediately dooms to failure any attempt by any rival of Zeus' to dispute his sovereign power.

28. *Theogony* 782–806. The comparison of this passage with *Works and Days* 190–200 emphasizes the difference in *eris* in the worlds of the gods and men. When *eris* arises among the gods, the procedure of the Oath automatically designates the guilty party, who is compelled to perjure himself (*epiorkos,* 793). Immediately the guilty party is "hidden" in an evil sleep (798) and expelled from the divine realm (801–804). Among men, when a bad *eris* has invaded everything and become the inseparable companion of poor men, the oath is no longer given any value, or *kharis* (*Works* 190). The evildoer will base his lies on perjuries, *epi d' horkon omeitai* (194), but this time it will not be the guilty one who will be hidden and excluded. On the contrary, it will be *Aidōs* and *Nemesis,* the two divinities still present in the human world as the last link to that of the gods, who will hide (198), abandoning men to *eris,* to regain the realm of the gods (199–200).

29. Among the gods, *eris* is deployed the moment Cronus commits violence against his father Uranus. Taking his children aside (*neikeiōn,* 208), Uranus tells them that in the future this heinous crime will require *tisis,* revenge. This *tisis* is the conflict that will set Titans against Olympians in the form of *eris* and *neikos.* Indeed, when Rhea is about to give birth to Zeus, she asks Gaea and Uranus to consider a plan, which will make it possible for the debt her father owed the Erinys to be paid by saving Zeus: *teisaito d'Erinus patros heoio* (472). As a result, everything will take place in the form of a power struggle between Cronus the king and his son with the violent heart (476) until the triumph of the latter. With Zeus' victory, the *tisis* is paid and order regained.

30. *Works* 29 and 30.

31. Ibid. 321–22, with the opposition between *khersi biēi* and *apo glōssēs.*

32. Ibid. 325–26 and 333–34.

33. Ibid. 18–19, with the opposition: *aitheri naiōn* / *gaiēs en rhizēisi.*

34. Ibid. 28.

35. *Bios* (31) =*Dēmēteros aktē* (32).

36. *Works* 44.

37. Ibid. 113–18. Men of the golden race live *ater ponōn,* without fatiguing work, content with what they have, *ethelēmoi,* tranquil and peaceful, *hēsukhoi,* that is, without jealousy or quarrels, without *eris.*

38. Ibid. 47–48.

39. Ibid. 47–48.

40. As Benedetto Bravo has pointed out to me, the terms *erga* and *ergazesthai* apply on two occasions in *Works and Days* to the activities of navigation and maritime commerce (45 and 641). It is nonetheless true that in the context of the poem these words refer essentially to agricultural labor (fifty examples, more or less).

41. *Works* 47–48.

42. Cf. J.-P. Vernant, *Mythe et pensée chez les Grecs* (Paris, 1974), 2: 19–20; M. Detienne, *Crise agraire et attitude religieuse chez Hésiode*, coll. Latomus 68 (Brussels, 1963), 34–51.

43. *Works* 300–301, 309: *kai ergazomenoi polu philteroi athanatoisin;* 826–28.

44. Ibid. 388: *pediōn nomos.*

45. Ibid. 226–27: *Eris* gives birth to *Ponos* and *Limos.*

46. *Iliad* 5.339–43: not eating bread, they do not have blood and are called Immortals. In *Convivium septem sapientium* Plutarch gives the following commentary on this passage of Homer: "By this he means that food is not only a means of living but a means of dying" (160 b 2–3).

47. Ibid. 21.464–65.

48. *Odyssey* 2.290 and 20.108: *alphita, muelon andrōn.*

49. *Works* 276–80.

50. After observing that cultivation cooks the food of plants and makes it active, Aristotle writes in *Problemata* 20.12.964 a. 19–21: "The fruits that result from this culture are said to be cultivated (*hēmera*) because they have benefited from this art as if they had received an education (*hōsper paideuomena*)."

51. See Detienne 1972, 31–34.

52. See P. Vidal-Naquet, "Valeurs religieuses et mythiques de la terre et du sacrifice dans l'*Odyssée*," *Annales E.S.C.* 25 (1970): 1278–97.

53. Aeschylus *Prometheus* 110–11 and 254.

54. Cf. *Odyssey* 5.488–90: "Deep in the countryside where one is without neighbors one hides the ember under the black ash, keeping the seed of the fire (*sperma puros sōzōn*) so that one does not have to light it from some other place"; and Homer, *Hymn to Hermes* 237–38; Pindar, *Pythian Odes* 3.66; and especially *Olympian Odes* 7.86–87: by founding the first sacrifice to Athena, the people of Rhodes "went up to the Acropolis without having taken with them the burning flame (*sperma phlogos*)." Thus by their fault the first use of a sacrifice without fire was begun—and Pindar comments on this forgetfulness in the following way: "It is by respecting Prometheus that men find virtue and joy" (79–81).

55. Cf. Herodotus 3.16: the Egyptians "reckon that the fire is a living animal that eats everything it takes and, gorged with food, itself perishes with what it devoured"; the Greek point of view is presented by Aristotle in the *Parva naturalia* (*On Youth and Old Age* 5.469 b 21–26): "When food (*trophē*) is lacking [for the fire] and the heat can no longer feed itself, the destruction of the fire occurs."

56. Cf. below, this chapter, and L. Graz, *Le feu dans l'Iliade et l'Odyssée* (Paris, 1965), 108–16 and 183–93.

57. On the use of the epithet *thespidaēs* to describe fire, see Graz, *Le feu,* 104–108.

58. Burkert 1971, 66–76.

59. *Iliad* 23.29 ff.

60. Ibid. 23.110.

61. Any more than one eats a part of the animals slaughtered on the pyre, whether they generally can be eaten (sheep and oxen) or not (horses and dogs), to say nothing of the Trojans.

62. *Iliad* 23.71, 75–76.

63. See *Iliad* 23.76: *epēn me puros lelakhēte.* On the use of *pur,* in the genitive, with *lankhanō,* see L. Graz, *Le feu,* 212–18.

64. Ibid. 23.177, 182, 183.

65. Ibid. 23.180–83; cf. Graz, *Le feu*, 213–17.

66. Ibid. 23.21.

67. Exactly what in the *Theogony* 538 Hesiod groups as flesh and entrails, *sarkes te kai enkata*, in contrast to the white bones. In the *Odyssey* the meal of the cannibal Cyclops, who eats like a wild animal, mixes and confuses flesh, entrails, and bones: *enkata te sarkas te kai ostea mueloenta* (9.293).

68. *Iliad* 23.237, 250; 24.791.

69. Ibid. 23.222, 224, 239, 252; 24.793.

70. Ibid. 23.251.

71. Ibid. 23.238–40: *autar epeita ostea Patrokloio Menoitiadao legōmen eu diagignōskontes: ariphradea de tetuktai.*

72. Ibid. 23.243: *diplaki dēmōi.*

73. Zeus hid the wheat in the earth; thus to have wheat, men must hide the seed, the *sperma*, in the ground. Cf. *Works* 470–71: while the peasant opens the furrow, "a small slave with a hoe gives *ponos* to the birds while hiding the seed well (*spérma katakruptōn*)."

74. See Detienne 1972, 29–35.

75. As Plutarch explains in a text of exceptional interest whose importance does not seem to us to have been recognized. In *Questiones Romanae* 109 (289 e–f), after commenting that flour is a food that is incomplete and uncooked, Plutarch continues, "For it has not remained what it was, wheat, *ho puros*, nor has it become what it should, bread, *ho artos*, but it has lost the power to germinate without gaining the usefulness of grain food, *tēn sitiou khreian*." Then going onto meat (*Questiones* 110, 289f–290a) and wondering if it is not the same for *to kreas* as for *to aleuron*, he adds, "For it is not a living creature without however having become a cooked food; for boiling and roasting, being alteration and change, remove the primary form; and the flesh of an animal that has been freshly killed, the raw flesh, does not have a pure, spotless aspect but is hideous like an ulcer." One could not say more clearly that bread is to the standing plant (live wheat) and flour (dead but still raw) what a dish of cooked food is to the animal on the hoof (the living animal) and to a piece of bloody flesh (dead but not yet cooked). In both cases, the food, whether vegetable or animal, to be made edible must undergo a kind of transmutation that brings it from one level to another. From its original state as a living being in nature, it must take on a new form of existence, that of a cultural object suitable for human consumption. This transmutation presupposes an intermediary stage where the killing of what was alive takes place. In this state of transition between nature and culture (flour, raw meat) resides an "impurity" that makes it untouchable for the person who took its life or killed it without giving it the full form of a human dish. By bringing this transformation to its end, only cooking and cookery will wipe out all trace of defilement and completely integrate the foods, whether vegetable or flesh, into the sphere of civilized human life, the "Promethean" life.

76. Herodotus 3.18. Cf. below, ch. 7.

77. The passage is found in line 592 of the *Theogony* (cf. 600), where the *thnētoi andres* replace the earlier *thnētoi anthrōpoi* (535, 552, 556, 564, 586, 588).

78. *Genos gunaikōn thēluterōn*—see, on this point, the comments of Nicole Loraux, "Sur la race des femmes et quelques-unes de ses tribus," *Arethusa* 11 (1978): 43–87. The author refers to the *Iliad* 8.520 and the *Odyssey* 8.324 for the *thēluterai gunaikes*, and to Bollack's commentary on fragment 616 of Empedocles for the corresponding formula: *andrōdesteroi andres (Empédocle 3. Les Origines, Commentaire* [Paris, 1969], 2: 545).

79. Which would also be called Aigialea, after Aigialeus, the first autochthonous king, and Telchinia, after Telchis, his grandson. Cf. Pausanias 2.5, 6 ff.; Strabo 8.6, 25; schol. on Pindar, *N.* 9.123; Stephanus of Byzantium, s.v. *Sikuōn.*

80. On the lottery of the gods, either of their cosmic domain or of earthly regions and cities, see *Iliad* 15.185 ff.; Pindar *Olympian Odes* 7.100 ff.; Callimachus *Hymn to Zeus* 1.60 ff. and fr. 119 Pfeiffer; Heraclitus *Allegories of Homer* 41.5.

81. According to the *Khronikōn Epitomē* of Castor; cf. *FGrHist*. 328 F 92 (vol. 3, 11 b [supplements], vol. 1, 383).

82. Strabo 8.6.23; 9.2.20; Athenaeus 219a; Cicero *De lege agraria* 1.2.5; Suidas, s.v. *ei to meson ktēsaio*.

83. *Works* 117–18.

84. Pausanias 2.11.3–4. On the use of *deinos* to characterize the intelligence of Prometheus, cf. Aeschylus *Prometheus* 59 and, above all, for the comparison with the Titan of Sicyon, 454–58.

85. Pausanias 2.1.6.

86. Pausanias 2.19.5; Clement of Alexandria *Protreptica* 44.

87. Pausanias 2.5.6.

88. Marathon is the plain of fennel, as Mecone is that of the poppy.

89. Pausanias 2.1.1. Different versions in 2.6.5.

90. Cf., lastly, Detienne 1977, 184–85.

91. According to the lexicons of Photius and Suidas, the expression "Titan earth" would refer to the land of Attica, "after Titenius, one of the oldest of the Titans, who lived near Marathon and who alone did not wage war against the gods, as Philochorus in the *Tetrapolis* and Ister in his *Atthides* indicate."

92. Detienne 1977, 184–86; *FGRHist*. 328 F 74 and 92; 334 F 1 with commentaries, vol. 3, 2 b (supplements), 354–55, 380 ff.; vol. 1, 627; vol. 2, 257–59 and 500 ff.

93. Detienne 1977, 185, with the sources cited in his notes 70 and 75–77.

94. When Diodorus of Sicily wants to justify the generally accepted opinion that the Ethiopians, inhabiting the region of the earth closest to the sun, were the first of all men to appear and arose directly from the soil as autochthonous beings, he reasons in the following way: "It seems obvious to all that the men who inhabit the south were probably the first to come out of the bosom of the earth. For since the heat of the sun dries the humid earth and makes it ready for the generation of animals, it is likely that the region closest to the sun was the first to be peopled with living beings" (3.2.1).

95. Aristotle *Problemata* 9.909 b 25 ff.; cf. Detienne 1972, 28 ff. Among mortals the Ethiopians, who reside in the country of the sun, are the closest to the primordial autochthonous beings, because of their natural dryness. From the picture that Herodotus gives, let us keep the following three equally meaningful details in mind: they are *makrobioi*, who live one hundred-twenty years or more; they have a naturally good smell because there is no rotting in them, thanks to a lack of humidity; lastly, when they are dead, their dried bodies are covered with a layer of gypsum that is painted to faithfully reproduce their features. Enclosed in the middle of a transparent glass column, the dead person maintains the appearance of a living person under his gypsum covering without exuding bad odors or anything unseemly (Herodotus 3.17–24; see below, ch. 7).

96. On this opposition, cf. Pierre Ellinger, "Le gypse et la boue," *Quaderni Urbinati di cultura classica* 29 (1978): 7–35.

97. *Works* 61: *gaian hudei phurein*.

98. Cf. the general definition in the *Theaetetus* that Plato gives to mud, *pēlos:* "earth moistened with water, *gē hugrōi phuratheisa*" (147 c), with the comments of P. Ellinger, "Le gypse et la boue."

99. *Iliad* 7.99; with the lines of Xenophanes referred to in the scholia: "We all came out of earth and water." It will be noted, however, that in haranguing his companions, "Be water and earth once more," Menelaus wishes to make them ashamed of forgetting their virility and of behaving like women. In their fear, the Achaian warriors have become Achaian

women. Cf. as well Plato, *Symposium* 190 b. In earliest humanity, according to Aristophanes, the male was a castoff from the sun, the female, from earth.

100. Aeschylus, fr. 369, Nauck²: *ek pēloplastou spermatos thnētē gunē.*

101. *Birds* 686. The expression "formed of clay" is found in the middle of a series of adjectives defining men as lowly, leaf-like, powerless, inconsistent, dreamlike phantoms.

102. Fr. 192 and 493 Pfeiffer. On the attribution of this forming of man from clay, to Prometheus, cf. (Apollodorus) *Bibliotheca* 1.7.2; Pausanias 10.4.4; Philemon, fr. 89 Kapp = Stobaeus *Florilegium* 2.27.

103. *Mimes* 2.28–30.

104. *Works* 63.

105. *Metamorphoses* 1.80 ff.

106. Servius, to Virgil (*Eclogues* 6.42); earlier with the same sense, Empedocles, fr. 454 and 460 Bollack, with commentary, *Empédocle 3. Les Origines, Commentaire*, 2.376 ff.; cf. as well Plato *Protagoras* 320 d.

107. *Works* 107–108.

108. Ibid. 200.

109. Detienne 1977, 163–217.

110. Cf. Eustathius 332.24 ff. (on *Iliad* 2.735); Olympiodorus (on Plato, *Phaedo* 61 c), *O.F.*, 220, Kern.

111. Olympiodorus: "For we are a part (of Dionysus) since we are formed from the ashes of Titans who had eaten his flesh."

112. At the end of his analysis about the place and functions of the heart in the sacrificial victim and animal life, Detienne (1977, 196) writes: "If the heart is the only part of Dionysus that escapes destruction, it is because the survival of this organ, the most alive in any living being, enables this god to be born again, even after he is eaten. To continue the discourse of the tradition recalled by Aristotle, the heart is only last because it is first of all primary." It would be interesting in this respect to compare two Orphic accounts that each bring in the theme of devouring: the Titans devour Dionysus whole except for the heart and from this heart Dionysus is reborn outside of them in his totality; Zeus swallows Metis-Phanes, the first god to have emerged from the cosmic egg. Having absorbed him in this way, Zeus "contained in his hollow belly (*eni gasteri koilēi*) the substance of all beings and he blended in his own limbs the strength and vigor of the god." The totality of the universe is once again found gathered within Zeus. To bring once again to light what he had hidden in himself by putting it in the hollow of his *gastēr* Zeus had to "take it out of his heart, *apo kradiēs*" (*O.F.* 167 a and 168.31–32 Kern).

113. Olympiodorus (on Plato, *Timaeus* 67 c), *O.F.*, 211, Kern: "to gather and assemble is, since the Titan's life, to move toward the unified life."

114. Cf. Pindar, fr. 21 Puech = Plato, *Meno* 81 b: Those who have paid ransom to Persephone for their ancient fault (*poinan palaiou pentheos*), with commentary by J.-P. Vernant, *Mythe et pensée chez les Grecs*, 1:93 and nn. 49–50.

115. Cf. Athenaeus 674 d–e; A. Brelich, "La corona di Prometheus," *Hommages à Marie Delcourt*, coll. Latomus 114 (1970), 234–42; Detienne and Vernant, *Les Ruses de l'intelligence. La métis des Grecs* (Paris, 1978): 95–96.

116. *Theogony* 519.

117. Ibid. 522: *meson dia kion' elassas.*

118. Pindar *Pythian Odes* 1.36–37: *kiōn d'ourania sunekhei*, the column of heaven masters him.

119. See Aristophanes *Birds* 1247: *purphoroisin aietois*, as in Aeschylus *Seven Against Thebes* 444–45: *purphoron keraunon* (cf. Pindar *Nemean Odes* 10.132–33).

120. On the relationship between the eagle and thunder, see A. B. Cook, *Zeus* (reprinted, New York, 1964), 1: 84 ff. and 2: 751 ff. As the "flame-bearing" eagle moves with lightning

speed, lightning itself is winged (Sophocles *Oedipus at Colonus* 1460); the arrows of Zeus fly (Euripides *Heracles* 179; *Suppliants* 860; *Bacchae* 90; Sophocles *Oedipus at Colonus* 1658; Aristophanes *Birds,* 1714).

121. *Theogony* 523–24.

122. *Prometheus* 1022–25: *Ptēnos kuōn, daphoinos aietos . . . diartamēsei.*

123. Cf. Euripides *Electra* 828–30.

124. Aeschylus *Prometheus* 493 ff: "I taught them about the polished viscera, the colors it must have to be agreeable to the gods, the various propitious aspects of the gall bladder and the lobe of the liver."

125. Plato *Timaeus* 70 d–71 d; cf. Luc Brisson, "Du bon usage du dérèglement," *Divination et rationalité* (Paris, 1974), 220–248.

126. *Timaeus* 70 e–71 a.

127. Aeschylus *Prometheus* 1025; Hesiod *Theogony* 523–25.

128. The uncertain nature of Promethean immortality is expressed in another legendary tradition. According to this version it would be Chiron, who, to escape his sufferings, would have given the Titan the gift of immortality the centaur enjoyed and would have agreed to perish in Prometheus' stead; cf. *Prometheus* 1026–29; (Apollodorus) *Bibliotheca* 2.5.4 and 2.5.11.

129. Hesiod, *Theogony* 211–12 and 227.

130. The verb *aexein* is also used in *Works* 377 to refer to the increase of wealth (in agricultural products, as the context indicates) in the house, and 773, to the increase of the moon. In *Theogony* 195, it is a matter of the growth of the grass, *poiē,* under the footsteps of Aphrodite. The term can also be applied to the growth of ardor, courage, and strength (*Theogony* 493 and 641; *Scutum* 96 and 434). In *Works and Days* 5–6 the omnipotence of Zeus is expressed in that "easily he gives force, easily he overcomes the strong, easily he reduces the illustrious and makes the lowly increase (*aexei*)."

131. See *Theogony* 557. These are long bones, especially the thighbones, the pelvis, the vertebral column or, lacking that, the two extremities, the cervical vertebrae and the tail, *osphus kai sphondulos.*

132. *Odyssey* 12.359 ff. On this episode, see below, ch. 7.

133. *Iliad* 18.348; *Odyssey* 8.437.

134. Herodotus 6.61; cf. Fr. Hartog, this volume, chapter 8, opening page.

135. *Odyssey* 18.44.

136. Cf. as well *Odyssey* 18.53; 20.25; Aristophanes *Clouds* 409.

137. *Odyssey* 18.54.

138. Ibid. 18.54; 17.287 and 473–74; 15.544; 7.216.

139. Jesper Svenbro, *La Parole et le marbre. Aux origines de la poétique grecque* (Lund, 1976), 50–60.

140. Pindar *Isthmian Odes* 1.69–70.

141. Epimenides, fr. B 1 Diels-Kranz. In the *Odyssey* 7.216–21, the text is as follows: "Is there anything more doglike than this odious belly? It always excites us, obliges us not to forget it, even at the height of our troubles and anguish. When I have sorrow in my heart, it commands and I must forget my ills; it claims its due."

142. *Timaeus* 73 a.

143. *Memorabilia* 1.6.8.

144. *Oeconomicus* 7.6 and 9.11.

145. *Theogony* 599 and 605; *Works* 374 and 704.

146. On the Hesiodic *theios anēr,* cf. *Works* 731, and M. Detienne, *Les Maîtres de vérité dans la Grèce archaïque* (Paris, 1973), 25–26; *Crise agraire et attitude religieuse chez Hésiode,* coll. Latomus 68 (Brussels, 1963), 35 ff.

147. *Theogony* 22–23, 36–39.
148. Ibid. 43–52.
149. Ibid. 31–34 and 104–115.
150. Ibid. 80–93.
151. Ibid. 88–90 and 98–103.
152. Ibid. 26.
153. Ibid. 28–34.
154. Here we must refer the reader to the study, mentioned earlier (n. 78, above), by Nicole Loraux, "Sur la race des femmes."
155. *Theogony* 585.
156. Ibid. 589.
157. *Works and Days* 62.
158. *Theogony* 575 and 581; cf. 584 and 588.
159. *Theogony* 583; *Works* 65.
160. *Works* 63 and 66.
161. Ibid. 58.
162. Ibid. 67 and 78.
163. *Theogony* 567–69.
164. *Works* 55–56.
165. Ibid. 58.
166. *Theogony* 591. Clearly indicated by Nicole Loraux, whom we follow on this point.
167. *Theogony* 607–608 and *Works* 702–703: "There is no better fortune for a man than a good wife."
168. *Theogony* 585.
169. Ibid. 602.
170. *Kakōn xunēonas ergōn* in line 595 (drones); *xunēonas ergōn argaleōn,* in 601 (women).
171. M. L. West, *Hesiod: Theogony* (Oxford, 1966), 329 and 333.
172. *Theogony* 605: "This one will never lack bread for as long as he lives."
173. *Theogony* 606–607: "But as soon as he dies, his wealth is divided among distant kin."
174. The only son, who takes his father's place, is his alter ego, his right hand; cf. in line 378, the father who has only one son dies leaving this son in his stead: *heteron paid' enkataleipōn.*
175. *Works* 377.
176. Ibid. 379.
177. *Theogony* 609.
178. *Lysistrata* 839 and 844.
179. *Works* 374; with the comment in line 375, "Whoever trusts a woman trusts a thief."
180. *Theogony* 594–99.
181. *Works* 705: *ōmōi gēraï dōken*—literally: to a raw old age, that is, the husband is already dried up by the labor and cares caused by his wife at an age when one is still green.
182. *Works* 302: *aergōi sumphoros andri.* Hunger "accompanies" the man who, doing nothing, does not have enough to feed himself. Women are defined (*Theogony* 593) as those who refuse the companionship of poverty but keep company with satiety, *peniēs ou sumphoroi, alla koroio.* When they see a poor, miserable old fellow, women, according to Hesiod, think he already has his companion, Hunger. It is when they see full storehouses that they wish to keep a man—and satiety—company.
183. *Works* 304: *kēphēnessi kothourois eikelos.*
184. Ibid. 363.
185. *Theogony* 324 and 867; *Scutum* 60; fr. 30.10 and 755 Merkelbach-West.
186. Fr. 43 a 5–10 Merkelbach-West and 43 b = Schol. on Lycophron, *Alexandra* 1393.

Cf. J. Schwartz, *Pseudo-Hesiodea* (Leiden, 1960), 268; also Athenaeus 10.416 b; cf. above all Aeschines 3.184 and Callimachus, *Hymns* 6.67, who follows Hesiod; also, *Etymologicum Magnum* 33.18 and the Suidas, s.v. *aithōn.*

187. *Odyssey* 7.216.

188. Ibid. 11.427.

189. Clement of Alexandria 6.2.5.3. = *O.F.,* 234, Kern.

190. Why the knees? The knee, *gonu,* is connected to the root *gonos,* seed, *gonē,* the generative act; see R. B. Onians, *The Origins of European Thought about the Body, the Mind, the Soul, the World, Time and Fate* (Cambridge, 1954), 174–86.

191. See Detienne, 1972, 222–26.

192. Franco Ferrari, "Prometeo, Esiodo et la 'lecture du mythe' di Jean-Pierre Vernant," *Quaderni di Storia* 7 (1978): 142.

193. Euripides, fr. 429 Nauck.[2]

194. *Works* 406.

195. Ibid. 519.

196. *Theogony* 572; *Works* 63 and 71.

197. *Works* 520.

198. Ibid. 81–85.

199. Ibid. 80–82.

200. Ibid. 88–89.

201. *Theogony* 592.

202. *Theogony* 512: *kakon . . . andrasin alphēstēisin*—which can be compared to *Works* 82, where Pandora is sent to Epimetheus as a *pēm' andrasin alphēstēisin.*

203. *Theogony* 512–14.

204. Ibid. 594.

205. Ibid. 600.

206. Ibid. 594: *en smēnessi katērepheessi.*

207. Ibid. 598: *entosthe menontes epērepheas kata simblous.*

208. Ibid. 599: *es gastēr' amōntai,* with a play on the verbs *amaō-amaomai,* which mean either to harvest or to store up, amass; cf. *Works* 775 and 778, where both meanings appear just a few lines apart. It is normally in the storehouse, *kalia,* where the harvested wheat is amassed (cf. *Works* 301 and 307); it is this storehouse the woman eyes (*Works* 374): like the drone she wants to store the wheat harvested by the male by putting it in the oven of her *gastēr.*

209. *Theogony* 595.

210. Ibid. 601–602.

211. Ibid. 595: *boskōsi.*

212. *Works* 304.

213. *Republic* 8.15.564 b. Cf. as well Euripides *Trojan Women* 192; *Bacchae* 1365; Herodotus 7.61.

214. Detienne 1972, 154–55, "Orphée au miel," *Quaderni d'Urbinati* 12 (1971): 8–23, reprinted in *Faire de l'histoire,* ed. J. Le Goff and P. Nora (Paris, 1974), 3: 56–75.

215. To kill one's father, to eat human flesh (especially those of one's children), to sleep with one's mother: these three crimes are all in a certain sense equivalent because they all equally express the ultimate degree of horror at the departure from the human. See Plato *Republic* 9.1.571 c–d: the soul, detached from all reason and modesty and given over to its wild and bestial part, "does not hesitate in thought to rape its mother . . . there is no murder that does not taint it, nor food that it shuns." Cf. as well 560 c, 569 b, and Plutarch *Moralia* 83 a and 101 a.

216. *Works* 90–105.

217. Ibid. 94: *kheiressi . . . aphelousa.*

218. *Theogony* 553: *khersi d' ho g' amphotereĩsin aneileto.* . . .

219. *Works* 95: *anthrōpoisi d' emēsato kēdea lugra* (Pandora); *Works* 49: *anthrōpoisin emēsato kēdea lugra* (Zeus).

220. *Works* 91: *nosphin ater te kakōn;* and for the golden race, *Works* 115: *kakōn ektosthen hapantōn.*

221. Ibid. 101: *pleiē men gar gaia . . . , pleiē de thalassa.*

222. Ibid. 102–103.

223. *Theogony* 527.

224. *Works* 176–78, which can be compared to line 102.

225. Ibid., 179: *all' empēs kai toisi memeixetai esthla kakoisin.*

226. In the *Theogony* she is created as an evil, *kakon,* a source of suffering, *pēma,* as works of anguish, *erga argelea,* or care, *mermēra erga;* she already contains in potential all the evils that will ever come out of the jar, in *Works and Days.*

227. *Works* 61 and 79; and especially 78, which defines the meaning of the feminine "voice" or "speech": in Pandora's heart Hermes puts "lies, deceiving words"; cf. 373–74, "let not a woman abuse your mind with her prattling flatteries."

228. Ibid. 104: "In silence, for Zeus the prudent one refused to let them speak."

229. On the value of the adverb *thuraze* indicating, with respect to the threshold of the house, what is outside, cf. *Theogony* 750 and *Works* 365, where the equivalent adverb, *thurē-phi,* refers to everything that is outside, in contrast to what is at home, in the house *(oikoi).*

230. Hesiod in three other passages also mentions, along with the *pithoi,* the *angea,* vases. In two cases they are intended to hold grain, *bios* (*Works* 600 and 475), and in one, wine (*Works* 613).

231. *Works* 815 and 819.

232. Ibid. 368. When one opens and when one finishes a jar, one eats one's fill; when it is opened, there is plenty, and when one finishes it, the game is up in any case—it is too late to be thrifty. Thrift, restraint, the strict measuring of the daily ration, take place between the two times. Once the jar is opened, before it is empty, one must go slowly in order to bring the *bios* of the belly of the *pithos* to the belly of the inhabitants of the house (*messothi pheides-thai,* 369).

233. Cf. *Theogony* 598: while the bees fly outside, the drones remain inside (*entosthe me-nontes*).

234. *Nosos* has a broader, less precise connotation than our term "sickness," understood in the technical and medical sense. We have already indicated that the punishment that the eagle inflicts on Prometheus is a *nousos* (*Theogony* 527): also *nousos* is the *kakon kōma,* the bad torpor, that "covers" the guilty god when he broke his oath (*Theogony* 798). In *Prometheus* the fear of death is called *nosos* (248).

235. *Works* 114: *aiei de podas kai kheiras homoioi.*

236. On the relationship between *kamatos* and *ponos,* cf. *Works* 113 and *Scutum* 351. On the value of *kamatos* as "hard-working," which describes the incessant work of the worker bees in contrast to the idleness of the drones, cf. *Theogony* 539 and *Works* 305. *Ponos* and *kamatos* are likewise associated as evils with *oizus,* suffering. It is the suffering of laborious effort.

237. *Works* 112.

238. Cf., for the golden race: *esthla de panta toisin eēn,* all the wealth was theirs, in line 116; cf. as well lines 119 and 123.

239. Cf. the *mega pēma* that constitutes Woman, in *Theogony* 592 and *Works* 56.

240. Cf. *Works* 577: He who during the harvest avoids the siesta and hastens to gather the harvest in his house, does it "so that his life (or his bread) is assured (*hina toi bios arkios eiē*)."

241. *Works* 475.

242. Ibid. 600.

243. Ibid. 475–78.

244. To repeat the formula of line 179; cf. above, n. 225.

245. Cf. *Works* 298–99.

246. Cf. Semonides, fr. 1.6 West; cf. as well Simonides, fr. 97 Ed. and 542.23 Page; Theognis 637.

247. Cf. Pindar *Nemean Odes* 11.59–61: speaking of the *elpides oknēroterai,* the too timid hopes of the relatives of Aristagoras who prevented him from trying his luck at Delphi and Olympia, the poet adds that some miss their chance out of presumptuous vanity, others because of a heart that is too fearful.

248. Aeschylus *Prometheus* 101.

249. *Nemean Odes* 11.46.

250. *Prometheus* 248–50.

251. Cf. Plato *Gorgias* 523 d, where Zeus declares, "The first thing to do is to take from men the knowledge of the hour of their death, for now they foresee it. I ordered Prometheus to stop that." Plato is directly inspired by Aeschylus, as is proved by the parallelism between the formulas used by the tragic poet and the philosopher: *Pausteon estin proeidotas autous tou thanatou; nun gar proïsasi,* Plato writes. *Pausteon* takes up *epausa; proeidotas* and *proïsasi* echo *proderkesthai.* If one wishes to use this text in to interpret Hesiodic *elpis,* it can only be in the sense given by Aeschylus. To cure men of prescience, the foresight of death, Prometheus is going to use blind *elpis.* Thus *elpis* is not foresight.

252. *Works* 475 and 273: *eolpa.*

253. Ibid. 500.

254. Ibid. 197–201, with the conclusion, *kakou d' ouk essetai alkē.*

255. Theognis 647; cf. 635.

256. Ibid. 1135–36.

257. Paul Mazon, *Les Travaux,* edited with commentary (Paris 1914), 54.

258. *Works* 103.

259. Ibid. 267.

260. Ibid. 289–91.

261. Ibid. 281: *olbon.*

262. As the beginning of the Promethean tale in *Works and Days* indicates, the gods have hidden the *bios* from men; otherwise, one would work effortlessly and in one day harvest enough to eat for a whole year, without doing anything, *kai aergon eonta.* . . . It would be the end of the work of the patient oxen and mules. But Zeus hid life when he found himself tricked by Prometheus (*Works* 42–48).

263. Ibid. 117–18: *zeidōros aroura automatē.*

264. Pandora's opening of the jar, the dispersion of the evils throughout all of man's territory, forms an explicit contrast to Poseidon's closing of Tartarus, which shut the Titans and Typhon away so that the powers of rebellion and chaos could not escape or again enter the domain of the gods (*Theogony* 726–35 and 868). Shut up in Tartarus, these "evils" always remain "away and distant" from the happy gods. The example of Typhon is particularly significant in this respect. If the monster had been able to surprise the vigilance of Zeus and defeat him, "then a work without remedy, *ergon amēkhanon,* would be accomplished that day" (*Works* 836), without hope for the gods or men. Typhon is defeated, struck down, and sent to the depths of Tartarus. But from his remains escape the chaotic and ill winds that sometimes blow across the human realm; when one encounters them at sea, "There is no recourse against this ill, *kakou d' ou gignetai alkē* (*Theogony* 876; compare to *Works* 201). When Pandora opens the jar to release the evils and shuts the lid on *Elpis,* she acts "by the will of Zeus, the assembler of the clouds" (*Works* 99). When Poseidon shuts the bronze doors of Tartarus on the Titans so that they cannot leave, he acts "by the will of Zeus, the assembler

of the clouds" (*Theogony* 730). Tartarus ends with a neck, *deirē*, like the *pithos* which opens with a mouth or lips, *kheilea*. In Tartarus there is no exit for the Titans, no way out: *ouk exiton esti;* Poseidon shut the doors on them, *thuras*. Pandora shut the lid of the jar on *Elpis,* which cannot fly beyond the door, *thuraze*.

If it were necessary to take the comparison to the limit, we would say that the evils (in the jar) correspond to the Titans and Typhon in Tartarus, the first escaping and the second remaining prisoner. But just as *Elpis,* joined with the evils although not itself an evil, remains at the bottom of the empty jar, in Tartarus there also remain, in the company of their brother Titans, the three Hundred-handed Giants, Gyes, Cottus, and Briareos, rallied to the cause of Zeus whose victory they assured (cf. *entha* in 729 for the Titans, *entha* in 724 for the Hundred-handed Giants). These three figures do not remain in the abyss as prisoners, always kept far away from the gods like the Titans; on the contrary, they live there (*naiousin*) permanently as Zeus' faithful guardians, *phulakes pistoi Dios* (*Theogony* 735). Zeus' reign implies, with the closing of Tartarus, the constant presence deep inside it of three representatives of his sovereign power, just as the human condition implies the continual presence of *Elpis* at the bottom of the jar that the evils have abandoned.

265. Here we repeat with slight modifications the text that we had placed in conclusion to an earlier study on the same theme, "Le mythe prométhéen chez Hésiode," Vernant 1974, 193–94.

266. *Works* 609: a man can find a good wife, "but even for him, throughout his whole life the bad will offset the good."

Chapter 3. Greek Animals

1. Cf. the entirety of the study by J.-P. Vernant, above, ch. 2.

2. This clearly emerges from the totality of the work by Berthiaume.

3. Cf. the analyses of M. Detienne, ch. 1, above.

4. Special circumstances made it possible for me to make that irreplaceable immersion in the logic of another, where one may always return by inquiring about what is incomprehensible and little understood. A series of long stays in Tunisia gradually made the difficult approach to the languages of the body possible. Professional butchers, as well as friends or acquaintances, never refused me information and instruction. Muslims, Jews, and lay people—the latter indeed the bearers of the Western system—all generously listened to me and answered my questions with immense patience for week after week. It is to them, as well as to the peasants of the Occitan and Catalan regions among whom I once had the privilege of being invited to the "pig festival," that these pages are very humbly dedicated.

5. On this point see below, n. 9.

6. Published by G. Ricci, "Una hydria ionica da Caere," *ASAA* 24–26 (1946–48): 47–57; here, figs. 1–4.

In the following discussion the vase will be referred to by the name of the editor. Cf. J. M. J. Hemelrijk, *De caeretaanse Hydriae,* thesis, (Amsterdam, 1956), 62. The interpretations proposed here are often different from the ones of G. Ricci. We will thus refer to this study as a whole regarding details of these differences, which will not be indicated. M. Detienne was the first to note the importance of this vase for an analysis of the internal structure of the sacrifice in "Dionysos orphique et le rôti bouilli," in Detienne 1977, 161–217.

7. On these two "instruments of oblation," cf. chapter 4, this volume.

8. I thank the authorities of the Villa Giulia for having made this possible on several occasions.

9. On this point and the more general problems of the death of the pig as a sacrifice in our rural societies, see the remarks of Y. Verdier, "Le langage du cochon," *Ethnologie française* 7 (1977): 143–52, and the entire issue of the journal *Ethnozootechnie* 16 on the "domestic

pig." Blood as the first element of the body that comes into men's hands is central to the representations that develop around the death of the animal.

10. As on the cup AFR, Louvre G 112, *ARV²* 117/7, here fig. 6.

11. Cf. the image of a warrior, sword in hand, slaughtering a sheep on the cup AFR, Cleveland 26422, *ARV¹* 918/7.

12. She can be seen in this pose on a small lekythos AFR, Boston, Museum of Fine Arts 9884; see H. Metzger, *Recherches sur l'imagerie athénienne.* 113/30.

13. As the Thyrenian amphora of London, 97.7.272 shows it for the sacrifice of Polyxena; cf. F. Brommer, *Vasenlisten,* 3d ed., 413/1, here fig. 7.

14. On this point one should reread the analyses of M. Detienne, "Entre bêtes et dieux," *Nouvelle Revue de psychanalyse* 6 (1972), reprinted in Detienne 1977, 135–57.

15. As Rudhardt explains, 262.

16. On the *haimation,* a preparation based on blood, see P. Stengel, *Die griechischen Kultusaltertümer,* 3d ed. (Munich, 1920), 113.

17. On this point one can reread the comments of M. Mauss in the fine text of 1936, "Les techniques du corps," reprinted in *Sociologie et anthropologie* (Paris, 1966), 363–86.

18. On this notion cf. P. Bourdieu, *Esquisse d'une théorie de la pratique,* (Paris, 1972), with its development, "Le sens pratique," *Actes de la recherche en sciences sociales* 1 (1976):43–86, where the author expresses a conception of the logic of practice that is in complete disagreement with "componential" analyses (43–44).

19. The *derma* very often figures in the prescriptions given in the statutes.

20. On-site research has enabled me to verify the effectiveness of this procedure on many occasions.

21. Amphora AFR, Boston 018109, *ARV²* 553/40, here fig. 8.

22. See on this point, chapter 4, this volume, section "Death-dealing Waters."

23. Recall that the sacrificed quadrupeds are taken from the domestic livestock and include only ruminants and pigs.

24. Pyxis AFN, Bonn, University, 62, here fig. 5.

25. Pelike AFN, Paris, Fondation Custodia (coll. F. Lught, Dutch Institute) 3650, here fig. 9.

26. Skyphos AFR, Warsaw, National Museum, 14.24.64, *ARV²* 797/142, here fig. 10.

27. It is exactly in this way that the extraction is described in Greek, with the arm being plunged in below: *katheis katō tēn kheïra* (Euphorion, fr. 1 Kock=Athenaeus 9.380 a).

28. On the skyphos AFN, Athens 12 626, see *Journal of Hellenic Studies* 75 (1955), pls. 6–7.

29. The whole of the tale of the sacrifice from the prayer to the death runs from lines 800 to 841. The French edition is by L. Parmentier and H. Grégoire, Collection des Universités de France.

30. The anguish of Aegisthus is explicit in the opening prayer of the rite (805–807).

31. On the purely tragic level, note the *use* of the sacrifice in the sacrifice—as a ritual moment where the pleasure that is to come from the sacrifice serves to divert the attention of the ex-sacrificer and future victim.

32. For manipulation during hieroscopy, see for example the amphora AFR, Wurzburg 507, *ARV²,* 181/1, here fig. 14.

For the theme of the *splankhnoptēs,* see the catalogue of G. Rizza, "Una nuove pelike a figure rosse e lo 'splanchonoptes' de Styppax," *ASAA* 37–38 (1959–60): 321–45. We can add the cup AFR, Bern, private collection, reproduced by R. Blatter, *Hefte des archäolgisches Seminars der Universität Bern* (1976), 5–10, pls. 1–13.

33. See on this point J.-P. Vernant, first page of chapter 2, this volume.

34. Aristotle *On the Parts of Animals* 673 b 1–3; cf. Detienne 1977, 175.

35. Aristotle *Parts of Animals* 667 b 10.

36. Ibid. 667 a 34–b 4.

37. Ibid. 665 a 27. The French edition is by P. Louis, Collection des Universités de France.

38. Ibid. 672 b 9–12.

39. Ibid. 672 b 19–24.

40. Ibid. 669 b 13–21.

41. Ibid. 669 b 25.

42. Ibid. 669 b 28, b 36–670 a 2.

43. Ibid. 670 a 10–16.

44. Ibid. 670 a 19–20.

45. The statutes mention them but in an unspecific context. They are distinguished from the *splankhna* on Cos, for example; cf. *LSG* no. 151 A.

46. Aristotle *Parts of Animals* 672 a 17.

47. Schol. on Oppian, *Halieutica* 2.622, ed. Bussemaker.

48. Plato *Phaedrus* 265 e.

49. This first moment is indicated in the Homeric texts by the verb *diakheō* (*Iliad* 7.316; *Odyssey* 3.456, 14.427).

50. Hydria AFN, Boston 99 257, *ABV,* 430/25, here fig. 12.

51. On cup AFR, Louvre C 10 918, *ARV²* 467/130, here fig. 23.

52. On crater AFN London, British Museum B 362, here fig. 11.

53. Aristotle *Parts of Animals* 672 a 16–20.

54. Cf. Chantraine, s.v. *osphus.*

55. Aeschylus *Prometheus* 496–97.

56. Athenaeus 4.169 b (= Anaxippes, fr. 6 Kock); Aristophanes *Wasps* 1155, *Knights* 772, *Palatine Anthology* 5.306.

57. *Palatine Anthology* 5.306.

58. Schloss Fasanerie, Adolphseck 120, cf. *CVA* Germany 16, Schloss Fasanerie 2, pl. 63/1–4, 64/1–2, here fig. 22.

59. Cf. the Attic fragment of the Acropolis, Athens Acr. 965, with a scene that is undoubtedly parallel, *ARV²*, 253/56.

60. Cf. Detienne 1977, 173–75.

61. As Plutarch attests in *Quaestiones conviviales* 3.10.696 e, when he asks, "Why do the parts hung from a fig tree become tender quickly?"

62. On this point note the arguments by Berthiaume.

63. *Quaestiones conviviales* 2.10.642 e–f.

64. Cf. a scene of the adjusting of skewers of meat on olpe AFN, Heidelberg, University 143, *CVA* Germany 10, Heidelberg 1, pl. 39/3.

65. Cf. Polycharmes, *FGrHist.*, 770 F 1 (= Athenaeus 8.333 d–f).

66. The sketch, directly traced from the vase by F. Lissarrague, makes their outline explicit.

67. On the possible developments concerning these practices with respect to coin origins, cf. N. Parise, "Segni premonetari, sacrificio et società nella Grecia arcaica," *Annali dell'Istituto Italico di Numismatica.*

On the *obeloi* as instrument and object, see U. Kron, "Zum Hypogäum von Paestum," *JDAI* 86 (1971): 117–48.

68. Cf. D. H. Gill, "*Trapezōmata:* A Neglected Aspect of Greek Sacrifice," *Harvard Theological Review* 67 (1974): 117–37.

69. It is often linked with the hide, *derma,* in the statutes.

70. See P. Stengel, "Die Zunge der Opfertiere," *Opferbräuche der Griechen* (Leipzig-Berlin, 1910), 172–77.

71. See Laurence Kahn, *Hermès passe ou les ambiguités de la communication* (Paris, 1978).
72. See Aristophanes *Peace* 1060.

Chapter 4. Ritual As Instrumentality

1. On this particular configuration of the Greek domain, see the introductory comments in Rudhardt (261).

2. On these questions of principle, cf. this volume, 88.

3. These relationships are at the heart of the thought of E. H. Gombrich. On the exact problem of the action of rite and image, see "Le geste et l'expression rituels dans l'art," in *Le Comportement rituel chez l'homme et l'animal,* ed. J. Huxley, French edition (Paris, 1971), 225–237.

4. This is why it will not be surprising to find line drawings traced from the figures instead of photographs. This old practice, which is revived for our purposes, makes the position of the elements of the image immediately visible. I warmly thank my friend François Lissarrague for having accepted this difficult task. The notion of the iconic sign extends the ideas of Claude Bérard, giving iconology a different orientation and sometimes offering new readings of identical images. In particular, the reader should refer to two texts: Bérard, "ΑΞΙΕ ΤΑΥΡΕ," *Mélanges Paul Collart* (Lausanne, 1976):61–73, and "Le liknon d'Athéna," *Antike Kunst* 19 (1976):101–114.

5. On this notion see the ideas of J. L. Schefer, *Semiotica* 4 (1971):193.

6. Having decided to consider image, there is a danger of slipping without any theoretical difficulty into an analysis of the discourse that it produces, for example, in the work of L. Porcher, *Introduction à une sémiotique des images, sur quelques exemples d'images publicitaires* (Paris, 1976). In the case of advertising images the anthropological competence of the spectator, speaker, producer of the image, and the one who analyzes it is the same. All of them function within the same culture. For Greek images, the interpreter absolutely must work from a strict iconic analysis or risk projecting his own representational system onto the image—a virtual falsification based on verisimilitude.

7. See E. Benveniste, *Problèmes du linguistique générale,* vol. 2 (Paris, 1974), 43–66.

8. On the convenient notions of process and system and their extralinguistic use, see L. Hjemslev, *Prolégomènes à une théorie du langage* (Paris, 1968), 175–227.

9. Cf. Lévi-Strauss, "Religions comparées des peuples sans écriture," in *Problèmes et méthodes d'histoire de religions* (Paris, 1968), 261.

10. On the problem of narrative time and the structure of myths, see the comments of J.-P. Vernant, "Raisons du mythe," in *Mythe et société en Grèce ancienne* (Paris, 1974), 244–50.

11. On the numerous possible circuits around the animals' bodies, cf. chapter 3, this volume, section "The Viscera as Center."

12. Cf. on this point Detienne 1977, 177–78.

13. Cf. ibid., 181–82.

14. The translation [into French was] adapted for the interpretation we propose here from L. Méridier's French translation, Collection des Universités de France. The meaning of the word *rhuthmos* poses a problem of historical semantics in Greek. Benveniste considers the musical value of the term to be the result of a recent development. But his study on "La notion de rythme dans son expression linguistique," in *Problèmes de linguistique générale* (Paris, 1966), 331, does not account for this text. The general meaning, "manner," proposed by Cl. Sandoz in a comprehensive work, *Les Noms grecs de la forme,* thesis (Neuchatel, 1971), 70, for this passage is of little help: the ogre uses two of them! The context seems indeed to impose a musical meaning on *rhuthmos.* Here it is a matter of the cadenced balancing of the two murderous acts of the wild man, of the esthetic proportion that orders the scene in a

horrible way and fascinates Odysseus. For this notion of cadence and symmetry expressed by *rhuthmos,* cf. L.S.J., s.v. For the overall history of the word, cf. Chantraine, s.v.

15. See for example concerning the table, *trapeza,* as a determining element of the sacrificial practice, the entire preceding article, ch. 3 above.

16. Oinochoë AFN, Boston (Museum of Fine Arts), 99527, cf. *ABV,* 430/25, here figure 12.

17. Cf. the reading "butcher" recently maintained by J. Boardman, *Athenian Black Figure Vases* (London, 1974), fig. 287, in caption.

18. On this instrument, cf. this chapter, section "Blood Vase."

19. On this practice and its rendering into image, cf. above chapter 3, this volume, section "The Dismantled Body."

20. This does not exhaust the lexical possibilities of the term "tree." It can for example provide information on the divinity engaged by the rite. Compare the following lekythoi of the Gela painter: Amsterdam APM 268, below, n. 23 (branches), Athens Agora P. 24067 (palm tree), for example. The palm tree can always refer to an Apollonian context.

21. On a lekythos AFN of the Gela painter, Amsterdam APM 8196, here fig. 15.

22. Amsterdam APM 268, here fig. 16. On the work of this painter, see J. M. J. Hemelrijk, "The Gela Painter in the Allard Pierson Museum," *Bulletin Antieke Beschaving* 49 (1974):117–58.

23. Olpe AFN, Paris (Louvre), F. 333; cf. R. Ginouves, *Balaneutikē* (Paris, 1962), pl. 11.

24. On the fascination caused by this aspect of Dionysianism, read the fine commentary on Euripides *Bacchae* written by H. Jeanmaire, *Dionysos* (Paris, 1951), 138–56.

25. Cloths spotted with blood comparable to the one held by the young officiant to the right on the Boston oinochoë are sometimes represented in carving scenes. Cf. for example: pelike AFN, Paris, Fondation Custodia (Dutch Institute), where the cloth is found together with the *trapeza* and *sphageion,* here fig. 9.

26. Its presence is striking in the series of scenes where Hercules, during a sacrifice connected with the maintenance of water in Egypt, is going to be sacrificed by the king of the country, Busiris; see F. Brommer, *Vasenlisten zur Griechischen Heldensage,* 3d ed. (Marburg, 1973), 34–36, for the list of vases.

27. As in the version of the Bouphonia in Athens in the tale of Theophrastus, *Peri eusebeias,* F 18, Pötscher ed.

28. Krater AFR, The Hague (Gemeente Museum) OC (ant) 5–71, here fig. 17.

29. Stamnos AFR, Munich 2412, cf. *Paralipomena* 443/5, here fig. 18.

30. On the questions posed by the *podaniptēr* and the interpretation of this stamnos, cf. R. Ginouves, *Balaneutikē* (Paris 1962), 73.

31. See on this point H. Froning, *Dithyrambos und Vasenmalerei in Athen* (Würzburg, 1971), 81–82.

32. Stamnos AFR Paris (Louvre), C. 10754, *ARV²*, 228/32, here fig. 13.

33. Caeretan hydria, Copenhagen (National Museum) 13567, published by K. Friis Johansen, *Opuscula romana* 4, 61–81, and especially 76, for water instruments. Here fig. 19.

34. On the basket and its representations, see J. Schelp, *Das Kanoun. Der griechische Opferkorb* (Würzburg, 1975).

35. On this instrument, see chapter 8, this volume, text at note 36.

36. Olpe AFN Berlin (Staatliche Museen), 1915, *ABV,* 377/247, here fig. 20.

37. On the eel, cf. Agatharchides in Athenaeus 7, 297 d (= FGrHist, 86 F 5); on the tuna, cf. Antigone of Carystus in Athenaeus, ibid., 297 d–e.

38. The most recent work that discusses this vase maintains the classic interpretation, a scene from daily life, fishmongers. See moreover the very useful little study by J. Chamay,

"Une scène de la vie quotidienne sur une peliké du peintre de Sylée," *Genava* 24 (1976):281–89.

39. Lekythos AFN New York (Metropolitan Museum), 41, 162, 29, cf. *CVA,* USA 8, Fogg Museum and Gallatin Collection, 44/1.

40. Olpe AFN Paris (Louvre) F 338, *ABV,* 536/35, here fig. 21.

41. Cup AFN Paris, *ABV,* 231/7. The presence of the skewer under a modern overpainting had been suspected by Brommer from the time of the *Vasenlisten,* 2d ed. (1960), 134/2. I am grateful to Alain Pasquier for the cleaning of the vase and confirmation of this hypothesis.

Chapter 5. The Violence of Wellborn Ladies

1. Formulation of the problem and bibliography in Burkert 1977, 365–70. Cf. also H. W. Parke, *Festivals of the Athenians* (London, 1977), 82–88. Archeological and epigraphic discoveries make the need for a monograph urgent.

2. Cf. Nicole Loraux, "Sur la race des femmes et quelques-unes de ses tribus," *Arethusa* 11 (1978):43–87.

3. Aelian, fr. 44 Hercher, the version of which is partly cited in Suidas, in two articles, "Thesmophoros" and "Sphaktriai." Cf. L. Vitali, *Fonti per la storia della religione cyrenaica, R. Università di Padova, Facoltà di Lettere et Filosofia* 1 (Florence, 1932), 70 and 136, who knows only Suidas, like F. Chamoux, *Cyrène sous la monarchie des Battiades* (Paris, 1953), 265.

4. The text distinguishes *ta aporrhēta* and *ha mē idein.*

5. *Ta prōta,* in this instance in the genitive, does not permit us to reconstruct an exact calendar of the ceremonies.

6. Battus is castrated by the women acting in concert. This excludes any confusion with practices in which a man cuts off his own genitals, such as the unfortunate occurrence in Athens at the altar of the twelve gods the night before the expedition to Sicily (Plutarch *Nicias* 13.3–4) or the ritual of the entourage of Cybele (cf. Er. Will, "Aspects du culte et de la légende de la grande Mère dans le monde grec," in *Eléments orientaux dans la religion grecque ancienne* [Paris, 1960], 95–111).

7. Pausanias 4.17.1.

8. It is to carry off the Athenian women of the best families that the people of Megara head toward Cape Colias, where all the women are gathered to offer their traditional sacrifice to Demeter. But the trap, which Solon set for them by replacing the women with young beardless boys who conceal daggers under their women's clothing (Plutarch, *Solon* 8.4–5), does not have the same meaning as the two tales under discussion here. Cf. as well the incident that pits the Ephesians against the Chians (Herodotus 6.16).

9. Two arguments come from F. Chamoux (*Cyrène,* 265), who finds in the story of Battus the echo of rites "going back to a distant past" (266). In 1906, M. P. Nilsson believed similarly (*Griechische Feste von religiöser Bedeutung mit Ausschluss der Attischen,* new ed. [Stuttgart, 1957], 324–25).

10. F. Chamoux, *Cyrène,* 265.

11. Cf. chapter 1, this volume.

12. Ph. Gauthier, *Symbola. Les étrangers et la justice dans les cités grecques* (Nancy, 1972), 45–47, as well as Casabona, 108–109.

13. *LSG,* no. 13, 1.25. In the deme of Scambonides (*LSG,* no. 10, ca. 7–10), foreigners receive a share of three obols in the agora. On Ceos (*LSG,* no. 98, 10), they take part with the freed slaves in the banquet that follows a sacrifice offered by the city.

14. D. M. Schaps, *Women's Rights in Ancient Greece* (London, 1979).

15. Inscription published by Cl. Rolley, "Le sanctuaire des dieux patrôoi et le Thesmophorion de Thasos," *BCH* 89 (1965):441 ff. The interpretation that we adopt was proposed in 1966 by Casabona (349–50).

16. *LSG Suppl.*, no. 20, 17–23, with commentaries by W. S. Ferguson, "The Attic Orgeones," *Harvard Theological Review* 37 (1944):73–77; "Orgeonika," *Commemorative Studies in Honor of Th. L. Shear, Hesperia, Suppl.* 8 (Baltimore and Athens, 1949), 130–31.

17. On line 21 the statute even foresees the case of a female servant, one per family, who receives the same share as the daughter.

18. Nothing indicates that the clause applies to those women who are absent.

19. The world is turned upside down when women begin to dispense justice (Ephorus *ap.* Strabo 9.2.2–5 = *FGrHist.*, 70 F 119).

20. G. Daux, "La grande démarchie: un nouveau calendrier sacrificial d'Attique (Erchia)," *BCH* 87 (1963):606 (A, 44–51); 609 (Δ, 33–40), with commentaries in 617 and 619. On the place of the feminine element in the dionysiac movement, we refer the reader, on the one hand, to the data gathered by K. Kérényi, *Dionysus: Archetypal Image of Indestructible Life,* Eng. ed. (Princeton and London, 1976), index, s.v., *Women* (443), and on the other, to very provisional conclusions in Detienne 1977 (203, 216) and in "Les chemins de la déviance: orphisme, dionysisme et pythagorisme," *Atti del XIV Convegno sulla Magna Grecia: Orfismo in Magna Grecia* (Naples [1974] 1978), 70–79.

21. P. Boyancé, "Dionysos et Sémélé," *Rendiconti. Atti della Pontificia Accademia Romana di Archeologia* 38 (1965–66):79–104; as well as Walter F. Otto, *Dionysos. Le mythe et le culte* (1933; Fr. ed. Paris, 1969), 180–87.

22. Pausanias 5.16.2–4.

23. Female age classes, related to a "tribal" system of initiation, are at the heart of an important book by C. Calame, *Les Chœurs de jeunes filles en Grèce archaïque,* vol. 1 (Rome, Athens, Bizzari, 1977), particularly 277–304; 441–43.

24. *Boos moiran tethumenēs tēi Hērai.* The olive crown (the *kotinos,* brought back from the country of the Hyperboreans) had been bestowed by Hercules Curetes on the victor of the first footrace in Olympia (Pausanias 5.7.7). Cf. M. Detienne, "L'Olivier: un mythe politicoreligieux," *Revue de l'histoire des religions* 3 (1970):5–23.

25. Pausanias 8.48: 4–5. Two points to be noted: 1) these "women warriors" are not *parthenoi* but married women; 2) this exchange of places is not marked by any exchange of clothing.

26. If the sacrificial perspective governs our remarks here, undoubtedly it is necessary to place the Tegean ritual in the field of relations that link Ares (instead of war) with certain feminine values.

27. Bread, cookies, pastries, *kukeōnes* are the business of women, who are confined to the house (cf. P. Herfst, *Le Travail de la femme dans la Grèce ancienne,* thesis [Utrecht, 1922]: 32). The oven, the pan for roasting grains, the portable brazier all are part of the mobile but domestic gear that women have in their charge along with slaves (equipment inventoried in B. A. Sparkes,"The Greek Kitchen," *Journal of Hellenic Studies* 82 [1962]: 121–37; 85 [1965]:162–63). For the "Homeric world," cf. G. Bruns, *Küchenwesen und Mahlzeiten, Archeologia homerica* 2:9 (Göttingen, 1970). But Greek houses are not generally equipped to prepare the meat of sacrificial victims (Vanna Svoronos-Hadjimichalis, "Fosses à rôtir dans des demeures helléniques du 4ᵉ siècle avant Jésus-Christ," *Hellénisme contemporain* 10 [1956]:106–124). The space of sacrificial cooking is neither private nor of the order of the household (cf. a whole oxen cooked in a bread oven—a sign of Barbarian eating in Aristophanes' *The Acharnians* [85–87]); it is organized around temples and public buildings specifically intended for banquets (cf., for example, G. Roux, "Salles de banquets à Délos," *Bulletin de correspondance hellénique. Suppl. 1. Etudes déliennes* [1973]:525–54; S. G. Miller, *The Prytaneion: Its Function and Architectural Form* [Berkeley and Los Angeles, 1978]).

28. The fact that a woman is a bad cook does not prevent the culinary symbolism from proliferating around the female body: her belly is a kettle (Herodotus 1.59), and sex a bread-

oven (ibid., 5.92.3) or a cooking hole, a hearth blackened with smoke (cf. J. Taillardat, *Les Images d'Aristophane,* 2d ed. [Paris, 1965], 76–77).

29. As in the *Dyscolus* of Menander, the sacrifice to Pan is offered by women, but it is the *mageiroi* who officiate, taking on the task of leading the victim as well as finding the indispensable caldron (456 ff.).

30. Cf. A.-J. Festugière, "La Grèce. Religion," in *Histoire générale des religions,* ed. M. Gorce and R. Mortier (Paris, 1944), 2:71.

31. The enumeration almost reproduces that of a decree of the deme of Cholargus (334–333 B.C.), published by E. Michon, "Un décret du dème de Cholargos relatif aux Thesmophories," *Mémoires de l'Académie des inscriptions et des belles-lettres* 13 (1923):1–24 (*LSG Suppl.,* no 24).

32. In the same way, the exclusively feminine character of the festival was to conceal the political dimension of the Thesmophoria.

33. Schol. on Lucian, ed. Rabe 276.3–28. Concerning the rite of the *megarismos,* its place on the first day of the Thesmophoria and not on the occasion of the *Skira,* see Burkert 1972, 284 and n. 5. Obviously, the "putrefied" remains are those from the preceding year.

34. In contrast to L. Deubner, Ph. Bruneau (285–290) has shown for Delos the importance of blood sacrifices in the Thesmophoria. Burkert 1977 (368–69) insists on the bloody aspect of the festival, citing the two accounts that we are analyzing, but he perhaps diminishes their meaning by displacing the problems of the women-slaughterer to the question of the pomegranate and the "blood-colored" grains that fall on the ground.

35. *Moralia* 298 b–c.

36. *Kalligeneia* is sometimes Earth, sometimes Demeter's nurse (*trophos*), at least if she is not her priestess or attendant (Apollodorus of Athens, *FGrHist.,* 244 F 141).

37. Schol. on Aristophanes, *Frogs* 388.

38. Bruneau, 285–90.

39. Ibid., 288.

40. On the *megara,* the rite of *megarizein,* and the different interpretations of *megaron,* cf. A.-J. Festugière, "Deux notes sur le 'De Iside' de Plutarque" (1959), in *Etudes de religion grecque et hellénistique* (Paris, 1972), 173–77; N. Kontoléon, "Mégaron," in *Mélanges O. et M. Merlier,* vol. 1 (Athens, 1956), 293–316; A. Heinrichs, "Megaron im Orakel des Apollon," *Zeitschrift für Papyrologie und Epigraphik* 4 (1969): 30–37; B. C. Dietrich, "A Religious Function of the Megaron," *Rivista storica dell'antichità* 3 (1973): 1–12; Bruneau, 276.

41. Lekythos 1695, National Museum of Athens, reproduced in L. Deubner, *Attische Feste* (1932; reprinted Berlin, 1956), pl. 2, which places the scene at the *Skira* (44). But nothing leads one to think that the animal is slaughtered before the "throwing" (cf. Pausanias 9.8.1 and Clement of Alexandria, *Protreptica* 2.17.1) or at the moment it is dropped. This whole phase is placed under the sign of decomposition in and by the earth, and the altar will serve as a table where the results of the "scoopers'" quest are placed.

42. Cf., e.g., G. Voza, in *Archeologia nella Sicilia Sud-Orientale* (Naples, 1973), nos. 395 and 397, table 41. Sicilian temples like that of Eloro where sacrificial pits have been inventoried: terra cotta statuettes, the remains of animal victims. Likewise in Sardinia the temple of Santa Margherita di Pula (Cagliari) (abstract published by G. Pesce, *Notizie dei Scavi* [1974], 506–513), where the pigs are drawn morphologically very close to boars. The ex-votos of the *Thesmophorion* of Thasos are quite remarkable (Cf. Rolley, *BCH* 89 [1965]: 470–71; figs. 30–31): the two halves of the opened animal are spread apart to show the entrails and the whole inner geography of the pig or the sow.

43. Bruneau, 288–89.

44. 692–95. The cakes (*popana*) contained in the basket (*kistē*) carried by the Thracian slave at the beginning of the *Thesmophoriazusae* (284–84) are intended for this blood sacrifice.

45. *Thesmophoriazusae* 754–55.

46. Ibid., 758. To the priestess who offers and carries out the blood sacrifice. But the presence of a knife does not indicate the person who wields it. The same remark applies to the sacrificial knives found at Bitalemi (Gela) in the temple of Demeter Thesmophorus, excavated by P. Orlandini (cf. *Kokalos* 12 [1965]:8–35; pl. 25, 3).

47. Aristophanes *Thesmophoriazusae* 1150–51. Burkert (1977, 370) recalls that on Paros the cult of the Thesmophoria is in the hands of male priests, the "Kabarnoi" (n. 51), while in Corinth American excavators have discovered statues of young boys standing in Demeter's temple holding offerings in their hands (n. 53).

48. Cf. J. Martha, *Les Sacerdoces athéniens* (Paris, 1881), passim. The old book by Adrian, *Die Priesterinnen der Griechen* (Frankfurt, 1822), has not inspired any recent research. Comments that are sometimes interesting are found in L. R. Farnell, "Sociological Hypotheses Concerning the Position of Women in Ancient Religion," *Archive für Religionswissenschaft* 7 (1904): 70–94.

49. J. Martha, *Les Sacerdoces athéniens*, 20–23.

50. Demosthenes *Contra Neaeram* 73–75. Cf. H. Jeanmaire, *Dionysos. Histoire du culte de Bacchus* (Paris, 1951; reprinted, 1970), 51–54; Burkert 1977, 361–64.

51. *LSA*, no. 73 (third century B.C.), and the analyses of L. Robert, *Hellenica* 5, 64–69; J. and L. Robert, *Bulletin épigraphique* 55 (1951): 144–45.

52. *LSA*, no. 73, 21.

53. Aristophanes *Thesmophoriazusae* 293–94; Isaeus 6.49–50. In other words, in this festival males are treated like slaves. This would probably lead to an extension of the "variations" discussed by P. Vidal-Naquet, "Esclavage et gynécocratie dans la tradition, le mythe et l'utopie," in *Recherches sur les structures sociales dans l'Antiquité classique,* ed. Cl. Nicolet (Paris, 1970), 63–80.

54. Fr. 63 Pfeiffer. A more important piece of evidence for the classical age than that of Lucian, *Dialogi Meretricii* 2.1, traditionally given, for example, in Burkert 1977, 365, n. 6.

55. Lysias 1.19.

56. Isaeus 8.19–20; 3.80 (*gametē*). Cf. Detienne 1972, 151–52.

57. *Eugeneis gunaikes,* as Aristophanes calls them (*Thesmophoriasuzae* 330). It is indeed the assembly of the eugeneia: the women of the best families, likewise called *gunaikes eleutherai* (cf. W. S. Ferguson, "Orgeonika," *Hesperia,* Suppl. 8 [1949]: 131, n.2). Moreover, the richer her husband the more likely it is that the wife will obtain the honor of offering—as a liturgy—the banquet of the Thesmophoria (*hestian:* Isaeus 3.80). For "nobility" and its values, see the analyses of J. Brunschwig of the Aristotelian treatise, *On Nobility* (*Peri Eugeneias*), in *Aristotle* (*Fragments*), ed. P. M. Schuhl (Paris, 1968), 81–98.

58. *IG* (Inscriptiones Graecae), 2², 1177 (fourth century B.C.); *LSG Suppl.,* no. 32 (fifth century B.C., which opens the series of documents related to the forbidding of luxurious clothing, jewels, or adornments in the enclosures of the temples to Demeter). In a statute of Arcesines of Amorgus (fourth century B.C.), Demeter is described as *dēmotelēs,* a divine power "at public expense" (cf. Herodotus 6.56). And her priestess has the right to bring suit before the prytaneis for an infraction, which is unreadable on the stone (*LSG,* no. 102, 4–7). In the same vein, it is not unimportant that the only woman admitted to the Olympic Games is a priestess of Demeter *Khamunē* (Pausanias 6.20.9), who is the model for the woman-theōrus who inspires an Ephesian tradition (L. Robert, "Les femmes-théores à Ephèse," *Comptes rendus de l'Académie des inscriptions et des belles-lettres* [1974]: 176–181).

59. Pausanias 9.16.5. Cf. F. Vian, *Les Origines de Thèbes. Cadmos et les Spartes* (Paris, 1963), 135–39.

60. Cl. Rolley, *BCH* 89 (1965): 441–83. Also see the comments on the "great families" by J. Pouilloux in *Archiloque, Entretiens sur l'antiquité classique* 10 (Vandoeuvres-Geneva,

1964), 23. The whole Miltiades affair on Paros, which involves a minor priestess of Demeter and her treason, seems to indicate that the city's fate is closely linked to the temple of the Thesmophoria (Herodotus 6.134–35). Elsewhere, the *Hymn to Demeter* of Callimachus shows a procession winding along a "Cyrenean" trail between two of the goddess' temples, one located on the agora and the other outside of town (cf. Cl. Meillier, *Callimaque. Hymnes 5 et 6. Texte, traduction et commentaire,* thesis, Paris IV [1971]: 154–55 [typescript, Sorbonne Library]). For Sicily, see D. White, "Demeter Sicilian Cult As a Political Instrument," *Greek, Roman and Byzantine Studies* 5 (1964): 261–79.

61. Detienne 1972, 151–58.

62. Schol. on Lucian, ed. Rabe, 276, 14–18; 280.

63. Detienne 1972, index, s.v., *sperma.*

64. The meaning of *thesmos* in the compound name of the festival has been extensively discussed among partisans of a concrete meaning (remains of piglets, seeds, objects designated by the "container" [Anacreon, Fr. 406 Page; *Odyssey* 23.296]) and those who insist on its abstract, "prescriptive" value (following the uses of *thesmia* and *thesmoi* in the political and constitutional vocabulary). Cf., for example, H. Jeanmaire, *Couroi et courètes* (Lille, 1935), 305–306; *Annuaire de l'Ecole pratique des hautes études, Sciences religieuses* (1952–53): 40–41; H. W. Parke, *Festivals of the Athenians* (London, 1977), 83–84. Material that perhaps should be reconsidered in light of the epigrams analysed in G. Mangaraon, "Due epigrafi rinvenute ad Egina," *ASAA* 37–38 (1959–60): 421–27, where *thesmia* seems to designate the *hiera,* sacred objects.

65. E. Michon, "Un décret du dème de Cholargos," 4–5, and B. Haussoullier, *La Vie municipale en Attique* (Paris, 1883): 139.

66. Isaeus 8.19–20.

67. *LSG Suppl.,* no. 124, 3. On women as priestesses and presiders (*arkhis, arkhēis, arkhinē, arkhousa*), cf. W. Volgraff, in *Mémoires présentés par divers savants à l'Académie des inscriptions et de belles-lettres* 14, 2 (1951): 329–30.

68. *LSG,* no. 36, 10–12.

69. Isaeus 8.19.

70. *LSA,* no. 61, 5.

71. The prayer opening the ceremonies asks the tutelary gods of the Thesmophoria that the gathering and assembly of that day have the finest and best effects, that they be full of advantages for the city of the Athenians and luck for the women (295–305). "May she who by her perspicacity and harangue has deserved the most *from the Athenian people and the people of women* be the one who takes it" (305–307). It is only in the final invocation addressed to Athena—before the Thesmophoria—that the "people of women" make the economy of the "city of Athenians" (1145–46).

72. Varro in Augustine *City of God* 18.9.

73. 181. The plot of Aristophanes' play blends the story of Battus and the account of Aristomenes.

74. 75–84.

75. *Psēphisasthai pasa androktonein* (Asclepiades of Tragilus, *FGrHist.,* 12 F 14). Another example of the assembly of women can be found among the Phocians during the war of extermination against the Thessalians. They have already adopted the plan of Daiphantus; women and children will be gathered next to an enormous woodpile that can, in case of defeat, remove them from the vengeance of the victors. It is at that moment that an unknown man suggests that it would be fair to ask the women what they think about this. They gather in an assembly and vote (*psēphisasthai*) in favor of the plan. Moreover, it is said, the children (*paides*), for their part, had the right to their own assembly (*idiai*) and they also decided upon this solution (*epipsēphisasthai*) (Plutarch *Moralia* 244 B–D).

76. Cf. this chapter, text at note 14.

77. *Heydemann* 2411. Reproduced and analysed in F. Cumont and A. Vogliano, "La grande iscrizione bacchica del Metropolitan Museum," *American Journal of Archaeology* 37 (1933): 242–43, pl. 31, 1.

78. For example, the sacrifice depicted on a *pinax* of wood from the grotto of Pitsa indeed shows women leading an animal victim toward the altar of the Nymphs accompanied by an *aulos*-player (cf. U. Hausmann, *Griechische Weihreliefs* [Berlin, 1960], 23, fig. 10), but none of them carry a visible "weapon"; and moreover, the procession is flanked by male servers (and not children, as N. Kontoléon believes, in *Aspects de la Grèce préclassique* [Paris, 1970], 15–16), as can be seen on several Corinthian vases. Further, the problem of the "Victories" remains: a winged woman sacrificing a bull and often by imposing her *kratos* on him (e.g., H. Metzger, *Recherches sur l'imagerie athénienne* [Paris, 1965], 112).

79. Obviously, it is necessary to consider the series of Maenads separately: women brandishing in one hand a *makhaira* and, in the other, half of the victim, cut in two, often in the middle (cf. H. Philippart, "Iconographie des bacchantes d'Euripide," *Revue belge de philologie et d'histoire* 9 [1930]: 5–72: nos. 99, 100, 106, 112, 132).

80. Cf. Detienne 1977, 199–200.

81. Possessed by Dionysus, on a small island at the mouth of the Loire, forbidden to men. Once a year they raise the roof of the temple, to replace it on the same day. "She who drops her burden on the ground is torn apart by others who walk with her limbs around the temple" (Strabo 4.4.6 = Posidonius, *FGrHist.*, 87 F 56).

82. For example, the oinochoë of Amphissa: a satyr grillmaster in a cave hallowed by a ribbon (*BCH* 89 [1965]: 780, fig. 4). It would be necessary to put the grillmasters opposite the hunter-satyrs.

83. M. P. Nilsson, *Griechische Feste*, 329–30.

84. Aelian, *De natura animalium* 11.4.

85. 2.35.4–8.

86. In the sacrifice to the *Despoina* of Lycosura in Arcadia, on the contrary, one of the victim's limbs is cut off at random instead of having its throat slit (Pausanias 8.37.8). But conditions are different; for the *Despoina*, to whom one sacrifices without counting, each slays an animal he owns, and his actions are as if disordered. While in the temple of Hermione, troubled by the furious charge of the "bull," each old woman strikes the throat with a precise blow.

87. And not in the suicidal form in Pausanias 4.13.1.

88. The weapon of Cronus or the tool forged by the Titans. The scythes (*drepana*), along with daggers (*encheiridia*), form part of the war equipment of the Carians (Herodotus 5.112; 7.93) who are, in the tradition of the fifth century, warriors who have invented weapons (cf. D. Fourgous, "L'invention des armes en Grèce ancienne," *Annali della Scuola normale superiore di Pisa* Cl. Lett. Filos. 3, 4, no. 4 [1976]: 1153–54).

89. The *Hymn to Demeter* of Callimachus separates the women more than sixty years old from the lot of the initiates, the only ones authorized to follow the *Kalathos* from the Prytaneum to the temple of the goddess located outside the town (129–30).

90. 40–41; 621–24. "Female murderer of the male" (*"thēlus arsenos phoneus"*) is of course Clytemnestra (Aeschylus *Agamemnon* 1231).

91. Nothing proves that the Vera Hydrophorus, for example, priestess of Artemis and daughter of a physician of Lebedos, herself sacrificed the fetuses of chosen goats mentioned in an inscription at Patmos (analyzed of late by H. D. Saffrey, "Relire l'Apocalypse à Patmos," *Revue biblique* [1975]:385–417). Inversely, it is certain that the women of Herondas sacrificing to Asclepius did not themselves slaughter the cock they came to offer. It is the *neōkoros*, the sacristan on duty, who has this task and receives the bird's thigh as the honored share (*Mimes* 4.89–90). We were unable to consult J. R. Oliver, "The Sacrificing Women in the Temple of Asclepios," *Bull. Inst. Hist. of Medicine* 1 (1934): 504–511.

92. See Durand 1977.
93. Jochen Schelp, *Das Kanoun. Der griechische Opferkorb* (Würzburg, 1975), 24–25.
94. Pherecrates, fr. 64 Kock (= Athenaeus 612 a–b). Cf. Berthiaume, 31.
95. Cf. the documents referred to by Bruneau (272–273) and again discussed by Berthiaume. The *mageiros* is documented from the middle of the third century up until the end of the Independence, 166 B.C.
96. As Bruneau, who does not linger over the problem posed by this *mageiros* in the middle of the Thesmophoria, believes (288).
97. *LSA,* no. 61, 5–10.
98. *LSA,* no. 61, 9. The text published by E. Hula and E. Szanto, "Bericht über eine Reise in Karien," *Sitz. ber. A. W. Wien* 132 (1895): 14, no. 5, reads as follows:
9 [. . . *spha*]*xamenos ta hiera apitō e*[*k*] *tō*[*n*
10 [*dei*]*pnon paratheōsi kai dede* [——
Before the form, "who slaughtered," one could construe either *mageiros* or *dēmosios* (?). In another inscription, of a later date (first century A.D.), coming from Cius Prusias in Bithynia (*LSA,* no. 6) and apparently concerning Demeter (mention is made of the *kalathos*), a male (*anēr*) is again given the function of "assistant" (latreuein: carry out the office of a servant; or *daitreuein:* fulfill the role of the one who carves and cuts up the parts.) But the reading of two letters is uncertain.
99. Cf. chapter 1, this volume, text at note 29.
100. As in the cultic calendar of Cos, around 350 B.C. (*LSG,* no. 151, A. 40–44), in which a distinction is made between a priest (*hiareus*), heralds (*kerukes*) gathered to offer a sacrifice, and a third person chosen to be the *slaughterer.* "Let the heralds choose among themselves one to slaughter the ox, *sphagē tou boos.*" In the statute of the Scambonides, early fifth century B.C. (*LSG,* no. 10, c. 13–14), the *slaughterer* receives a sausage (*khordeion*) as an honorarium. The ambiguity of *sphageus* (slaughterer/assassin) is central to the sacrificial action (Casabona, 174–80). Cf. "Wolves at the Feast," chapter 6, this volume.
101. Cf. Aelian, fr. 44 Hercher: "the part of the ceremonies that contained nothing but the ordinary for the spectators as well as for the actors."
102. Herodotus 6.134–35. Herodotus' account marks the homology between "reveal things forbidden (*arrhēta hira*) to the male sex" and "put one's hand on what one must not touch" (*kinein ta akinēta*). Objects and gestures are mobilized in a ritual action where showing, *deiknunai* (Aristophanes *Thesmophoriazusae* 629), does not involve the absence of words.
103. *Iliad* 3.189; 6.186. And the story of the double interpretation between Aeschylus and Aristarchus, in Th. Drew-Bear, "Imprecations from Kourion," *Bull. Amer. Soc. Papyrology* 9 (1972):88–92.
104. Herodotean tradition (cf. F. Vian, *La Guerre des géants. Le mythe avant l'époque hellénistique* [Paris, 1952], 268–274). In the novel of Dionysios Skytobrachion (Diodorus 3.71.3–4, *FGrHist.,* 32 F 8), Athena commands a detachment of Amazons in the war against the Titans of Cronus.
105. Diodorus 3.53.1–3. Cf. Jeannie Carlier, "Les Amazones font la guerre et l'amour," *Ethnographie* 76 (1980–81): 11–33.
106. 17–18; 59 (*hosa Skirois edoxen*).
107. Cf. the indications given by P. Vidal-Naquet, "Le Chasseur noir et l'origine de l'éphébie athénienne," *Annales E. S. C.* 23 (1968):958.
108. *Thesmophoriazusae* 121.
109. Detienne 1972, 154–55; "Orphée au miel," in *Faire de l'histoire,* ed. J. Le Goff and P. Nora, vol. 3 (Paris, 1974), 56–75.
110. Cf. abstracts of the seminars that we have devoted to "La Violence au féminin," in *Annuaire de l'Ecole pratique des Hautes Études, Sciences religieuses,* 1975–76 (Paris, 1977), 279–80.

111. 2.171.

112. "Orphée au miel," 70–71.

113. An idea of the iconographic documentation can be had by consulting Felix M. Schoeller, *Darstellungen des Orpheus in der Antike,* thesis (Freiburg, 1969), 55–65. But an analysis of the approximately forty vases depicting the killing of Orpheus can only be done with the catalogue of E. Panyagua, "Catálogo de representaciones de Orfeo en el arte antiguo," *Helmantica* 70 (1972): 83–135, particularly nos. 39, 40, and 41, where the sacrificial skewers are associated at times with the *makhaira,* at times with the double ax. A spit for roasting an ox is a formidable weapon (cf. Xenophon *Anabasis* 7.8.14); it has its place in the equipment of the Delphians who surround Neoptolemus, who had come to sacrifice to Apollo (Euripides *Andromache* 1132–34. Cf. E. K. Borthwick, "Two Scenes of Combat in Euripides," *Journal of Hellenic Studies* 90 [1970]: 15–17).

114. 7.1.581 a 31–b 2.

115. Detienne 1972, 153–54; Detienne 1977, 130, n. 197 (where we summarize an interpretation, outlined in "Potagerie de femmes ou comment engendrer seule," *Traverses* 5–6 [1976]: 75–81, but which remains to be developed). The two flows provoked by the agnus castus—milk and menstrual blood—have the same sanguinary origin but in a body where they reveal the fundamental incapacity of the feminine race to produce anything but "failed" sperm, in the culinary sense, since here indeed it is a question of women who are bad cooks (in Aristotle *De Generatione Animalium* 728 a 18–21.774 a 2–3).

Chapter 6. The Feast of the Wolves

1. Material concerning the wolf appears in R. de Block, "Le loup dans les mythologies de la Grèce et de l'Italie anciennes," *Revue de l'instruction publique en Belgique* 20 (1877): 145–58, 217–34; M. Schuster, "Der Werwolf und die Hexen. Zwei Schauermärchen bei Petronius," *Wiener Studien* 48 (1930): 149–78; L. Gernet, "Dolon le loup" (1936), in *Anthropologie de la Grèce antique* (Paris, 1968): 154–71 [Eng. ed., "Dolon the Wolf," in *The Anthropology of Ancient Greece,* trans. John Hamilton, S.J., and Blaise Nagy (Baltimore and London, 1981), 125–39]; G. Piccaluga, *Lykaon. Un tema mitico* (Rome, 1968); Burkert 1972, particularly, 97–108; W. Richter, s.v., "Wolf," *R.E.,* Suppl. 15, (1978): 960–87.

2. Aristotle *Historia Animalium* 1.1.488 b 17–20.

3. On the different nuances of nobility, cf. Aristotle's treatise, *On Nobility,* with commentaries by J. Brunschwig, in the collective volume, *Aristotle, De la richesse,* etc., ed. P.-M. Schuhl (Paris, 1968):84–89.

4. A contrast that has already been observed by H. Fränkel, *Die homerischen Gleichnisse* (Göttingen, 1921):60, and more recently by U. Dierauer, *Tier und Mensch im Denken der Antike* (Amsterdam, 1977):8–9.

5. *Iliad* 4.471–72.

6. Ibid. 11.67–73.

7. Ibid. 16.155–65.

8. Aristophanes of Byzantium *Epitome* 1.11, ed. Lambros: the wolf is both *epithetikos* and *epiboulos.*

9. Xenophon, *On the Cavalry Commander* 4.18–20.

10. Artemidorus *Oneirocritica* 2.12, ed. Pack, 124.3–13; 4.56, ed. Pack, 279.12–14. Cf. as well Solon, fr. 36, 27 West.

11. Pindar, *P.,* 2.84–85. "His right eye concealed under clothing . . . enables him to flee from the midst of his enemies without being seen": Cyranides, in *Lapidaires grecs,* ed. de Mély and Ruelle, 1.65.

12. A series of terms refers to the "human" way of hunting wolves: *kunēgein* in two variants of Aesop's fable 229, ed. Chambry, 2 (1926):371–72; *Kunēgesia* in Aristotle *Historia Animalium* 8.594 a 30–32; *agreuein* in Xenophon, *On the Cavalry Commander* 4.18–20.

13. Cf. Aesop, fable 230, ed. Chambry (unless otherwise indicated, we cite the one-volume edition published by Belles Lettres with a French translation, second edition published in 1960).

14. Aesop, fable 229, ed. Chambry 2 (1926):371–372.

15. Aesop, fable 215, ed. Chambry.

16. Cf. M. Detienne, "La Phalange: problèmes et controverses," in *Problèmes de la guerre en Grèce ancienne,* ed. J.-P. Vernant (Paris-The Hague, 1968):119–42.

17. See J.-P. Vernant, *Les Origines de la pensée grecque,* 3d ed. (Paris, 1975):125–30, et al.

18. See M. Detienne, *Les Maîtres de vérité dans la Grèce archaïque,* 2d ed. (Paris, 1973):82–93.

19. Herodotus 3.142–43.

20. Generally stubborn and not very intelligent, the ass is hardworking (fables 262, 273), peaceable (268, 269), a simple private person (141, 279); jealous of people who obtain advantages, he seems to represent arithmetic equality (cf. Plutarch *Quaestiones conviviales* 2.10.643 c, etc.): fables 209, 228, 272 (cf. 207). Cf. as well Aelian *De natura animalium* 8.6, who says that the ass is easy prey for wolves.

21. Cf. Herodotus 2.134.

22. (Apollodorus) *Bibliotheca* 3.11.2. Meleager keeps the hide of the boar of Calydon as the share of honor and distributes the pieces among his companions (*dianeimas ta krea*), according to Antoninus Liberalis, *Metamorphoses* 2.3. In this case as elsewhere (*Odyssey* 9.159–60), the division of the game is made according to the same rules as the division of booty (cf. G. Glotz, *La Solidarité de la famille dans le droit criminel en Grèce* (Paris, 1904):201 n.2. On some occasions the booty is devoured (*katadēmoborēsai: Iliad* 18.301).

23. Athenaeus 1.12 d–e.

24. Cf. above, chapter 1, text at notes 35–39.

25. Cf. for Crete, for example, Dosiadas, *FGRHist.,* 458 F 2.

26. Fable 281, ed. Chambry. Cf. Babrius 122.14–16, ed. Crusius.

27. Fable 107, ed. Chambry. For *makellarios,* cf. the article *makellon* in Chantrine.

28. Herodotus 6.60.

29. Aristotle *Historia Animalium* 9.6.612 b; Xenophon *On the Cavalry Commander* 4.19. Since P.-L. Courier, there has been an inclination to correct the form *aposphaxas* in the manuscripts to *apospasas* (from the verb "to tear," "tear up") on the pretext that the verb *aposphazein,* "to slaughter," put to death," is used only for human victims; but cf. Aristotle *Politics* 5.9.1305 a 25: *ta ktēnē aposphaxas,* "after he slaughtered the flocks." Ed. Delebecque, the editor of the Collection des Universités de France (1973) is correct in refusing to banish a verb that is perhaps unusual but confirms Aristotle's testimony. Elsewhere, we can note that (Apollodorus) *Bibliotheca* 3.8.1 uses *sphazein* for the sacrifice of a child slain by the sons of Lycaon.

30. Aristotle *Historia Animalium* 9.6.612 b. Our texts do not explicitly say that the wolf's jaw is his knife, but the association between jaw and *makhaira* is referred to, for example, in the expression *oxustomon makhairan,* in Euripides *Suppliants* 1206 (cf. Chr. Collard, *Euripides: Suppliants* [Groningen, 1975] 2:416, for other references).

31. Plutarch *Quaestiones conviviales* 2.10.624 b–c.

32. Cf. R. de Block, "Le Loup," 151–57; A. B. Cook, *Zeus* 1, reprint (New York, 1964), 63–68; L. Gernet, "Dolon le loup," 157 and n. 18.

33. Cf. Br. Lincoln, "Homeric Lyssa, Wolfish Rage," *Indogermanische Forschungen* 80 (1975): 98–105. W. Burkert 1972, 127, n. 11, refers to a bell crater in Boston (00.346 = *ARV²*, 1045.7) representing Lyssa with a wolf's hairdo.

34. Plutarch *Quaestiones conviviales* 6.10.696 e.

35. On a terra cotta from Tanagra, from the last quarter of the sixth century B.C., pub-

lished by S. Mollard-Besques, *Catalogue raisonné des figurines et reliefs en terre cuite grecs, étrusques et romains.* 1.1–2: *Epoques préhellénique, géométrique, archaïque et classique. Musée national du Louvre* (Paris, 1954), pl. xvi B 123. We are grateful to Jean-Louis Durand for indicating this document to us.

36. Timotheus of Gaza 8.27–29, ed. Haupt (*Hermes* 3 [1869]:1–30).

37. Aesop, fable 229, ed. Chambry, 2 (1926), 371–72.

38. Aelian *De natura animalium* 7.20.

39. For the material on Lycaon, which we are not treating here, cf. G. Piccaluga, *Lykaon;* for Lycosura, see Chantraine, s.v. *lukos.* The Arcadian traditions surrounding Lycaon, Pelasgus, and Pan or Arcas are the subject of chapter 2 of Philippe Borgeaud, *Recherches sur le dieu Pan* (Rome, 1979) [trans. Kathleen Atlas and James Redfield as *The Cult of Pan in Ancient Greece* (Chicago, 1988)].

40. (Apollodorus) *Bibliotheca* 1.9.2. Cf. schol. on Plato, *Minos* 315 c (ed. Greene, 293); Tzetzes, ad Lycophron, *Alexandra* 22 (ed. Scheer, 21–22); *Etymologicum Magnum,* s.v., *Athamantion; Schol. ad Apollonius of Rhodes, Argonautica* 2.513 (ed. Wendel, 170); Stephanus of Byzantium, s.v., *Alos.* The descendants of Athamas were forbidden to the prytaneum that was found in the temple of Zeus Laphystius, on pain of being sacrificed (*thusesthai:* Herodotus 7.197) when they exited. A punishment that was provoked by the "execution" of Phrixus, who had convinced his father to follow Ino's counsel. As a space for hospitality, the "Achaian" prytaneum evokes both the "table" set by the wolves and the table of Lycaon overturned by his divine guest. In the histories of Arcadia, the table plays an essential role, midway between its sacrificial uses and its communal symbolism.

41. Cf. Pausanias 2.19.3–5: Danaus against Agenor is the wolf combatting the bull because in the eyes of the Argives he appears to be a man without a country, an exile, a fugitive. Aristotle *Historia Animalium* 6.35.580 a 18, and Aelian *De natura animalium* 10.26, tell the story of Leto, who is transformed into a shewolf when she flees Hera's anger. Other accounts revolve around the wolf and exile: in the surroundings of the Athenian tribunals (Plato *Phaedrus* 271 c–d; Aristophanes *Wasps* 389–93; *Paroemiographi Graeci,* ed. Leutsch-Schneidewin 1.115, s.v., *Lukou dekas*); in a poem by Alcaeus (fr. 130 Lobel-Page). Cf. as well G. Glotz, *La Solidarité de la famille,* 22–23.

42. Aristotle, *Historia Animalium* 8.5.594 a 30–32.

43. The discussion of the "four constitutions" begins in the *Republic* 8.1.544 b.

44. Plato *Republic* 8.16.565 d–566 a.

45. Cf. Plato *Republic* 9.1.571 c–572 b; 10.16.619 c. Cf. as well *Phaedo* 82a.

46. *Iliad* 16.160.

47. Aristotle *Historia Animalium* 1.1.488 a 7–10. Cf. Plato *Phaedo* 82 b5.

48. Aristotle *Historia Animalium* 6.18.571 b 27–30: *mē agelaios.*

49. Aristotle *Historia Animalium* 1.1.488 a 5. The wolf is a plunderer, *harpax* (Lycophron *Alexandra* 1309). To lead a wolf's life is to live by pillaging (Polybius 16.24.4). Cf. *Paroemiographi Graeci,* ed. Leutsch-Schneidewin 2.243.10–11, s.v., *agora lukios.*

50. A. Alföldi, "La Louve du Capitole. Quelques remarques sur son mythe à Rome et chez les Etrusques," *Hommage à la mémoire de Jérome Carcopino* (Paris, 1977):1–11, pl. 3.2 (Etruscan document in the Museo Nazionale di Civitavecchia, inv. no. 1290, published by Lisa Hannestad, *The Followers of the Paris Painter* [Copenhagen, 1976], pl. 16. We thank Fr. Lissarrague for bringing it to our attention).

Some benchmarks among pictorial representations of the wolf: the vase in the Dipylon series showing two wild animals tearing a young warrior apart with wide open jaws (analyzed by H. Jeanmaire, "Un Thème initiatique sur un vase du Dipylon," *Mélanges G. Glotz* 2 [Paris, 1932]:483; *Couroi et Courètes* [Lille, 1939]: 565–66); a "hairy monster" (wolf?) among armed hunters on a Boeotian kantharos (8th/7th century B.C.), in F. Canciani, "Böotische Vasen aus dem 8. un 7. Jahrhundert," *JDAI* 80 (1965):45; a wolf behind a tree overlooking a scene where two cattle face each other near a cowherd (Attic vase in the Metropolitan Museum, published by Gisela M. Richter, "Two Recent Acquisitions by the Metropolitan Museum of Art," *American Journal of Archaeology* 43 [1939]:6–9, fig. 4–5); assorted Etruscan wolf demons in E. Simon, "Die Tomba dei Tori und der etruskische Apollokult," *JDAI* 88 (1973):27–42, pl. 8 and 9.

51. *Paroemiographi Graeci,* ed. Leutsch-Schneidewin, 2, 186, s.v., *lukōn philia;* cf. Plato, *Letters* 3.318 e, *lukophilia.*

52. According to Aristotle's expression (*Historia animalium* 1.1.488 a 8) for the "political ones."

53. *Paroemiographi Graeci,* ed. Leutsch-Schneidewin, 1:431, s.v., *Lukos kreas nemei: epi tou pleonektein kai didonai boulomenou.*

54. This is the title of Lycaon stabbing his son Nyctimus, in Lycophron *Alexandra* 481.

55. It is the opposite of the *isomoiria* (Xenophon *Cyropaedia* 2.2.22; 2.3.5). Cf. B. Borecky, "The Primitive Origin of the Greek Conception of Equality," *Festschrift G. Thomson* (Prague, 1963), 59.

56. Cf. Plutarch *Quaestiones conviviales* 2.10.643 c, etc.

57. Euripides, *Rhesus* 254. For the analysis of pictorial documents, cf. Fr. Lissarrague, "L'iconographie de Dolon le loup," *Revue archéologique,* 1980, 3–30.

58. *Sphageus* (Casabona, 178–79, 335).

59. Casabona, 174–78.

60. Aristotle *Historia animalium* 1.14.493 b 7.

61. Cf. Andocides *De Mysterii* 78, quoted by Casabona, 178.

62. Xenophon *Constitution of the Lacedaemonians* 13.8. Cf. Rudhardt, 274.

63. Plutarch *Aristides* 17.5–10.

64. Polyaenus 1.23.1, ed. Melber. Cf. J. Labarbe, "Un putsch dans la Grèce antique: Polycrate et ses frères à la conquête du pouvoir," *Ancient Society* 5 (1974):21–41, which compares the text of Polyaenus with a passage of Aeneas Tacticus (*Poliorcetica* 17.2–4).

65. Herodotus 6.60.

66. Cf. Durand, 1977.

67. Cf. above, chapter 1, text at note 25.

68. As the essential study by Roux has demonstrated.

69. Herodotus 7.225, quoted by Roux, 35.

70. Finally we must add to Roux's study, for both Neoptolemus and Aesop, the analyses of Gregory Nagy in his book, *The Best of the Achaeans: Concepts of the Hero in Archaic Greek Poetry* (Baltimore, 1981).

71. Aristophanes, fr. 684, ed. Edmonds, quoted by Roux, 37. Cf. the Apollo of the Penthesilea painter on the Munich cup 2689, where the god is represented striking a suppliant with his *makhaira* (reproduced and cited in Roux, 35 and pl. 10.5).

72. *Oxyrhynchus Papyrus* 1800, fr. 2, col. 2, 32 ff., which we use in light of the analyses of Gregory Nagy. It is in this context that we must recall Heracles at the banquet, holding the *makhaira* before a table laden with carved meat (cf. R. Blatter, "Herakles beim Gelage," *Archäologischer Anzeiger* 91 [1976]:49–52), a Heracles, however, who sacrifices the working ox that he wrested from Theodamas the day after his Egyptian adventure, when he himself was nearly turned into a sacrificial animal by the no less impious Busiris who treated foreigners as choice victims ([Apollodorus] *Bibliotheca* 2.5.11).

73. Athenaeus 1.12 d–e.

74. Cf. Theophrastus, fr. 18, ed. Pötscher.

75. Asclepiades of Tragilus, *FGrHist.,* 12 F 15. Cf. Burkert 1972, 136.

76. Euripides, fr. 482, ed. Nauck².

77. It is a wolf's shape that Apollo takes on to carry off Cyrene (Servius, ad Virgil, *Aeneid*

4.377), and in the city of Argos, where he is Apollo Lyceius, wolves are sacrificed to him (schol. on Sophocles, *Electra* 6). Cf. W. Richter, s.v. "Wolf," *R.E.,* Suppl. 15 (1978):975–77.

78. Of which G. Roux speaks in *Delphes, Son oracle et ses dieux* (Paris, 1976), 16.

79. Aratus *Phenomena,* ed. J. Martin, 130–32. To be added to the dossier compiled by D. Fourgous, "L'invention des armes en Grèce ancienne," *Annali della Scuola Normale Superiore di Pisa, cl. Lett. Filos.,* ser. 3, 6, no. 4 (1976):1123–64. The two lines are quoted by Plutarch (*De esu carnium* 2.4.998 a) and A. Delatte has mistakenly attributed them to the author of a Pythagorean *Sacred Discourse* (*Etudes sur la littérature pythagoricienne* [Paris, 1914]:41–42).

80. This is the scholiasts' reading, which influenced the translation of J. Martin.

81. Cf. M. Foucault, *Annuaire du Collège de France* (1976):361–66.

Chapter 7. Food in the Country of the Sun

1. *Odyssey* 1.5–9.

2. In Hesiod's *Theogony, Huperiōn* is the name of a Titan whose son is *Hēlios.* Whether the epithet *Huperiōn* applies to *Hēlios* himself or refers to him as the son of his father, it characterizes him by his position high in the sky; things are different when *Hēlios* is considered and defined as setting or rising.

3. *Histories* 3.17–26.

4. *Odyssey* 1.24; cf. Strabo 1.1.5 and 1.2.24–29. In a passage of the *Odyssey* (12.380–81), perhaps interpolated, the island of the Sun, by its position both east and west, seems to be likened to the land of the Ethiopians.

5. *Iliad* 1.423–24; 23.205; *Odyssey* 1.25–26.

6. *Odyssey* 12.283, 292, 307 ff. For the Greeks it is the island of the *dorpon,* supper.

7. *Odyssey* 12.279–83.

8. Ibid. 301.

9. They must remain "intact." Nothing must be undertaken that threatens to harm their physical integrity; cf. the use of *asinēs* ("intact") in the *Odyssey* 11.110 and 12.137; similarly, in 11.112 and 12.139, the prohibitions against harming them (*sinomai*).

10. The beauty of the cattle, in Homer: *Odyssey* 12.129, 262, 365; of the Ethiopians, in Herodotus 3.20.7.

11. *Odyssey* 12.129–31: "Seven herds of cattle, of fifty head each, live there, always beautiful, knowing neither birth nor death (*gonos d' ou ginetai autōn oude pote phthinuthousi*)." Cf., for men of the golden race, Hesiod *Works and Days* 112–115: "They lived like gods, their hearts free of care, apart from and sheltered from painful labor and misery; miserable old age did not weigh upon them, but arms and calves always young, they made merry in feasts, far from all misfortunes."

12. Homer, *Hymn to Hermes* 7.1: *theōn makarōn boes ambrotoi,* "immortal cattle of the fortunate Gods."

13. Ibid. 103: *admētēs,* "untamed."

14. The verb *aulizomai* and all the terms grouped around *aulē* are related, as P. Chantraine writes (s.v., *aulē,* 1.140), "to the central idea of spending the night out in the open air." In this respect one can compare *Odyssey* 12.265 (*aulizomenaōn*) to the *Homeric Hymn to Hermes* 71 (*aulin*).

15. Homer, *Hymn to Hermes* 72.

16. Ibid. 497–98: Apollo gives Hermes "a shining whip and entrusts him with the herd."

17. Animals are no longer kept in the open but brought inside a stable built with a high ceiling (*es aulion hupsimelathron*) next to deep troughs (*lēnoi*) (*Hymn to Hermes* 103–104, 106, 134, 399).

18. The portion of the divine herd that Hermes stole forms the *genos boōn* (*Hymn to Hermes* 335); cf. Hesiod, *Theogony* 444: with Hecate, Hermes knows "how to make the stock grow in the stables," with *Hymn to Hermes* 491–94: Hermes proclaims that he will have the wild cattle graze in the mountains and concludes: "It is there that the cows, coupling with the bulls, will produce a quantity of both males and females."

19. *Hymn to Hermes* 130–35.

20. *Iliad* 5.339–43: "Since they eat no bread (*siton*) and drink none of the wine of the dark fires (*aithopa oinon*), they (the gods) have no blood and are called Immortal (*athanatoi*)."

21. Hesiod *Works and Days* 276–78: "The fish, wild beasts, and the winged birds eat one another (*esthemen allēlous*), since for them there is no justice; but to men Zeus gave justice." Cf. in the *Odyssey*, the Cyclops, who does not know of the wine of the cultivated grape but drinks curdled milk, eats human flesh like a lion of the mountains, and "resembles in no way a man, a bread-eater" (*sitophagōi*) (9.190–91).

22. The ship contains food and drink, *brōsis te posis te* (12.320), i.e., bread and water, *sitos kai oinos* (12.327).

23. Triply cooked: by an internal cooking; by cultivation, which makes the sun's heat penetrate into the worked earth, and by the cooking fire for grains and the fermentation of the fruit of the vine for wine.

24. Cf. Detienne 1972, 29–35; J.-P. Vernant, "Sacrifice et alimentation humaine. A propos du Prométhée d'Hésiode," *Annali della Scuola Normale Superiore di Pisa* (1977): 938–39 (and above, chapter 2, section 2).

25. *Odyssey* 12.328; 302.

26. Ibid. 330–32. On the island of the Sun there is no earthly animal except for the creatures comprising the gods' sacred herds. Hunting and fishing, then, can only concern the animal species that are the farthest removed from man by their aquatic or aerial habitat. As a result, the distance separating normal sacrifice from hunting and fishing is all the more emphasized.

27. Ibid. 342: "Any death is cruel to unhappy humans, but is there a more dreadful fate than to die of hunger (*limōi thaneein*)?"

28. Ibid. 344.

29. Ibid. 343 and 353–56, with the use of the verbs *elauno*, to drive before one, and *periistēmi*, to surround. Pierre Vidal-Naquet has clearly seen and deftly analyzed these perverted aspects of the sacrifice in his study entitled "Valeurs religieuses et mythiques de la terre et du sacrifice dans l'*Odyssée*," *Annales E.S.C.* 25 (1970): 1278–97, esp. 1288–89.

30. *Odyssey* 12.357–58. On the "wild" value of the oak, its leaves and acorns (as the food of still primitive man), cf. Herodotus 1.66: the Arcadians, because of their "primitive" character, are called *balanēphagoi*, acorn-eaters, and not *sitophagoi*, bread-eaters. On the opposition in the marriage ritual between the wild life, *bios agrios*, symbolized by oak leaves, and civilized life, *bios hēmeros*, or life "of milled wheat," *bios alēlesmenos*, cf. Detienne 1972, 216–17, and references.

31. *Odyssey* 12.362–63.

32. Ibid. 395: the skins were walking.

33. Ibid. 395–96: the flesh on the skewers lowed, cooked as well as raw (*optalea te kai ōma*).

34. Ibid. 396: *boōn d' hōs gineto phōnē*.

35. In line 396, the lowing of the cattle (although they are already dead, cf. 393) recalls the bellowing that signaled their living presence to the crew while the ship was still at sea, even before they landed on the island; cf. line 265: "from the dark ship, still on the waves, we heard the cattle lowing. . . ."

36. Ibid. 12.415–19: "Zeus thunders and strikes the vessel with lightning and it capsizes,

filled with sulfur; all my companions are in the water; they float around the black ship like crows carried off by the waves. Zeus denied them the trip homeward."

37. On the Ethiopians in Greek tradition and in Herodotus, cf. Moses Hadas, "Utopian Sources in Herodotus," *Classical Philology* 30 (1935): 113–21; T. Säfve-Söderbergh, "Zu den äthiopischen Episoden bei Herodot," *Eranos* 44 (1946): 68–80; A. Lesky, "Aithiopika," *Hermes* 87 (1959): 27–38; Franck M. Snowden, *Blacks in Antiquity: Ethiopians in the Greco-Roman Experience* (Cambridge, 1970).

38. In their justice and felicity the Ethiopians, according to Herodotus, are on the side of "nature." They are the only people to accord royal dignity "to the one they have recognized as tallest and strongest" (3.20); cf. Plato, *Politics* 1290 b 5: "If magistratures were divided according to size, as they do, it is said, in Ethiopia, or to beauty"; Nicolas of Damascus, after Stobaeus, *Florilegium* 44.25: they choose the most handsome and warlike among them for their king; they are pious and just. At the end of the second century B.C., Agatharchides will write that the Ethiopians, following a divine way of life, have not sought to distort nature with false ideas. They are happy following nature's logic. They are not ruled by laws; they have no need of them, since they are honest without being taught (*On the Red Sea* 49).

39. Herodotus 3.20.2–5: "They carried presents consisting of a purple garment, a golden necklace and bracelets, a vase of perfume and a jar of Phoenician wine." Taking the purple garment and learning it was dyed, the king of the Ethiopians "declared that false were these men and false their garments" (3.22.2–6); the same words on the subject of the perfume (3.22.11–12).

40. It is the very meaning of their name: *Aithiopes*, "burned faces, fire-blackened faces."

41. There is a dual reason for this *euōdia:* on the one hand, the dryness of the climate and their constitution; on the other, their use of a water for bathing that exudes "an odor similar to that of violets" (Herodotus 3.23.8).

42. Herodotus 3.23.14–17.

43. Cf. J.-P. Vernant, "Sacrifice et alimentation humaine."

44. Herodotus 3.18.1–7: "There is in front of the town a field (*leimōn*) full of the boiled meat of all four-legged animals (*epipleos kreōn hephthōn pantōn tōn tetrapodōn*)". The people of the land claim "that it is the earth itself that, each night, produces the meats (*tēn gēn autēn anadidonai hekastote*)". Cf., for the Golden Age, Hesiod *Works and Days* 117: the fertile row produces an abundant and generous harvest by itself (*zeidōros aroura automatē*).

45. On the higher degree of perfection represented by the boiled in comparison to the roasted, cf. Detienne 1977: 180–82.

46. The term *makrobioi* or *makraiōnes* defines the status of beings midway between gods and men with respect to lifespan: e.g., *Numphai*, wood and water nymphs.

47. The Ethiopians' diet is composed exclusively of boiled meat and milk (3.23.4–5).

48. 3.22.19: the Ethiopian, upon hearing what wheat is and how it grows, replied "that he was not surprised that, since they lived on dung, *kopros,* they lived such a short time."

49. On the use of *aithops* for wine, see *Iliad* 4.259, and above all, Euripides, fr. 896 Nauck[2] = Athenaeus 11.465 b: "Euripides states that one of the horses of the Sun is *Aithiops,* who ripens (*pepainō* = cook) the autumnal vineyards of the bacchic god, friend of the flowers; hence, mortals call wine *aithops.*"

50. Herodotus 3.22.20.

51. Ibid. 3.23.5–14.

52. Aeschylus, fr. 192 Nauck[2] = Strabo 1.2.27, 22–27.

53. Herodotus 3.24.7–8.

54. Ibid. 3.24.2–12, esp. in line 8: *Kai ekhei panta phanera homoiōs autōi tōi nekuï.*

55. Ibid. 3.25.15–25.

56. Ibid. 3.25.16.

57. Ibid. 3.25.20–21.

58. Ibid. 3.25.23 and 25 (*allēlophagein*).

59. Ibid. 3.25.23: *deinon ergon . . . ergasanto.*

Chapter 8. Self-Cooking Beef

1. Vernant 1974, 171; cf. as well Durand.

2. Herodotus 4.61–62.

3. Ibid. 4.59 (based on slight modification of the Legrand French translation).

4. I. M. Linforth, "Greek Gods and Foreign Gods in Herodotus," *University of California Publications in Classical Philology* 9 (1926):6–7.

5. Hesiod *Theogony* 454.

6. F. Hartog, "La mort de l'autre: les funérailles des rois Scythes," *Actes du Colloque sur l'idéologie funéraire* (Ischia, 1977).

7. Herodotus 2.52.

8. Herodotus believed that Hesiod and Homer lived four hundred years before him.

9. Herodotus 2.52.

10. Ibid. 4.59.

11. Ibid. 1.131.

12. Ibid. 4.108.

13. Ibid. 2.4.

14. Ibid. 4.59.

15. Plato *Protagoras* 322 a.

16. Herodotus 3.18.

17. Ibid. 4.60. Casabona (61) shows that for Herodotus *erdō* is equivalent to *poieō:* "We shall see in the way Herodotus uses *erdō,* even with a religious sense, one of these Homerisms of vocabulary spoken of by the Ancients."

18. Herodotus 2.39.

19. Neither do the Persians (1.132) build any temples or altars; however, they choose a "pure place" (*khōron katharon*) in which to sacrifice. Thus their space is divided into zones of differing quality.

20. Herodotus 4.60.

21. Ibid. 1.132.

22. According to Casabona (249), *epispendō* for Herodotus means "to pour libations on something and refers to an act rather than to a ceremony. It is the equivalent of *kataspendō,* which Herodotus uses in another sense."

23. Herodotus 2.39.

24. Ibid. 4.62.

25. Ibid. 4.61; cf. as well 3.24.

26. Ibid. 4.188.

27. Ibid. 4.103.

28. Ibid. 2.45 (slightly modified from the Legrand French translation): for Herodotus it is a question of "foolishness" told by the Greeks.

29. *Odyssey* 3.445.

30. Durand 1977, 51–59.

31. Vernant 1974, 191; see also above, chapter 2, section 2.

32. P. Stengel, *Opferbräuche der Griechen* (Leipzig-Berlin, 1910), 155 ff.

33. Herodotus 1.216. Strabo repeats this information (11.3.6). Moreover, in a completely exceptional way, the Persians once made a sacrifice of horses; to obtain favorable omens seers slaughtered white horses in the waters of the Strymon (7.213).

34. Pausanias 1.21.6.

35. Herodotus 4.60.

36. The absence of the *pelekus* can be connected with the lack of cultivated land. Durand 1977 (49 and n. 5) remarks that the ax is perhaps seen as a tool for clearing land.

37. Herodotus 2.169. Apries is strangled by Egyptians who after rising up against him defeated him.

38. Ibid. 3.150. When they rise up in rebellion, the Babylonians choke the women.

39. Ibid. 4.160. Arcesilas is strangled by his brother.

40. Ibid. 7.85.

41. *Odyssey* 22.471–73. This death seems to be the feminine equivalent of that meted out to Melanthius, who had his nose, ears, sex (which was given to the dogs), hands, and feet cut off (474–77).

42. Euripides *Andromache* 412.

43. Sophocles *Oedipus Rex* 1374. There is probably a relationship between hanging and blood, or the fear of blood; thus in the *Suppliants* (788): "Hanged, I would like to find death in a noose, before a despised husband could place a hand on my body."

44. The meat of an ox that had not been bled would not be fit for eating.

45. Herodotus 2.39.

46. Ibid. 4.188.

47. Ibid.; as *ōmon* is a conjecture, the manuscripts have *domon*.

48. Ibid. 1.132: neither altar, fire, libation, flute, banners, or barley; however, the Persians are not presented as nomads, even if there are nomadic "tribes" among them, such as the Dai, Mardi, Dropici, Sagartii (1.125).

49. Ibid. 4.60, 61.

50. Rudhardt, 262.

51. Herodotus 4.76.

52. Ibid. 4.62.

53. Ibid. 4.69.

54. Aristotle *De Partibus Animalium* 661 b.1 ff. and 673 b.1 ff.: the *splankhna* are the "vital" parts of the animal and comprise the liver, lungs, spleen, kidneys, and heart. Cf. Detienne 1977, 177–78, and above, chapter 3, section "The Viscera as Center."

55. Detienne 1977, 173 ff. We encounter the question of the cultural representation of the boiled and the roasted: "Just as the cooked," writes Detienne (1977, 182), "distinguishes man from the animal that eats its food raw, boiled food separates the truly civilized man from the lout condemned to grilled fare." We would thus expect the Scythians to practice roasting rather than boiling; however, this is not the case. They do not know about roasting (it appears) and only know about boiling food. Similarly, the Persians, when they sacrifice, boil the meat (Herodotus 1.132); but they use roasting for birthday meals. Among the Ethiopians the Table of the Sun bears boiled meats (Herodotus 3.18). No details are given in the case of the Libyan sacrifice; as for the Egyptian sacrifice, nothing is explicitly said, even though it appears elsewhere (Herodotus 2.77) that the Egyptians are familiar with roasted and boiled dishes. We can even mention the Indians who feed on grasses (*poiēphageousi*) and boil a grain with its husk, which they eat (Herodotus 3.100); they eat food either raw or boiled. When they sacrifice the old men, the Massagetae include the flesh with that of the *probata* and boil it all together (Herodotus 1.216); they are milk-drinkers.

56. Herodotus 4.61.

57. Idem.

58. Menander *Dyscolus* 456, 519.

59. Hesiod *Theogony* 538–39, 188. The tricksters (*Odyssey* 18.44–45) have on the fire "stomachs (*gasteres*) of goats stuffed with fat and blood": a kind of blood sausage. Metro-

dorus (*FGrHist.*, 43 F 3) reports that the people of Smyrna, originally Aeolians, sacrifice to Boubrostis a black bull that after it is carved is completely cooked in its skin (*autodoron*); this is, then, something different (holocaust).

60. Herodotus 4.61.

61. Porphyry, *Peri eusebeias*, fr. 18. The only time that Herodotus speaks of a feast (*dais*) is concerning the Egyptian sacrifice; nothing is said about the Libyan sacrifice. Among the Persians, it is specified that the sacrifier "carries the meat home and uses it as he sees fit" (Herodotus 1.132).

62. Curiously, Rudhardt (220) uses this Scythian example to show that this is a normal Greek practice.

63. Herodotus 2.41: Having other sacrificial customs, the Egyptians would not wish "either to kiss a Greek on the mouth or use the knife of a Greek or his skewers or his kettle, or eat of the flesh of an ox free of signs if it has been carved with a Greek knife."

64. Ibid. 1.73.

65. Ibid. 1.119: Astyages, king of the Medes, "as soon as the son of Harpagus came to him, stabbed him, cut him into pieces, had part of the flesh roasted and the rest boiled. . . ."

66. Lucian *Peri thusiōn* 13.

67. *Iliad* 13.301; *Odyssey* 8.361; Sophocles *Antigone* 970; *Oedipus Rex* 196.

68. Apollonius of Rhodes *Argonautica* 2.989 ff.: the Amazons "liked only fatal immoderation and the works of Ares, for they were of the race of Ares and Harmonia, this nymph who had borne warlike daughters to Ares. . . ."

69. Herodotus 5.7.

70. Ibid. 2.63: a group defends the entry of the temple while another tries to penetrate within. According to the people of the country, the origin of the combat is as follows: Ares' mother lived in this place; Ares had been brought up elsewhere. Once a man, Ares returns, desirous of visiting or uniting with (*summeixai*) his mother. The servants wished to prevent him from approaching, which gave rise to the combat. There also exists an oracle of Ares, still in Egypt (2.83) and another among the Pisidians (7.76).

71. Ibid. 7.140; 8.77.

72. Ibid. 4.62: *thusias . . . prosagousi probatōn kai hippōn;* cf. Casabona, 135.

73. Herodotus 4.62.

74. Wood with which moreover nothing is done, since his sacrifices call for no cooking. *Marae*, by "analogy" with Polynesian temples.

75. G. Dumézil, *Romans de Scythie et d'alentour* (Paris, 1978), 31–32.

76. Herodotus 4.62, 71, 101.

77. Ibid. 7.54, in which *akinakēs* is defined as a Persian sword. Moreover, a connection exists between iron and Scythia. The chorus in *Seven Against Thebes* links the two several times: "The one who rattles the dice, the stranger Chalybus, emigrant from Scythia, hard divider of patrimonies, the Iron with the cruel heart . . ." (726–30); "Cruel was the judge of their dispute [between Eteocles and Polynices], the stranger of the Bridge, the Iron that emerges sharpened from the flame; cruel the hard divider of their patrimony, Ares, who today makes the curse of their father come true" (942–46). Thus Scythia, iron, and Ares are associated; we understand even better, under these conditions, that the Scythians can be seen as "warrior beings" and that a saber serves as an *agalma* of Ares.

78. Herodotus 2.63.

79. Sophocles *Oedipus Rex* 215.

80. These comments on Scythian sacrifices refer to a more extensive study in progress on Scythians and the representation of the nomad in the Greek imagination.

81. Herodotus 4.62.

82. Ibid. 4.103.

83. Ibid. 9.119.

84. P. Ducrey, *Le Traitement des prisonniers de guerre* . . . (Paris, 1968), 204–205: a sacrifice carried out in honor of a dead person (Patrocles, Achilles, Philopoemen), or before a battle (the three Persians who probably were stabbed on the altar by Themistocles).

85. *Aposphazein:* Casabona (167) notes that there are only two uses of the term related to sacrifice; this one is from Aristophanes *Thesmophoriazusae* 750; but cf. above, ch. 6, n. 29.

86. Herodotus 4.62. On the meaning of *aperxantes*, see Casabona (65), for whom *aperdō* is an equivalent to *apergazomai*.

87. J.-P. Vernant, "La belle mort et le cadavre outragé," in *La mort, les morts dans les sociétés anciennes*, ed. G. Gnoli and J.-P. Vernant (Cambridge and Paris, 1982), 45–76.

88. Cf. n. 70, if one admits that *summeixai* can mean to sleep with his mother.

Chapter 9. Sanctified Slaughter

1. Reading the folklorists, one has the impression that the practice of blood sacrifice was almost exclusively limited to the Greek populations of northeast Thrace and Asia Minor prior to their forced departure from these lands imposed by historical vicissitudes in 1914 and 1922—a custom that the refugees would continue to practice in their new homes in Greece. In reality it is much more widespread, since it is found—although given only cursory mention—in Macedonia and Thessaly, in Epirus and in the Peloponnesus, as well as in the islands (Euboea, Samos, Lesbos, Amorgos, Ikaria, Skyros, Crete, Paxoi, etc.). The preference the folklorists display for Thrace, endowing its customs with detailed descriptions, conceals, it seems to us, a preconceived opinion: Thrace is considered the "reservoir" of the cults of ancient Greece, as the "kernel" par excellence that has kept its "memory."

2. We do not claim, of course, to draw up the "map of topographical diffusion" of this cultic practice, or to make a diachronic and exhaustive study that would attempt to define its extent and duration. Such an inquiry would instead be the work of on-site researchers, who perhaps could utilize the various unpublished reports deposited every year at the Center for Research on Greek Folklore in Athens, documents inaccessible to an outsider such as a Hellenist! In addition to the published annual reports and the articles of the folklorists, a variety of information can be found in the contributions written by amateurs describing the customs of their native country and in some books on regional history and customs. Cf. as well a comprehensive work by the folklorist G. A. Megas, *Greek Calendar Customs* (Athens, 1958).

3. Here we will speak only of public sacrifices, described by folklorists as *dēmoteleis* (from *dēmos*, people); indeed, the village community, as such, taking on the role of protagonist, plays a part in many ways. Let us specify, however, that private sacrifices also exist, made by private individuals on various occasions: in case of the sickness of a person or an animal, for the health of a child, for the development of an enterprise, for the birth of a male child, when one has lost an animal or builds a house, at a marriage or after the mass commemorating a death, etc. But private and public sacrifices have, as we will see, common and complementary aspects, and the boundary between them is fluid.

4. A word borrowed by the Greeks from the Turkish, *kurban*, "sacrifice," (according to a passage from the Koran, [*The Encyclopaedia of Islam*, vol. 2, s.v. *ḳurbān*, p. 1129]), which derives in turn from the Hebrew *qorban*, a "general term to designate the gifts that one offers to God when presenting oneself before him . . .; it includes all sacrifices properly speaking, bloody and nonbloody, voluntary or obligatory, as well as first fruits and gifts of money" (note to Leviticus 1:2, page 95 of the *Bible de Crampon*, new ed., 1960). The term has been translated in the Septuagint as *dōron*, "gift." Cf. as well the Gospel according to Mark 7:11: *korban, ho esti dōron*. The long Turkish occupation could explain the name but not the origin of the neo-Greek blood sacrifice, for this practice was noted several centuries before the fall of Constantinople in 1453.

For the Turkish ritual (Muslim), cf. *Encyclopaedia of Islam*; Skarlatos Byzantios, *Constantinople* (in Greek) (1852), 3: 577; *Thr.* 42 (1968): 161. Before 1922, the Turks often took part in Greek *kourbánia* (especially during the feast of Saint George) in some regions of Thrace and Asia Minor (D. Petropoulos and E. Andreadis, *Religious Life in the Akseraï-Gelveri Region* [in Greek] [Athens, 1971]); see also n. 55, below.

5. Cf. a "prayer for the victim (sacrificed) in memory of a saint," A. Dmitrievsky, *Euchologia*, (Kiev, 1901), 2:113.

6. On this milieu, as well as on the multiple aspects of space within the framework of traditional neo-Greek civilization, see Alki Kyriakidou-Nestoros, *Studies in Folklore* (in Greek), (Athens, 1975), particularly the chapter, "Signes de lieu ou de la logique du paysage grec," 15–40.

7. Some descriptions place the slaughter behind the church to the east or next to the belltower (sometimes separated from the church); cf. *Laogr.* 15 (1953): 160; *ELA* 13–14 (1960–61): 405.

8. A white sheep, the victim sacrificed to Saint George every year in a village of Thrace, used to spend the night in front of the icon of the saint, *Mes. Gram.* 1 (1931): 157.

9. G. Megas, "Sacrifice de taureaux et de béliers en Thrace du Nord-Est," *Laogr.* 3 (1911): 170. (This fundamental article will be referred to henceforth as "Sacrifice"). S. Imellos, in *ELA*, 406. Even extreme cases are noted, all in the Greek village of Farassa (Cappadocia), where the victim—always some small animal—was sometimes slaughtered inside the country chapels next to a large square or round stone raised before the altar. But this exceptional practice, which one has a tendency to generalize arbitrarily, is probably explained by regional peculiarities and lies outside our subject because of its private and familial character. See D. Loukopoulos and D. Petropoulos, *Folk Religion of Farassa* (in Greek), coll. of the French Institute of Athens 34 (Athens, 1949). In this village almost everyone sacrificed animals. Of course, when several private individuals, often heads of families, brought and sacrificed promised animals for an important religious feast, the private character of the sacrifice seemed to diminish. However, even in this case, each one slaughtered *his own* animal (Loukopoulos and Petropoulos, *Folk Religion,* 131) while the community per se had no role.

10. This factor can contribute to breathe new life into this practice today. The mayor of Melissochori, a small village of 1300 inhabitants near Salonika, spoke to us in 1976 with pride about his efforts to revive the local *kourbánia* celebrated on the *hagíasma* of Saint Paraskevi on July 26. During the festival twelve goats and sheep had been slaughtered (but not at the site), the number of participants was estimated at 5000, and the *panigíri* had brought in 45,000 drachmas (about 6000 French francs).

11. At the "miraculous" springs in Thrace, the period of the sacrifices generally began April 23 (feast of Saint George) and ended October 26 (Saint Dimitrios) (see E. Stamouli-Sarandi, "Thracian Hagiasmata" [in Greek] *Thr.* 18 [1943]: 219–90). On the importance in general of annual religious festivals, the most frequent of which are those that occur in spring and summer, see Rennel Rodd, *The Customs and Lore of Modern Greece* (1892; reprt. Chicago, 1968), 82 ff. Sacrifices are not completely absent in the winter. Especially notable is the *kourbánia* of Saint Athanasius on January 18; but often the common meal does not take place.

12. Cf. S. Paraskevaïdis, *Survivals of Ancient Greek Life on Lesbos* (in Greek) (Mytilene, 1956), 37–38, whose torturous reasoning to explain these displacements by the "fusion" of a Christian and an ancient pagan cult cannot be taken seriously. Cf. as well Chr. Chatjiyannis, *The "Panigiri" of Taurus of Saint Paraskevi, on Lesbos* (in Greek) (Mytilene, 1969), 7. On the shifting of festival dates due to weather, cf. K. Marinis, *Nea Hestia* 11 (1932): 586, and *ArThTh* 25 (1960): 209.

13. See *Megas Synaxaristis,* "December," ed. Loukakis, (Athens 1896), 437–45; G. Megas, *Greek Festivals,* 36.

14. Anna Maraba-Chatjinikolaou, *Saint Mamas* (in Greek), ed. Institut français d'Athènes, 57 (Athens, 1953), 30 ff., 41 ff., and 86 ff. On Skyros, the shepherds bring him

small sheep so that "he also has his flock, does not complain, is not jealous, and so that he protects theirs" (Niki Perdika, *Skyros* [in Greek] [Athens, 1940], 1:140).

15. Migne, *Patrologia Graeca*, 115, 156 b. *Miracula S. Georgii*, ed. Aufhauser (Leipzig, 1913), 44 ff. The resurrection of the ox is part of a more general context of prodigious feats that result in conversion of the pagans. In our opinion the story of Theopistos revolves around a rather common theme, also present in neo-Greek sacrifice: one must always sacrifice the animal that has been promised and never another (see this chapter, text at note 118). On these miracles, cf. two articles by Fr. Cumont (*Revue de l'histoire des religions* 114 [1936]: 5–41, and *Journal of Roman Studies* 27 [1937]: 63–71), which link Saint George with Mithra and Mazdaism and are consequently beyond the scope of the questions examined here.

16. On this point see our article, "Quelques problèmes de la transhumance dans la Grèce ancienne," *Revue des études grecques* 87 (1974): 169. An opposing view is found in G. Spyridakis, "Saint Georges dans la vie populaire," *L'Hellénisme contemporain*, 2d ser., 6 (1952): 140 ff. Popular tradition, moreover, very often attributes various functions to a saint that hagiography had never recognized, because some activities coincide with the date of the feast day. This is again the case of Saint George, nicknamed "Sower" or "Drunk," for in some regions on the day of another feast in his honor (November 3) the seed is readied or the new wine tasted (Megas, *Greek Festivals* 27–28; *Laogr.* 11 [1934–37]: 230 ff.).

17. In contrast to the common opinion of the folklorists, who consider the saint the Christian form of Helios or Zeus, see S. Georgoudi, "Sant'Elia in Grecia," *Studi e materiali di Storia delle Religioni* 39 (1968): 293–319.

18. Who, however, has no relationship with animals, according to his hagiography.

19. Cf. Megas, *Greek Festivals*, 223.

20. On diseases, healer saints, and popular therapeutics, see the bibliography compiled by D. Loukatos, *Introduction to Greek Folklore* (in Greek) (Athens, 1977), 238–40.

21. On the cult of this saint, see D. Oikonomidis, "Saint Paraskevi among the Greeks and Roumanians" (in Greek), in *ELA* 9–10 (1955–57), particularly 88 ff.

22. Sometimes a small scroll with the donor's name is hung from the victim's forehead (Chatjiyannis, *Panigiri*, 11).

23. Megas, "Sacrifice," 155; see n. 118, below.

24. As C. A. Romaios has done, in *Cultes populaires de la Thrace*, French trans., coll. of the Institut français d'Athènes, (Athens, 1949), 50 ff.

25. Cf. Stamouli-Sarandi, "Hagiasmata," 223; C. A. Romaios, *Cultes populaires de la Thrace*, 52: sacrifice to Saint Christopher. But these scanty indications do not permit us to resolve the question of color, for it seems in general that color is not important: "The bull can be of any color," said the peasants of the village of Bana (northeastern Thrace) (Megas, "Sacrifice," 170). As for the color black, one would look in vain for these "chthonian gods" to whom "in olden days" (?) "black lambs" were sacrificed (Megas, "Sacrifice"); perhaps one could think of the analogy that the popular mind sometimes establishes between the black garb of a sacrificial animal and its blood, a powerful prophylactic element (see this chapter, text at note 42).

26. See Loukopoulos and Petropoulos, *Folk Religion*, 44. But the choice of the sex can also be linked to very commonplace issues: for the *kourbáni* of Saint Paraskevi on July 26 in Melissochori, ewes are preferred, for male sheep smell bad at this first part of the breeding season (July–August).

27. *Thr.* 18 (1943): 249, n. 2. On this widespread tradition that in its different versions attempts to explain the physical and moral differences between the sheep (the creature of Christ) and goat (the devil's creature), see N. Politis, *Traditions* (in Greek), vol. 1, no. 191 (Athens, 1904; reprinted 1965), 107; and D. Loukopoulos, *Pastorals of Roumeli* (in Greek) (Athens, 1930), 217–19. Moreover the Devil's flock is made up of wild goats (I. Sanders, *Rainbow in the Rock: The People of Rural Greece* [Cambridge, Ma., 1962], 17). On goats as

262 *Notes to Pages 188–90*

diabolical animals tamed by Christ, as well as on their affinities with women, other creatures of the Devil, see J. K. Campbell, *Honour, Family and Patronage: A Study of Institutions and Moral Values in a Greek Mountain Community* (Oxford, 1964), 26, 31, 347.

28. Megas, *Greek Festivals,* 182–83. The promised animal is often marked with a distinctive sign (for example, holes in its ears), *Eos* 76–85 (1964): 320.

29. *Laogr.* 3 (1911): 505–506.

30. See *ELA* 13–14 (1960–61): 380. The church sometimes buys animals, if the number of *támata* is insufficient (Imellos in *ELA* 13–14 [1960–61]: 405). The victims could come from vast flocks in earlier times belonging to the churchs or monasteries (cf. Romaios, *Cultes populaires de la Thrace,* 52).

31. Cf. *Thr.* 37 (1963):295.

32. As for the *kourbáni* of Our Lady of Euboea at Cyme (*Laogr.* 3 [1911]: 505–506). The responsibility for the fundraising is often taken on by a commission of inhabitants or by the church committee (*Thr.* 41 [1967]: 303–305; *ELA* 17 [1964]: 199) or else it is entrusted to the children of the village, whose happy procession from door to door asking for all types of contributions takes the place of the public herald (*Thr.* 13 [1940]: 338).

33. For the ox sacrificed to Saint Elisaios, cf. *Mikrasiatika Chronika* 6 (1955): 202. Elsewhere a peasant chosen by lottery raises the animal at his own expense, thereby assuming a task regarded as beneficial to himself and his family (*Thr.* 37 [1963]: 40). The bull or ram that will be sacrificed May 21 during the famous ceremony of the *Anastenária* (see n. 38, below) is bought on January 18, the feast of Saint Athanasius (K. Kakouri, *Dionysiaka: Concerning Modern Popular Religious Practices in Thrace* [in Greek] [Athens, 1963], 18).

34. Cf. K. Kakouri, *Dionysiaka,* 19; K. Makistos, *I Sellada Hagias Paraskevis Lesbou* (Athens, 1970), 65; *ArThTh* 16 (1951): 318; Chatjiyannis, *Panigiri,* 10.

35. Megas, "Sacrifice," 159.

36. *Thr.* 18 (1943): 223 and n. 2. *Mes. Gram.* 1 (1931): 157.

37. On these aspects see Makistos, *I Sellada,* 65–66; Loukatos, in *ArThTh* 12 (1945–46): 160–61; *ArThTh* 5 (1938–39): 140, and 18 (1953): 144. Megas, *Questions of Greek Folklore* (in Greek), fasc. 3 (Athens, 1950), 63–64. That these luxurious cloths are indeed gifts made to the church is shown by the example of Melissochori, where the day of the sacrifice to Saint Paraskevi, such gifts (cloths embroidered by hand) are sold at auction for the benefit of the church (see n. 10, above). Stratis Myrivilis evokes the solemn procession of the animal in some very fine pages of his novella *Vassilis Arvanitis.*

38. Things are different in the sacrifice offered in the context of the *Anastenária,* a group of very complex rites that has not ceased to excite ethnographers, folklorists, historians of religion, and psychologists: here the protagonists of the sacrifice are naturally the members of the confraternity of the *Anastenárides.* Let us note that the most important rite of the *Anastenária* takes place May 21, the feast of Saints Constantine and Helen; the *Anastenárides* walk barefoot on burning coals (see p. 275, below).

39. Megas, "Sacrifice," 152–54.

40. Matthew 7:6. Cf. Psalm 22 (Vulg. 21):17.

41. Megas, "Sacrifice," 154. What is involved here is not the notion of "above" and "below," but the care to keep the bones away from the dogs, for one could just as well bury the bones or burn them (Megas, "Sacrifice," 171).

42. *Kourbáni* of Saint Charalambos on Lesbos (Makistos, *I Sellada,* 69). P. Nikitas, *Menologus of Lesbos* (in Greek) (Mytilene, 1953), 39. Local customs reveal other uses of the blood of the victim: for divinatory ends (private sacrifice) or as an element protecting the church (in earlier days one anointed the four corners of the church with the blood of a ram sacrificed to Saint George) (Megas, *Greek Festivals,* 182).

43. The viscera are sometimes prepared separately. Roasted on the spit or cooked with rice, they are served to all as an hors d'oeuvre, or else only to those who worked, as a "tasty"

reward (Megas, "Sacrifice," 154; *ELA* 13–14 [1960–61]: 406; Loukopoulos and Petropoulos, *Folk Religion,* 48, 131).

44. The number of one hundred and one caldrons is cited for boiling the oxen sacrificed to Our Lady of Euboea at Cyme (*Laogr.* 3 [1911]:506).

45. On Samos, *ELA* 17 (1964): 199; in the village Kornopholia, *Thr.* 41 (1967): 304, etc.

46. D. Loukatos, *ArThTh* 12 (1945–46): 161. The priest can also bless a small quantity of the food and then mix it with the rest (*ELA* 13–14 [1960–61; cb:406). Sometimes he sprinkles holy water in the kettles (*ELA* 17 [1964]: 199).

47. Megas, *Greek Festivals,* 197; *Thr.* 18 (1943): 224; *EKEL* 18–19 (1965–66): 328; *Thr.* 8 (1937): 390, and 37 (1963): 295. In Farassa the victim's head, feet, and a thigh, all wrapped in its hide, were set aside for the priest (Loukopoulos and Petropoulos, *Folk Religion,* 131). Special portions are also set aside for the police chief, the village mayor, and other officials (*Laogr.* 15 [1953]: 158).

48. Megas, "Sacrifice," 152 and 169–70; Megas, *Questions of Greek Folklore,* 29. In the extreme but rare case where the group of celebrators is composed solely of heads of families, it is difficult to speak of a common meal, e.g., sacrifice to Saint Athanasius on Didymoteichon (*Thr.* 13 [1940]: 338).

49. *ELA* 13–14 (1960–61): 406.

50. Before the distribution, the priest blesses the raw pieces, as he normally does for prepared food (*ArThTh* 18 [1953]: 281).

51. *ELA,* 13–14 (1960–61): 406; Megas, "Sacrifice," 154.

52. *ArThTh* 18 (1953) 281.

53. Cf. *ELA* 13–14 (1960–61): 405–406.

54. Music, an essential element in neo-Greek sacrifice, sometimes even accompanies the skinning of the victim (Megas, "Sacrifice," 154), preparation of the food, or the cooking of the meat in the caldrons (Melissochori).

55. In some villages in Thrace, the Turks often celebrated with the Greeks and took part in the games (*Thr.* 18 [1943]: 240; *Mes. Gram.* 1 [1931]: 154; see n. 4, above).

56. *Thr.* 18 (1943): 239; *Mes. Gram.* 1(1931): 153; *ELA* 9–10 (1955–57): 408.

57. Cf. M. Godelier, *Horizon, trajets marxistes en anthropologie* (Paris, 1973), 29.

58. Cf. G. Spyridakis, "Saint George," 145. A. Maraba-Chatjinikolaou, *Saint Mamas,* 17, 29 ff.; Megas, "Sacrifice," 169–70, etc. To be objective, we must specify that the idea of "survivals" is not the prerogative of some Greek folklorists. Several non-Greek authors who write about the Greece of yesterday and today make great use of it. For example, the following titles are revealing: J. C. Lawson, *Modern Greek Folklore and Ancient Greek Religion: A Study in Survivals* (1910, reprinted New York, 1964); W. W. Hyde, *Greek Religion and Its Survivals* (1923, reprinted New York, 1963). Cf. in the same vein, on "unbroken continuity," the sociological study of I. Sanders, *Rainbow in the Rock: The People of Rural Greece,* 258 ff.

59. Cf. M. Meraklis, *Contemporary Greek Popular Culture* (in Greek) (Athens, 1973): 37, 51–52, where the author, to attenuate in some way the absolute character of the theory of survivals, does not forget the familiar formula of the "Christianization" of customs. Why, if the machine of survivals is to be activated, not go all the way back to Sumer to explain ancient Greek sacrifice in turn? This is how G. Korres proceeds in "Survivances des sacrifices de taureaux," *Athena* 73–74 (1972–73): 879–913.

60. Thus if the victim's age in years is odd-numbered, the Pythagorean theory of numbers is invoked (*ArThTh* 18 [1953]: 144; K. Kakouri, *Dionysiaka,* 18); the distribution of raw meat refers to Dionysian omophagia (see this chapter, text at notes 109–10); the black color of the victim evokes Dionysus *Melanaigis* (Kakouri, *Dionysiaka,* 161–62); the ditch—far from being present everywhere, however—is evidence of the "chthonian" character of the neo-Greek sacrifice (S. Kyriakidis, *Laogr.* 6 [1917]: 213). To our knowledge the only serious

attempt to interpret the blood sacrifices taking the Christian framework into consideration is the book of the archeologist and Byzantinist D. Pallas, *Church "Thalassa": A Study of the History of the Christian Altar and of the Morphology of the Mass* (in Greek), coll. of the French Institute of Athens (Athens, 1952), esp. pp. 102 ff. See also *Epetiris Etairias Byzantinon Spoudon* 20 (1950): 268 ff. Although one cannot accept some of his interpretations, his study is very stimulating, especially in the domain of paleo-Christian and Byzantine archaeology, where a Hellenist feels incompetent (I would like to thank the archaeologist Ilias Kolias for having indicated this book to me).

61. Sometimes it is enough to find an ancient inscription on the site for "continuity" to be assured (Megas, "Sacrifice," 161 ff.). This tendency has often provided the basis for conservative and reactionary attitudes in different arenas of neo-Greek life.

62. A. Kyriakidou-Nestoros justly remarks that for a folklorist "the height of success used to consist (and still does to a certain extent) in being able to prove that a contemporary custom or belief has its roots in classical antiquity" (*Studies in Folklore*, 96).

63. Cf. the prohibition against the *kourbáni* in Melissochori by the metropolitan of Salonika (*Laogr.* 15 [1953]: 159; but see n. 10, above); the prohibition made by another metropolitan against the participation of priests in blood sacrifices (*Thr.* 13 [1940]: 339). As N. Svoronos says (see n. 71, below), "On the social level, if the high clergy identifies itself with the leading classes of society, the lower clergy, which from an institutional point of view has never formed its own social 'order,' has always identified itself with the people." On the village priest, see I. Sanders, *Rainbow in the Rock*, 261 ff.

64. See Megas, "Sacrifice," 171. On Lesbos the bishop himself used to bless the victims or distribute the prizes to the winners of the competitions that ended the sacrificial ceremony (*Laogr.* 15 [1953]: 160; Megas, *Questions of Greek Folklore*, 64).

65. One can cite the case of a public sacrifice where the priest slaughtered the victim, skinned it, and cut it up (*ArThTh* 15 [1948–49]: 282). In Mandamados on Lesbos, the sheep of the private *kourbáni* is killed by the priest (*Laogr.* 15 [1953; cb: 160). The same act is attributed to the priest in a version of the myth of the stag (see below, p. 197) (*EKEL* 18–19 [1965–66]: 327–28).

66. *Laogr.* 3 (1911): 506.

67. *ArThTh.* 18 (1953): 145.

68. Chatjiyannis, *Panigíri*, 8–9.

69. A note by the same Nicodemus in his edition with commentary of the apostolic and conciliary Canons (*Pēdalion*), 1st ed. (Lipsiae, 1800), 211 (99th Canon of the 6th Eucumenical Council). This note is not found in the eighth edition of the book (Athens, 1976).

70. Often an auction was organized to sell the hides (see *ArThTh* 8 [1941–42]: 145). When the church did not own any flocks, the churchwardens also would sell the *támata* that had not been sacrificed (*Archeion Pontou* 21 [1956]: 115; *ELA* 13–14 [1960–61]: 406 and 15–16 [1962–63]: 257). On monastic flocks and sacrifice, see Megas, "Sacrifice," 159; *Thr.* 41 (1967): 91–92. Cf. as well, Ph. Koukoules, *Eusthates of Salonika. Ta laographika* (in Greek) (Athens, 1950), 2:4.

71. As N. Svoronos has remarked in a lecture given at the E.H.E.S.S. (Ecole des Hautes Etudes supérieures) (June 1978) on "Religions et identité culturelles en Europe centrale et orientale: le cas de l'Orthodoxie."

72. It must be recalled that throughout nearly four hundred years of Turkish occupation, from 1453 to 1821, sacred texts as well as liturgical books were widespread and read among the Christian populations of the regions of presentday Greece, and for many generations they were the only reading.

73. M. Carrez, in *Vocabulaire biblique*, ed. J.-J. von Allmen, 2d ed. (Lausanne, 1956), s.v. *Sacrifices*, 269.

74. The prophets do not condemn blood sacrifices but rather the conviction "that sacrifices act by themselves, without equivalent acts" (cf. H. Ringgren, *La religion d'Israël* [Fr. trans., Paris, 1966]: 190–91).

75. 1 Cor. 10:14 ff. Such conceptions are also found in the pure Hebraic tradition of the rejection of the worship of idols.

76. Cf. the third apostolic canon, with the explanations of Zonaras, Balsamon, and Aristinos, in *Syntagma* (collection of sacred canons), ed. Rallis-Potlis, Athens, 1852–59 (reprinted, 1952), 2:4.

77. *Syntagma*, 2:543.

78. A. H. M Jones, *Le Déclin du monde antique* (Fr. trans., Paris, 1970): 248 ff., 252 ff. According to testimony dating from the twelfth century, villagers gave the priests meat and other food in return for communion (Ph. Koukoules, *Byzantine Life and Civilization* [in Greek] Athens, 1955, 6: 160).

79. *Syntagma*, 5: 387–88.

80. Cf. K. Kakouri, *Dionysiaka*, 21.

81. For example, "Prayer for a Sacrifice" or "for a Sacrifice of Animals," "Prayer for a Victim in Memory of a Saint," "Prayer for Victims" or "for a Victim," "Prayer for Those Who Offer a Sacrifice," "Prayer for the Sacrifice of an Ox," etc. (A. Dmitrievsky, *Euchologia*, Kiev [1901], 2: 451 and 1014, 113, 6, and 46). The title of a prayer can be variously formulated in different manuscripts: for example, "Prayer for a Sacrifice of Oxen" or "Oxen and Rams" or "Oxen and Other Four-legged Animals" (Fr. Conybeare, "Les sacrifice d'animaux dans les anciennes églises chrétiennes," *Revue de l'histoire des religions* 44 [1901]: 109–110).

82. D. Pallas notes that the number and relative variety of these prayers indicate that they represent different local traditions (*Church "Thalassa,"* 111); consequently, the sacrificial usage would be rather widespread.

83. Cf. Gen. 4:4: "Abel, for his part, brought the first-born of his flock and some of their fat"; Heb. 11:4: "Abel offered God a better sacrifice than Cain . . . God made acknowledgment of *his offerings.*"

84. Dmitrievsky, *Euchologia*, 2:46: "Prayer for a Victim" (cf. Jer. 31 [Greek 38]:12–14).

85. Megas, "Sacrifice," 152, 164. The episode is in 2 Kings 2:19–22. See two versions of the prayer in *Euchologion to Mega*, ed. N. Papadopoulos (Athens, 1927): 375 a; and in Dmitrievsky, *Euchologia*, 2:113.

86. D. Pallas, *Church "Thalassa,"* 111.

87. Cf. Levit. 2:13; Num. 18:19; Ez. 43:24. On its therapeutic virtue, see this chapter, penultimate paragraph (salt water). Cf., among other, E. Jones, *Psycho-Myth, Psycho-History* (New York, 1975), vol. 2, chap. entitled "The Symbolic Significance of Salt in Folklore and Superstition"; Koukoules, *Eustathes*, 1:285 ff.

88. *Euchologion to Mega*, 382 a–b. Cf. Luke 15:23 ff.

89. See the article by S. Kyriakidis, "Deer Sacrifice in the Neo-Hellenic Tradition and in the Synaxaries" (in Greek), *Laogr.* 6 [1917]: 189–215; *ELA* 9–10 [1955–57]: 90–91; *EKEL* 18–19 [1965–66]: 327–28; *ArThTh* 7[1940–41]: 168; *Thr.* 42 [1968]: 120).

90. See Kyriakidis, "Deer Sacrifice." Cf. in the same vein, Fr. Cumont, "L'Archevêché de Pédachtoé et le sacrifice du faon," *Byzantion* 6 (1931): 521–33.

91. L. Charbonneau-Lassay, *Le Bestiaire du Christ* (Bruges, 1940), 241–60. Cf. H.-Ch. Puech, "Le Cerf et le serpent. Note sur le symbolisme de la mosaïque découverte au baptistère de l'Henchir Messaouda," *Cahiers archéologiques* 4 (1949): 17–60, art. "Idées et recherches" reprinted in *Sur le manichéisme et autres essais*, coll. (Paris, 1979). For the stag as messenger, see *Epetiris Etairias Byzantionōn Spoudōn* 28 (1958): 566–67 (Spyridakis).

92. Pursued by "idolaters" he was saved by the Angel and led into the mountains where

he lived, fed by the does who hurried to him to be milked; with their milk the saint also made cheese, which he gave to the poor (*Megas Synaxaristis*, ed. Loukakis [Athens, September 1894]: 36–37).

93. Chatjinikolaou, *Saint Mamas*, 81–82. The saint sent nothing after his order to always spare one of his goats was broken. Another figure associated with stags, the martyr Athenogenus, who had raised a doe in his monastery, prayed God to always keep the progeny of this animal safe and sound so that every year a doe could bring a fawn to the church to be eaten by the faithful in memory of it (*Megas Synaxaristis* [July 1893]:218; *Mēnaion tou Iouliou*, ed. B. Koutloumousianos [Athens, 1905]: 77–78.

94. *ArThTh* 13 (1946): 159–60. The story of Abraham and Isaac, blended with miraculous elements, appears to underlie another tradition of Thrace also belonging to the legend cycle of the stag, a tradition in which the theme of the testing of Christian faith is clearly apparent: Saint George not only sends no more stags but, furious, claims as a *kourbáni* the child of a woman. She obeys, stabs the child, prepares it by stuffing it, and puts it in the oven only to find the child the following morning safe and sound and reading a book. Henceforth Saint George gives a sheep every year, "so that you make the *kourbáni* during my feast day" (*Thr.* 7 [1936]: 252). On the motif of the oven, see below, n. 106, regarding the type of cooking of the *kourbáni* of Saint George in Thrace. In the same context we must cite another tradition, notable because of the species of animal sacrificed: on the feast of Saint Bissarion, patron saint of the island of Meganisi, near Leucas, a large fish appears in the port, which is then caught and eaten by the inhabitants (Loukatos, *ELA* 11–12 [1958–59]: 266). To our knowledge in contemporary practice the only example of the sacrifice of a fish is found in a village in Thrace, where a kind of carp was brought to Saint Nicholas, protector of sailors and fishermen, as a *kourbáni* the priest blessed and distributed to all (*Thr.* 18 [1943]: 223, n. 1).

95. The animal dies full of bitterness at such brutality, a bitterness that is revealed by the black foam that comes forth with its blood (tradition from Jannina) (Kyriakidis, "Deer Sacrifice," 191).

96. Apparently the sin committed by the faithful in the story of the goats of Saint Mamas. See above, n. 93.

97. Cf. Megas, "Sacrifice," 152. *Thr.* 46 (1972–73): 86; *ArThTh* 16 (1951): 319. I. Sanders, *Rainbow in the Rock*, 51 ff.

98. *Tameion orthodoxias* (*Treasure of Orthodoxy*) (Venice, 1804, new ed. Salonika, 1959), 135–38.

99. In two sacrificial prayers, God is asked to accept the sacrifice of his servant "in agreeable odor" (*eis osmēn euōdias*). See A. Dmitrievsky, *Euchologia*, 2: 46 and 113. But this does not necessarily mean that a part of the victim, set aside for God, is consumed in his honor on the fire (an interpretation that none of our sources can confirm). It seems that this expression has the value of a cliche, repeating the known formula of Leviticus (1:9, etc.), in the tradition of the Septuagint. It is more difficult to decide concerning the expression in another prayer, "may its fat (of the animal)—*stéar*—be received as an incense before your holy glory" (Fr. Conybeare, "Les sacrifices d'animaux," 109). D. Pallas (*Church "Thalassa,"* 130) concludes from this that the fat of the animal was burned. But if one also considers the metaphorical meaning of the phrase that follows it ("that the effusion of his blood be the bread of the richness of mercy") as well as the unique character of the expression, it is highly uncertain that this is the evidence of a specific sacrificial practice that would be the separate treatment of the fat as a portion set aside for God.

100. In a "prayer for the sacrifice of oxen" (8th century ms.) prayers are made to God to fill the storehouses of the faithful with fruit, wheat, wine, and oil, to multiply their flocks, to fill their souls with faith and justice, to heal the bodily sufferings (Conybeare, "Les sacrifices d'animaux," 109). To fail to give this food to all and thereby deprive some people constitutes

a serious fault that the saint severely punishes, as is shown in the anecdote of the cook punished for having set aside the boiled meat for only a part of the crowd (P. Nikitas, *Menologus of Lesbos*, 144).

101. They were often kept in the church (*Thr.* 9 [1938]: 325).

102. The caldrons and the spoons played a particularly important role in the *kourbáni* of Saint Athanasius in Kornopholia (*Thr.* 41 [1967]: 304); since there was no common meal, the food was divided into three large caldrons, which were taken to the three corners of the village for a spectacular distribution: each family took as many spoons as it had people. A fourth caldron was reserved for the families of the cooks, the churchwardens, and the young people who had worked as helpers.

103. The relationship between victims and grains can appear yet another way: with the wheat or the corn, which has been gathered by going among the inhabitants of the village Chandra, one buys an ox or cow for the sacrifice to Saint Athanasius (*ArThTh* 18 [1953]: 281).

104. The ram sacrificed to the Anargyroi saints, protectors of children, is roasted, but this case displays special characteristics: the absence of a common meal and the auction of the roasted pieces of meat, an operation undertaken by the young people ages twelve to twenty (*ELA* 13–14 [1960–61]: 380–81).

105. Boiled sheep (*Thr.* 9 [1938]: 324, and 18 [1943]: 239, 242; *Mes. Gram.* 1 [1931]: 153, etc.

106. In neo-Greek culinary practice a covered pan is used for cooking lamb, but the spit and the oven are often preferred; on the other hand, in sacrificial cookery these are extremely rare (cf. the sheep sacrificed to Saint George and prepared in the oven stuffed with raisins and pine nuts, *Mes. Gram.*, 157–58).

107. See Ph. Koukoules, *Vie et civilisation des Byzantins,* 6:161. The paschal lamb is not however presented as a sacrificial victim in current practice, as J. K. Campbell mistakenly believes (*Honour, Family, and Patronage,* 344). Other data show, moreover, a close relationship between Easter and the feast of Saint George: the liturgy of the mass for these two feast days, the transfer of the saint's feast day until after Easter if it falls beforehand, and the Thracian family custom of slaughtering the paschal lamb not at Easter but on the feast of Saint George (*ArThTh* 18 [1953]: 280–81).

108. Regions of Kozani and Florina, Deuteraios (*ELA* 17 [1964]: 235–36, and *EKEL* 18–19 [1965–66]: 255).

109. However, the hide is often given to the priest or sold to enrich the coffers of the group of the *Anastenárides* (Kakouri, *Dionysiaka,* 83 and 161; *Thr.* 46 [1972–73]: 85).

110. Romaios, *Cultes populaires de la Thrace,* 67. Cf. in the same vein *ArThTh* 5 (1938–39): 92 and 15 (1948–49): 282; Kakouri, *Dionysiaka,* 22.

111. As has been rightly remarked in *Thr.* 46 (1972–73): 85. Sheep and goats are also common victims.

112. *Thr.* 46 (1972–73): 85; *ArThTh* 5 (1938–39): 140 and 14 (1947–48): 348: part of the victim is distributed boiled to the families of the village.

113. See on this point the evidence of one of the *Anastenárides,* in *ArThTh* 5 (1938–39): 140.

114. This is a tradition that is rather widespread in Greece (*ELA* 15–16 [1962–63]: 239–40).

115. Cf. *Thr.* 8 (1937): 390. In Tenos, various families promise to slaughter a lamb on the Sunday of Saint Thomas, "so that people have something to eat" (A. Floriakis, *Tenos, Popular Culture* [in Greek] [Athens, 1971]: 196–97).

116. Chatzopoulos, *Thrakiki Epetiris* (1897), 1:195.

117. Cf. Loukatos, *ELA* 9–10 (1955–57): 420, and Spyridakis, *ELA* 9–10 (1955–57): 408.

118. For these contractual obligations, see Megas, "Sacrifice," 164, 166; cf. 155: the sacrifice of a ram instead of a bull—traditional victim of the *kourbáni* in a village in Thrace—led to the death of thirty-five people, it was said. The shepherd who had sacrificed a he-goat that was larger than the one he had promised found the latter dead when he came back from the festival (*Eos* 76–85 [1964]: 320). See also *Kritika Chronika* 10 (1956): 37, 45.

119. *Kritika Chronika* 10 (1956): 34, 45; *Eos* 76–85 (1964): 320; *ELA* 13–14 (1960–61): 261. Saint Paraskevi is known for her terrible punishments (cf. *ELA* 9–10 [1955–56]: 91, tradition from Naxos); for as a healer of eyes, she blinds the impious, such as the man who, instead of sacrificing the promised calf, brought her the animal dead and furthermore kept the animal's hide (*ELA* 15–16 [1962–63]: 345).

120. *ELA* 17 (1964): 232–34 (Saints Modestus, Spyridon, and Mamas); *Laogr.* 11 (1934–37): 233 (Saint George).

121. *ELA* 17 (1964): 233; *Mikrasiatika Chronika* 6 (1955): 202; *ArThTh* 13 (1946–47): 160; during the feast of Saint George, the outside door is covered with cow manure (*Mes. Gram.* 1 [1931]: 155). On saints who are healers of animals, see Koukoules, *Eustathe*, 2: 5.

122. Dmitrievsky, *Euchologia*, 2: 804–805; *Euchologion to Mega*, 509 b, 512b ("prayer of Saint Mamas recited for animals") and 381 b–382 a.

123. *Euchologion to Mega*, 510–511 b (to Saint Modestus). In these prayers we once again find multiple references to the flocks of Israel that God has protected and multiplied, as well as several names of diseases that threaten the animals (cf. as well *Euchologion to Mega*, 509 b–510 a, and Dmitrievsky, *Euchologia* 2:124–26: prayer to Saint Mamas).

124. Dmitrievsky, *Euchologia*, 2: 473.

125. They are also present, in great quantity, in the form of ex-votos in silver or gold.

Index

269

Woman (*continued*)
  Promethean myth, 62–68. *See also*
  Feminine; Women
Women: as carnivorous, 134; as citizens,
  137–39; confined to the house, 243;
  covered with blood, 147; in Demeter's
  ritual, 140–41; different tribes of, 63;
  one race of, 63; as priestesses, 135–36;
  as slaughterers, 140; in Thesmophoria,
  129–47; vegetarian, 133, 145; without
  political rights, 131; god of, 182. *See
  also* Feminine; Woman
Worker bee: drone contrasted to, 70–71.
  See also Bees; Drone
Works and Days (Hesiod), 21–26, 32, 37,
  46

Xenophon, 60
Xiphos, 130, 161

Yoke, 10

Zagreus-Dionysus, 18
Zeus: creates women, 62–68; duping of,
  41; eagle sent by, 54; evil introduced
  by, 76–78; lightning of, 51; as Olympian, 21, 28, 29; and Prometheus, 7,
  21–26, 29–30, 38–59, 52; protection
  of, 9; in relation to humanity, 28–29;
  sacrifice offered to, 13; victory
  of, 26